Foundations for Scientific Investing:

Multiple-Choice, Short-Answer, and Long-Answer Test Questions

Foundations for Scientific Investing:

Multiple-Choice, Short-Answer, and Long-Answer Test Questions

Timothy Falcon Crack
PhD (MIT), MCom, PGDipCom, BSc (HONS 1st Class), IMC

Published by:
Timothy Falcon Crack, P.O. Box 6385, Dunedin North, Dunedin 9059, New Zealand

Editions: 1st Ed. Nov 2014, 2nd Ed. Sept 2015, 3rd Ed. Nov 2016, 4th Ed. Sept 2017 revised/corrected Feb 2018, 5th Ed. Feb 2019, 6th Ed. Nov 2019, 7th Ed. Jan 2021.

Cover image: United States coin image from the United States Mint (used with permission).

ISBN: 978-0-9951173-5-8

Typeset by the author.
www.FoundationsForScientificInvesting.com
timcrack@alum.mit.edu

Contents

Preface

THIS BOOK ACCOMPANIES *Foundations for Scientific Investing* (see advertisements at the end of this book). It provides 607 multiple-choice, and 125 short-answer questions to accompany the long-answer questions already appearing in *Foundations*. Most of the long-answer questions are repeated here.

The suggested solutions to the multiple-choice and short-answer questions appear here and are also available, free of charge, at the Web site for the book: `www.FoundationsForScientificInvesting.com`. You may need to use the password "gosset" without the quotes to access the solutions. Note that the suggested solutions to the long-answer questions already appear at the Web site, and are not repeated here.

If you have purchased an eBook version of this book which is not able to be printed, it might be easiest to print out the Web-based solutions to consult while viewing the eBook questions.

Note that if any errors in the solutions in this book are discovered, then they will be amended and corrected in the Web-based solutions.

I thank the thousands of undergraduate, masters, and PhD students who were guinea pigs for the classroom testing of the material in this book. I thank ASB Securities for kindly allowing me to include online brokerage screen shots.

TFC/OU/2021

Tables

Figures

Introduction

The questions in this book are arranged in three chapters: Chapter 1 contains multiple-choice questions, Chapter 2 contains short-answer questions, and Chapter 3 contains long-answer questions. The questions in each chapter are classified according to the chapters of *Foundations For Scientific Investing*, or according to major topics or themes. These classifications are somewhat arbitrary in some cases because some questions overlap multiple topics. Multiple-choice and short-answer questions that have proven difficult to many students are indicated by a diamond symbol: ◇. Very difficult questions are indicated with two diamonds: ◇◇ . Equations from *Foundations* appear in Appendix A for reference.

The suggested solutions to the multiple-choice and short-answer questions appear in Chapter 4. The suggested solutions to all questions in this book appear, along with the spreadsheets that accompany *Foundations*, at the Web site www.FoundationsForScientificInvesting.com. These files may need to be accessed using the password "gosset" without the quotes. The suggested solutions to the long-answer questions appear only at the Web site, and are not repeated here.

I use the club suit symbol, ♣, to draw your attention to a spreadsheet download, and that you will need the above-mentioned password for some of these sheets.

The multiple-choice and short-answer questions often assume you have already answered some of the long-answer questions (especially the Markowitz/Tobin problem in Question 3.2.1 and the active alpha optimization in Question 3.2.2). The reason for this is that these long-answer questions appear in *Foundations* already to reinforce the material there, and the multiple-choice and short-answer questions are designed to test your understanding of the material in *Foundations*. So, many of the multiple-choice and short-answer questions refer explicitly to the long-answer questions and what you found there.

Note that when I use multiple-choice questions in an exam at this level, I give the students a special answer sheet where they get to choose, for any question, whether to give a multiple-choice answer or a multiple-choice answer accompanied by an explanation of any length. Something like 90% of students choose to treat the exam as a fully multiple-choice exam, and write nothing in the explanation section. Another 5% choose to give a written explanation for only one or two of the multiple-choice questions. The remaining 5% write a great deal in support of their multiple-choice answers. Such exams have an endogenous nature about them that students like because each student's preference determines the nature of their exam.

Each multiple-choice question has a best answer. You may need to read all choices before picking it. Note that some answers are rounded.

The short-answer questions typically require only a sentence or two in response, but the long-answer questions in Chapter 3 typically require an Excel spreadsheet or MATLAB code, or something similar.

Getting your hands dirty with spreadsheets serves to improve basic spreadsheet construction skills. My experience is that most students do not know how to build a spreadsheet that is dynamic and that can be easily audited. A dynamic spreadsheet is one that has, for example, a set of raw inputs in a raw data tab or in the top left-hand corner of the first tab, and those raw inputs are never copied and pasted anywhere else in the sheet; the contents of the spreadsheet and every other tab flow from those inputs only via cell referencing. As soon as a spreadsheet builder veers away from this model, various risks (operational and otherwise) are introduced. A spreadsheet is easy to audit as long as the auditor can see how the raw inputs are transformed into the outputs. This requires, for example, that the spreadsheet be dynamic and clearly labeled.

I am hopeful, therefore, that the long-answer questions allow you both to review the more difficult concepts in *Foundations*, and to simultaneously improve your spreadsheet skills.

Please feel free to send me e-mails with queries, corrections, alternative methods, etc. I reply to most e-mails, though sometimes with considerable delay. The errata (with corrections and comments) can be found at the Web site below.

www.FoundationsForScientificInvesting.com
timcrack@alum.mit.edu

If you found the material in this book to be beneficial to you, then please go to Amazon.com and leave a positive book review so that other people may similarly benefit from it. Just find the book on Amazon's Web site and then click on the box labeled "Write a customer review." Thank you.

Chapter 1

Multiple-Choice Test Questions

1.1 Foundations I: Quantitative

1. You have 40 years until retirement. Very roughly speaking, an extra 1% return per annum (after taxes and T-costs) does what to your wealth at retirement?

   (a) Increases wealth by 1%

   (b) Increases wealth by 25%

   (c) Increases wealth by 50%

   (d) Increases wealth by 100%

   (e) Decreases wealth.

2. Assume that Miss Bebe Nouveaune is born on April 1 (the first day of the N.Z. financial year). On this day her parents deposit $1,000 into a KiwiSaver account for her, and she also gets an additional $1,000 deposit from her grandparents. That is $2,000 deposited at $t = 0$. Assume that on every subsequent birthday up to and including her 16th birthday Bebe's parents deposit an additional $1,000 into her KiwiSaver scheme. That is $1,000 deposited on each of $t = 1$ through $t = 16$. There are no more contributions. Assume Bebe's KiwiSaver scheme returns a steady $R = 6\%$ every year after all taxes and expenses. What will be the balance in the scheme at Bebe's 65th birthday (rounded to whole dollars)?

   (a) $446,124

   (b) $517,037

   (c) $534,414

   (d) $550,808

   (e) None of the above is correct.

---

3. Suppose you are multiplying matrices to work out a Markowitz-type problem. You come to some algebra that looks like this:

$$\vec{h}_P = \vec{H}\mu_P + \vec{G} \text{ where}$$
$$\vec{H} = \frac{1}{D}\{[C(V^{-1}\vec{\mu}) - A(V^{-1}\vec{\iota})]\},$$
$$\vec{G} = \frac{1}{D}\{[B(V^{-1}\vec{\iota}) - A(V^{-1}\vec{\mu})]\},$$
$$A = \vec{\iota}'V^{-1}\vec{\mu},\ B = \vec{\mu}'V^{-1}\vec{\mu},\ C = \vec{\iota}'V^{-1}\vec{\iota},\ \text{and}\ D = BC - A^2.$$

If you have 20 stocks, what are the dimension of A, $\vec{H}$, and $\vec{h}_P$

(a) 1x1, 1x20, and 1x20, respectively.

(b) 20x20, 1x20, and 1x20, respectively.

(c) 1x1, 20x1, and 20x1, respectively.

(d) 1x1, 20x20, and 20x1, respectively.

(e) 1x20, 1x20, and 1x20, respectively.

4. Suppose you had plugged numbers into most of the algebra in Question 3, and you now want to locate the portfolio on the Markowitz frontier at $\mu_P = 0.15$. So, you plug $\mu_P = 0.15$ into the formula for $\vec{h}_P$. Now what formulas do you put $\vec{h}_P$ into to get the mean and standard deviation at this level of return?

(a) $\vec{h}'_P\vec{\mu}$ and $\vec{h}'_P V \vec{h}_P$, respectively.

(b) $\vec{h}'_P\vec{\mu}$ and $\vec{h}'_P V \vec{h}_B$, respectively.

(c) $\vec{h}'_P\vec{\iota}$ and $\vec{h}'_P V \vec{h}_P$, respectively.

(d) $\vec{h}'_P\vec{\mu}$ and $\sqrt{\vec{h}'_P V \vec{h}_P}$, respectively.

(e) $\sqrt{\vec{h}'_P\vec{\mu}}$ and $\vec{h}'_P V \vec{h}_P$, respectively.

5. You think riskier stocks probably have wider relative bid-ask spreads. So, you collect data on the relative size of the bid-ask spread (i.e., spread/price) of stocks and on the standard deviation (i.e., risk) of returns of stocks. You think the relationship is not linear. Which test is appropriate?

(a) Regress relative spread on standard deviation and look at the t-statistic of the slope.

(b) Look at the traditional Pearson product-moment correlation between relative spread and standard deviation and calculate its t-statistic.

(c) Look at the Spearman rank-order correlation between relative spread and standard deviation and calculate its t-statistic.

(d) All of the above.

(e) None of the above.

6. Table 1.1 contains the function $f(x) = 5 \times \mathrm{erf}(1/x)$ where $\mathrm{erf}(x) = \frac{2}{\sqrt{\pi}} \int_{t=0}^{t=x} e^{-t^2} dt$. Please show me that you understand elementary calculus by estimating the slope of $f(x)$ at $x = 6$ using a *numerical* technique.

x	$f(x)$
5.000	1.1135129
5.010	1.1113488
5.100	1.0922388
5.200	1.0717521
5.300	1.0520103
5.400	1.0329742
5.500	1.0146069
5.600	0.9968743
5.700	0.9797444
5.800	0.9631873
5.900	0.9471750
6.000	0.9316814
6.010	0.9301596
6.100	0.9166819
6.200	0.9021535
6.300	0.8880744
6.400	0.8744244
6.500	0.8611843
6.600	0.8483361
6.700	0.8358627
6.800	0.8237481
6.900	0.8119772
7.000	0.8005356
7.010	0.7994091

Table 1.1: Function $f(x) = 5 \times \mathrm{erf}(1/x)$

The table shows the function $f(x) = 5 \times \mathrm{erf}(1/x)$, where $\mathrm{erf}(x) = \frac{2}{\sqrt{\pi}} \int_{t=0}^{t=x} e^{-t^2}$.

(a) The slope of $f(x)$ at $x = 6$ is approximately -0.18183

(b) The slope of $f(x)$ at $x = 6$ is approximately -0.15218

(c) The slope of $f(x)$ at $x = 6$ is approximately -0.13115

(d) The slope of $f(x)$ at $x = 6$ is approximately +0.93168

(e) The slope of $f(x)$ at $x = 6$ is approximately +0.15218

7. "Spearman's rank-order correlation coefficient (SROCC) is a valid tool only where the relationship being tested is non-linear." Is this statement TRUE or FALSE.

(a) TRUE

(b) FALSE

8. In the active alpha optimization problem in Question 3.2.2, the objective function was $RTAA = \alpha_P - \lambda_R \cdot \omega_P^2 - TC$. This objective function measures what?

   (a) Expected utility of our active portfolio.

   (b) Choice variables and constraints.

   (c) Risk-adjusted return.

   (d) Return out-performance adjusted for risk and T-costs.

   (e) The CAPM expected return on our portfolio adjusted for costs and risks.

   This information is for questions 9 and 10:
   Suppose you have analyzed a time series of 500 continuously compounded daily returns on an individual small-cap stock, and you find the following sample statistics. Sample mean=0.00064, sample standard deviation=0.013308, sample first-order autocorrelation=0.056773. Assume 251 trading days in a year.

9. The value of the t-statistic to test the value of the mean against the null that the true mean is zero is given by:

   (a) 0.04809

   (b) 1.07535

   (c) 1.26948

   (d) 4.26608

   (e) 24.04568

10. The value of the t-statistic to test the value of the autocorrelation against the null that there is no autocorrelation is given roughly by:

    (a) 0.048

    (b) 1.075

    (c) 1.269

    (d) 4.266

    (e) 24.046

11. You have 40 years until retirement. Roughly speaking, an extra 2% return per annum (after taxes and T-costs) does what to your wealth at retirement?

    (a) Increases wealth by 2%

    (b) Increases wealth by 25%

    (c) Increases wealth by 50%

    (d) Increases wealth by 100%

    (e) Increases wealth by 200%

12. Table 1.2 contains the function $f(x) = sin(x \cdot \pi) - \Gamma(x, \pi)$ where $\Gamma(x, \nu) \equiv \frac{1}{\Gamma(\nu)} \int_{s=0}^{x} s^{\nu-1} e^{-s} ds$, for $x > 0$. Please show me that you understand elementary calculus by estimating the slope of $f(x)$ at $x = 7$ using a *numerical technique* and telling me which of the following is the **best answer**.

x	$f(x)$
6.00	-0.928310
6.01	-0.897401
6.20	-0.349955
6.40	0.005043
6.60	-0.002198
6.80	-0.371797
7.00	-0.965099
7.01	-0.996766
7.20	-1.557687
7.40	-1.925131
7.60	-1.928751
7.80	-1.568616
8.00	-0.983543
8.01	-0.952257
8.20	-0.398100
8.40	-0.036850
8.60	-0.038591
8.80	-0.403361
9.00	-0.992435

Table 1.2: Function $f(x) = sin(x \cdot \pi) - \Gamma(x, \pi)$

The table shows the function $f(x) = sin(x \cdot \pi) - \Gamma(x, \pi)$ where $\Gamma(x, \nu) \equiv \frac{1}{\Gamma(\nu)} \int_{s=0}^{x} s^{\nu-1} e^{-s} ds$, for $x > 0$.

(a) The slope of $f(x)$ at $x = 7$ is approximately -3.17

(b) The slope of $f(x)$ at $x = 7$ is approximately -2.98

(c) The slope of $f(x)$ at $x = 7$ is approximately -0.64

(d) The slope of $f(x)$ at $x = 7$ is approximately -0.04

(e) The slope of $f(x)$ at $x = 7$ is approximately -0.02

13. Which of the following is TRUE?

(a) In a sample of 500 daily large-cap stock returns, the t-test of the sample mean requires that the data are normally distributed.

(b) In a sample of 30 daily small-cap stock returns, the t-test of the sample mean requires that the data are normally distributed.

(c) In a sample of 500 daily large-cap stock returns, the t-test of the sample mean does not require that the data are normally distributed.

(d) (a) and (b), but not (c).

(e) (b) and (c), but not (a).

14. Figure 1.1 shows a Bloomberg screen print out from the command `UXG <EQUITY> GIP <GO>` for the U.S. stock UXG. I have labeled seven trades as A–G. Which of the following is TRUE?

    (a) B, D, and F are most likely customers selling.

    (b) A and G are most likely customers selling.

    (c) E is clearly a customer sale.

    (d) All of the above are true.

    (e) None of the above is true.

15. Looking again at Figure 1.1, which of the following is TRUE?

    (a) A, B, C, and D are most likely customers buying.

    (b) A, D, and F are most likely customers buying.

    (c) A, D, and G are most likely customers selling.

    (d) B, C, and F are most likely customers buying.

    (e) None of the above.

16. Looking again at Figure 1.1, I have labeled seven trades as A–G. Which of the following is FALSE?

    (a) The width of the bid-ask spread is a penny (i.e., $0.01) when trades A, B, C, and D occur.

    (b) The width of the bid-ask spread is a penny when trades F and G occur.

    (c) Trade C likely involves some price improvement.

    (d) We cannot immediately tell whether trade E was a customer sell or buy.

    (e) None of the above is false; they are all true.

17. You want to test whether large-capitalization stocks are less risky than small-capitalization stocks. So, you collect data on market capitalization and on the standard deviation (i.e., riskiness) of returns of stocks. You are sure that the relationship is not linear. Which test is appropriate?

    (a) Use a standard OLS to regress market capitalization on standard deviation of returns and then look at the t-statistic of the slope from the OLS regression.

    (b) Look at the traditional Pearson product-moment correlation between market capitalization and standard deviation and calculate its t-statistic.

    (c) Standardize both variables by subtracting the cross-sectional mean and dividing by the cross-sectional standard deviation. Now plot the two on an X-Y scatter plot, find the line of best fit, and calculate the R^2 as your statistic.

    (d) All of the above.

    (e) None of the above.

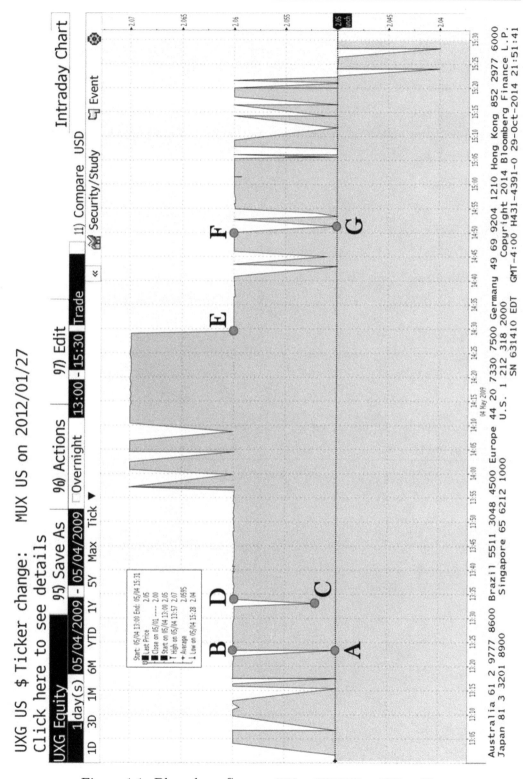

Figure 1.1: Bloomberg Screen: UXG <EQUITY> GIP <GO>

A UXG Corporation Bloomberg GIP screen from May 4, 2009, showing a series
of trades.

This information is for questions 18 and 19:
Suppose you have analyzed a time series of 500 continuously compounded daily returns on an individual small-cap stock, and you find the following sample statistics. Sample mean=−0.000327, sample standard deviation=0.017007, sample first-order autocorrelation=−0.092763. Assume 251 trading days in a year.

18. The value of the t-statistic to test the value of the mean against the null that the true mean is zero is given by:

    (a) −0.007322

    (b) −0.027177

    (c) −0.429937

    (d) −6.821446

    (e) −108.072028

19. The value of the t-statistic to test the value of the autocorrelation against the null that there is no autocorrelation is given roughly by:

    (a) 22.36

    (b) -2.08

    (c) -7.70

    (d) -121.97

    (e) None of the above is within 0.10 of the correct answer.

20. Suppose you are multiplying matrices to work out the Tobin frontier part of a Markowitz-type problem. You come to some matrix algebra that looks like this:

$$
\left[\begin{array}{c} \min_{\vec{h}} \ \vec{h}'V\vec{h} \\ \text{s.t.} \ \ \underbrace{\vec{h}'\vec{\mu}}_{risky} + \underbrace{(1 - \vec{h}'\vec{\imath})R_F}_{riskless} = \mu_P \end{array} \right] \Rightarrow \left[\vec{h}_P = \underbrace{\frac{\mu_P - R_F}{(\vec{\mu} - R_F\vec{\imath})'V^{-1}(\vec{\mu} - R_F\vec{\imath})}V^{-1}(\vec{\mu} - R_F\vec{\imath})}_{\text{column vector of weight in risky assets for given } \mu_P} \right]
$$

    If you have 20 stocks, what are the dimensions of $\left[\frac{\mu_P - R_F}{(\vec{\mu} - R_F\vec{\imath})'V^{-1}(\vec{\mu} - R_F\vec{\imath})}V^{-1}(\vec{\mu} - R_F\vec{\imath}) \right]$ and $\left[V^{-1}(\vec{\mu} - R_F\vec{\imath}) \right]$?

    (a) 1x1 and 1x1.

    (b) 1x1 and 20x1.

    (c) 20x1 and 1x1.

    (d) 20x1 and 20x1.

    (e) 20x1 and 20x20.

21. The difference between analytical and numerical derivatives is that:

    (a) Numerical derivatives use high-level Math skills; analytical derivatives just use a simple computer routine.

    (b) Analytical derivatives use high-level Math skills; numerical derivatives just use a simple computer routine.

    (c) Analytical derivatives are time-consuming to work out and prone to errors; numerical derivatives can be worked out quickly and checked easily.

    (d) (a) and (c), but not (b)

    (e) (b) and (c), but not (a)

22. Suppose you calculate an autocorrelation of -0.040 from a time series of 500 daily stock returns. Suppose the sample standard deviation is 0.015, and the sample mean is 0.001. Which number is closest to a good estimate of the standard error of the autocorrelation estimate?

    (a) -0.89442

    (b) 0.04472

    (c) 0.00067

    (d) 0.01500

    (e) 1.49071

23. Suppose you download two years of daily returns data on all stocks listed on the N.Z. Stock Exchange (NZX). For roughly what proportion of these stocks would you expect that you could reject the null hypothesis that the returns are drawn from a normal distribution? Assume a 5% level of significance if you wish.

    (a) 90%

    (b) 50%

    (c) 20%

    (d) 5%

    (e) 0%

24. Suppose you download two years of daily data on all stocks listed on the NZX. For what proportion of these stocks would you expect that you could reject the null hypothesis that the returns are drawn from a distribution with zero mean? Assume a 5% level of significance if you wish.

    (a) 100%.

    (b) Almost all.

    (c) About half.

    (d) A small proportion.

    (e) 0%.

25. Suppose I go to the Bloomberg terminal and download the time series of daily stock prices on IBM for the last 250 trading days. Suppose I use them to work out the correlation between P_t and P_{t-1}. That is, the correlation between the prices on the first 249 days and the last 249 days of my 250-day sample. This tells me whether I can use today's stock price to forecast tomorrow's stock price. Which of the following is a likely number for this correlation?

    (a) 1.050

    (b) 0.975

    (c) 0.500

    (d) 0.000

    (e) -0.500

26. We can distinguish between statistical techniques that are distributionally parametric or non-parametric and functionally parametric or non-parametric. Which ONE of the following statements is the best answer?

    (a) The traditional t-test for the population mean is always distributionally non-parametric regardless of sample size.

    (b) The traditional t-test for the population mean is always distributionally parametric regardless of sample size.

    (c) The traditional t-test for the population mean is distributionally non-parametric in small samples.

    (d) The traditional t-test for the population mean is distributionally parametric in small samples.

    (e) The traditional t-test for the population mean is always functionally non-parametric.

27. Suppose you download one month of daily returns data to a stock. Suppose you calculate the skewness and kurtosis Z-statistics. Suppose that the skewness Z-statistic is very large and you reject the null hypothesis of no skewness at the 5% level. Suppose however that the kurtosis Z-statistic is tiny, and you cannot reject the null hypothesis that there is no excess kurtosis. Please assume the data are independent and identically distributed. Given all this information, if you want to test the null hypothesis that the population mean return is zero,...

    (a) The traditional t-test for the population mean is valid.

    (b) The traditional t-test for the population mean is invalid.

    (c) The traditional t-test for the population mean is invalid, but a small adjustment using the autocorrelation coefficient will solve the problem.

    (d) We do not have enough information to judge whether the traditional t-test for the population mean is valid or not.

    (e) None of the above is correct.

This information is for questions 28 and 29:
Suppose you have analyzed a time series of 500 continuously compounded daily returns on an individual small-cap stock, and you find the following sample statistics. Sample mean=0.0014360, sample standard deviation=0.0181796, sample first-order autocorrelation=0.0252561. Assume 251 trading days in a year.

28. The value of the t-statistic to test the null hypothesis that the true mean is zero is given by:

    (a) 0.07899

    (b) 1.76449

    (c) 1.76626

    (d) 12.65981

    (e) 39.49482

29. The value of the t-statistic to test the value of the autocorrelation against the null that there is no autocorrelation is given roughly by:

    (a) 31.06

    (b) 1.96

    (c) 1.39

    (d) 0.56

    (e) None of the above is close to the correct answer.

30. Suppose you think that there is a U-shaped relationship between time of day and T-costs to trade stocks. You think it is costly to trade in the morning when investors are worried about what information may arrive during the day, cheap to trade in the middle of the day when not much new information arrives, and costly to trade in the afternoon when panicked investors may be trying to get out of stocks ahead of the uncertain overnight period. You want to demonstrate the U-shaped relationship by looking at the relationship between time of day and measured T-costs (e.g., relative spreads). You want to use a correlation measure and you think about using the Spearman rank-order correlation coefficient (SROCC) or the traditional Pearson product-moment correlation coefficient (PPMCC) or both. Which one(s) make sense in this situation?

    (a) Only the PPMCC.

    (b) Only the SROCC.

    (c) Both the PPMCC and the SROCC.

    (d) Neither the PPMCC nor the SROCC.

    (e) None of the above makes sense.

31. Suppose you download 500 days of returns to a stock. Suppose that you test for normality and cannot reject normality. Suppose that you now want to test whether the variance in the second half of the sample is different from the variance in the first half of the sample. Suppose that you take a test statistic of form $STAT \equiv \frac{s_1^2}{s_2^2}$, where s_1^2 and s_2^2 are the estimators of variance from the first and second halves of the sample and $s^2 \equiv \frac{1}{N-1}\sum_{i=1}^{N}(X_i - \bar{X})^2$ is the small-sample-adjusted variance estimator. Then in this case, the test statistic $STAT$ should be compared with which of the following tables?

    (a) The standard normal distribution.

    (b) The t-distribution.

    (c) The chi-squared distribution.

    (d) The F-distribution.

    (e) None of the above; it is non-parametric.

32. The t-test for a mean is...

    (a) "Distributionally parametric" in small sample but "distributionally non-parametric" in large sample.

    (b) "Distributionally parametric" in large sample but "distributionally non-parametric" in small sample.

    (c) "Distributionally parametric" in small sample and "distributionally non-parametric" in small sample.

    (d) "Distributionally parametric" in large sample and "distributionally non-parametric" in large sample.

    (e) None of the above; the correct statement was about being functionally parametric or not.

33. We have 30 daily continuously compounded returns to a small-capitalization stock. We want to use a standard t-test of the null hypothesis that the mean return is different from zero. We run some other tests first and discover that the returns data display significant excess skewness, but not excess kurtosis. Which of the following is the best answer.

    (a) We have no evidence that there is any problem with the assumptions or robustness of the standard t-test of the mean.

    (b) We have some evidence that there is a violation of one of the assumptions of the standard t-test of the mean, but the t-test should be robust to this violation.

    (c) We have some evidence of a violation of one of the assumptions of the standard t-test of the mean, and the t-test is likely *not* robust to this violation.

    (d) We have evidence that there is a violation of *two* of the assumptions of the standard t-test of the mean, and the t-test is *not* robust to these violations.

    (e) None of the above is correct.

This information is for questions 34 and 35:
You have analyzed a time series of 503 continuously compounded daily returns on an individual N.Z. stock, and you find the following sample statistics. Sample mean=−0.0003568, sample standard deviation=0.0204594, sample first-order autocorrelation=−0.0532845. Assume 251 trading days in a year.

34. The t-statistic to test the null hypothesis that the true mean is zero is given by:

    (a) −0.3911

    (b) −6.1963

    (c) −2.6044

    (d) −8.7717

    (e) −0.2763

35. Assuming the given sample statistics, and rounding to the nearest 100, how big would the sample size N have had to have been for the quoted autocorrelation to be statistically significant at the 5% level? Assume a two-sided test.

    (a) 500

    (b) 1,400

    (c) 12,700

    (d) None of the above is close to the correct answer.

    (e) We do not have enough information to calculate this answer.

36. We may interpret the exponential function and continuously compounded returns in terms of APRs and frequent compounding. Suppose we write down the following where r is the continuously compounded return per annum:

$$e^r \approx \left[1 + \frac{\boxed{A}}{\boxed{B}} \right]^{\boxed{C}} = 1 + \boxed{D} = \boxed{E}$$

    Which one of the following is FALSE?

    (a) $A = r$ is like an APR (annual percentage rate)

    (b) $B = n$, but only for large n

    (c) $C = t$ counts the number of years.

    (d) $D = EAR$ (effective annual rate)

    (e) $E =$ multiplicative compounding factor that shows economic growth.

37. Table 1.3 gives stock price and option price for a range of stock prices. Please give me an estimate of the delta of the option at stock price equal to $5. Please round to two decimal places.

   (a) -0.24

   (b) -0.46

   (c) -0.48

   (d) -0.72

   (e) None of the above is close to correct.

Stock Price x	Option Price $f(x)$
$ 4.0000	$ 0.9965
$ 4.0100	$ 0.9873
$ 4.1000	$ 0.9053
$ 4.2000	$ 0.8171
$ 4.3000	$ 0.7324
$ 4.4000	$ 0.6519
$ 4.5000	$ 0.5760
$ 4.6000	$ 0.5051
$ 4.7000	$ 0.4395
$ 4.8000	$ 0.3796
$ 4.9000	$ 0.3252
$ 5.0000	$ 0.2766
$ 5.0100	$ 0.2720
$ 5.1000	$ 0.2333
$ 5.2000	$ 0.1954
$ 5.3000	$ 0.1624
$ 5.4000	$ 0.1339
$ 5.5000	$ 0.1097
$ 5.6000	$ 0.0892
$ 5.7000	$ 0.0720
$ 5.8000	$ 0.0578
$ 5.9000	$ 0.0460
$ 6.0000	$ 0.0364
$ 6.0100	$ 0.0356

Table 1.3: Stock Price and Option Price (both in dollars per share)

38. In *Foundations*, we said that $1 invested in the S&P 500 stocks grew to be worth $108.45 over the 50-year period from mid-1963 to mid-2013. We said this was an average rate of return of approximately 9.83% per annum. Do you think this is an arithmetic average rate of return or a geometric average rate of return?

   (a) Arithmetic.

   (b) Geometric.

   (c) Both.

   (d) Neither.

39. In Chapter 1 of *Foundations* there is a naive coin toss strategy where at the end of each day you decide whether to be invested in T-bills or the S&P 500 for the next business day. Suppose, instead, that your coin has a $(50 + x)\%$ chance of choosing the better investment. Using your intuition, how big do you think x has to be to add 1% per annum to your returns? Please ignore T-costs.

    (a) $x = \frac{1}{2}\%$ so the coin is correct 50.5% of the time.

    (b) $x = 5\%$ so the coin is correct 55% of the time.

    (c) $x = 10\%$ so the coin is correct 60% of the time.

    (d) $x = 25\%$ so the coin is correct 75% of the time.

    (e) $x = 45\%$ so the coin is correct 95% of the time.

40. I have the following data for standard deviation and sample size for samples of daily returns drawn from 2010 and from 2011; note that they are not full-year samples. Sample stats: $\hat{\sigma}_{2010} = 0.025$, $N_{2010} = 60$, $\hat{\sigma}_{2011} = 0.015$, $N_{2011} = 200$. If I want to conduct a two-sided F-test of the null hypothesis that the standard deviations are the same (H_0: $\sigma_{2010} = \sigma_{2011}$), what is the value of the F-statistic? Note that I give below the F-statistic and also $1/(F\text{-statistic})$, because both are F-statistics, and I am not sure which one you will calculate.

    (a) F=1.67 (or F=0.60 if you invert it)

    (b) F=2.78 (or F=0.36 if you invert it)

    (c) F=0.83 (or F=1.20 if you invert it)

    (d) F=0.50 (or F=2.00 if you invert it)

    (e) None of the above is reasonable.

41. We may interpret the exponential function and continuously compounded returns in terms of APRs and frequent compounding. Suppose we write down the following where r is the continuously compounded return per annum:

$$ e^r \approx \left[1 + \frac{\boxed{A}}{\boxed{B}} \right]^{\boxed{C}} = 1 + \boxed{D} = \boxed{E} $$

    Which ONE of the following is FALSE?

    (a) $A = r$ is like an APR (annual percentage rate)

    (b) $B = n$ for large n

    (c) $C = n$ for large n.

    (d) $D = APR$ (annual percentage rate)

    (e) $E = $ multiplicative compounding factor that shows economic growth.

42. Suppose you are multiplying matrices to work out the Tobin frontier part of a Markowitz-type problem. You come to some matrix algebra that looks like this:

$$
\left[\begin{array}{c} \min_{\vec{h}} \vec{h}'V\vec{h} \\ \text{s.t. } \underbrace{\vec{h}'\vec{\mu}}_{\text{risky}} + \underbrace{(1 - \vec{h}'\vec{\iota})R_F}_{\text{riskless}} = \mu_P \end{array} \right] \Rightarrow \left[\vec{h}_P = \underbrace{\frac{\mu_P - R_F}{(\vec{\mu} - R_F\vec{\iota})'V^{-1}(\vec{\mu} - R_F\vec{\iota})}V^{-1}(\vec{\mu} - R_F\vec{\iota})}_{\text{column vector of weight in risky assets for given } \mu_P} \right]
$$

If you have 20 stocks, what are the dimensions of $\left[\frac{\mu_P - R_F}{(\vec{\mu}-R_F\vec{\iota})'V^{-1}(\vec{\mu}-R_F\vec{\iota})}V^{-1}(\vec{\mu} - R_F\vec{\iota}) \right]$ and $\left[(\vec{\mu} - R_F\vec{\iota})'V^{-1}(\vec{\mu} - R_F\vec{\iota}) \right]$?

(a) 20x1 and 1x1.
(b) 20x1 and 20x1.
(c) 20x1 and 20x20.
(d) 1x1 and 1x1.
(e) 1x1 and 20x1.

43. ◇◇ To analyze the portfolio on the Tobin frontier at $\mu_P = 0.15$, you plug $\mu_P = 0.15$ into the formula for $\vec{h}_P$ in Question 42. Which formulas can you put this $\vec{h}_P$ into to get the **mean** and **variance** of returns at this level of return?

(a) $\vec{h}'_P\vec{\mu}$ and $\vec{h}'_PV\vec{h}_P$, respectively.
(b) $\vec{h}'_P\vec{\mu}$ and $\vec{h}'_PV\vec{h}_B$, respectively.
(c) $\vec{h}'_P\vec{\iota}$ and $\vec{h}'_PV\vec{h}_P$, respectively.
(d) $\vec{h}'_P\vec{\mu}$ and $\sqrt{\vec{h}'_PV\vec{h}_P}$, respectively.
(e) $\sqrt{\vec{h}'_P\vec{\mu}}$ and $\vec{h}'_PV\vec{h}_P$, respectively.
(f) None of the above.

44. ◇ Suppose you take five large-capitalization NZX stocks and five small-capitalization NZX stocks. The five small-cap NZX stocks will have something in common when we look at their autocorrelation of daily returns. What is it?

(a) Most of the small-cap stocks will have positive autocorrelations and most of these will be significantly different from zero.
(b) Most of the small-cap stocks will have negative autocorrelations and most of these will be significantly different from zero.
(c) Most of the small-cap stocks will have positive autocorrelations and most of these will be insignificantly different from zero.
(d) Most of the small-cap stocks will have negative autocorrelations and most of these will be insignificantly different from zero.
(e) None of the above is true.

45. I download 500 daily returns on a stock and I test the returns to see if there is any skewness and also I test for any kurtosis. Suppose I find very significant excess kurtosis but I find no skewness at all. I can conclude what:

    (a) I cannot tell whether the returns are normally distributed or not.

    (b) The returns are not normally distributed because there is kurtosis.

    (c) The returns are normally distributed because although we found kurtosis, there is no skewness.

    (d) The returns are normally distributed because although there is kurtosis, the sample size is large enough that it does not matter.

    (e) We cannot reject normality because there is no skewness.

46. Suppose I give you daily returns data for 10 randomly selected U.S. or N.Z. stocks for 3 years. For how many of these stocks do you think a statistical test would reject normality of returns? Which is the best answer?

    (a) Most if not all of them. Say nine or 10.

    (b) Perhaps two thirds of them.

    (c) Half of them.

    (d) A third of them.

    (e) Few if any. Say zero, one, or two.

47. Suppose you find that the first order autocorrelation of daily returns to FPH is 6.68%. The count of daily returns is 504. The mean of daily returns is 0.0002165, and the standard deviation of daily returns is 0.0146541. Use these data to calculate a t-statistic, denoted t, to test the null hypothesis that the first order autocorrelation of daily returns is zero.

    (a) $t = 0.33$

    (b) $t = 1.50$

    (c) $t = 4.56$

    (d) $t = 22.45$

    (e) $t = 102.34$

48. In Chapter 1 of *Foundations*, we discussed the realized equity risk premium in the U.S. over the 50-year period May 1963 to May 2013. We said it was roughly how much?

    (a) 14–16%.

    (b) 12–14%.

    (c) 10–12%.

    (d) 8–10%.

    (e) 4–6%.

49. In Chapter 1 of *Foundations*, we said that the dividend yield on the S&P 500 varied between L and H over the 50-year period May 1963 to May 2013. How big were L and H?

    (a) $L = 0.0110$; $H = 0.0167$.

    (b) $L = 0.0110$; $H = 0.0670$.

    (c) $L = 0.0310$; $H = 0.0375$.

    (d) $L = 0.0375$; $H = 0.0885$.

    (e) $L = 0.0510$; $H = 0.0885$.

50. Which of the following is TRUE?

    (a) In a sample of 500 daily large-cap stock returns, the t-test of the sample mean requires that the data are normally distributed.

    (b) In a sample of 500 daily large-cap stock returns, the t-test of the sample mean does not require that the data are normally distributed.

    (c) In a sample of 150 daily small-cap stock returns, the t-test of the sample mean may require that the data are normally distributed.

    (d) (a) and (b), but not (c).

    (e) (b) and (c), but not (a).

51. ◇ Suppose I take a two-year time series of daily prices and returns on a typical stock. You could download these data and do the same. Suppose I regress prices on themselves with one day's lag, $P_t = a + bP_{t-1} + \epsilon_t$, and I regress returns on themselves with one day's lag, $R_t = c + dR_{t-1} + \eta_t$. What will the coefficients of the respective regressions be (roughly speaking)?

    (a) $\hat{b} \approx 0$ and $\hat{d} \approx 0$

    (b) $\hat{b} \approx 0$ and $\hat{d} \approx 1$

    (c) $\hat{b} \approx 1$ and $\hat{d} \approx 0$

    (d) $\hat{b} \approx 1$ and $\hat{d} \approx 1$

    (e) Neither $\hat{b}$ nor $\hat{d}$ will be close to either 0 or 1.

52. On Monday October 19, 1987, the Dow Jones Industrial Average fell 22.6% from the previous Friday's closing level. Given your knowledge of the parameters of the distribution, how many standard deviations of daily return was that day's move?

    (a) Less than two standard deviations.

    (b) Roughly 2.26 standard deviations.

    (c) Roughly 22.6 standard deviations.

    (d) Notably more than 22.6 standard deviations.

    (e) None of the above are even close to the correct answer.

53. Suppose that we randomly select 10 stocks from the S&P/NZX50 and download two years of daily stock returns data on each stock. For how many of these 10 stocks do you think we should be able to reject the null hypotheses that the daily mean return is zero? Choose the ONE best answer.

    (a) Definitely none of them.

    (b) Probably 0, 1, 2, or 3 of them.

    (c) Probably 5, 6, 7, or 8 of them.

    (d) Probably 8, 9, or 10 of them.

    (e) Definitely all 10 of them.

54. Suppose you download the most recent 250 trading days of daily prices on Fletcher Building (FBU) stock. Suppose you want to see whether you can use FBU prices to predict FBU prices one day ahead. So, you regress observations $t = 2$ through $t = 250$ on observations $t = 1$ through $t = 249$ using a simple linear regression: $P_t = \alpha + \beta P_{t-1} + \epsilon$. Roughly what should the R^2 of the regression be?

    (a) R^2 essentially zero, because you should not be able to predict tomorrow's stock price using today's stock price.

    (b) R^2 slightly positive, maybe $0 < R^2 \le 0.25$, because there should be some light positive relationship.

    (c) R^2 close to a half, because there should be some sort of positive relationship, but it is not likely to be linear.

    (d) R^2 close to a one, maybe $0.90 \le R^2 \le 0.99$, because the relationship is nearly perfectly linear.

    (e) R^2 exactly one, because the relationship is perfectly linear.

55. In *Foundations* we used the spreadsheet MIN-VAR-OBJ.XLS to minimize portfolio variance (i.e., $\sigma_P^2 = \vec{h}'V\vec{h}$) for varying level of return μ_P, and the spreadsheet MAX-UTIL-OBJ.XLS to maximize utility (i.e., $+\vec{h}'\vec{\mu} - \lambda\vec{h}'V\vec{h}$) for varying risk aversion λ. Each optimization produced a frontier. Which ONE of the following describes the relationship between these frontiers when short selling is allowed?

    (a) The minimum variance frontier was a "batwing" shape inside the maximum utility frontier.

    (b) The minimum variance frontier was identical in all respects to the maximum utility frontier.

    (c) The minimum variance frontier did not agree at any point with the maximum utility frontier.

    (d) The minimum variance frontier was the upper part only of the maximum utility frontier.

    (e) The maximum utility frontier was the upper part only of the minimum risk frontier.

56. ◇ Suppose that I am going to run a Monte Carlo simulation of an investor's 45-year horizon until retirement, simulating the time series of annual continuously compounded returns. Suppose I am going to simulate the first time series of 45 independent normally distributed annual after-tax continuously compounded returns r_t to his investments for $1 \leq t \leq 45$. I will know the true mean and variance of these returns because I am going to create the returns myself (let me assume they are fixed at $\mu = 0.05$ and $\sigma = 0.1075$). Suppose I plan to then standardize the simulated returns by calculating $z_t = \frac{r_t - \mu}{\sigma}$ for each continuously compounded return r_t, for $1 \leq t \leq 45$. Suppose I then plan to square the standardized returns and add them up to get the sum $S = \sum_{t=1}^{45} z_t^2$. What will be the simulated statistical distribution of S?

   (a) S is distributed Student-t with 44 degrees of freedom.

   (b) S is distributed Student-t with 45 degrees of freedom.

   (c) S is distributed chi-squared with 44 degrees of freedom.

   (d) S is distributed chi-squared with 45 degrees of freedom.

   (e) S is distributed normal with mean $45 \cdot \mu$ and standard deviation $\sqrt{45} \cdot \sigma$.

57. I collected market capitalizations and relative bid-ask spreads for the 500 stocks in the S&P 500 index, and I calculated the traditional PPMCC correlation between relative spread and market capitalization, and also the rank-order SROCC correlation (see the figure in Chapter 1 of *Foundations*). Which ONE of the following did I find?

   (a) $0 <$ PPMCC $<$ SROCC

   (b) $0 <$ SROCC $<$ PPMCC

   (c) SROCC $<$ PPMCC < 0

   (d) PPMCC $<$ SROCC < 0

   (e) Each of the above must be incorrect.

58. Two matrices are given as follows:

$$B = \begin{pmatrix} 1 & 2 & 3 & 4 \\ 5 & 6 & 7 & 8 \end{pmatrix}, \quad C = \begin{pmatrix} 9 & 10 \\ 11 & 12 \end{pmatrix}.$$

   I want to multiple them together as $B \times C$. Which ONE of the following is correct?

   (a) They are conformal and the answer has size 4×2.

   (b) They are conformal and the answer has size 2×2.

   (c) They are conformal and the answer has size 2×4.

   (d) They are conformal and the answer has size 4×4.

   (e) They are not conformal.

59. You have a sample of 500 daily continuously compounded stock returns. The mean return is 0.0016278. The sample standard deviation is 0.0212155 (calculated using division by $N-1$). The sample autocorrelation is -0.1973230 (i.e., first-order autocorrelation). What is the value of the t-statistic to test the null hypothesis that the true mean is zero? Please round to two decimal places.

(a) -207.97

(b) -4.41

(c) 0.04

(d) 1.72

(e) 38.36

60. Which are the three standard assumptions that go into any t-test of the mean? In answering this question, do not worry about whether the test is robust to violations of the assumption or not, just choose the option that names the assumptions.

(a) The data are normally distributed, independent of each other, and identically distributed.

(b) The distribution of the data is stable, the parameters of the distribution are stable, and the data are independent.

(c) The data are elliptically distributed, the parameters of the distribution are stable, and the data are independent.

(d) The data are chi-square distributed, independent, and identically distributed.

(e) None of the above is correct.

61. Assume that Miss Bebe Nouveaune is born on April 1 (the first day of the N.Z. financial year). On this day her parents deposit $1,000 into a KiwiSaver account for her, and she also gets an additional $1,000 deposit from her grandparents. That is $2,000 deposited at $t = 0$. Assume that on every subsequent birthday up to and including her 18th birthday Bebe's parents deposit an additional $1,200 into her KiwiSaver scheme. That is $1,200 deposited on each of $t = 1$ through $t = 18$. Assume there are no more contributions and no MTC match. Assume Bebe's KiwiSaver scheme grows at 6% every year after all taxes and expenses. What will be the balance in the scheme at Bebe's 65th birthday?

(a) $573,581.10

(b) $611,895.60

(c) $643,311.94

(d) $661,871.04

(e) None of the above.

62. ◇ In Chapter 1 of *Foundations*, we said that given a random variable X, we could view the continuous integral

$$E(X) = \int x f_X(x) dx$$

as a discrete probability-weighted average summation $\sum_i x_i \cdot p_i$, where probability $p_i = h_i \cdot w_i$, and which ONE of the following holds?

(a) $p_i = f_X(x_i)$, $w_i = x_i$ and dx is an infinitesimal step in x at x_i, and the summation is valid only in the limit as $dx \to 0$.

(b) $h_i = f_X(x_i)$, $w_i = $ a non-infinitesimal step in x at x_i, and the summation is valid only in the limit as $w_i \to 0$.

(c) $p_i = f_X(x_i)$, $w_i = dx$ is an infinitesimal step in x at x_i, and the summation is valid only in the limit as $w_i \to 0$.

(d) $h_i = x_i$, $w_i = f_X(x_i)$, and the summation is valid only in the limit as $dx \to 0$.

(e) None of the above makes good sense.

63. ◇◇ Suppose that there exist two well-known and heavily traded stocks in the same industry in the same country. They are Stock S and Stock F. Suppose that Stock S is well managed and successful and that its stock price steadily increases over 10 years. Suppose that Stock F is mis-managed and is somewhat of a failure, and its stock price declines steadily over those same 10 years. Suppose, however, that, being in the same industry and in the same country, their stock prices tend to move together on a day-to-day basis, relative to their respective trends. That is, on a day when good industry news or good macro-economic news comes out, the price of Stock S tends to rise a bit more than usual, and the price of Stock F tends to fall a bit less than usual. Similarly, for bad news days, when the price of Stock S tends to rise a little less than usual, and the price of Stock F tends to fall a little more than usual. Which ONE of the following best describes the sign of the correlation of the prices and the correlation of the returns (i.e., between Stock S and Stock F in each case) over the full 10-year sample at the sampling frequencies indicated in Table 1.4?

	Daily Prices	Daily Returns	Annual Prices
(a)	−	+	−
(b)	+	−	+
(c)	+	+	+
(d)	−	−	−
(e)	None of the above is correct.		

Table 1.4: Possible Correlations Between Prices and Correlations Between Returns

64. Stock returns and stock index returns are not normally distributed. This has particularly important implications for risk management models and for models that price options. We can almost always reject normality because of excess kurtosis (that is, kurtosis in excess of what you find in a normal distribution). Which ONE of the following answers best describes typical excess kurtosis (also called "leptokurtosis") seen in stock returns and stock index returns distributions?

    (a) There are many more very small returns than if the distribution were normal with the same mean and variance.

    (b) There are many more very large returns than if the distribution were normal with the same mean and variance.

    (c) There are fewer very small returns than if the distribution were normal with the same mean and variance.

    (d) There are fewer very large returns than if the distribution were normal with the same mean and variance.

    (e) Both (a) and (b).

65. ◇ Suppose that I have a large sample of daily stock returns, 500 observations, say. Suppose I calculate the t-statistic for the mean return to test the null hypothesis that the mean return is zero. Suppose that the only violation of the assumptions of the t-statistic is that there is significant autocorrelation (at lag 1) of +15% in the daily returns. Ignoring any other possible violations of the assumptions underlying the t-statistic, which ONE of the following is roughly true?

    (a) The calculated t-statistic is over-stated (i.e., of too big a magnitude) by a factor of about 15%.

    (b) The calculated t-statistic is under-stated (i.e., of too small a magnitude) by a factor of about 15%.

    (c) The calculated t-statistic is roughly correctly stated (i.e., of neither too big nor too small a magnitude) because the sample size is large enough that the t-statistic is robust to the stated violation.

    (d) We cannot tell whether the t-statistic is over- or under-stated based on the above information.

    (e) None of the above is true.

66. A U.S. mutual fund that passively tracks the S&P 500 charges an annual fee (or "expense ratio") of 9 bps. On an investment of $100,000 this amounts to...

    (a) $0.90 per year

    (b) $9.00 per year

    (c) $90.00 per year

    (d) $900.00 per year

    (e) None of the above

67. You download a sample of 100 daily stock returns for a small stock. The standard t-statistic for the sample mean is 3.2, which is well beyond the critical value for a 5% test. The standard t-statistic for the autocorrelation is -3.4, which is also well beyond the critical value for a 5% test. Based only on this information, what can you conclude about whether the data are normally distributed or not?

    (a) We can reject normality, given the statistically significant results mentioned.

    (b) We do not have enough evidence to reject normality, but if we had a smaller sample, the statistically significant results mentioned would lead us to reject normality.

    (c) We do not have enough evidence to reject normality, but if we had a larger sample, the statistically significant results mentioned would lead us to reject normality.

    (d) We do not have any evidence to reject normality, and even if we had a larger sample, the statistically significant results mentioned would not lead us to reject normality.

    (e) None of the above makes any sense.

68. True diversification is obtained when

    (a) Riskless assets are combined with risky assets to give a less risky portfolio. At the optimum weights, the risk of the portfolio is reduced.

    (b) Risky assets from different asset classes are combined. We hope that the returns to the different assets classes are lightly, or even negatively, correlated.

    (c) Riskless assets are combined into a riskless portfolio.

    (d) Risky assets from a single asset class are combined together using weights that give the optimum risk reduction (e.g., a Markowitz-type optimization).

    (e) None of the above is correct.

69. Suppose you have three matrices, A, B, and C as follows.

$$A = \begin{pmatrix} 1 \\ 2 \\ 3 \end{pmatrix}, \quad B = \begin{pmatrix} 4 & 5 & 6 \\ 7 & 8 & 9 \\ 10 & 11 & 12 \end{pmatrix}, \quad C = \begin{pmatrix} 13 & 14 & 15 \\ 16 & 17 & 18 \end{pmatrix}$$

Which of the following are ALL valid matrix operations, where I used the notation "×" to denote matrix multiplication?

    (a) $A \times B$, $B \times C$, and $A \times C$.

    (b) $C \times B$, $B \times A$, and $C \times A$.

    (c) $A \times C$, $B \times C$, and $A \times B$.

    (d) $A \times B$, $B \times C$, and $C \times A$.

    (e) All of the above.

70. In Chapter 1 of *Foundations* we noted that the average annual return to the S&P 500 over the 91 years from 1928 to 2018 was 9.49% including reinvested dividends. In how many of those years did the actual return on the S&P 500 come within 1% of this average (i.e., between 8.49% and 10.49%)?

    (a) 1 year.

    (b) 10 years.

    (c) 21 years.

    (d) 43 years.

    (e) More than 43 years.

71. The correlation between the daily returns to an all-stock portfolio and a 60/40 stock/bond portfolio is roughly what? Assume high-quality bonds in the bond portfolio.

    (a) 2%

    (b) 20%

    (c) 50%

    (d) 70%

    (e) 98%

72. An Excel spreadsheet contains $N = 25$ continuously compounded returns on a stock. You want to build a t-test to test the null hypothesis that the mean return is zero: $t = \bar{X} \big/ \left(\hat{\sigma} \big/ \sqrt{N} \right)$. You build your t-statistic using Excel functions for the sample mean, $\bar{X}$, the sample standard deviation, $\hat{\sigma}$, and the sample size. Assume that there are no missing data and no violations of the assumptions of the t-test. You are trying to choose between two Excel functions for the standard deviation. The first function is =STDEV() (which is the same as =STDEV.S() in the latest Excel version), and it calculates sample standard deviation using division by $N - 1$. The second function is =STDEVP (which is the same as =STDEV.P() in the latest Excel version), and it calculates population standard deviation using division by N. Which Excel function should you use?

    (a) =STDEV()(i.e., =STDEV.S() in the latest Excel version).

    (b) =STDEVP()(i.e., =STDEV.P() in the latest Excel version).

    (c) Either =STDEV() or =STDEVP(), there is no particular reason why it matters.

    (d) Either =STDEV() or =STDEVP(), but if you use =STDEVP, then you need to exclude either the first or last observation so that it applies to $N - 1$ observations.

    (e) Neither =STDEV() nor =STDEVP() is correct. The t-statistic has $N - 2$ degrees of freedom, and so we need division by $N - 2$.

73. Suppose that I collect monthly returns data R_t^{GM} for investing in the stock of General Motors (a big auto company in the U.S.) and monthly returns data R_t^{CCA} for investing in the stock of Corrections Corp. of America (a prison stock). During good times, the autos sell well and not many folks go to jail, and during bad times the reverse happens. Suppose I find that the correlation between the monthly returns is $\rho(R_t^{GM}, R_t^{CCA}) = -80\%$. What will I find if I regress R_t^{GM} on R_t^{CCA} and plot R_t^{GM} versus R_t^{CCA} including a line of best fit?

(a) Upward sloping plot, $R^2 \approx 0.80$, scatter plot quite close (but not extremely close) to the line.

(b) Upward sloping plot, $R^2 \approx 0.64$, scatter plot basically a big round ball of points.

(c) Downward sloping plot, $R^2 \approx 0.80$, scatter plot quite close (but not extremely close) to the line.

(d) Downward sloping plot, $R^2 \approx 0.64$, scatter plot quite close (but not extremely close) to the line.

(e) Downward sloping plot, $R^2 \approx 0.64$, scatter plot basically a big round ball of points.

74. Table 1.5 shows stock prices S and option prices $f(S)$ for a range of stock prices. Use a numerical technique to estimate the slope of the pricing function $f(S)$ at $S = \$4$. What is the best estimate of the slope $f'(S)$ at $S = 4$ to two decimal places?

(a) -90.85

(b) 90.85

(c) 100.00

(d) -100.00

(e) None of the above.

75. We need to use natural logs because, among other things, we need to use continuously compounded returns in our backtest regressions in Question 3.2.3. Suppose r is the continuously compounded return on a stock over one month, ignoring dividends. Suppose that R is the traditional simple net return on the stock over the same time period. Suppose that the stock went up in price by only a few pennies, so that $R > 0$ is a very small number, and quite close to zero. In this case, which ONE of the following is true? (Note that $\ln(\cdot)$ is the natural logarithm function and that "$\approx$" means approximately equal to.)

(a) $r \approx \ln(1 + R)$ and $r = R$

(b) $r = \ln(1 + R)$ and $r \approx R$

(c) $r \neq \ln(1 + R)$ and $r \approx R$

(d) $r \neq \ln(1 + R)$ and $r \neq R$

(e) $r \approx \ln(1 + R)$ and $r \approx R$

Stock Price S	Option Price $f(S)$
$ 4.0000	$ 98.1285114
$ 4.0100	$ 97.1285114
$ 4.1000	$ 88.1285151
$ 4.2000	$ 78.1285786
$ 4.3000	$ 68.1293168
$ 4.4000	$ 58.1353427
$ 4.5000	$ 48.1708017
$ 4.6000	$ 38.3250496
$ 4.7000	$ 28.8335604
$ 4.8000	$ 20.1365537
$ 4.9000	$ 12.8012325
$ 5.0000	$ 7.2765060
$ 5.0001	$ 7.2719521
$ 5.1000	$ 3.6457918
$ 5.2000	$ 1.5942159

Table 1.5: Stock Price and Option Price

The first column shows the stock price in dollars per share. The second column shows the total price of a derivatives option contract in dollars.

76. In Chapter 1 of *Foundations* we invested $1 into a portfolio of 500 stocks and held for 50 years. At the end of the 50 years we had $108.45 (assuming all dividends were reinvested back into the stock portfolio). The average dividend yield was only 3.1% over this time period. Roughly what proportion of the ending wealth was as a result of the reinvested dividends?

(a) 3.1% of the $108.45 was from reinvested dividends.

(b) 10% of the $108.45 was from reinvested dividends.

(c) Roughly one third of the $108.45 was from reinvested dividends.

(d) Roughly one half to two thirds of the $108.45 was from reinvested dividends.

(e) Roughly 80% of the $108.45 was from reinvested dividends.

77. ◇ In *Foundations*, we said that a chi-squared random variable χ^2_ν with ν degrees of freedom is built using which one of the following operations, where the Z_i are independent $N(0,1)$ random variables?

(a) $\chi^2_\nu = Z_1 + Z_2 + \cdots + Z_\nu$

(b) $\chi^2_\nu = Z_1^2 + Z_2^2 + \cdots + Z_\nu^2$

(c) $\chi^2_\nu = Z_1 \times Z_2 \times \cdots \times Z_\nu$

(d) $\chi^2_\nu = \frac{Z_1^2 + Z_2^2 + \cdots + Z_\nu^2}{\nu}$

(e) None of the above is correct.

78. ◇ In Chapter 1 of *Foundations* we discussed the expected value of a continuous random variable $E(X)$. I drew a density function and sliced it up into small vertical rectangles of probability mass, and then labeled the terms in the integral as shown below—to show that the continuous integral was analogous to the easier-to-understand discrete case.

$$E(X) = \int \quad x \quad \underbrace{\underbrace{f_X(x)}_{h_i} \underbrace{dx}_{w_i}}$$

$$\uparrow \qquad \uparrow \qquad \qquad$$

$$\text{sum}_i \quad x_i \quad \cdot \quad p_i$$

We said, however, that this labelling was true only in a limiting sense as...

(a) $E(X) \to 0$

(b) $x_i \to 0$

(c) $h_i \to 0$

(d) $w_i \to 0$

(e) None of the above is correct.

79. Suppose I download a recent sample of 250 daily prices on the stock Spark (SPK). Suppose I regress daily stock price on daily stock price with one day's lag. In what range will the R^2 of that regression fall, roughly?

(a) 0.00–0.05

(b) 0.05–0.25

(c) 0.25–0.50

(d) 0.50–0.95

(e) 0.95–1.00

80. Chapter 1 of *Foundations* gives an economic interpretation of a continuously compounded return. Assume that r is the continuously compounded return on a stock over one year. Then we may think of r as which ONE of the following?

(a) r is like a traditional simple net return. So, for example, if a stock price moves from \$10 to \$15, then r would be very close to +50%.

(b) r does not have an economic interpretation. Instead, it is just given by a mathematical transformation that removes any economic interpretation.

(c) r is given by a logarithmic transformation, and so r must always be a positive number, even when the stock price falls.

(d) r is much like a quoted APR but with extremely frequent (in fact, continuous) compounding.

(e) In fact, more than one of the above answers is correct.

81. In Chapter 1 of *Foundations* we said that if you could add an extra 1% to the annual return on a lump sum buy-and-hold investment of $1 for 50 years this would increase your wealth by something like half as much again by the end of the investment horizon. This is true for almost any reasonable rate of return on your investment. Suppose that instead of a lump sum buy-and-hold strategy, your deposits are made at regular intervals (e.g., monthly) over the 50 years. What should be the impact on your ending wealth of an extra 1% per annum return over the 50 years?

    (a) The same impact (i.e., roughly half as much wealth again after 50 years), because the total investment horizon in unchanged.

    (b) A greater impact on ending wealth because all the intermediate deposits can now earn interest on interest.

    (c) A lesser impact on ending wealth because of time value of money arguments.

    (d) We cannot answer without specific numbers.

    (e) None of the above is correct.

82. The empirical density function for the S&P 500 index daily returns data in Chapter 1 of *Foundations* had what?

    (a) Many more observations in the tails than would be expected if the returns were normally distributed with the same mean and variance.

    (b) Many fewer observations in the tails than would be expected if the returns were normally distributed with the same mean and variance.

    (c) Many fewer observations close to zero than would be expected if the returns were normally distributed with the same mean and variance.

    (d) More than one of the above.

    (e) None of the above.

83. You want to conduct a *t*-test of the mean of a sample of daily continuously compounded large-cap stock returns. You tested for skewness and kurtosis first and you rejected normality because of excess kurtosis (and assume there was no skewness). You have 750 observations and you have no reason to think that there is any dependence in your data or that there is any instability in the distributions. So, you have independent and identically distributed leptokurtic (i.e., displaying excess kurtosis) returns. Is the *t*-test of the mean a VALID test?

    (a) No, because the assumptions of the test are violated.

    (b) No, because it is a small-sample test, not a large sample test.

    (c) Yes, because the test is robust to this violation of the assumptions.

    (d) It is not obvious. We need to test for autocorrelation.

    (e) None of the above is correct.

CHAPTER 1. MULTIPLE-CHOICE TEST QUESTIONS

84. When we perform a Monte Carlo simulation to estimate, say, the value of an option, we get what? Pick the ONE best answer.

   (a) An estimate of the option value only.

   (b) An estimate of the uncertainty in the option value only.

   (c) An estimate of the option value and a confidence interval about that value.

   (d) An analytical formula to value the option as a function of the value of the underlying security and other inputs, like the Black-Scholes formula.

   (e) None of the above is correct.

85. Which correlation estimator is generally MOST sensitive to outliers in the data? Note that PPMCC is the traditional Pearson product-moment correlation coefficient and SROCC is the Spearman rank-order correlation coefficient.

   (a) PPMCC

   (b) SROCC

   (c) In fact, PPMCC and SROCC are both insensitive to outliers.

   (d) In fact, PPMCC and SROCC are both very sensitive to outliers.

   (e) None of the above is a good answer.

86. You take a sample of 20 stock returns to IBM and 20 stock returns to MSFT. You calculate the correlation between their returns as $\hat{\rho} = 0.60$. What is the t-statistic for the correlation to two decimal places? (Assume null hypothesis $H_0 : \rho = 0$. Assume $\hat{\sigma} = 0.03$ for each stock. Assume all assumptions of the test are satisfied.)

   (a) 3.18

   (b) 2.68

   (c) 89.44

   (d) We do not have enough information to work out the t-statistic.

   (e) None of the above is correct.

87. If you plot relative bid-ask spread against market capitalization for the 20 stocks from Question 3.2.2, you would expect to find the Spearman rank-order correlation coefficient between these observations to be roughly what?

   (a) -0.9

   (b) -0.5

   (c) 0.0

   (d) 0.5

   (e) 0.9

88. ◇◇ Suppose that $g(x) = x^2$. Suppose that $X \sim N(0, 1)$ with density function $f_X(x)$. Use your intuition to figure out the rough value of $E[g(X)]$. That is, what is the value of the following integral?

$$E[g(X)] = \int_{-\infty}^{+\infty} g(x)f_X(x)dx = \int_{-\infty}^{+\infty} g(x)\frac{1}{\sqrt{2\pi}}e^{-\frac{1}{2}x^2}dx = \int_{-\infty}^{+\infty} x^2 \frac{1}{\sqrt{2\pi}}e^{-\frac{1}{2}x^2}dx.$$

Sketching a careful picture to scale may help.

(a) 0.0

(b) 0.1

(c) 1

(d) 10

(e) 100

89. In terms of capitalization, roughly how big was the global stock market compared with the global bond market in 2013?

(a) The global stock market was about 3.5 times the size of the global bond market.

(b) The global stock market was about 50% bigger than the global bond market.

(c) The global stock market was about the same size as the global bond market.

(d) The global stock market was about two-thirds to three-quarters the size of the global bond market.

(e) The global stock market was about one-quarter to one-third the size of the global bond market.

90. A client asks you what is the historical long-term average rate of return to investing in broadly diversified stocks, including dividends. You tell him is it roughly 9% per annum before taxes, but that it varies slightly depending upon the time period sampled. He then asks if that 9% average is a good estimate of the *actual* return he will receive next year in those stocks. The best answer for him is that...

(a) Actual stock market returns are extremely volatile from year to year. In practice, we almost never get an average year.

(b) Actual stock market returns are quite volatile from year to year. In practice, however, your return is unlikely to be more than about five percentage points away from the historical average return.

(c) Actual stock market returns have some volatility from year to year. In practice, however, your return is unlikely to be more than about two percentage points away from the historical average return.

(d) Because our historical average is based on a very large sample, our estimator has a tiny standard error. So, in practice, your actual return next year is likely to be extremely close to the historical average return.

(e) None of the above is a good answer.

91. ◇ The general functional form of a Z- or t-statistic is $\frac{\hat{\phi} - \phi_{H_0}}{\widehat{SE(\hat{\phi})}}$ where ϕ is some population parameter with a null hypothesis value ϕ_{H_0} and a sample estimator $\hat{\phi}$. In this general case, the denominator $\widehat{SE(\hat{\phi})}$ represents what?

   (a) The estimated standard deviation of the underlying data sample.

   (b) The estimated standard deviation of the estimator $\hat{\phi}$.

   (c) The estimated standard deviation of the null hypothesis value ϕ_{H_0}.

   (d) The estimated standard deviation of the sample mean, given by $s/\sqrt{N}$, where s is the sample standard deviation.

   (e) None of the above.

92. In Chapter 1 of *Foundations*, we examined a 50-year (1963–2013) sample of daily returns to the S&P 500 index. Roughly speaking, during this time period, the broad U.S. stock market was what?

   (a) About as likely to go up as down on any randomly selected day.

   (b) Much more likely to go up than down on any randomly selected day.

   (c) Much more likely to go down than up on any randomly selected day.

93. What was the average dividend yield on the S&P 500 index portfolio over the 50-year period 1963–2013?

   (a) A number close to 1% per annum.

   (b) A number close to 3% per annum.

   (c) A number close to 5% per annum.

   (d) A number close to 8% per annum.

   (e) A number close to 10% per annum.

94. Looking at stock market runs in the 50-year (1963–2013) sample of daily returns to the S&P 500 index...

   (a) There are many occasions where an investment in the portfolio of index stocks outperformed T-bills every consecutive day for three or more weeks in an unbroken winning streak.

   (b) There are many occasions where an investment in the portfolio of index stocks outperformed T-bills every consecutive day for many years in a row in an unbroken winning streak.

   (c) There are no occasions where an investment in the portfolio of index stocks outperformed T-bills every consecutive day for three or more weeks in an unbroken winning streak.

   (d) Both of (a) and (b) are correct.

   (e) None of the above is correct.

95. In Chapter 1 of *Foundations*, we showed that $1 invested for 50 years in the S&P 500 stocks (and with all dividends reinvested) grew to be worth $108.45 before taxes. If, however, dividends were consumed over time, rather than reinvested, the ending wealth did what?

    (a) Dropped very little, because the average dividend yield was a tiny number.

    (b) Dropped to $85.42 (i.e., only about 80% of the original balance), because of the power of compounding and reinvested dividends.

    (c) Dropped to $23.03 (i.e., only about 20% of the original balance), because of the power of compounding and reinvested dividends.

    (d) Dropped to $13.25 (i.e., only about 12% of the original balance), because of the power of compounding and reinvested dividends.

    (e) None of the above is correct.

96. ◇ Your research assistant, Miss Gosset, has collected data on market capitalization and dividend yields on small-capitalization U.S. stocks over the last year. You have not seen the data. She tells you only that the SROCC (Spearman rank-order correlation coefficient) between market capitalization and dividend yield is -91%. You can conclude what?

    (a) There is a strong negative non-linear relationship between market capitalization and dividend yield in the sample.

    (b) There is a weak negative non-linear relationship between market capitalization and dividend yield in the sample.

    (c) There is no relationship between market capitalization and dividend yield in the sample.

    (d) There is a positive non-linear relationship between market capitalization and dividend yield in the sample.

    (e) None of the above is a fair conclusion.

97. Which of the following is correct regarding dividend yield on a broad market index (e.g., the S&P 500)?

    (a) Dividend yield on the index tends to fall when the index level rises and rise when the index level falls.

    (b) Dividend yield on the index tends to rise when the index level rises and fall when the index level falls.

    (c) Dividend yield on the index changes through time, but it does so in a manner that is largely unrelated to moves in the index.

    (d) No, in fact, dividend yield on the index tends to be quite stable over time because dollar dividends are quite "sticky."

    (e) None of the above is correct.

98. ◇◇ You are given a spreadsheet with two columns of data from some economic variables labeled only as A and B. You run an OLS regression of A against B. The regression equation fits extremely closely, with an R^2 of 95%. Estimate the traditional Pearson product-moment correlation coefficient (PPMCC) between A and B.

    (a) $PPMCC = 100\%$.
    (b) $PPMCC \approx 97.5\%$.
    (c) $PPMCC = 95\%$.
    (d) $PPMCC \approx 90.25\%$.
    (e) None of the above is a good answer.

99. At the close of business Monday, the stock of Priceline (PCLN) is priced at $1,200 per share and the Stock of Chesapeake Energy (CHK) is priced at $4.00 per share. You have $10,000 to invest and you put 60% of your money into PCLN and 40% of your money into CHK at these prices, and you do not rebalance the portfolio. By the close of business Tuesday, suppose that PCLN is up $30 per share, and CHK is down $0.25 per share. By the close of business Wednesday, PCLN is up another $30 per share, and CHK is down another $0.25 per share. You sell at these prices. What is the simple net return on your portfolio from close of business Tuesday to close of business Wednesday? Please ignore all T-costs. My answers are rounded.

    (a) -1.01010%
    (b) -1.01523%
    (c) -1.20325%
    (d) -1.31386%
    (e) None of the above.

100. You have a sample of 500 daily continuously compounded stock returns for Stock X. You calculate the t-statistic for the mean. It takes the value 2.4, which appears significant. You discover, however, that there is significant first-order autocorrelation in the daily returns with estimated autocorrelation coefficient of $\hat{\rho} = 0.25$. Using only this information, can you provide an adjusted t-statistic to amend for the violation of the underlying assumption?

    (a) Yes, the amended t-statistic is $t=1.35$
    (b) Yes, the amended t-statistic is $t=1.80$
    (c) Yes, the amended t-statistic is $t=3.00$
    (d) Yes, the amended t-statistic is $t=3.75$
    (e) In fact, no adjustment is needed.

101. Dividend yield is usually defined as what?

    (a) The dollar value of the most recent dividend per share.

    (b) The dollar value of the sum of dividends per share over the last 12 months.

    (c) The dollar value of the sum of dividends per share over the last 12 months divided by the most recent stock price.

    (d) The dollar value of the sum of dividends per share over the last 12 months divided by the forecast of stock price one year from now.

    (e) The proportion of a firm's after tax net income over the last 12 months that has been paid out as cash dividends.

102. Given a single lump sum initial investment, an extra 1% per annum added to your return adds about half as much again to an ending wealth over a 50-year period. In practice, however, most people save as a growing annuity, not a lump sum. In this case, an extra 1% per annum has a...

    (a) greater effect on ending wealth than in the case of the lump sum.

    (b) same effect on ending wealth as in the case of the lump sum.

    (c) lesser effect on ending wealth than in the case of the lump sum.

    (d) unclear effect on ending wealth, because it depends upon whether the market goes up or down.

    (e) none of the above is correct.

103. Looking at our 50-year sample of daily returns to the S&P 500 index, roughly speaking, an initial lump sum investment of $1 into the broad U.S. stock market grew to be worth N times as much as an initial lump sum investment of $1 into T-bills. How big was N? Assume all dividends are reinvested and ignore taxes.

    (a) 88

    (b) 44

    (c) 22

    (d) 8

    (e) 5.5

104. Suppose an N.Z. mutual fund that actively tries to beat the S&P/NZX50 charges an annual fee of 85 bps. On an investment of $100,000 this fee is expected to amount to something like what?

    (a) $8.50 per year.

    (b) $85.00 per year.

    (c) $850.00 per year.

    (d) $8,500.00 per year.

    (e) None of the above is correct.

105. In *Foundations*, we agreed that we can read the simple integral

$$\int x\,dx$$

as the limiting value of a summation of terms, where x and dx are what?

(a) x is the height of a small lump of probability mass and dx is the width of a small lump of probability mass.

(b) x is the height of a probability density function and dx is the width of a small slice of probability mass under the probability density function.

(c) x is the height of the function $y = x$ and dx is the width of a small slice of probability mass under the probability density function.

(d) $\int$ denotes a summation and $x\,dx$ is the area of a small slice of probability mass under the probability density function.

(e) x is the height of the function $y = x$ and dx is the width of a small step in the value of x, but no probability density function is involved.

106. In *Foundations*, we discussed the integral $E(X)$ where X is a random variable with probability density function (pdf) $f_X(x)$. We said that sometimes the integral converges and sometimes the integral does not converge. Convergence in mathematics is always something that happens or does not happen side-by-side with some other variable that goes off to some limit. That is, we have convergence, or not, in the limit as "some variable" $\longrightarrow$ "some limit." What was the variable, and what was the limit, as presented in *Foundations* for convergence of $E(X)$?

(a) Width of a small step in x under the pdf goes to zero.

(b) Count of the number of slices of probability mass under the pdf goes to zero.

(c) Height of a small slice of probability mass under the pdf goes to zero.

(d) (a) and (b) but not (c).

(e) (b) and (c) but not (a).

107. You are given a spreadsheet with two columns of data from some economic variables labeled only as A and B. You run an OLS regression of A against B. The regression equation fits extremely closely, with an R^2 of 95% and a positive slope. Estimate the traditional Pearson product-moment correlation coefficient (PPMCC) between A and B.

(a) $PPMCC = 100\%$.

(b) $PPMCC \approx 97.5\%$.

(c) $PPMCC = 95\%$.

(d) $PPMCC \approx 90.25\%$.

(e) None of the above is a good answer.

108. Suppose that the correlation coefficient between the daily returns to a broadly diversified stock ETF and an investment-grade bond ETF is -15%, and that this correlation is strongly statistically significant, with a t-statistic of -8. May we conclude that combining the bond ETF with the stock ETF in a 60/40 stock/bond portfolio will bring significant diversification benefits compared with investing only in the stock ETF?

    (a) Yes, certainly, because the significant negative correlation coefficient means that the bond returns move contrary to the stock returns.

    (b) Yes, certainly, because when stocks have returns below their mean, bonds tend to have returns above their mean.

    (c) Yes, certainly, because holdings in high-quality bonds have long been known to diversify stock holdings.

    (d) Yes, all of the above.

    (e) No, none of the above.

109. If you plot relative bid-ask spread against market capitalization for the 20 stocks in Question 3.2.1, you would expect to find the Spearman rank order correlation coefficient between these observations to be roughly what?

    (a) 0.90

    (b) 0.50

    (c) 0.00

    (d) -0.50

    (e) -0.90

110. An Economic Policy Institute report released in March 2016 (but using 2013 figures) showed that for U.S. families headed by a person in the 32–37-year old age group, the average retirement account savings was \$31,644.[1] Almost half of all working-age families have a zero balance in these accounts, however. So, the *median* savings was only \$480. For families headed by someone in the 56–61-year old age group (i.e., those folks approaching retirement), the average was \$163,577, and the median was only \$17,000. The distribution of savings, for either age group, is most likely distributed how?

    (a) Left skewed.

    (b) Right skewed.

    (c) Symmetric, but with fat tails relative to a normal distribution.

    (d) Normally distributed, because of the large sample size involved.

    (e) It is impossible to tell.

---

[1] Available here: `http://www.epi.org/publication/retirement-in-america/`

CHAPTER 1. MULTIPLE-CHOICE TEST QUESTIONS

111. In the perfect foresight example in *Foundations*, we found that if you had perfect foresight one day out of every M months, you could add 1% per annum to your investment performance over my 50-year sample. Roughly how big was M?

    (a) 3
    (b) 5
    (c) 7
    (d) 9
    (e) 11

112. ◇◇ You use OLS to regress daily stock return, $y = R(t)$, on return with one day's lag, $x = R(t-1)$. Which ONE of the following is FALSE in a large sample? (Note: ρ_{xy} is the correlation between x and y, and ρ_1 is the autocorrelation of y.)

    (a) $\hat{\beta}_{xy} \approx \hat{\rho}_{xy}$.
    (b) $R^2 \approx \hat{\rho}_{xy}^2$.
    (c) $\hat{\beta}_{xy}^2 \approx R^2$.
    (d) $\hat{\rho}_{xy} \approx \hat{\rho}_1$.
    (e) $\hat{\rho}_1 \approx \hat{\beta}_{xy} \big/ \hat{\rho}_{xy}$.

113. ◇◇ Stock S and Stock F are two well known and heavily traded stocks in the same industry in the same country. Stock S is well managed and successful and that its stock price steadily increases over 10 years. Stock F is mis-managed and is somewhat of a failure, and its stock price declines steadily over those same 10 years. Being in the same industry and in the same country, however, their stock prices tend to move together on a day-to-day basis relative to their trends. So, on a day when good industry news or good macro-economic news comes out, the price of Stock S tends to rise a bit more than usual, and the price of Stock F tends to fall a bit less than usual. Similarly, on bad news days the price of Stock S tends to rise a little less than usual, and the price of Stock F tends to fall a little more than usual. Which ONE of the following in Table 1.6 best describes the sign of the traditional Pearson product-moment correlation (PPMCC) of the prices and returns (i.e., between Stock S and Stock F) over the full 10-year sample?

	Daily Prices	Daily Returns
(a)	+	+
(b)	+	−
(c)	−	+
(d)	−	−
(e)	None of the above is correct.	

Table 1.6: Possible Correlations

114. Assume we have two normally distributed samples of returns, each of size N, hypothesized to be independent of each other. Suppose that we calculate the t-statistic to test the correlation of returns between the two samples. Using our usual notation, the estimator of the standard error of the two-sample correlation estimator is given by what?

    (a) $s/\sqrt{N}$

    (b) $\hat{\rho}$

    (c) $\sqrt{1-\hat{\rho}^2} \cdot \sqrt{\frac{1}{N-2}}$

    (d) σ^2/N

    (e) $\sqrt{1-\hat{\rho}^2}$

115. ◇ Consider a typical right-skewed distribution. For example, the distribution of real estate sales prices or the distribution of bitcoin transaction sizes. As we walk from LEFT to RIGHT (i.e., from the origin towards the right tail in the examples just mentioned), in which order do we come across the three standard measures of central tendency?

    (a) Mean, median, mode.

    (b) Median, mean, mode.

    (c) Mode, median, mean.

    (d) Mode, mean, median.

    (e) Mean, mode, median.

    (f) Median, mode, mean.

116. ◇◇ In Chapter 1 of *Foundations*, we arrived at Z-statistics (i.e., standard normally distributed statistics) for testing for excess skewness excess kurtosis. We labeled them as Z_{skew} and Z_{kurt}, respectively (see Appendix A on p. 289). How did we say that we could build a Jarque-Bera test statistic (distributed χ_2^2) by combining the two Z-statistics? Please assume a very large sample size.

    (a) $Z_{skew} + Z_{kurt}$.

    (b) $Z_{skew} - Z_{kurt}$.

    (c) $N \times \left[Z_{skew}^2/6 + (Z_{kurt} - 3)^2/24 \right]$, where N is the sample size.

    (d) $Z_{skew}^2 + Z_{kurt}^2$.

    (e) $\sqrt{Z_{skew}^2 + Z_{kurt}^2}$.

Test/Statistic	Distributionally	Functionally
Parametric	A	B
Non-Parametric	C	D

Table 1.7: Examples of Parametric and Non-Parametric Techniques

117. In Chapter 1 of *Foundations*, we discussed distributionally parametric (and non-parametric) tests/techniques and functionally parametric (and non-parametric) tests/techniques. Table 1.7 is taken from the textbook, but with the letters A, B, C, and D in place of the names of tests or techniques. Which ONE of the following is the best answer?

   (a) A could be a large-sample t-test of the mean.

   (b) B could be the Spearman rank-order correlation coefficient (SROCC).

   (c) C could be a small-sample t-test of the mean.

   (d) D could be the traditional Pearson product-moment correlation coefficient (PPMCC).

   (e) None of the above is correct.

118. ◇◇ You download a sample of 30 daily stock returns for a small-cap stock. The standard t-statistic to test the null hypothesis that the population mean is zero (i.e., $H_0 : \mu = 0$) takes the value $t = 2.8$, which is well beyond the critical value for a two-sided 5% t-test. You test for skewness and kurtosis and find no significant departures from normality. You test for dependence, and find no autocorrelation or ARCH/GARCH type effects. You also conduct an F-test to see whether the variance is the same in the first and second halves of the sample (i.e., $H_0 : \sigma_1^2 = \sigma_2^2$, where σ_1^2 and σ_2^2 are the true variances in the first and second halves of the sample, respectively). The standard F-statistic for equality of variances, however, takes the value 3.2, which is well beyond the critical value for a two-sided 5% F-test. Can you reject the null hypothesis that the true mean return is zero?

   (a) Yes, we can reject $H_0 : \mu = 0$ immediately.

   (b) Yes, we can reject $H_0 : \mu = 0$ immediately. In fact, rejecting $H_0 : \sigma_1^2 = \sigma_2^2$ just strengthens our rejection of $H_0 : \mu = 0$.

   (c) No, we cannot reject $H_0 : \mu = 0$ because the sample size is not large enough for us to be confident. We need more data.

   (d) No, we cannot reject $H_0 : \mu = 0$ because we need to choose a non-parametric test instead.

   (e) No, we cannot reject $H_0 : \mu = 0$ because the rejection of $H_0 : \sigma_1^2 = \sigma_2^2$ means that the t-test for the mean is invalid.

119. We described $E(X)$ as a probability-weighted sum of possible values of the random variable X. Suppose that $f(x)$ is the probability density function (pdf) of X. We described small slices of probability mass under the pdf and a limiting argument. Which bit of Equation (1.1) represents the small <u>slices of probability mass</u> under the pdf in the limit, according to our limiting argument?

$$E(X) = \int_{x=-\infty}^{x=+\infty} xf(x)dx. \qquad (1.1)$$

   (a) $E(X)$

   (b) $\int_{x=-\infty}^{x=+\infty}$

   (c) x

   (d) $xf(x)$

   (e) $f(x)dx$

120. We simplified integral calculus by breaking down the integral into component parts, and associating these parts with a summation using a discrete approximation that employs thin slices of area under the function (these are slices of probability mass in the random variable case, but just slices of area in the general case). There were, however, two conditions that had to be satisfied for the approximation to be valid in the case of a convergent integral. What were they?

   (a) The widths of the thin slices must go to zero, and as they do so, the discrete sum must converge to a single value (and this latter result must be true no matter how the widths of the thin slices go to zero).

   (b) The heights and the widths of the thin slices under the function must both go to zero.

   (c) The heights of the thin slices under the function must go to zero, and the product of height times width (of these thin slices) must also go to zero.

   (d) The widths of the thin slices under the function must go to zero, and the product of height times width (of these thin slices) must equal probability mass, or area, no matter how the slices are formed.

   (e) In fact, each of the above is true.

121. Which one of the following represents the proportion of days where the S&P 500 index was up, down, and unchanged, respectively, over our 50-year sample from mid-1963 to mid-2013? Note that this question is about price level data only, and that dividends are ignored.

   (a) Up 27.5%, down 67.5%, unchanged 5.0%.

   (b) Up 52.7%, down 47.0%, unchanged 0.3%.

   (c) Up 75.2%, down 22.7%, unchanged 2.1%.

   (d) Up 66.0%, down 33.0%, unchanged 1.0%.

   (e) Up 33.0%, down 66.0%, unchanged 1.0%.

122. We argued that if you hold a passive S&P 500 investment for 50 years with dividends reinvested, but you miss out on the 10 best days in the market, your ending wealth would be cut in half relative to the ending wealth of a buy-and-hold investor. This empirical fact is an argument against what sort of strategy?

    (a) Actively trying to time the market by going to cash when you feel bearish.

    (b) Passively buying and holding the market.

    (c) Holding a broadly diversified ETF, because ETFs, unlike mutual funds, can be bought and sold during the trading day.

    (d) Actively stock picking while remaining fully invested.

    (e) A value strategy like the one used by Benjamin Graham.

123. Over the 50-year 1963–2013 sample of U.S. daily stock market data from Chapter 1 of *Foundations*, the stocks returned $\bar{R}_S$ per annum, and the T-bills returned $\bar{R}_T$ per annum. The extra returns on stocks, over and above T-bills, $\bar{R}_S - \bar{R}_T$, is referred to as what?

    (a) The equity market default risk premium.

    (b) The equity market credit risk premium.

    (c) The equity market liquidity risk premium.

    (d) The equity market maturity risk premium.

    (e) The equity market risk premium.

    (f) The equity market inflation risk premium.

    (g) The equity market interest rate risk premium.

    (h) The equity market expropriation risk premium.

124. ◇ When we introduced transaction costs of 25 bps per trade to the perfect foresight strategy, we found that we did not need to look beyond $N = 12$ days to determine an optimal investment strategy because of what?

    (a) Beyond a one-day horizon, initial T-costs matter only because you might wish to capitalize on runs, but runs of more than 12 days are almost unheard of.

    (b) Nobody can predict the market beyond 12 days (just like we rarely see meaningful weather forecasts at this horizon).

    (c) The computational complexity required to solve the problem means that beyond 12 days, no computer can resolve differences in the solution.

    (d) Accumulated wealth accrues only slowly over time, so the first 10–12 days are simply not relevant. It is compounding *after* this horizon that leads to the massive ending wealth of the perfect foresight investor.

    (e) From a time value of money (TVM) perspective, an initial T-cost of 25 bps is magnified so much after 12 days, that it swamps any possible stock market move beyond that horizon.

125. Assume that you have two independent samples of data, each of which is IID normally distributed. Let s_i^2 be the usual unbiased sample variance estimator, estimating σ_i^2, for sample i, for $i = 1, 2$. Assume sample sizes $N_1 = 500$, and $N_2 = 400$. Which one of the following is an F-statistic to test for differences in dispersion under the null hypothesis $H_0 : \sigma_1 = \sigma_2$?

(a) $F = s_1/s_2$

(b) $F = s_1 - s_2$

(c) $F = s_1^2 - s_2^2$

(d) $F = s_1^2/s_2^2$

(e) $F = \dfrac{s_1^2/(N_1-1)}{s_2^2/(N_2-1)}$

126. Stock returns are so volatile that...

(a) Realized broad market annual return is rarely close to long-run averages.

(b) Stock market returns suffer from mean blur (i.e., their standard deviation is typically much bigger than their mean).

(c) It can be difficult to reject $H_0 : \mu = 0$ for individual stocks.

(d) Stocks supply more than 90% of the risk in a 60/40 stock/bond portfolio.

(e) All of the above.

127. ◇ You download a sample of 300 daily stock returns for a small-cap stock. The standard t-statistic to test the null hypothesis that the population mean is zero (i.e., $H_0 : \mu = 0$) takes the value $t = 2.2$, which is beyond the critical value for a two-sided 5% t-test. You test for skewness and kurtosis and find no significant departures from normality. You test for dependence, however, and find significant autocorrelation of $\hat{\rho} = -0.15$. You also conduct an F-test to see whether the dispersion is the same in the first and second halves of the sample (i.e., $H_0 : \sigma_1 = \sigma_2$, where σ_1^2 and σ_2^2 are the true variances in the first and second halves of the sample, respectively). The standard F-statistic for equality of variances takes the value $F = 1.02$, which is well within the critical values for a two-sided 5% F-test. Can you reject the null hypothesis that the true mean return is zero?

(a) Yes, we can reject $H_0 : \mu = 0$ immediately, and we may use the original $t = 2.2$ value to determine our p-value.

(b) No, we cannot reject $H_0 : \mu = 0$ immediately, because we need to shuffle the data randomly to remove the autocorrelation, and then we need to recalculate the t-statistic value to see whether we reject or not. We might not reject.

(c) Yes, we can reject $H_0 : \mu = 0$, but we need to adjust the $t = 2.2$ value to account for autocorrelation first, and I can see that I will still get a rejection.

(d) No, we cannot reject $H_0 : \mu = 0$. I can see that if I adjust the $t = 2.2$ value for autocorrelation, I do not get a rejection.

(e) No, we cannot reject $H_0 : \mu = 0$ because the presence of autocorrelation means that the t-test for the mean is invalid.

128. ◇ Figure 1.2 looks similar to Figure 1.14 in the text book, with the simulated daily prices of two stocks over a year. What is the correlation between the daily returns to the two stocks?

 (a) Positive, large, and close to 1.

 (b) Positive, small, but not close to zero.

 (c) Negative, small, but not close to zero.

 (d) Negative, large, and close to -1.

 (e) We cannot tell from the picture.

129. In Chapter 1 of *Foundations* we discussed numerical techniques versus analytical techniques in several contexts. For example, we discussed these for the simple integral problems, for evaluation of $E[g(W)]$ where $g(\cdot)$ is the weird function and W is distributed standard normal, for valuing a European-style call option, and for numerical optimization. We said that one hallmark of a numerical technique is that it gives no analytical formula. We also said that numerical techniques are

 (a) Easy to check, and easy to change.

 (b) Dangerous, because they can behave in misleading ways (e.g., a numerical optimizer sticking at a local maximum or minimum).

 (c) Widely accessible, because you do not need to master high-level analytical mathematics to use them.

 (d) Often used to check analytical work.

 (e) All of the above.

130. ◇ I have just calculated the mean daily continuously-compounded return to the S&P 500 broad market index in the U.S. using 9,000 observations (I used daily data from 1974 to 2009). I calculated the mean as $\bar{R} = 0.000307$. Gosh, that seems close to zero! **Roughly how big is the t-statistic** for testing the null hypothesis that the mean daily return to the S&P 500 actually equals zero? Note that the t-statistic is positive because the sample average $\bar{R}$ is positive, that I have called the t-statistic "t" for short below, and that the following ranges are NOT confidence intervals. Please ignore any and every possible violation of the assumptions underlying the t-statistic calculation.

 (a) $0.00 \le t \le 1.96$

 (b) $1.97 \le t \le 2.50$

 (c) $2.60 \le t \le 2.95$

 (d) $t \ge 3.00$

 (e) I need more information to be able to work out the t-statistic.

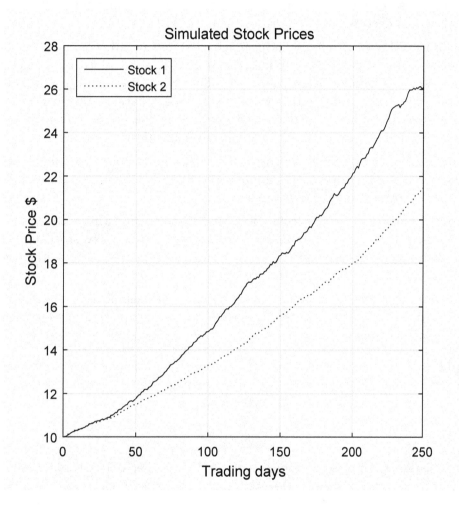

Figure 1.2: Simulated Stock Prices

The figure plots the simulated prices of two stocks over 250 trading days. The prices of Stock 1 and Stock 2 have similar volatility, but Stock 1's price grows at a higher rate.

131. We argued that investment-grade bonds should not be held to diversify stock positions, and that bonds should, instead, be held as part of the "second step of two-fund separation." Which ONE of the following best explains this further?

    (a) Bonds are risky right now, because it is difficult to forecast anything other than a 20-year secular rise in interest rates looking forward, and this will increase, rather than decrease, portfolio risk for anyone with a significant bond holding.

    (b) Ignoring TIPS (i.e., inflation-adjusted bonds), bonds are nominally denominated securities, paying a nominal coupon that is undermined by unexpected increases in inflation. Stocks, however, offer ownership of real assets that increase in nominal value terms when unexpected inflation occurs. So, bonds undermine the value of a stock-bond portfolio in the presence of unexpected inflation, and should not be included for diversification purposes.

    (c) Bonds are issued by the same corporations that issue stocks, so holding bonds does not diversify a stock portfolio, but rather provides claims on the cash flows generated by the same underlying assets.

    (d) True diversification comes from combining risky assets with lightly correlated returns, rather than from adding low-risk bonds to a risky stock portfolio. High-quality bonds are added only to reduce risk and thus cater to the degree of investor risk aversion, not to diversify a stock position.

    (e) We have no frame of reference to determine what should be the correlation between the returns to stocks and bonds. So, we cannot estimate covariances to include in the risk model needed for diversified portfolio formation.

132. ◇◇ Let *RS* denote relative bid-ask spread. Let *DTV* denote dollar trading volume. Economist A suggests to you that lower spreads attract and drive dollar trading volume, and so the linear regression model

$$DTV = \alpha + \beta \cdot RS + \epsilon$$

    makes sense. Economist B argues that, in fact, higher dollar trading volumes force down relative spreads, and so the linear regression model

$$RS = \alpha + \beta \cdot DTV + \epsilon$$

    makes sense. Economist C argues that you can sensibly pick between the above two models by choosing the regression with the highest R^2. Which of the three economists do we know to be definitely incorrect?

    (a) Economist A.

    (b) Economist B.

    (c) Economist C.

    (d) No, in fact, each economist's argument seems reasonable.

    (e) I need more information in order to be able to answer this question.

133. The average dividend yield over the stocks of the S%P 500 from 1963 to 2013 was 3.1% per annum. Given how small this dividend yield is, **am I correct to argue that reinvesting these dividends is not very important**? Assume you are a 20-year old lump-sum investor trying to build future long-term wealth by investing in stocks. Ignore taxes and transaction costs.

    (a) Yes. Whether you consume the dividends or reinvest them back into the stocks has almost no effect on future long-term wealth.

    (b) Not entirely. If you choose to consume the dividends instead of reinvesting them, you will be worse off at retirement, but only by about 3–4 percentage points of ending wealth.

    (c) Not entirely. If you choose to consume the dividends instead of reinvesting them, you will be worse off at retirement, but only by about 10 percentage points of ending wealth.

    (d) Not at all. If you choose to consume the dividends instead of reinvesting them, you will be significantly worse off at retirement, possibly losing as much as 75–80% of your potential future wealth.

    (e) Not at all. If you choose to consume the dividends instead of reinvesting them, you will be very significantly worse off at retirement, losing as much as 95–99% of your potential future wealth.

    (f) None of the above is correct.

134. During the COVID-19-driven market panic of 2020:Q1, the stock of Fletcher Building (FBU) **fell slowly and very steadily in price**, recording a 33% drop in price over the quarter. Fisher and Paykel Healthcare (FPH) stock, however, **increased slowly and very steadily in price**, recording a 34% rise in price over the quarter. I downloaded daily prices for these stocks and I used them to calculate daily returns. Neither stock paid dividends during the quarter. For these stocks, I calculated the traditional Pearson correlation (PPMCC) between the time series of **daily prices** (I call it ρ_{PRICES}) and the traditional Pearson correlation (PPMCC) between the time series of **daily returns** (I call it ρ_{RETURNS}). Given my description of the data, which ONE of the following describes these correlation numbers? Hint: I found that it helped very much when I drew a time series plot of the prices.

    (a) $\rho_{\text{PRICES}} = -73\%$ and $\rho_{\text{RETURNS}} = +5\%$

    (b) $\rho_{\text{PRICES}} = +5\%$ and $\rho_{\text{RETURNS}} = -73\%$

    (c) $\rho_{\text{PRICES}} = +73\%$ and $\rho_{\text{RETURNS}} = +5\%$

    (d) $\rho_{\text{PRICES}} = +5\%$ and $\rho_{\text{RETURNS}} = +73\%$

    (e) $\rho_{\text{PRICES}} = -5\%$ and $\rho_{\text{RETURNS}} = +5\%$

    (f) In fact, there are two likely candidates above, and I do not have enough information to distinguish between them.

135. Suppose my underlying data are $X_1, X_2, \ldots, X_N$ independent and identically distributed $N(\mu, \sigma^2)$. Then

$$\frac{s^2}{\sigma^2} = \frac{\frac{1}{N-1}\sum_{i=1}^N (X_i - \bar{X})^2}{\sigma^2} = \sum_{i=1}^N \left(\frac{X_i - \bar{X}}{\sigma}\right)^2 \bigg/ (N-1),$$

where $s^2 \equiv \frac{1}{N-1}\sum_{i=1}^N (X_i - \bar{X})^2$ is the usual sample variance estimator, and $\bar{X}$ is the usual sample mean. Then, it follows that

$$\frac{(N-1)s^2}{\sigma^2} = \sum_{i=1}^N \left(\frac{X_i - \bar{X}}{\sigma}\right)^2.$$

What distribution does $\frac{(N-1)s^2}{\sigma^2}$ follow?

(a) Student-t distribution with N degrees of freedom.

(b) Student-t distribution with $N-1$ degrees of freedom.

(c) Chi-squared distribution with N degrees of freedom.

(d) Chi-squared distribution with $N-1$ degrees of freedom.

(e) A normal distribution.

(f) An F-distribution.

(g) None of the above is correct.

136. Suppose that you download a sample of S&P 500 stock index returns data from the first half of 2019 ($N_1 = 175$) and you download a second, independent sample of S&P 500 stock index returns data from the first quarter of 2020 ($N_2 = 86$). Note that 2020:Q1 has been reported to be the worst first quarter for the U.S. stock market in history! You already know that the *returns* are different in these two samples, but now you want to test whether the *volatility* levels are different. Let s_i^2 be the usual unbiased sample variance estimator, estimating σ_i^2, for sample i, for $i = 1, 2$. Which one of the following is an F-statistic to test for differences in dispersion under the null hypothesis $H_0 : \sigma_1 = \sigma_2$? Do not worry about violations of the assumptions of the test; just pick the test statistic of the correct form.

(a) $F = s_1/s_2$

(b) $F = \frac{N_1 s_1^2}{N_2 s_2^2}$

(c) $F = s_1^2/s_2^2$

(d) $F = \frac{s_1^2/\sqrt{N_1}}{s_2^2/\sqrt{N_2}}$

(e) $F = \frac{s_1^2/N_1}{s_2^2/N_2}$

(f) $F = \frac{s_1^2/(N_1-1)}{s_2^2/(N_2-1)}$

137. Why is it that when we combine stocks with investment-grade bonds, the bonds do not help very much to diversify the stock investment? That is, why do the bonds fail to provide true diversification?

    (a) It is because the bonds have low risk.

    (b) It is because the bond returns are *highly* correlated with the stock returns.

    (c) It is because the bond returns are *positively* correlated with the stock returns.

    (d) Both of (a) and (b).

    (e) Both of (b) and (c).

    (f) None of the above is correct.

138. I want you to estimate a numerical derivative to a function. Unlike the example in Chapter 1 of *Foundations*, where I gave you a table of values and no explicit functional form, here I am giving you the functional form but no table of values. The principle is, however, exactly the same. Suppose that $f(x) = \ln\left[\sqrt{x}\left(e^{\sqrt{x}}\right)\right]$, where $\ln(\cdot)$ is the natural logarithm function. Please use a numerical method to estimate the slope at $x = 10$. Which answer is closest?

    (a) 0.088

    (b) 0.090

    (c) 0.183

    (d) 0.184

    (e) 0.196

    (f) 0.208

    (g) 0.311

    (h) A larger answer than any of the above.

    (i) None of the above is close to being correct.

139. Suppose that $f(x) = x^2 + x + 2$. In Chapter 1 of *Foundations* we argued that we can think of an integral, say, $\int_{x=0}^{x=3} f(x)\,dx$ as the limiting value as $w_i \to 0$ of a summation of the form $\sum_i h_i w_i$, for some discretization $x_1, x_2, \ldots, x_N$ of the range over which the integral is executed, where...

    (a) h_i is the height of a probability density function.

    (b) $h_i = f(x_i)$ and $h_i w_i$ is a small area under the curve for $f(x)$.

    (c) $h_i = f(x_i)$ and $h_i w_i$ is a small probability mass under the probability density function.

    (d) (a) and (b)

    (e) (a) and (c)

    (f) (b) and (c)

    (g) None of the above is correct.

140. ◇ We argued that investment-grade bonds do not properly diversify a stock portfolio. So, what could we add to a stock portfolio to diversify its returns? Pick the best answer.

    (a) A safe asset whose returns have a low or negative correlation of returns with stocks, like five-year Treasury bonds (i.e., a medium-term government obligation).

    (b) A cash position, like cash in the bank.

    (c) A T-bills position (i.e., a short-term government obligation).

    (d) All of the above.

    (e) None of the above.

141. ◇◇ Suppose we use a normal distribution to approximate the distribution of height of females in the U.S. The vertical axis of this normal distribution displays what?

    (a) Count

    (b) Ethnicity

    (c) Frequency

    (d) Height

    (e) Kurtosis

    (f) Probability

    (g) Probability density

    (h) Weight

142. Suppose that you use the CAPM to calculate the expected return on a stock as follows: $E(R) = R_F + \beta[E(R_M) - R_F]$. If the beta of the stock is 1.2, and we replace R_F with the average return on U.S. T-bills from 1963–2013 (see Chapter 1 of *Foundations*), and we replace $[E(R_M) - R_F]$ with the U.S. equity market risk premium calculated over 1963–2013 (see Chapter 1 of *Foundations*), which range does the expected return on the stock fall into? Even if you do not recall the exact numbers, your capital markets intuition should lead you to the right answer. Remember that the CAPM ignores all taxes and fees. (Note that the historic level of R_F is arguably too high going forward, but there is no reason to think that the historic equity market risk premium is inappropriate.)

    (a) $4\% \leq E(R) < 6\%$

    (b) $6\% \leq E(R) < 9\%$

    (c) $9\% \leq E(R) < 13\%$

    (d) $13\% \leq E(R) < 16\%$

    (e) None of the above is within two percentage points of the correct answer.

143. On any given day, the probability that the level of the broad U.S. stock market (e.g., the S&P 500) rises is what?

    (a) About one-quarter. Although stocks are less likely to rise than fall on any given day, when they do rise, it is by much more than when they fall, giving a long-term upward trend in stock market levels.

    (b) About one-half. That is, stocks are, roughly speaking, about as likely to rise as they are to fall.

    (c) About three-quarters. We know that stock market levels rise over the long term, and one symptom of this is a notable bias towards index levels rising rather than falling on any given day.

    (d) A lower probability number than any of the above.

    (e) A higher probability number than any of the above.

144. In Chapter 1 of *Foundations*, we saw that reinvested dividends accounted for a significant proportion of the *ending value* of a passive 50-year lump sum investment in the portfolio of S&P 500 stocks. We also found, however, that reinvested dividends had very little impact on the *probability* that your investment in this same portfolio would increase in value over short or long horizons. Why are dividends so important in the value context and not in the probability-of-a-rise context?

    (a) At short-term horizons, dividend yields are so low that reinvesting dividends for a short period has little impact on wealth.

    (b) At long-term horizons, time and compounding mean that wealth in stocks grows so dramatically that with or without reinvested dividends, your investment, at least historically, was almost certain to increase in value.

    (c) At short horizons, the probability of a wealth increase is basically zero. A small dividend yield does not change that.

    (d) At long horizons, the probability of a wealth increase is basically a half, like a coin toss. A small dividend yield does not change that.

    (e) (a) and (b) are correct.

    (f) (c) and (d) are correct.

145. For a 21-year old, what is a very rough estimate of the impact of earning an extra one percentage point per annum on your retirement-date wealth at age 65 if you save via a *lump sum*, or if you save via an *annuity* of monthly deposits, respectively? Ignore taxes and T-costs.

    (a) about 30% extra and 50% extra at retirement, respectively.

    (b) about 50% extra and 50% extra at retirement, respectively.

    (c) about 50% extra and 30% extra at retirement, respectively.

    (d) about 50% extra and 100% extra at retirement, respectively.

    (e) about 100% extra and 50% extra at retirement, respectively.

146. Figure 1.3 shows a scatter plot of 5,000 points for jointly normally distributed Y and X. Roughly what do you think the correlation (i.e., the traditional PPMCC measure) is between Y and X?

    (a) +1.00
    (b) +0.90
    (c) +0.30
    (d) 0.00
    (e) -0.30
    (f) -0.90
    (g) -1.00

147. ◇ Figure 1.3 shows a scatter plot of 5,000 points for jointly normally distributed Y and X. What do you think the R^2 is for the relationship in Figure 1.3, at least roughly?

    (a) +100%
    (b) +80%
    (c) +9%
    (d) 0%
    (e) -9%
    (f) -80%
    (g) -100%

148. Suppose that an OLS time-series regression $y_t = \alpha + \beta x_t + \epsilon_t$ yields estimates $\hat{\alpha}$ and $\hat{\beta}$. Suppose that you also estimate the traditional Pearson correlation (PPMCC) $\hat{\rho}$ between y and x. Under which circumstances do you get that $\hat{\beta} \approx \hat{\rho}$? Note that "$\approx$" means approximately equal to. Hint: Go back to first principles and compare the formulas for beta and for correlation.

    (a) If $var(x) \approx var(y)$.
    (b) If x and y are both standardized variables. That is, if x and y both have sample mean 0 and sample standard deviation 1.
    (c) If x and y are both trending up over time.
    (d) If x and y are both trending down over time.
    (e) (a) and (b)
    (f) (c) and (d)
    (g) All of the above are correct.
    (h) None of the above is correct.

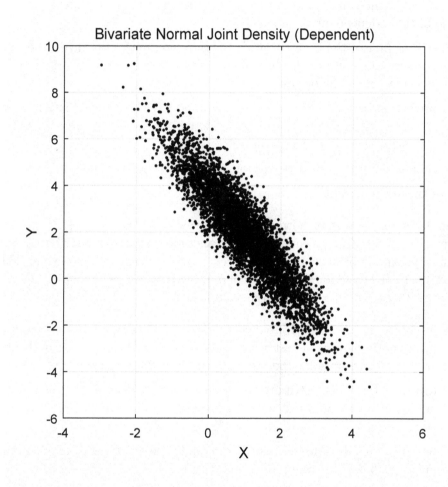

Figure 1.3: Bivariate Normal Joint Density (Dependent)

This figure shows 5,000 points drawn from the joint density of Y and X which are jointly bivariate normal. The parameters of the joint density are $\mu_X = 1$, $\sigma_X = 1$, $\mu_Y = 2$, $\sigma_Y = 2$, and correlation ρ_{XY} (not given to you).

149. What does it mean if you get a very low R^2 in your OLS regression but you have high t-statistic(s) on the coefficient(s) of the independent variable(s)?

    (a) The high t-statistics mean that your regression has good predictive power (i.e., a narrow confidence interval for a predicted dependent variable value given a new value of the independent variable(s)).

    (b) In a scatter plot of the data (if in a univariate context), you have little uncertainty about the slope of the line of best fit, but the data vary dramatically around the obvious line of best fit.

    (c) Any prediction based on such a regression must have a wide prediction interval (i.e., a wide confidence interval for a predicted dependent variable value given a new value of the independent variable(s)).

    (d) You cannot claim that your regression has high "predictive power."

    (e) All of the above except (a).

150. ◇ The Jarque-Bera test of normality of returns is $JB = Z_{skew}^2 + Z_{kurt}^2$, where each of Z_{skew} and Z_{kurt} is independently standard normally distributed under the null hypothesis of normally distributed data (see Appendix A on p. 289 or Section 1.3.10 of *Foundations*). When conducting this test, which of the following is correct? Please assume a very large sample size.

    (a) The test statistic JB is distributed chi-squared with 2 degrees of freedom under the null hypothesis, and a test with 5% level of significance uses both upper and lower critical values for the test statistic (i.e., 2.5% in each tail).

    (b) The test statistic JB is distributed chi-squared with 2 degrees of freedom under the null hypothesis, and a test with 5% level of significance uses only an upper critical value for the test statistic (i.e., 5% in the upper tail).

    (c) The test statistic JB is distributed chi-squared with 2 degrees of freedom under the null hypothesis, and whether a test with 5% level of significance uses only an upper critical value or upper and lower critical values depends upon the form of the alternative hypothesis.

    (d) The test statistic JB is distributed chi-squared with 750 degrees of freedom under the null hypothesis, and a test with 5% level of significance uses both upper and lower critical values for the test statistic (i.e., 2.5% in each tail).

    (e) The test statistic JB is distributed chi-squared with 750 degrees of freedom under the null hypothesis, and a test with 5% level of significance uses only an upper critical value for the test statistic (i.e., 5% in the upper tail).

    (f) The test statistic JB is distributed chi-squared with 750 degrees of freedom under the null hypothesis, and whether a test with 5% level of significance uses only an upper critical value or upper and lower critical values depends upon the form of the alternative hypothesis.

    (g) None of the above is correct.

151. Mean blur appears in many stylized facts in finance and it also has an impact on investment techniques. What is the *definition* of mean blur in stock returns? Read carefully and choose the ONE best answer. Be sure to choose the definition of mean blur, and not simply an example of it.

    (a) The fact that we almost never get an average year in the stock market.

    (b) The frequent difficulty in rejecting the null hypothesis that mean $\mu_i = 0$ for individual stocks.

    (c) The importance of the implicit equilibrium returns in the first step of the Black-Litterman technique.

    (d) The impossibility of reaching the ex post minimum-variance frontier.

    (e) The empirical observation that the mean returns on stocks are very small relative to the standard deviation of returns on stocks.

    (f) The importance of the global minimum-variance portfolio (MVP) on the Markowitz minimum-variance frontier as the only point on the frontier not needing $\vec{\mu}$ as an input to locate it.

152. This question is about mean blur. You should have the capital markets intuition to answer it, even if you do not remember the numbers from Chapter 1 of *Foundations*. Over period 1928–2018, data from Damodaran (2019) tell us that there were X years in this 91-year sample when the S&P 500 return including dividends was within 1 percentage point of its average return over the sample, and Y years in this 91-year sample when the S&P 500 return including dividends was within 5 percentage points of its average return over the sample. What are X and Y?

    (a) $X = 1$ and $Y = 17$

    (b) $X = 5$ and $Y = 27$

    (c) $X = 20$ and $Y = 57$

    (d) $X = 43$ and $Y = 77$

    (e) $X = 60$ and $Y = 86$

153. In the 50-year 1963–2013 sample of U.S. daily stock market data (see Chapter 1 of *Foundations*), roughly how many daily returns were there on the S&P 500 index? Work it out by estimating the count of trading days.

    (a) Between 5,000 and 10,000.

    (b) Between 10,001 and 12,459.

    (c) Between 12,500 and 12,750.

    (d) Between 12,751 and 18,249.

    (e) Between 18,250 and 18,300.

    (f) Fewer than any of the above numbers.

    (g) More than any of the above numbers.

154. The distribution of daily returns to stock market indices in developed countries is not normally distributed. Which of the following is the best explanation, or partial explanation?

    (a) There are too many tail events, like the extreme positive and negative returns seen during October 2008 (GFC) and the first quarter of 2020 (COVID-19).

    (b) No, in fact, there are not as many extreme-return days as we would expect if returns were normally distributed. These extreme returns stand out, and make headlines, *because* they are so rare.

    (c) There are too many calm days, with returns of small magnitude, compared with what we would expect if returns were distributed normally (e.g., all of 2017).

    (d) No, in fact, there are not enough calm days for returns to be normally distributed. That is because we see so many extreme-return days and not enough small-return days.

    (e) (a) and (c) are correct.

    (f) (b) and (d) are correct.

    (g) None of the above is correct.

155. You are a portfolio manager running a passively-managed S&P ETF. An investor is worried about the risk of changes in the value of their investment in your ETF on any day. They have measured the mean return on your ETF as 3 bps per day, and the standard deviation of returns as 100 bps per day. They ask you to quantify the risk of moves in the value of their investment of greater than 400 bps in a day, in either direction. You model returns as normally distributed and you conclude that a move in the value of their investment of this size or more will happen only about once every 40 years. What is wrong with your analysis?

    (a) Stock returns are not normally distributed, and it matters in this case.

    (b) In fact, a return of this magnitude could easily happen more frequently than once per annum.

    (c) Extreme returns of this sort are in fact much less likely than is suggested by a model assuming normality, perhaps happening only once every 1000 years, because there are many more returns close to zero than is suggested by a normal distribution with these parameters.

    (d) Both (a) and (b).

    (e) Both (a) and (c).

156. Consider two long-term passive investors in stocks, Connor and Reinar. They each invest a lump sum in a passive S&P 500 index fund with negligible fees. Connor consumes all his dividends as they are paid out, but Reinar reinvests all his dividends back into the fund. Based on our analysis of the 50-year S&P 500 sample, after 50 years, roughly what will be the ratio of Reinar's ending wealth (including all reinvested dividends) divided by Connor's ending wealth (with no dividends)?

To answer this question, think of Reinar's ending wealth as $100, and ask yourself how much of that is reinvested dividends (call this X). Then conclude that Connor must have only $100 - X$. I am asking for the ratio $100/(\$100 - X)$. Ignore taxes. Which rounded answer below is best?

(a) 4.75

(b) 3.00

(c) 2.25

(d) 1.25

(e) 0.50

157. Which ONE of the following statements about "true diversification" is FALSE?

(a) True diversification requires that the assets be diverse and that the assets be risky.

(b) If you can find assets whose returns are lightly correlated with the returns to the risky assets in your risky-asset portfolio, then adding these assets to your portfolio is an example of true diversification.

(c) High-quality bonds add a minimal diversification benefit to your portfolio; ultimately they are adjusting the overall portfolio risk, driven by risk aversion, and are not part of true diversification.

(d) Adding low-risk assets to a risky-asset portfolio does not further true diversification as this action fails to diversify unsystematic risk.

(e) We do not necessarily need many assets to achieve the coveted effect of true diversification, but they have to be well chosen.

158. You have 100 observations of stock returns on large-capitalization stock FBU, but only 50 observations of stock returns on small-capitalization stock SEA. The sample standard deviation of stock returns to FBU is $s_{FBU} = 0.015111819$. The sample standard deviation of stock returns to SEA is $s_{SEA} = 0.045336066$. You want to conduct an F-test for differences in variance. What is the value of the F-statistic? I have rounded my answers to three decimal places. (Note that if you invert an F-statistic, it is still an F-statistic. So, if your answer does not appear here, be sure to try inverting it before resorting to the "none of the above" answer.)

(a) 1.485

(b) 3.000

(c) 4.455

(d) 9.000

(e) None of the above is correct.

159. In a traditional Student-t test of the mean, under which of the following scenarios is your usual test statistic most likely to be INVALID? Treat each option as a completely separate scenario.

    (a) You cannot reject normality of the underlying data.

    (b) You can reject normality of the underlying data, but you have a large sample ($N > 500$) of large-capitalization stock returns and no other violations of assumptions are suspected.

    (c) You can reject independence of your returns data because of significant first-order auto-correlation. The auto-correlation is given by $\rho = -0.25$ and no other assumptions are violated.

    (d) You have a small sample ($N < 30$) and there is significant skewness in your sample ($Z_{skew} = +3.7$ using the skewness test from Appendix A on p. 289 or Section 1.3.10 of *Foundations*).

    (e) You have a large sample ($N > 500$) and there is insignificant kurtosis in your sample ($Z_{kurt} = +0.6$ using the kurtosis test from Appendix A on p. 289 or Section 1.3.10 of *Foundations*).

    (f) In fact, the Student-t test statistic is invalid in **two of the above cases**.

160. $\diamond$ Suppose that the only violation of the assumptions of the Student-t test of the mean is that there is negative first-order auto-correlation in your returns data. So, your data are still normally distributed and identically distributed. What happens to the standard error of the sample mean? That is, what happens to the standard error (or the estimated standard error) sitting in the denominator of the Student-t test statistic for the mean? You may assume that your data are a very large sample of large-capitalization stock returns.

    (a) The standard error of the mean is immune to this violation of the assumptions because of the large sample size.

    (b) The standard error of the mean is immune to this violation of the assumptions because you cannot reject normality.

    (c) Both of the above are correct.

    (d) The true standard error is likely larger than is indicated by the usual calculation, because of the negative auto-correlation.

    (e) The true standard error is likely smaller than is indicated by the usual calculation, because of the negative auto-correlation.

1.2 Foundations II: Financial Economics

161. The quotes (i.e., the best bid and ask prices) for CMO at 2:00PM on Friday April 1, 2016 were $6.25–$6.34. Assume that your broker charges you a $30 commission (and this includes the exchange fee) every time you trade. Assume that you buy 100 shares. Calculate the T-costs of the trade in dollars assuming that fair value is in the middle of the spread. Account for both the T-costs of the spread and the commission, but not for anything else.

    (a) $19.50

    (b) $26.00

    (c) $30.00

    (d) $34.50

    (e) $39.00

162. ◇ On April 13, 2015, Vanguard offered an ETF that mimics the S&P 500 and charges an annual expense ratio of only 5 bps. Investors had USD208.8b invested in it (c.f. the NZD100b capitalization of the entire NZX on the same day). Assume that the annual return on the fund before fees will be 8.00% for the next 10 years (it was exactly this on average over the last 10 years). Suppose I put USD10,000 into this fund. How much worse off will I be at the end of 10 years because of this expense ratio? I have rounded all the answers below to the nearest dollar. You do not have to worry about taxes or any other transaction costs or dividends.

    (a) $10

    (b) $50

    (c) $100

    (d) $629

    (e) $979

163. In Question 3.2.1 you constructed a Markowitz frontier for 20 stocks. The frontier your constructed showed what?

    (a) It showed naive consensus expected return versus standard deviation of returns for minimum-risk portfolios of the 20 stocks.

    (b) It showed skilled expected return versus standard deviation of returns for minimum-risk portfolios of the 20 stocks.

    (c) It showed active return versus active risk for portfolios of the 20 stocks.

    (d) It showed historical sample mean returns versus sample standard deviation of returns for minimum-risk portfolios of the 20 stocks.

    (e) None of the above is correct.

164. In Question 3.2.2 you built value alphas using price-earnings (P/E) ratios and dividend yield (DY). Which way around were the raw alphas?

   (a) $\alpha = P/E$ and $\alpha = DY$.

   (b) $\alpha = \frac{1}{P/E}$ and $\alpha = DY$.

   (c) $\alpha = P/E$ and $\alpha = \frac{1}{DY}$.

   (d) $\alpha = \frac{1}{P/E}$ and $\alpha = \frac{1}{DY}$.

   (e) It does not matter; the transformations we did took care of this issue.

165. Which ONE of the following is TRUE?

   (a) A value stock is a stock whose price has been beaten down relative to fundamental variables, but its price is expected to rebound (i.e., grow) in the future.

   (b) A value stock is a stock whose price has been optimistically over-inflated relative to fundamentals and its price is expected to collapse in the future.

   (c) The definition of a growth stock is that it is a stock whose price has been beaten down relative to fundamental variables, and whose price is expected to rebound (i.e., grow) in the future.

   (d) Value stocks and growth stocks are mutually exclusive; a stock cannot be both.

   (e) All of the above are true.

166. In the Markowitz problem we solved in Question 3.2.1, the return on the tangency portfolio "T" was given by:

   (a) $\vec{h}'_T \mu_P$ where μ_P was the return to the frontier portfolio that had the highest Sharpe ratio out of all the portfolios we constructed.

   (b) $\vec{h}'_B \vec{\mu}$ where $\vec{h}_B$ was the capitalization-weighted benchmark portfolio weights.

   (c) $\vec{h}'_T \vec{\mu}$ where $\vec{h}_T = \frac{V^{-1}(\vec{\mu} - R_F \vec{\iota})}{\vec{\iota}' V^{-1}(\vec{\mu} - R_F \vec{\iota})}$ and $\vec{\mu}$ was the vector of mean stock returns.

   (d) $\vec{h}'_{mvp} \vec{\mu}$ where $\vec{h}_{mvp} = \frac{1}{C} V^{-1} \vec{\iota}$ was the weights in the minimum variance portfolio.

   (e) $\mu_{mvp} = \frac{A}{C}$ where "mvp" stands for minimum variance portfolio.

167. New Zealand's KiwiSaver retirement savings scheme offers *which* investors a matching tax credit of up to $521.43 per annum? Please ignore investors over age 65.

   (a) All KiwiSaver scheme participants who contribute at least $1042.86 per annum

   (b) Only KiwiSaver scheme participants under age 18 who contribute at least $1042.86 per annum

   (c) Only KiwiSaver scheme participants over age 18 who contribute at least $1042.86 per annum

   (d) Only employed KiwiSaver scheme participants over age 18 who contribute at least $1042.86 per annum

   (e) None of the above.

Day	Date	Stock BUY Price	Stock SELL Price	Dividend
Mon	January 10	1074	1080	None
Tue	January 11	$10.76	$10.82	None
Wed	January 12	$10.24	$10.28	None
Thu	January 13	$2.56	$2.60	None
Fri	January 14	$2.25	$2.30	$0.25

Table 1.8: Stock ABC Price and Dividends (Dollars Per Share)

168. Table 1.8 gives closing bid and ask prices for stock ABC, and the amount of a cash dividend (Friday is the ex-date). If you think a stock split took place this week, then please guess the ratio. You buy stock ABC at Monday's close, and sell it at Friday's close, using market orders. Assuming sufficient depth, what is your total simple net return over this four-day period? Ignore broker commissions and exchange fees.

    (a) -1.9%

    (b) -6.2%

    (c) -7.4%

    (d) -11.5%

    (e) None of the above.

169. On April 22, 2008, the FX quotes were 1.97950/1.97983 USD/GBP (in literal terms) or GBP/USD 1.97950/1.97983 (using the standard FX quoting convention) on www.oanda.com.[2] How wide is the bid-ask spread?

    (a) 3 pips

    (b) 3.3 pips

    (c) 30 pips

    (d) 33 pips

    (e) None of the above

170. If you have gone short 100 shares of stock and you now want to close out your position, which best describes the order you give your broker to close out?

    (a) Buy 100 shares

    (b) Sell 100 shares

    (c) Buy to cover 100 shares

    (d) Sell short 100 shares

    (e) Limit order on 100 shares

---

[2]You must be flexible enough to work with literal quotes (e.g., for dimensional analysis) and standard FX quoting conventions. To better understand standard FX quoting conventions, please see https://www1.oanda.com/forex-trading/learn/getting-started/first-trade.

171. One semester, when talking about the television commercials for trading your way to riches, I showed my students the CFTC's warnings on trading scams. Find the CFTC warnings and tell me which are on the list?

    (a) Stay away from opportunities that seem too good to be true.

    (b) Stay away from companies that promise little or no financial risk.

    (c) Don't trade on margin unless you understand what it means.

    (d) Currency scams often target members of ethnic minorities.

    (e) All of the above.

172. ◇ When building the objective function for our quantitative active alpha optimization, we removed the benchmark return (i.e., κ_B) and benchmark risk (i.e., σ_B^2) components from the candidate objective function because:

    (a) Investors are resigned to facing the risk of the benchmark.

    (b) The benchmark return and risk components are not a function of our choice variables.

    (c) Most U.S. institutional asset managers and a growing majority of non-U.S. institutional asset managers do not use benchmark timing.

    (d) All of the above.

    (e) (a) and (b), but neither (c) nor (d).

173. Suppose I want to estimate a variance-covariance matrix (VCV) using daily returns on the 100 largest N.Z. stocks. Suppose I use the most recent three months of daily returns to estimate the sample VCV. May I now use this VCV to estimate a Markowitz efficient frontier allowing short selling?

    (a) Yes, it should work fine because three months of daily data is a good-sized sample.

    (b) No, certainly not.

    (c) Not enough information is given to answer the question.

174. An order experiences "price impact" (also called "market impact") when...

    (a) the time delay between placing the order and having it filled leads to an unfavorable price move.

    (b) there is more than enough depth at the posted quotes to fill the order immediately.

    (c) the order "walks up the limit order book" consuming depth and pushing prices against the favor of the trader.

    (d) a designated market maker crosses the order with another client order strictly within the spread.

    (e) when the order is broken down into smaller orders and the firm's trading desk "works the order" effectively.

175. The "Fundamental Law of Active Management" says that if we double the number of independent forecasts of active return we make during a year (e.g., by doubling the number of stocks we cover), our IR will roughly:

    (a) Halve.

    (b) Stay the same.

    (c) Double.

    (d) Triple.

    (e) None of the above.

176. If R_B is benchmark return, and β_P is portfolio beta relative to the benchmark, and R_P is portfolio return, then:

    (a) Active return is $R_B - R_P$ and active beta is $1 - \beta_P$

    (b) Active return is $R_P - R_B$ and active beta is $\beta_P - 1$

    (c) Active return is $(R_B - R_F) - \beta_P \cdot (R_B - R_F)$ and active beta is $1 - \beta_P$

    (d) Active return is $(R_B - R_F) - \beta_P \cdot (R_B - R_F)$ and active beta is $\beta_P - 1$

    (e) None of the above.

177. We "neutralized" our alphas when we built them for our active alpha optimization. That is, we replaced $\vec{\alpha}$ with $\vec{\alpha}_{\text{neut}} = \vec{\alpha} - (\vec{h}'_B \vec{\alpha}) \cdot \vec{\beta}$, where $\vec{\alpha}$ is the column vector of original alpha forecasts, $\vec{h}_B$ is the column vector of weights in the benchmark, $\vec{h}'_B \vec{\alpha}$ is the benchmark average alpha, and $\vec{\beta}$ is the column vector of betas of the stocks with respect to the benchmark. We did this because:

    (a) We didn't want our alphas to have any beta.

    (b) We wanted our alphas to have a mean and standard deviation that was comparable to that of the benchmark.

    (c) We wanted our alphas to have a mean of zero and a standard deviation of one.

    (d) We did not want to be able to capture any alpha by holding the passive benchmark.

    (e) We wanted our portfolio weights to sum to one, and this transformation ensures that.

178. Suppose you buy shares of a stock on 50% margin. If the stock price falls dramatically, you might expect the broker to...

    (a) ask you for more margin money.

    (b) close out your position without even consulting you.

    (c) buy more shares on your behalf to lower your average purchase price.

    (d) (a) or (b), but certainly not (c).

    (e) (a) or (c), but certainly not (b).

179. Figure 1.4 shows a possible plot of the Markowitz and Tobin frontiers with the following labels: 12 different stock ticker symbols, "T" for the theoretical tangency portfolio, and "B" for the benchmark. Which of the following is TRUE?

    (a) Betas of the 12 stocks calculated relative to "B" will fall perfectly on a straight line.

    (b) The tangency portfolio T is NOT mean-variance efficient.

    (c) Stocks TEL, FPH, and PPG have betas relative to "T" that are less than 1.

    (d) Stocks FBU and RNS have betas relative to "T" that are less than 1.

    (e) None of the above is true.

180. In the Markowitz plot in Figure 1.4, the tangency portfolio "T" was on the upper Markowitz frontier, and the benchmark portfolio "B" was strictly within the interior of the Markowitz frontier. Which of the following is TRUE.

    (a) The correlation between the sample means of the stocks and their sample betas calculated with respect to "T" was +1.

    (b) The correlation between the sample means of the stocks and their sample betas calculated with respect to "B" was +1.

    (c) The correlation between the sample betas of the stocks calculated with respect to B and their sample betas calculated with respect to "T" was +1.

    (d) The correlation between the sample means of stocks and their sample standard deviations was +1.

    (e) None of the above is true.

181. Which of the following is TRUE?

    (a) Smaller tick sizes make it easier for a sell side agent to pass private information to their proprietary colleagues and front run the trade via "time priority."

    (b) "Market fragmentation" refers to the breaking up of large orders into smaller orders to try to avoid price impact.

    (c) Electronic trading platforms (e.g., ECNs) involve lower direct costs (i.e., spreads plus commissions plus fees) than traditional brokers.

    (d) Buy side managers with large orders prefer sell side firms with proprietary trading divisions to agency-only firms because agency-only firms tend to be smaller.

    (e) None of the above.

182. Suppose you sell a stock on the ex-dividend day. Do you expect to get the dividend?

    (a) Yes, I am entitled to the dividend.

    (b) No, I am NOT entitled to the dividend.

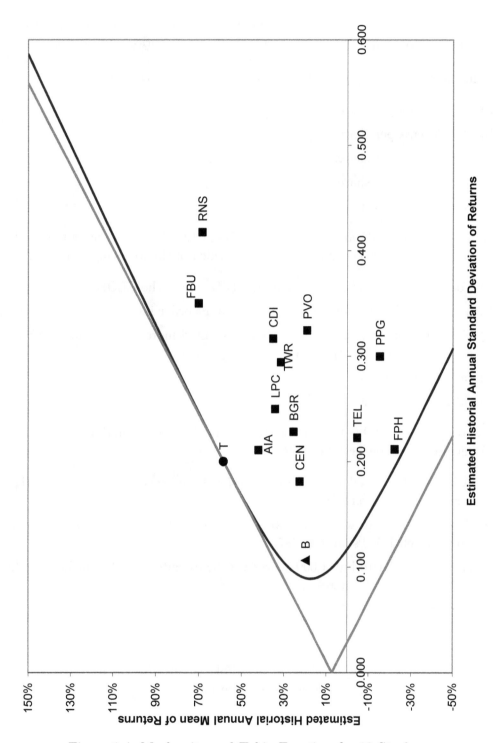

Figure 1.4: Markowitz and Tobin Frontiers for 12 Stocks

Markowitz (curved) and Tobin (kinked) minimum variance plots for 12 N.Z. stocks. A riskless rate of 7.25% is used.

183. Table 1.9 shows the Centralized Limit Order Book (CLOB) for TEL stock on April 23, 2008. Suppose you can trade at the quoted prices and depths. Suppose you submit a *market order* to buy 100,000 shares. Ignoring the broker commission and the NZX exchange fee, the average cost to buy those shares is:

    (a) 387.00 cents per share.

    (b) 387.45 cents per share.

    (c) 388.45 cents per share.

    (d) 389.00 cents per share.

    (e) None of the above.

184. Ignore Question 183 and look again at Table 1.9. Suppose you submit a *limit order* to buy 100,000 shares at 386. Then which of the following is TRUE?

    (a) You become the market maker on the BID side of the CLOB.

    (b) You risk non-execution by submitting a limit order instead of a market order.

    (c) Your limit order to buy will surely be executed more quickly than the market order to buy in Question 183.

    (d) (a) and (b), but not (c).

    (e) (a) and (c), but not (b).

185. Looking again at Table 1.9, suppose you can trade at the quoted prices and depths. Which of the following is/are TRUE?

    (a) A limit order to sell 1,000 shares at 387 will be executed more quickly than a market order to sell 1,000 shares.

    (b) A market order to sell 1,000 shares will be executed more quickly than a limit order to sell 1,000 shares at 387.

    (c) A market order to buy 1,000 shares will be executed just as quickly as a limit order to buy 1,000 shares at 387.

    (d) (a) and (c), but not (b).

    (e) (b) and (c), but not (a).

186. Which of the following numbers is a credible number for the average annual expense ratio for actively managed equity mutual funds in N.Z. or the U.S.?

    (a) 10 bps

    (b) 50 bps

    (c) 125 bps

    (d) 250 bps

    (e) 500 bps

Telecom Corporation of New Zealand Limited (NS)
Share prices at 17:30:00 Wednesday, April 23, 2008   <u>View Depth</u>

Stock	Exchange	Bid	Offer	Last	Change*	Open	High	Low	Volume	Turnover
TEL	NZX	385	387	386	▲ 7	376	386	376	14937801	$56,938,965

Buy >>   Sell >>   Announcements >>   Research & Graphs >>   Add to Watchlist >>

🖻 Print >>

Buy	**Market Depth**		**Sell**
Buy Quantity	Prices	Prices	Sell Quantity
108,292	385	387	75,000
34,513	384	388	10,000
9,556	383	389	10,000
5,250	376	390	82,750
5,273	371	394	4,090
50,000	370	395	4,500
35,875	368	397	4,000
5,500	365	399	1,000
9,156	360	400	20,668
13,300	358	401	2,000
2,000	357	403	5,000
12,200	356	404	5,000
66,066	355	405	3,000
2,400	350	409	11,053
7,000	340	410	*91,036
700	335	411	1,000
322	300	415	6,540
0	0	420	26,044
0	0	430	1,612
0	0	450	7,780
0	0	490	1,003
367,403			373,076

*Limit orders can be placed onto the market with an undisclosed quantity. The undisclosed quantity of the order must be a value equal to or greater than $100,000.

Table 1.9: Centralized Limit Order Book for TEL NZ

The CLOB for Telecom N.Z. (now renamed "Spark") from April 23, 2008. All prices are in cents per share. Source: ASB Securities, used with permission.

187. Figure 1.5 shows a Bloomberg screen using the command `MSFT <EQUITY> OV <GO>`. An options market maker who sold this American-style call option (covering 100 shares) would trade roughly how many shares to hedge his/her position?

    (a) Go long 7 shares

    (b) Go short 7 shares

    (c) Go long 86 shares

    (d) Go short 86 shares

    (e) Not enough information is given to be able to figure it out.

188. Suppose you own 100 shares of Boeing and you want to buy a protective put option to put a floor on your downside. You see a put option contract with ticker ZBOMC trading with posted quotes of $0.85–$0.95 per share. You know that a single contract of ZBOMC covers 100 shares of stock. Your broker charges an options trading commission of $10 plus $0.75 per option contract traded. What would be your total expenditure (i.e., premium + commission) to purchase a single contract of ZBOMC?

    (a) $95.75

    (b) $105.75

    (c) $850.75

    (d) $960.75

    (e) None of the above

189. Who earns the bid-ask spread for S&P/NZX50 stocks on the NZX?

    (a) Nobody does; there is no designated market maker in any S&P/NZX50 stock.

    (b) We can think of whoever posted the best bid or offer as collecting half the spread (if their order is executed) because they are acting like a market maker.

    (c) The NZX collects the spread as a transaction fee.

    (d) The customers who are buying or selling (via market orders) get half the spread.

    (e) The broker who handles the trade collects the spread.

190. Suppose Fisher Funds' New Zealand Growth Fund charges an annual fee (i.e., expense ratio) of 125 bps per annum. On an investment of $100,000 this fee is expected to amount to something like...

    (a) $0.125 per annum

    (b) $1.25 per annum

    (c) $12.50 per annum

    (d) $125.00 per annum

    (e) None of the above

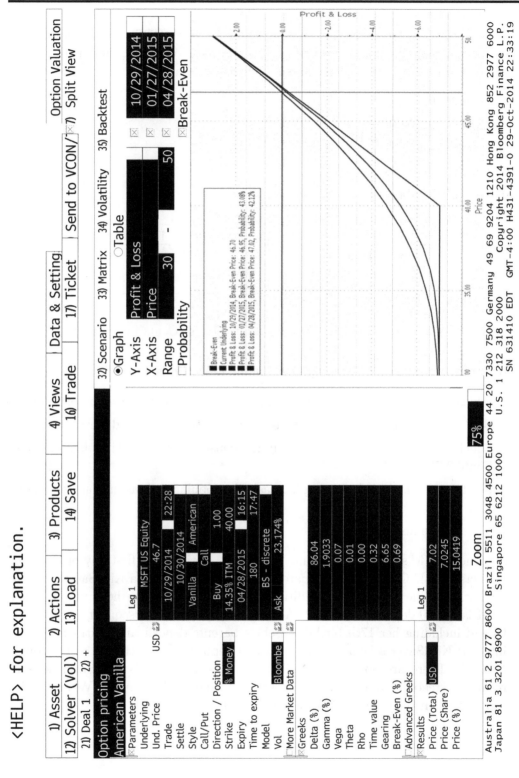

Figure 1.5: Bloomberg Screen: MSFT <EQUITY> OV <GO>

A MSFT Corporation Bloomberg OV screen from October 29, 2014, showing an option valuation.

191. Table 1.10 gives end of day mid-spread prices for stock DEF, and the amount of a cash dividend. Wednesday is the ex-dividend date. Which of these is the times series of simple net returns calculated from these data?

    (a) 0.01099, -0.01163

    (b) 0.01099, -0.07609

    (c) -0.05495, -0.07609

    (d) -0.05495, -0.01163

    (e) None of the above.

Day	Date	Stock Mid-Spread Price	Dividend
Tue	January 11	455	None
Wed	January 12	430	30
Thu	January 13	425	None

Table 1.10: Stock DEF Price and Dividends (Cents Per Share)

192. Regarding "benchmark timing," which of the following is TRUE?

    (a) Benchmark timing refers to choosing how often to rebalance your portfolio.

    (b) Benchmark timing is when you actively choose to have beta different to 1.

    (c) Benchmark timing is when you apply the constraint beta=1 (just like in Question 3.2.2).

    (d) Benchmark timing is becoming increasingly popular with asset managers globally.

    (e) None of the above is true.

193. Assume that Miss Bebe Nouveaune is born on April 1 (the first day of the N.Z. financial year). On this day her parents deposit $2,000 into a KiwiSaver account for her, and she also gets an additional $1,000 deposit from her grandparents. That is $3,000 deposited at $t = 0$. Assume that on every subsequent birthday up to and including her 17th birthday Bebe's parents deposit an additional $1,000 into her KiwiSaver scheme. That is $1,000 deposited on each of $t = 1$ through $t = 17$. There are no more contributions. Assume Bebe's KiwiSaver scheme returns a steady $R = 7\%$ every year after all taxes and expenses. What will be the balance in the scheme at Bebe's 60th birthday?

    (a) $739,583

    (b) $756,727

    (c) $1,037,304

    (d) $1,061,349

    (e) None of the above.

194. Suppose $\sigma_B = 0.1063$ (benchmark std deviation), $\sigma_P = 0.1240$ (portfolio std deviation), $\beta_P = 1$ (portfolio beta), $\alpha_P = 0.04300$ (forward looking portfolio alpha), and $\lambda = 10$ (residual risk aversion assuming return and risk are in decimals). What is the forward looking IR (information ratio) to three decimal places?

    (a) 0.347

    (b) 0.405

    (c) 0.673

    (d) 10.549

    (e) There is not enough information here to work it out.

195. The EUR/NZD exchange rate is quoted right now (3:48PM NZT April 27, 2009) as 0.43173/0.43373 on www.oanda.com. The width of the bid-ask spread is

    (a) 0.2 pips

    (b) 2.0 pips

    (c) 20 pips

    (d) 200 pips

    (e) None of the above

196. Table 1.11, below, gives close of business bid (buy) and ask (sell) prices for stock ABC, and the amount of a cash dividend. Friday is the ex-dividend date. If you think a stock split took place this week, then you should guess the ratio. Assume you bought stock ABC at the close of business Monday, and sold out at the close of business Friday. What is your actual total rate of return over this four-day period? Please ignore broker commissions and exchange fees. Note that I am asking for a simple net return over this holding period and it is not annualized.

Day	Date	Stock BUY Price	Stock SELL Price	Dividend
Mon	January 10	560	564	None
Tue	January 11	562	566	None
Wed	January 12	567	571	None
Thu	January 13	280	282	None
Fri	January 14	265	267	25

Table 1.11: Stock ABC Price and Dividends (Cents Per Share)

    (a) -5.3381%

    (b) -1.5957%

    (c) 2.8369%

    (d) 3.5587%

    (e) None of the above.

197. In *Foundations*, we compared a portfolio manager's investment strategy with a positive ex-ante RAA to a CFO's future investment project with a positive NPV. We said that they are similar because:

(a) Both will surely add value.

(b) Both are risky.

(c) Both require skill to manage.

(d) All of the above.

(e) (b) an (c) only.

198. You just went short 1,000 shares of stock using the traditional 150% cash margin. Oh no! The stock price just jumped up $10 a share. You close out immediately. What is your gain or loss?

(a) $1,000 loss.

(b) $5,000 loss.

(c) $10,000 loss.

(d) $15,000 loss.

(e) None of the above is correct; I made a gain.

199. A firm issues $1M in debt and uses the proceeds to buy back $1M in equity. Assuming no change in stock or bond prices, what is the impact on EV?

(a) EV increases by $2M.

(b) EV increases by $1M.

(c) No change in EV.

(d) EV decreases by $1M.

(e) EV decreases by $2M.

200. Different stocks should have different price-earnings (P/E) ratios because P/E is a function of the following variables and these variables are different from stock to stock:

(a) riskiness of the stock **and** PV of growth opportunities of the stock (e.g., a stock in a hot industry may have high growth prospects and a stock in a mature industry may have low growth prospects).

(b) riskiness of the stock **and** the impact of the general level of interest rates in the economy on the stock's price and earnings.

(c) The forecast rate of growth of earnings in a stock **and** the discount rate for the stock's future cash flows.

(d) All of the above.

(e) (a) and (c) only.

201. Lynch (2000) says that corporate diversification is usually "diworsification" because

   (a) It is only in concentrated portfolios of a few stocks that we are likely to find dramatic outperformance because most diversified portfolios have been dragged down by the global recession.

   (b) Investors have a home country bias and fail to hold enough shares in overseas firms.

   (c) Diversification in a portfolio requires that you buy many different stocks and you incur many transactions costs to do so.

   (d) Firms that buy businesses outside their core competency tend to manage them poorly.

   (e) The "winners curse" means that firms that acquire other firms tend to pay too much for them.

202. ◇ Lynch (2000) discusses Kellogg's as a recession-proof stock because people still eat cornflakes during a recession. Can you guess, or discover, which of Kellogg's and McDonald's best held its value during the recent global financial crisis?

   (a) Both Kellogg's and McDonald's.

   (b) Neither Kellogg's nor McDonald's.

   (c) Kellogg's only.

   (d) McDonald's only.

   (e) None of the above is correct.

203. Suppose you submit a market order into the New Zealand Stock Exchange (NZX) via your broker. Suppose you are going to buy a large block of shares (with money you just inherited from a rich aunt). Suppose you have no special informed/private information about the stock. Suppose that your buy order walks up the centralized limit order book (CLOB) pushing prices against you as you go. This means that you are going long and the price is going up. Is this **price rise** good for you?

   (a) Yes, obviously, because I am long and price is rising; This is a clear benefit to me.

   (b) No, obviously not. This is clearly a cost to me.

   (c) Whether it is a cost or benefit depends upon when I plan to sell the stock.

   (d) Whether it is a cost or benefit depends upon whether I break my position down into smaller orders when it is time to sell.

   (e) None of the above answers is correct.

204. NZT was an ADR for Telecom New Zealand trading on the NYSE. Each share of NZT corresponded to how many shares of Telecom New Zealand (TEL) bundled together? Hint: On April 28, 2009, NZT traded at USD7.67 (NYSE), TEL traded at NZD2.69 (NZX), and the exchange rate was NZD/USD 0.57191 (using standard FX quoting conventions) or 0.57191 USD/NZD (in literal terms). (See footnote 2 on p. 63 regarding FX quotes.)

    (a) 2

    (b) 4

    (c) 6

    (d) 8

    (e) None of the above is correct.

205. Which of the following is TRUE?

    (a) Continuously-compounded returns compound using addition and simple gross returns compound using addition

    (b) Continuously-compounded returns compound using addition and simple gross returns compound using multiplication

    (c) Continuously-compounded returns compound using multiplication and simple gross returns compound using addition

    (d) Continuously-compounded returns compound using multiplication and simple gross returns compound using multiplication

    (e) None of these makes sense.

206. In a competitive market, the bid-ask spread is not reduced to zero because the market makers need to be compensated for...

    (a) Order processing costs

    (b) The risk that the market maker is trading with better-informed people.

    (c) Inventory holding costs/risks.

    (d) All of the above.

    (e) (a) and (c), but not (b).

207. The "Fundamental Law of Active Management" says that if we halve the number of independent forecasts of active return we make during a year (e.g., by halving the number of stocks we cover), our IR will roughly:

    (a) Be multiplied by 0.50.

    (b) Be multiplied by 0.71.

    (c) stay the same.

    (d) Be multiplied by 2.

    (e) Be multiplied by 4.

208. Recall the result due to Robert C. Merton concerning the behavior of estimators of mean and variance as we sample a year's data more and more finely (e.g., going from monthly, to weekly, to daily data, etc.). The general implication of the result was that as we sample returns from a random walk more finely:

   (a) The standard errors of estimators of both mean and variance decrease.

   (b) The standard errors of estimators of both mean and variance increase.

   (c) The standard error of the estimator of the mean increases but the standard error of the estimator of the variance decreases.

   (d) The standard error of the estimator of the mean decreases but the standard error of the estimator of the variance increases.

   (e) None of these is correct.

209. With reference to retirement plans' matching "free money" and "vesting," vesting is what?

   (a) Contributing enough to your retirement savings scheme to get the maximum match from your employer.

   (b) Always taking the free money when it is offered to you.

   (c) Living within your means so that you can make the minimum contribution needed to obtain the maximum match from your employer.

   (d) Taking possession of some benefit (e.g., ownership of matching funds) after some set period of time.

   (e) Receiving compensation in the form of options contracts.

210. Which of the following is usually FALSE for individual daily stock returns?

   (a) The returns usually display excess positive kurtosis.

   (b) You often cannot reject the null that the returns are normally distributed.

   (c) Small-cap stock returns are usually more volatile than large-cap stock returns.

   (d) Small-cap stock returns are more likely to be negatively autocorrelated than large-cap stock returns.

   (e) You often cannot reject the null that the mean is zero.

211. If R_B is benchmark return, and β_P is portfolio beta relative to the benchmark, and R_P is portfolio return, then:

   (a) Active return is $(R_B - R_F) - \beta_P \cdot (R_B - R_F)$ and active beta is $\beta_P - 1$

   (b) Active return is $(R_B - R_F) - \beta_P \cdot (R_B - R_F)$ and active beta is $1 - \beta_P$

   (c) Active return is $R_B - R_P$ and active beta is $\beta_P - 1$

   (d) Active return is $R_P - R_B$ and active beta is $1 - \beta_P$

   (e) None of the above is correct.

212. Who earns the commission for S&P/NZX50 equity trades executed on the NZX?

    (a) Nobody does; there is no designated market maker in any S&P/NZX50 stock.

    (b) We can think of whoever posted the best bid or offer as collecting the commission because they are acting like a market maker.

    (c) The NZX collects the full commission as a transaction fee.

    (d) The customers who are buying or selling (via market orders) get half the commission each.

    (e) The broker who handles the trade gets most of the commission with a small portion going to the NZX.

213. ◇ Here is a question based on life insurance quotes for New Zealanders in the 16–28 age group. Which of the following is the correct life insurance coverage for a monthly premium of $19.95 (M=Male, F=Female, S=Smoker, NS=Non-Smoker)?

    (a) MS=$91,210, MNS=$149,662, FS=$161,000, FNS=$236,131

    (b) MS=$91,210, FS=$149,662, MNS=$161,000, FNS=$236,131

    (c) FNS=$91,210, MNS=$149,662, FS=$161,000, MS=$236,131

    (d) FS=$91,210, MS=$149,662, MNS=$161,000, FNS=$236,131

    (e) MS=$91,210, MNS=$149,662, FNS=$161,000, FS=$236,131

214. An active bond portfolio manager has an IR of 60%. Suppose that she wants to charge expenses and fees totaling 100 bps. Suppose she wants to generate 50bps of active return after these fees. What level of active risk should she take on?

    (a) 83.33bps

    (b) 166.67bps

    (c) 250bps

    (d) 375bps

    (e) None of the above.

215. When building the objective function for our quantitative active alpha optimization, we removed the benchmark return (i.e., κ_B) and benchmark risk (i.e., σ_B^2) components from the candidate objective function because:

    (a) The benchmark return and risk components are not a function of our choice variables.

    (b) Most U.S. institutional asset managers and a growing majority of non-U.S. institutional asset managers do not use benchmark timing.

    (c) Clients fear "maverick risk" (i.e., the risk of the manager having returns materially different from his or her peers) more than they fear benchmark risk.

    (d) All of the above.

    (e) (a) and (b) only.

216. Suppose you buy shares of a $2.00 stock on 50% margin. How low does the stock price have to fall for you to lose half of your investment? That is, how low does the stock have to fall for you to lose half the personal wealth you put into the trade? Please ignore all taxes and transactions costs.

    (a) The stock price dropping to $0.50 would mean I lose half my money.

    (b) The stock price dropping to $1.00 would mean I lose half my money.

    (c) The stock price dropping to $1.25 would mean I lose half my money.

    (d) The stock price dropping to $1.50 would mean I lose half my money.

    (e) The stock price dropping to $1.75 would mean I lose half my money.

217. Suppose I have a 10-year semi-annual bond with a 7% coupon rate per annum, and the ask price is a 6.00% YTM and the bid price is a 6.10% YTM. What is the relative bid-ask spread on the bond (i.e. $\frac{ASK\ less\ BID}{MIDSPREAD\ PRICE}$) to two decimal places?

    (a) 70.27 bps

    (b) 70.99 bps

    (c) 71.72 bps

    (d) 72.37 bps.

    (e) None of the above is correct.

218. $\diamond$ Suppose that Matthew instructs his U.S. broker to borrow and short sell 100 shares of NZT (the old N.Z. Telecom ADR) trading in New York. Suppose the broker borrows the 100 shares from a passive U.S. fund manager named Mark, and then sells the shares in the market to a U.S. investor named Luke. Suppose that NZT then declares and pays a dividend. Suppose no other trades take place that have any importance to this question. Which of the following is true.

    (a) Luke gets the dividend directly from NZT, whereas Matthew's broker extracts the dividend from Matthew's brokerage account and then pays it to Mark.

    (b) Mark gets the dividend directly from NZT (after all, he only lent the stock to Matthew's broker and is still the owner), and Matthew's broker extracts the dividend from Matthew's brokerage account and pays the dividend to Luke.

    (c) Matthew does not have any involvement in the dividend payment, and Mark, who lent the stock out and thus no longer holds it must pay the dividend to Luke who bought it.

    (d) Luke gets the dividend directly from NZT because he bought the stock and owns it, and neither Mark nor Matthew have rights or obligations in respect of the dividend.

    (e) Mark gets the dividend directly from NZT because he never sold the stock (he only lent it out). Neither Matthew nor Luke have any involvement in the dividend payments, and Luke misses out because he bought borrowed stock.

219. Table 1.12 shows a commission schedule for an N.Z. broker. You call them on the telephone to give a market order to buy 6,000 shares of an NZX stock. The ask price is $2.00 per share and the depth at the ask is 10,000 shares, and these are available to you. What will the commission be?

    (a) $30

    (b) $35

    (c) $36

    (d) $70

    (e) $84

220. I want you to conduct a commission calculation for a trade. Please consult Table 1.12. Tell me what my **total** commission expenses will be for today if I buy 10,000 shares of N.Z. stock SPK at 220 cents per share, and then a few minutes later sell 1,000 SPK shares (one tenth of my position) at 210 cents per share. Assume that I submit internet-based orders to be executed on the NZX.

    (a) $96.00

    (b) $72.30

    (c) $66.00

    (d) $60.00

    (e) None of the above is correct.

221. With a 40-year horizon, an extra 0.5% return per annum (after taxes and T-costs) does what to your wealth at retirement? Assume a lump sum investment.

    (a) Increases wealth by roughly 2%

    (b) Increases wealth by roughly 20%

    (c) Increases wealth by roughly 50%

    (d) Increases wealth by roughly 100%

    (e) Increases wealth by roughly 200%

222. The Japanese yen exchange rate was quoted at 3:01PM NZT May 4, 2010 as USD/JPY 94.8990/94.9090 on www.oanda.com (using standard FX quoting conventions). The width of the bid-ask spread was how many pips? (See footnote 2 on p. 63 regarding FX quoting conventions.)

    (a) 0.1 pips

    (b) 1 pip

    (c) 10 pips

    (d) 100 pips

    (e) None of the above

	Internet	Telephone	Advisory	One-off Trade
New Zealand Trades	0.3% with a minimum of NZD30.00 per trade	0.7% with a minimum of NZD35.00 per trade	Negotiable and will vary	1.0% with a minimum of NZD40.00
Australian Trades	0.3% with a minimum of AUD30.00 per trade	0.7% with a minimum of AUD35.00 per trade	Negotiable and will vary	1.0% with a minimum of AUD40.00
United States Trades for orders up to USD50,000	N/A	0.8% with a minimum of USD50.00 per trade **plus** Agency Fee 0.4% with a minimum of USD40.00 per trade	Negotiable and will vary	
United States Trades for orders above USD50,000	N/A	Negotiable	Negotiable and will vary	
United Kingdom Trades for orders up to GBP50,000	N/A	1.0% with a minimum of GBP50.00 per trade **plus** Agency Fee 0.4% with a minimum of GBP40.00 per trade	Negotiable and will vary	
United Kingdom Trades for orders above GBP50,000	N/A	Negotiable	Negotiable and will vary	
International Market	N/A	Please call us		

Table 1.12: Brokerage Rates

These are brokerage rates offered by an N.Z. broker observed on May 4, 2010. Note that to trade outside N.Z., there is an additional "agency fee." This is just the commission your broker pays to *their* broker overseas. The above rates are exclusive of U.K. Government Stamp Duty of 50 bps or GBP0.50 per GBP100.00 applying only to purchase orders. The further from home the trade is, the more expensive is the commission.

223. Table 1.13 contains the CLOB for Contact Energy (CEN) at 3:47PM on Thursday April 30th, 2009. Suppose you own 1,000 shares that you wish to sell. Which of the following seems like a sensible way (i.e., there exists a logical justification) to try selling the 1,000 shares?

    (a) Submit a market order to sell 1,000 shares.

    (b) Submit a limit order to sell 1,000 shares at 575.

    (c) Submit a limit order to sell 1,000 shares at 580.

    (d) All of the above can be justified as being sensible.

    (e) One or more of the choices (a), (b), or (c) does not make sense.

224. Table 1.13 contains the centralized limit order book (CLOB) for Contact Energy (CEN) at 3:47PM on Thursday April 30th, 2009. Suppose you submit a limit order to buy 1,000 shares at 575. Suppose that immediately after this another customer submits a market order to sell 1,000 shares. Assume there are no other orders submitted to the CLOB; just these two. Is your limit order crossed with the incoming market order to give you an execution? Which is the BEST answer?

    (a) YES, my limit order to buy 1,000 shares IS crossed with the market order that arrived immediately after my limit order.

    (b) NO, my limit order to buy 1,000 shares is NOT crossed with the market order that arrived immediately after my limit order.

    (c) We do not have enough information to answer the question.

    (d) It may or may not; it depends upon what happens next.

    (e) None of the above is correct.

225. Table 1.13 contains the centralized limit order book (CLOB) for Contact Energy (CEN) at 3:47PM on Thursday April 30th, 2009. Suppose you look at the CLOB and submit a limit order to sell 1,000 shares at 575. Suppose, however, that another customer sent in a market order to buy 20,000 shares just a few seconds before you (it has not yet been reflected in the CLOB) and that their order is going to be executed first. There are no other orders submitted. What price will your order be executed at and when will it be executed?

    (a) 560 immediately after the 20,000-share order is filled.

    (b) 575 immediately after the 20,000-share order is filled.

    (c) 575 if other incoming order(s) can be crossed with it later (but it might not be executed at all).

    (d) 580 immediately after the 20,000-share order is filled.

    (e) 584 if other incoming order(s) can be crossed with it later (but it might not be executed at all).

Contact Energy Limited

Share prices at 15:47:00 Thursday, April 30, 2009 — View Depth

Stock	Exchange	Bid	Offer	Last	Change*		Open	High	Low	Volume	Turnover
CEN	NZX	575	580	580	▲	2	580	595	580	706121	$4,115,802

Buy >>   Sell >>   Add to Watchlist >>   Announcements >>   Research & Graphs >>

🖨 Print >>

Buy		Market Depth		Sell
Buy Quantity	**Prices**		**Prices**	**Sell Quantity**
5,000	575		580	6,785
7,800	565		581	3,282
2,669	563		582	2,000
17,958	560		584	9,685
10,453	555		585	8,239
2,000	554		587	12,000
718	553		588	4,194
3,948	552		589	301
8,500	551		590	12,751
46,645	550		594	2,623
2,000	549		595	4,000
500	548		599	3,500
1,800	547		600	21,282
1,118	546		605	9,000
8,300	545		610	1,500
500	543		625	10,195
2,815	540		627	3,220
8,000	539		630	493
6,050	530		645	2,000
1,000	528		649	1,000
3,000	510		650	2,381
340	500		700	800
0	0		725	510
0	0		730	2,014
0	0		900	103
141,114				123,858

*Limit orders can be placed onto the market with an undisclosed quantity. The undisclosed quantity of the order must be a value equal to or greater than $100,000.

Table 1.13: Centralized Limit Order Book for CEN NZ

The CLOB for Contact Energy from April 30, 2009. All prices are in cents per share. Source: ASB Securities, used with permission.

226. Figure 1.6 shows a Bloomberg Quote (BQ) screen for AIR NZ (Air New Zealand). The figure for Price to Cash Flow (P/CF) is 2.99. This default CF number uses TTM cash flow from operations per share. Ideally we want a P/CF ratio using CF that adjusts for CAPEX and changes in NWC etc., but setting that aside, and judging by Peter Lynch's standards, this P/CF number is

   (a) Attractive.

   (b) Neither attractive nor unattractive.

   (c) Unattractive.

   (d) We cannot tell from the information given.

   (e) None of the above is correct.

227. ◇ Looking again at Figure 1.6. Please tell me which of the following is true based on Peter Lynch's simple rules. Ignore any gearing-related concerns.

   (a) The stock is attractive based on its P/CF and is attractive based on its P/E ratio relative to its Bloomberg peers.

   (b) The stock is attractive based on its P/CF but is un-attractive based on its P/E ratio relative to its Bloomberg peers.

   (c) The stock is un-attractive based on its P/CF but is attractive based on its P/E ratio relative to its Bloomberg peers.

   (d) The stock is un-attractive based on its P/CF and is un-attractive based on its P/E ratio relative to its Bloomberg peers.

   (e) None of the above is true. Justify this choice with a note on the answer sheet.

228. Suppose we have N risky stocks. Suppose we locate the Markowitz historical minimum variance frontier, and the tangency portfolio T on the risky asset frontier. Let $\vec{h}_T$ be the $N \times 1$ vector of portfolio weights in the tangency portfolio. Suppose that, as in Question 3.2.1, the only constraints for any risky asset frontier portfolios P are that $\vec{h}'_P \vec{\iota} = 1$ and that $\vec{h}'_P \vec{\mu} = \mu_P$ for level of return μ_P. Two questions: Can any of the weights in $\vec{h}_T$ be negative? Can the sum of the weights in $\vec{h}_T$ be different from 1?

   (a) Yes, some weights in $\vec{h}_T$ can be negative. Yes, the sum of the weights in $\vec{h}_T$ can be different from 1.

   (b) Yes, some weights in $\vec{h}_T$ can be negative. No, the sum of the weights in $\vec{h}_T$ cannot be different from 1.

   (c) No, no weights in $\vec{h}_T$ can be negative. Yes, the sum of the weights in $\vec{h}_T$ can be different from 1.

   (d) No, no weights in $\vec{h}_T$ can be negative. No, the sum of the weights in $\vec{h}_T$ cannot be different from 1.

   (e) Not enough information is given to answer the question.

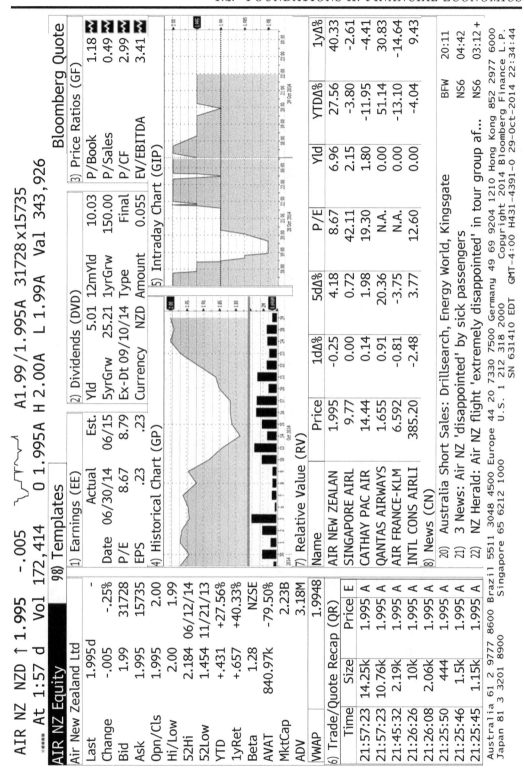

Figure 1.6: Bloomberg Screen: `AIR NZ <EQUITY> BQ <GO>`

An Air New Zealand Bloomberg BQ screen from October 29, 2014, showing some fundamental information.

229. Figure 1.7 shows the print out of the Bloomberg command `FPA NZ <EQUITY> BQ <GO>`. Please tell me which of the following is true based on Peter Lynch's simple rules. Ignore any gearing-related concerns.

    (a) The stock is attractive based on its P/CF and is attractive based on its P/E ratio relative to its Bloomberg peers.

    (b) The stock is attractive based on its P/CF but is un-attractive based on its P/E ratio relative to its Bloomberg peers.

    (c) The stock is un-attractive based on its P/CF but is attractive based on its P/E ratio relative to its Bloomberg peers.

    (d) The stock is un-attractive based on its P/CF and is un-attractive based on its P/E ratio relative to its Bloomberg peers.

    (e) None of the above is true. Justify this choice with a note on the answer sheet.

230. Suppose $\sigma_B = 0.13501$ (benchmark std deviation), $\sigma_P = 0.14453$ (portfolio std deviation), $\beta_P = 1$ (portfolio beta), $\alpha_P = 0.056741$ (forward looking portfolio alpha), and $\lambda = 10$ (residual risk aversion assuming return and risk are in decimals). What is the forward looking IR (information ratio) to four decimal places?

    (a) 0.3926

    (b) 1.0999

    (c) 5.9602

    (d) 21.3214

    (e) None of the above is correct.

231. Of the assumptions that underlie the one-sample t-test of the mean, other things being equal, which assumption are we LEAST likely to be worried about in a large sample (e.g., 600 observations) of returns to a large-capitalization stock?

    (a) The data are normally distributed.

    (b) The data are independent of each other.

    (c) The data are drawn from the same family of distributions.

    (d) The data are drawn from distributions with the same parameters.

    (e) None of the above is a good answer.

232. What does a portfolio active beta of 0.50 represent?

    (a) We have aggressively tilted the portfolio toward higher beta stocks.

    (b) We have aggressively tilted the portfolio toward lower beta stocks.

    (c) We have defensively tilted the portfolio toward higher beta stocks.

    (d) We have defensively tilted the portfolio toward lower beta stocks.

    (e) Our portfolio has a beta that is very small relative to the benchmark's beta.

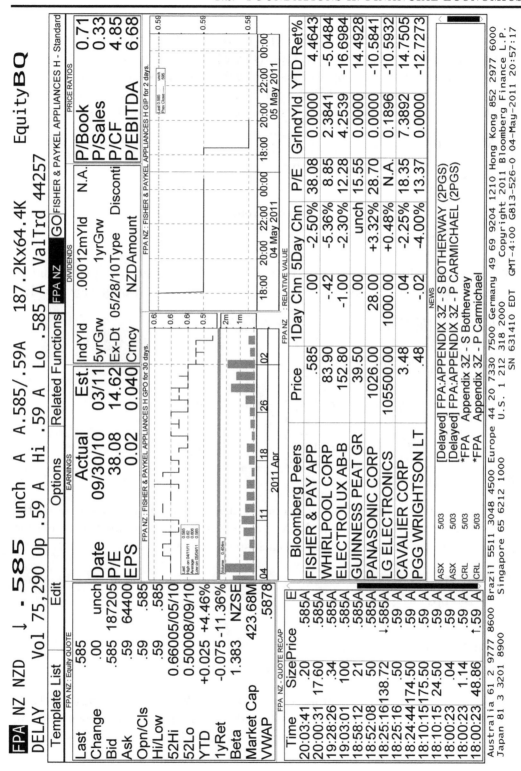

Figure 1.7: Bloomberg Screen: FPA NZ <EQUITY> BQ <GO>

An FPA NZ Bloomberg BQ screen from May 4, 2011, showing some fundamental information.

233. Figure 1.8 shows a Bloomberg Quote (BQ) screen for CAR (Avis Budget Group, Inc.). The figure for Price to Cash Flow (P/CF) is 2.50. This default CF number uses TTM cash flow from operations per share. Ideally we want a P/CF ratio using CF that adjusts for CAPEX and changes in NWC etc., but setting that aside, and judging by Peter Lynch's standards, this P/CF number is

(a) Attractive.

(b) Neither attractive nor unattractive.

(c) Unattractive.

(d) We cannot tell from the information given.

(e) None of the above is correct.

234. Which of the following is the objective function used in the active alpha optimization in Question 3.2.2? All notation is as in *Foundations* and frequency $F = 1$.

(a) $\vec{h}'_P\vec{\alpha}_P - \lambda\left[\vec{h}'_P V \vec{h}_P - \vec{h}'_B V \vec{h}_B\right] - |\vec{h}_P - \vec{h}_B|'\vec{\gamma}$

(b) $\vec{h}'_P\vec{\alpha}_P - \lambda\sqrt{\left[\vec{h}'_P V \vec{h}_P - \vec{h}'_B V \vec{h}_B\right]} - \frac{1}{2}|\vec{h}_P - \vec{h}_B|'\vec{\gamma}$

(c) $\vec{h}'_P\vec{\alpha}_P - \lambda\left[\sqrt{\vec{h}'_P V \vec{h}_P} - \sqrt{\vec{h}'_B V \vec{h}_B}\right] - \frac{1}{2}|\vec{h}_P - \vec{h}_B|'\vec{\gamma}$

(d) $\vec{h}'_P\vec{\alpha}_P - \lambda\left[\sqrt{\vec{h}'_P V \vec{h}_P} - \sqrt{\vec{h}'_B V \vec{h}_B}\right]^2 - \frac{1}{2}|\vec{h}_P - \vec{h}_B|'\vec{\gamma}$

(e) None of the above is correct.

235. Roughly what was the arithmetic average **closing** relative bid-ask spread on the largest 50 stocks listed on the NZX during 2017? Assume we collect closing relative spreads daily over a year for each stock.

(a) 5–20 bps

(b) 25–150 bps

(c) 150–250 bps

(d) 250–500 bps

(e) Larger than 500 bps

236. According to Peter Lynch, suppose you see a stock with a P/E ratio of 12, a dividend yield of zero (it does not pay dividends), and a forecast growth rate in earnings of 6% per annum, then, ignoring all other information, this is a signal that the stock may be

(a) Overpriced.

(b) Underpriced.

(c) Fairly Priced.

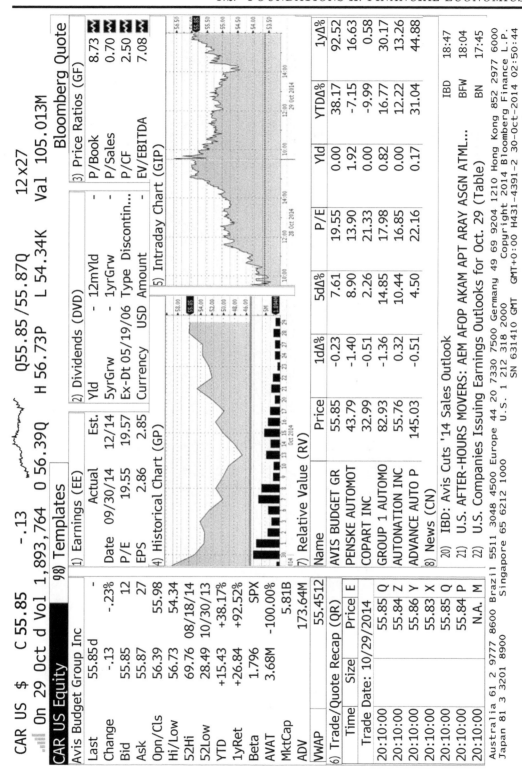

Figure 1.8: Bloomberg Screen: CAR <EQUITY> BQ <GO>

An Avis Budget group Inc. Bloomberg BQ screen from October 29, 2014, showing some fundamental information.

237. Figure 1.9 shows a Bloomberg screen print out from the command VG <EQUITY> GIP <GO>. I have labeled seven trades as A–G. Which of the following is TRUE?

   (a) A, B, C, and D are customer buys.

   (b) A, D, and F are customer buys.

   (c) A, D, and G are customer sells.

   (d) B, C, and F are customer buys.

   (e) None of the above.

238. Looking again at Figure 1.9, I have labeled seven trades as A–G. Which of the following is TRUE?

   (a) The width of the bid-ask spread was a penny (i.e., $0.01) when trades A, B, C, and D occurred.

   (b) The width of the bid-ask spread was a penny when trades F and G occur.

   (c) Trade E likely involved price improvement.

   (d) The stock closed down 5 pennies on this day.

   (e) All of the above.

239. Suppose that I ask you to re-run the active alpha optimization from Question 3.2.2 with the same objective, same constraints, and same choice variables, but with a different set of 20 stocks from the NZX. Which of the following is UNREASON-ABLE in an optimal solution?

   (a) You find the RTAA objective function is 0.0250, and the residual risk ω equals 0.0450

   (b) You find the portfolio alpha is only 0.0100, but the portfolio beta is 1.0000

   (c) You find the RTAA objective function is 0.2500, and the IR = 1.1000

   (d) You find the optimizer wants to underweight the small-capitalization stocks

   (e) You find the portfolio alpha and residual risk ω are very nearly equal to each other.

240. Suppose you perform an active alpha optimization like that in Question 3.2.2 (i.e., using the same five constraints). Which of the following is NOT a correct possible outcome from the optimization for alpha (α), active risk (ω), Information Ratio (IR), and Risk-Adjusted Alpha (RAA), respectively?

   (a) $\alpha = 0.0234$, $\omega = 0.0345$, $IR = 0.6783$, $RAA = 0.0145$.

   (b) $\alpha = 0.0537$, $\omega = 0.0678$, $IR = 0.7920$, $RAA = 0.0345$.

   (c) $\alpha = 0.0342$, $\omega = 0.0334$, $IR = 1.0240$, $RAA = 0.0352$.

   (d) $\alpha = -0.0034$, $\omega = 0.0104$, $IR = -0.3269$, $RAA = 0.0055$.

   (e) Neither (c) nor (d) are correct possible outcomes.

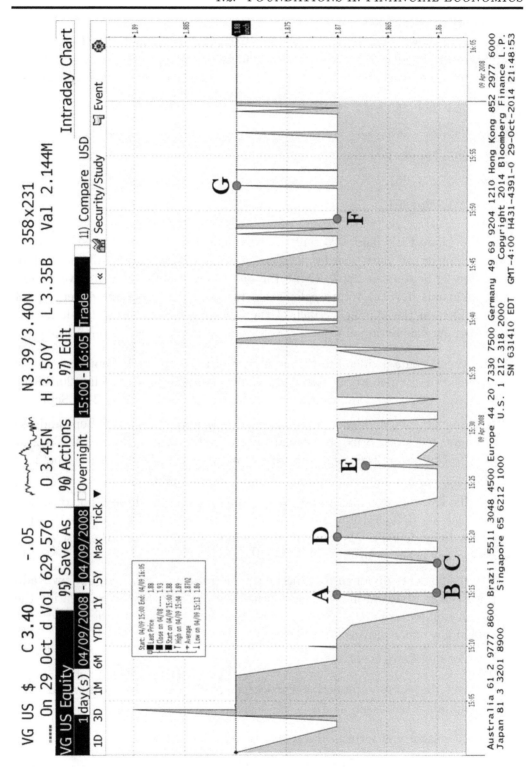

Figure 1.9: Bloomberg Screen: VG <EQUITY> GIP <GO>

A Vonage Group Bloomberg GIP screen from April 9, 2008, showing a series of trades.

241. Figure 1.10 shows a candlestick graph for Telecom New Zealand (TEL NZ), now renamed Spark (SPK NZ). Which one of the following represent the Open, High, Low, and Close, respectively, on May 1, 2009? All numbers are in cents per share.

    (a) 261, 263, 283, 285.

    (b) 283, 285, 261, 263.

    (c) 263, 285, 261, 283.

    (d) 285, 283, 263, 261.

    (e) 283, 261, 285, 263.

242. The N.Z. share FBU paid a 23 cent cash dividend per share on Thur 11 October 2007. The record date was Fri 21 September 2007 and the ex-dividend date was Mon 24 September 2007. (Note the old rec-ex timeline.) You have to add cash dividends into the return calculation to reflect the economic experience of shareholders in the market. Which of the following is the correct technique for adjusting our calculation of returns? Note that "close" means "close of business."

    (a) Add the 23 cents dividend to the close price of FBU on Fri 21 Sept and use the amended stock price to calculate both of the returns from close Thur 20th Sept to close Fri 21st Sept and from close Fri 21st Sept to close Mon 24th Sept.

    (b) Add the 23 cents dividend to the close price of FBU on Mon 24 Sept and use the amended stock price to calculate both of the returns from close Fri 21st Sept to close Mon 24th Sept and from close Mon 24th Sept to close Tue 25th Sept.

    (c) Use the 23 cents dividend to adjust only one return calculation, not two: add the 23 cents dividend into the close price Fri 21st Sept when calculating the return from close Fri 21st Sept to close Mon 24th Sept, but otherwise do not amend any other returns.

    (d) Use the 23 cents dividend to adjust only one return calculation, not two: add the 23 cents dividend into the close price Mon 24th Sept when calculating the return from close Fri 21st Sept to close Mon 24th Sept, but otherwise do not amend any other returns.

    (e) None of the above is correct.

243. We expect that large-capitalization stocks typically have what (compared with small-capitalization stocks)?

    (a) Higher volatility of returns and higher relative bid-ask spreads.

    (b) Higher volatility of returns and lower relative bid-ask spreads.

    (c) Lower volatility of returns and higher relative bid-ask spreads.

    (d) Lower volatility of returns and lower relative bid-ask spreads.

    (e) None of the above.

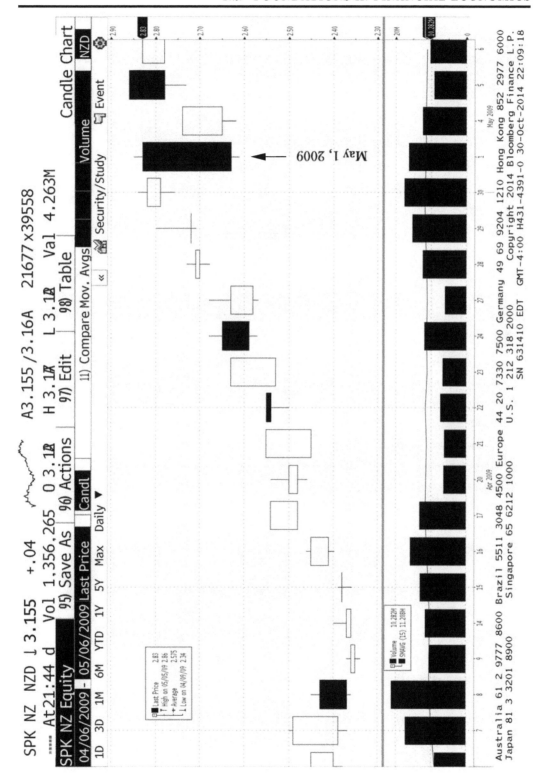

Figure 1.10: Bloomberg Screen: `TEL NZ <EQUITY> GPC <GO>`

A Telecom New Zealand Bloomberg GPC screen from April 6, 2009 to May 6, 2009. Note Telecom N.Z. renamed itself "Spark" in 2014.

244. Figure 1.11 shows a European call option valuation. Suppose that a corporate client wants a long position in this call option on 1,000 shares of FBU. Suppose the corporation buys the call from an investment bank. How many shares of FBU does the investment bank trade to hedge exposure to the call it sold (rounded to the nearest share)?

   (a) Go short 2,299 shares of FBU.

   (b) Go short 1,000 shares of FBU.

   (c) Go short 100 shares of FBU.

   (d) Go short 28 shares of FBU.

   (e) None of the above is close to the correct answer.

245. ◇ There are two well-known items of market lore concerning takeover offers. They are that you can make money by buying the target on the announcement of the offer, and that...

   (a) Upon announcement, the target's stock price rises immediately and the acquirer's stock price rises immediately.

   (b) Upon announcement, the target's stock price rises immediately and the acquirer's stock price falls immediately.

   (c) Upon announcement, the target's stock price falls immediately and the acquirer's stock price rises immediately.

   (d) Upon announcement, the target's stock price falls immediately and the acquirer's stock price falls immediately.

   (e) None of the above is true.

246. Which of the following appears to be a market neutral fund?

   (a) A fund that actively tries to outperform an S&P/NZX50 benchmark by chasing alpha, and which imposes the restriction that the fund's beta equals 1.

   (b) A fund that passively tries to match an S&P/NZX50 benchmark, and which imposes the restriction that the fund's beta equals 1.

   (c) A fund that goes long but also short sells high-beta stocks in sufficient quantity to obtain an overall beta of -1 for the fund.

   (d) A fund that is long $1,000,000 worth of stock and short $1,000,000 worth of stock, so that overall fund beta is zero.

   (e) A fund that invests only in low volatility stocks, like utility stocks.

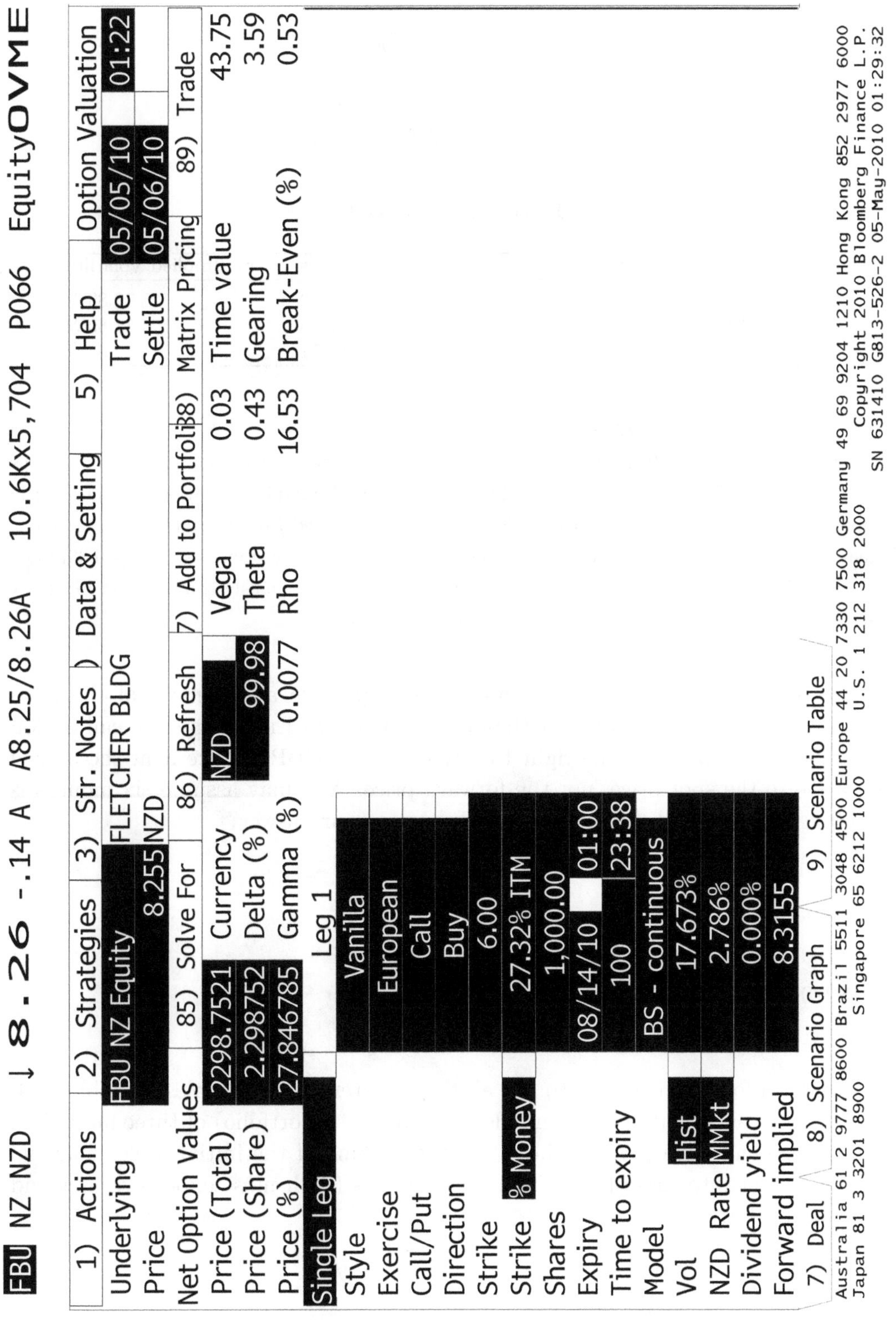
FBU NZ NZD ↓ 8.26 -.14 A A8.25/8.26A 10.6Kx5,704 P066 EquityOVME
1) Actions
2) Strategies
3) Str. Notes
) Data & Setting
5) Help
Option Valuation
Underlying FBU NZ Equity FLETCHER BLDG
Trade 05/05/10 01:22
Price 8.255 NZD
Settle 05/06/10
Net Option Values
85) Solve For
86) Refresh
7) Add to Portfoli
88) Matrix Pricing
89) Trade
Price (Total) 2298.7521 Currency NZD Vega 0.03 Time value 43.75
Price (Share) 2.298752 Delta (%) 99.98 Theta 0.43 Gearing 3.59
Price (%) 27.846785 Gamma (%) 0.0077 Rho 16.53 Break-Even (%) 0.53
Single Leg
Leg 1
Style Vanilla
Exercise European
Call/Put Call
Direction Buy
Strike 6.00
Strike % Money 27.32% ITM
Shares 1,000.00
Expiry 08/14/10 01:00
Time to expiry 100 23:38
Model BS - continuous
Vol Hist 17.673%
NZD Rate MMkt 2.786%
Dividend yield 0.000%
Forward implied 8.3155
7) Deal
8) Scenario Graph
9) Scenario Table
Australia 61 2 9777 8600 Brazil 5511 3048 4500 Europe 44 20 7330 7500 Germany 49 69 9204 1210 Hong Kong 852 2977 6000
Japan 81 3 3201 8900 Singapore 65 6212 1000 U.S. 1 212 318 2000 Copyright 2010 Bloomberg Finance L.P.
SN 631410 G813-526-2 05-May-2010 01:29:32

Figure 1.11: Bloomberg Screen: `FBU NZ <EQUITY> OV <GO>`

An FBU NZ Corporation Bloomberg OV screen from May 5, 2010, showing an option valuation.

Currency	Amount of A/R
GBP	6,500,000
EUR	7,500,000
JPY	900,000,000

Table 1.14: FX A/R

FX	Spot	6-mo Interest (p.a.)	6-mo Forward Points	6-mo Implied Volatility
GBP	1.5019	0.807753%	-35.59	13.834%
EUR	1.3622	0.855497%	-35.55	11.865%
JPY	90.02	0.392493%	+2.51	12.942%

Table 1.15: Your FX Desk's Quotes

The forward exchange rate (the "outright") is equal to spot plus the forward points (these are in pips which differ for the JPY). The implied volatilities are annualized standard deviations of continuously compounded returns to investing in the FX and they are inferred from foreign currency options of maturity six months. The six-month continuously compounded USD interest rate is 0.337136% per annum. All interest rates in the table are annualized and continuously compounded LIMEAN rates taking full account of the different day count conventions.

247. Use the numbers in Tables 1.14 and 1.15 to provide an estimate of the total value of a USD-denominated at-the-money six-month European-style call option on 6,500,000 GBP (i.e., the right to buy 6,500,000 GBP). Make it at-the-money relative to the spot price, not the forward price. You may assume six months is 0.50 years. Which of the following is closest to your answer?

(a) $0.041555

(b) $0.058767

(c) $169,342

(d) $270,105

(e) $381,986

248. Consider a forward contract to sell all three currencies receivables in Table 1.14, and also a basket put option, and also a strip (i.e., a portfolio) of three individual currency put options. What should be the ranking of the initial direct financial cost to enter into these three financial contracts (with most expensive first and cheapest last)?

(a) basket put, strip, forward

(b) forward, strip, basket put

(c) forward, basket put, strip

(d) strip, basket put, forward

(e) strip, forward, basket

249. Which one of the following was NOT one of the five constraints in the active alpha optimization you implemented in Question 3.2.2?

    (a) The optimal portfolio is to be fully invested in the risky stocks.

    (b) The alphas are to be constructed to be benchmark neutral. That is, $\vec{h}'_B \vec{\alpha} = 0$.

    (c) The beta of the optimal portfolio equals one.

    (d) The absolute magnitude of the active percentage holdings in each stock is restricted.

    (e) The two-sided turnover of the portfolio is restricted.

250. Ignore T-costs. Suppose that I ask you to run the active alpha optimization from Question 3.2.2 using risk aversion of each of $\lambda = 1$ and $\lambda = 10$. In theory, the lower λ gives optimal solutions with what characteristics?

    (a) Different alpha and residual risk ω, but essentially the same RAA as with $\lambda = 10$.

    (b) Lower alpha, lower ω, and lower RAA, than with $\lambda = 10$.

    (c) Higher alpha, higher ω, and higher RAA, than with $\lambda = 10$.

    (d) Essentially the same alpha and ω, but a higher RAA than with $\lambda = 10$.

    (e) It is impossible to say without running the optimization.

251. When discussing skewness and kurtosis in *Foundations*, we said that the Cauchy distribution was a well behaved "normal looking" symmetric bell-shaped distribution, but that

    (a) Its median is not defined.

    (b) Its mode is not defined.

    (c) Its mean is not defined.

    (d) Its skewness (i.e., scaled third central moment) is zero because it is symmetric.

    (e) Its kurtosis (i.e., scaled fourth central moment) is greater than three (the figure for a normal) because it has fat tails.

252. Who determines how wide the bid-ask spread is for the S&P/NZX50 stocks listed on the NZX?

    (a) It is the designated market makers standing on the floor of the NZX.

    (b) It is the brokers who route order flow from traders to the limit order book.

    (c) It is the customers who submit market orders to the NZX and who willingly pay for liquidity.

    (d) It is the traders who submit limit orders to the NZX, specifying the price as which they wish to trade.

    (e) It is determined as a matter of policy by the NZX because they require that a fair and orderly market exist.

253. Figure 1.12 shows a European call option valuation for FBU NZ stock. Suppose that a corporate client buys this call option covering 1,000 shares of FBU from an investment bank. Roughly how many shares of FBU does the investment bank trade to hedge exposure to the call it sold (rounded to the nearest share)?

    (a) Go long 8,500 shares of FBU.

    (b) Go long 1,000 shares of FBU.

    (c) Go long 866 shares of FBU.

    (d) Go long 75 shares FBU.

    (e) None of the above is close to the correct answer.

254. You want to test whether large-capitalization stocks are less risky than small-capitalization stocks. So, you collect data on market capitalization and on the standard deviation (i.e., riskiness) of returns of stocks. You are sure that the relationship is not linear. Which test is appropriate?

    (a) Use a standard OLS to regress market capitalization on standard deviation of returns and then look at the t-statistic of the slope from the OLS regression.

    (b) Look at the Spearman rank-order correlation between market capitalization and standard deviation and calculate its t-statistic.

    (c) Standardize both variables by subtracting out the cross-sectional mean and dividing by the cross-sectional standard deviation. Now plot the two on an X-Y scatter plot, find the line of best fit, and calculate the R^2 as your statistic.

    (d) All of the above.

    (e) None of the above.

255. My N.Z. broker tells me that I can buy stock WHS NZ (The Warehouse) with a 70% "margin lending ratio" (i.e., a 30% margin rate). My broker will lend me 70% of the purchase price of the stock, with the balance (i.e., my investment) coming out of my brokerage account. The ask price for WHS is $3.75, with plenty of depth. Suppose I purchase 1,000 shares of WHS at $3.75 using the 70% lending ratio. What level would the bid price of WHS have to fall to for me to lose 100% of my investment if I sell? Please ignore any margin call that my broker might make, brokerage commissions, price impact when I sell, any dividends, and any margin interest charged. For this question, assume that WHS trades with a tick size (i.e., minimum price variation, or "price step") of one penny (i.e., $0.01), so that your answer must be in whole pennies.

    (a) 112

    (b) 131

    (c) 187

    (d) 262

    (e) None of the above is correct.

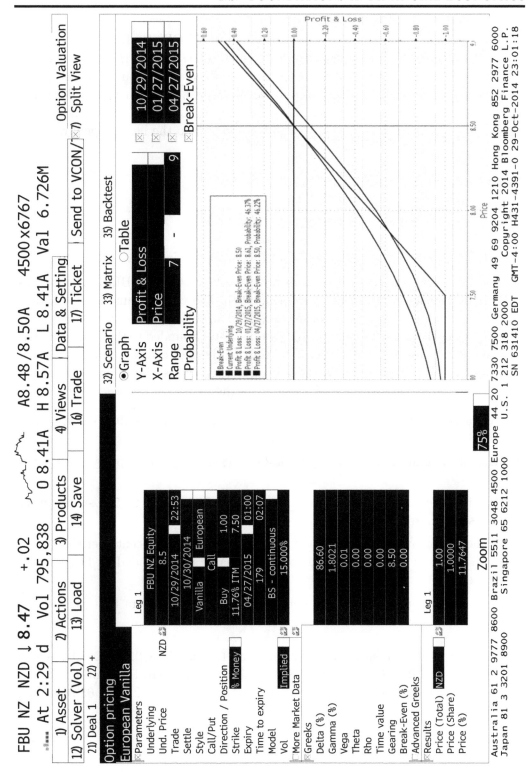

Figure 1.12: Bloomberg Screen: FBU NZ <EQUITY> OV <GO>

A FBU NZ Corporation Bloomberg OV screen from October 29, 2014, showing an option valuation.

256. Table 1.16 shows the centralized limit order book (CLOB) for BLIS Technologies (BLT) on May 5, 2010. Suppose that you own 100,000 shares of BLT, and that you want to sell them. Please calculate the sales proceeds from your order assuming that you submit a market order to sell 100,000 shares, and that your order is the only order being sent in to be executed against the CLOB as shown in with no price slippage or execution risk. Round your answer to the nearest penny.

    (a) $11,912.52
    (b) $11,100.00
    (c) $11,000.00
    (d) $10,822.01
    (e) $10,819.51

257. Table 1.16 shows the centralized limit order book (CLOB) for BLIS Technologies (BLT) at the close of business on May 5, 2010. The volume number reported as 41,998 is a count of the number of shares traded on this day. The turnover number quoted gives the *dollar* value of those traded shares—rounded to the nearest dollar. I want you to use all the information given in the figure to determine which, if any, of the following could NOT have been the order or series of orders executed on this day that yielded the CLOB shown in the figure at the close of business.

    (a) A market order or series of marker orders to <u>sell</u> a total 41,998 shares, all of which were executed at 11 cents per share.
    (b) One or more limit orders to <u>sell</u> a total 41,998 shares at limit price 11 cents per share.
    (c) Partial execution (41,998 shares) of a limit order to <u>buy</u> 97,500 shares at 11 cents per share.
    (d) Some combination of limit orders to <u>sell</u> at limit price 11 cents per share, and market orders to <u>sell</u> which led to 41,998 shares being traded at 11 cents per share.
    (e) In fact, any one of the above could be the order or orders that yielded the CLOB as shown at close of business.

258. On May 5, 2011, the spot exchange rate was 1.48291/1.48299 USD/EUR (read literally), or EUR/USD 1.48291/1.48299 (using the standard FX quoting convention). How wide is the bid-ask spread in pips? (See footnote 2 on p. 63 regarding FX quotes.)

    (a) 0.008 pips
    (b) 0.080 pips
    (c) 8.000 pips
    (d) 80.000 pips
    (e) None of the above

BLIS Technologies Limited

Share prices at 17:05:08 Wednesday, May 05, 2010

Stock	Exchange	Bid	Offer	Last	Change*	Open	High	Low	Volume	Turnover
BLT	NZX	11	11.1	11	0	11	11	11	41998	$4,620

Buy >> Sell >> Add to Watchlist >> Announcements >> Research & Graphs >>

Print >> View Depth

Market Depth

Buy			Sell
Buy Quantity	Prices	Prices	Sell Quantity
55,502	11	11.1	2,670
42,000	10.6	11.9	63,450
100,000	10.5	12	121,353
50,000	10.2	17	10,000
100,000	7	0	0
100,000	4.5	0	0
100,000	4	0	0
547,502			197,473

Table 1.16: Centralized Limit Order Book for BLT NZ

The CLOB for Blis Technologies from May 5, 2010. All prices are in cents per share. Source: ASB Securities, used with permission.

259. Figure 1.13 shows the print out of the Bloomberg command NZT <EQUITY> OVX <GO>. Assume the options market maker just sold this call option covering 100 shares of stock to a customer. Using only the numbers in Figure 1.13, and ignoring all T-costs, estimate the number of shares of stock the market maker has to hold to hedge his or her exposure to the option just sold. Round to the nearest share.

    (a) Long 81 shares.

    (b) Short 81 shares.

    (c) Long 71 shares

    (d) Short 71 shares

    (e) None of the above is correct.

260. Suppose you have 100 observations of daily returns to two stocks in the same industry: $\{R_{A1}, R_{A2}, R_{A3}, \ldots, R_{A100}\}$ and $\{R_{B1}, R_{B2}, R_{B3}, \ldots, R_{B100}\}$. Let $\bar{R}_A$ and $\bar{R}_B$ be the averages of these two time series, respectively. Suppose someone asserts that these two time series of returns are very highly positively correlated with each other. For this to be true, which of the following is the best answer?

    (a) The averages $\bar{R}_A$ and $\bar{R}_B$ must both be either high or low at the same time.

    (b) The individual returns R_{At} and R_{Bt} must tend to be high or low at the same time.

    (c) The individual returns R_{At} and R_{Bt} must tend to be above their respective means, $\bar{R}_A$ and $\bar{R}_B$, at the same time.

    (d) The individual returns R_{At} and R_{Bt} must tend to be below their respective means, $\bar{R}_A$ and $\bar{R}_B$, at the same time.

    (e) The individual returns R_{At} and R_{Bt} must tend to be above their respective means, $\bar{R}_A$ and $\bar{R}_B$, at the same time, and also below their respective means, $\bar{R}_A$ and $\bar{R}_B$, at the same time.

261. ◇ Assume the width and level of the bid-ask spread on a New York Stock Exchange (NYSE) stock are constant during the trading day. Assume the width of the bid-ask spread was one penny ($0.01). Assume supply and demand are stable and the designated market maker (DMM) ends the day with the same inventory of stock that he started the day with. Assume a volume of 500,000 shares that day (a total count of all shares in all customer orders that arrived that day). Assume no customer got any price improvement and that the DMM was a counterparty to every trade. How much revenue did the DMM make?

    (a) $50,000

    (b) $25,000

    (c) $5,000

    (d) $2,500

    (e) $500

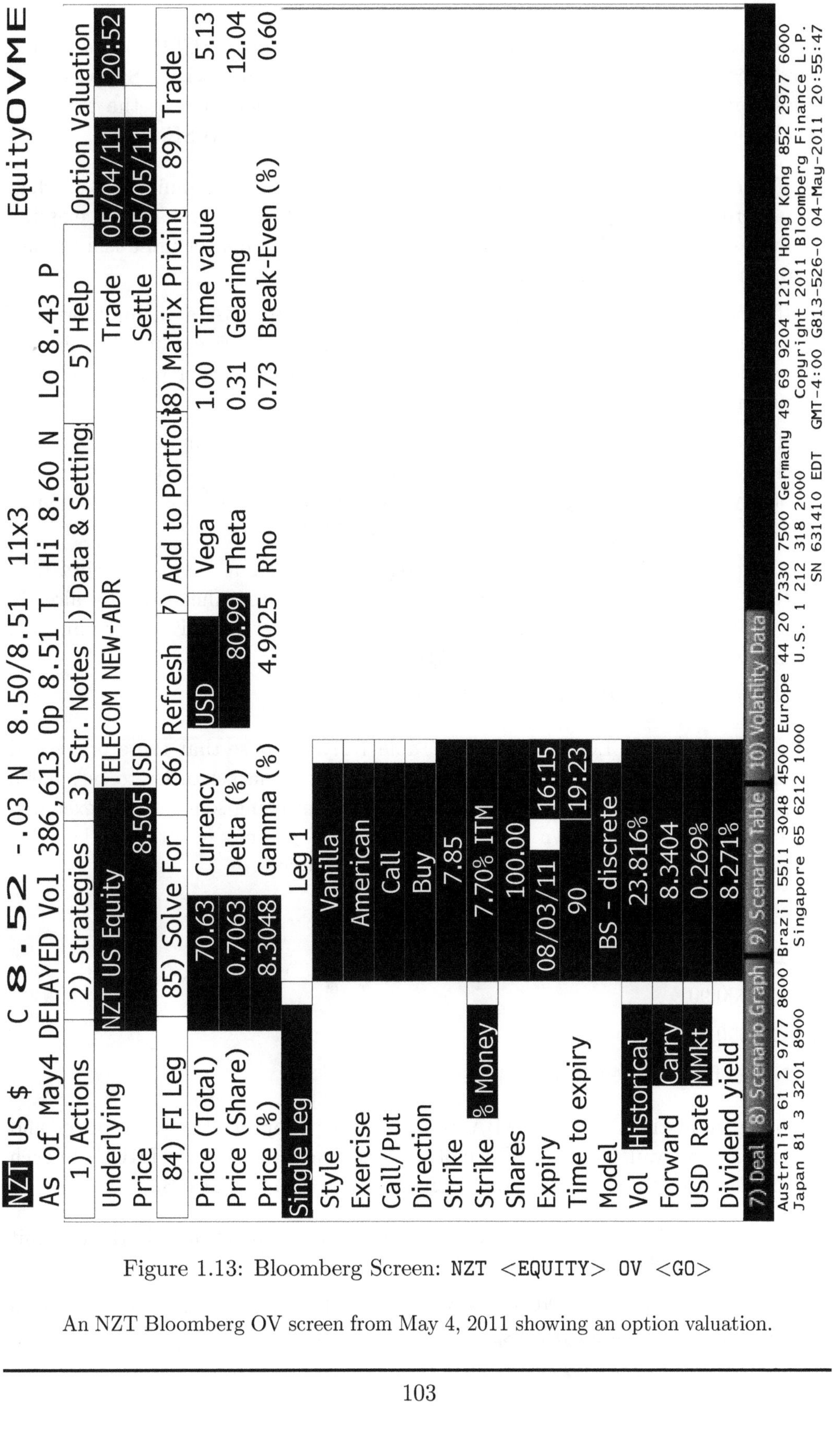
NZT US $ C 8.52 -.03 N 8.50/8.51 11x3 EquityOVME
As of May4 DELAYED Vol 386,613 Op 8.51 T Hi 8.60 N Lo 8.43 P
1) Actions 2) Strategies 3) Str. Notes) Data & Setting 5) Help Option Valuation
Underlying NZT US Equity TELECOM NEW-ADR Trade 05/04/11 20:52
Price 8.505 USD Settle 05/05/11
84) FI Leg 85) Solve For 86) Refresh 7) Add to Portfol 8) Matrix Pricing 89) Trade
Price (Total) 70.63 Currency USD Vega 1.00 Time value 5.13
Price (Share) 0.7063 Delta (%) 80.99 Theta 0.31 Gearing 12.04
Price (%) 8.3048 Gamma (%) 4.9025 Rho 0.73 Break-Even (%) 0.60
Single Leg Leg 1
Style Vanilla
Exercise American
Call/Put Call
Direction Buy
Strike 7.85
Strike % Money 7.70% ITM
Shares 100.00
Expiry 08/03/11 16:15
Time to expiry 90 19:23
Model BS - discrete
Vol Historical 23.816%
Forward Carry 8.3404
USD Rate MMkt 0.269%
Dividend yield 8.271%
7) Deal 8) Scenario Graph 9) Scenario Table 10) Volatility Data
Australia 61 2 9777 8600 Brazil 5511 3048 4500 Europe 44 20 7330 7500 Germany 49 69 9204 1210 Hong Kong 852 2977 6000
Japan 81 3 3201 8900 Singapore 65 6212 1000 U.S. 1 212 318 2000 Copyright 2011 Bloomberg Finance L.P.
SN 631410 EDT GMT-4:00 G813-526-0 04-May-2011 20:55:47

Figure 1.13: Bloomberg Screen: NZT <EQUITY> OV <GO>

An NZT Bloomberg OV screen from May 4, 2011 showing an option valuation.

262. Table 1.17 shows the entire centralized limit order book (CLOB) for Abano Healthcare (ABA) on May 5, 2011; Nothing is hidden from view. Suppose that these prices and quantities are available now. Consider each of the following choices independently of each other choice. Which one is FALSE.

   (a) If I now submit a limit order to sell 100 shares of ABA at a limit price of $4.42 my order will get price priority and be executed ahead of any already existing limit order to sell ABA if the very next order to arrive after mine is a market order to buy 100 shares of ABA.

   (b) If I now submit a limit order to sell 100 shares of ABA at a limit price of $4.50, then my order will get time priority at that limit price, but other already existing limit orders to sell ABA will rank ahead of my order because of price priority.

   (c) If I now submit a limit order to sell 100 shares of ABA at a limit price of $4.45, then my order will get price priority and time priority and be executed ahead of any already existing limit order to sell if the very next order to arrive after mine is a market order to buy 100 shares of ABA.

   (d) If I now submit a limit order to buy 100 shares of ABA at a limit price of $4.42, then my order will get price priority and be executed ahead of any already existing limit order to buy ABA if the very next order to arrive after mine is a market order to sell 100 shares of ABA.

   (e) No, in fact, all of the above are TRUE.

263. Look again at the CLOB for ABA in Table 1.17. Suppose that these prices and quantities are available now. Suppose you submit a market order to buy 5,000 shares of ABA, and that your order is the only order being sent in to be executed against the CLOB as shown in Figure 4. What will you pay in total for the 5,000 shares? Please ignore any commissions or exchange fees.

   (a) $22,377.89
   (b) $22,250.00
   (c) $22,030.90
   (d) $22,050.00
   (e) None of the above is correct.

264. Look again at the CLOB for ABA in Table 1.17. Suppose that these prices and quantities are available now. Which of the following statements is TRUE? In each case assume it is a new order (or orders) submitted to the CLOB.

   (a) A market order to buy 3,090 shares will be executed more quickly than a limit order to buy 3,090 shares at $4.41.

   (b) A limit order to sell 1000 shares at a specified limit price risks non-execution regardless of the limit price specified (ignore possible price slippage).

(c) A market order to buy 1,000 shares will be executed just as quickly as a market order to sell 1,000 shares.

(d) All of the above are TRUE.

(e) (a) and (c) are TRUE, but not (b)

265. Look again at the CLOB for ABA in Table 1.17. Note that this is the entire CLOB and nothing is hidden from view. Suppose that these prices and quantities are available now. Suppose you submit a limit order to sell 10,000 shares of ABA at a limit price of $4.35 or better, and that your order is the only order being sent in to be executed against the CLOB as shown in Figure 4. What will be the best bid price and best ask price after your order is submitted and executed (or partially executed)?

(a) Best bid of $4.35; Best ask of $4.45.

(b) Best bid of $4.35; Best ask of $4.38.

(c) Best bid of $4.41; Best ask of $4.45.

(d) Best bid does not exist; Best ask of $4.35.

(e) None of the above is correct.

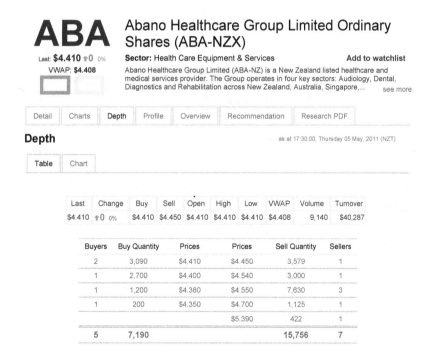

Table 1.17: Centralized Limit Order Book for ABA NZ

The CLOB for Abano Healthcare from May 5, 2011. Source: ASB Securities, used with permission.

266. Figure 1.14 shows a plot of average relative bid-ask spread versus average market capitalization for 12 N.Z. stocks using two years of daily data over 2009–2010. Which one of the following do you think shows the traditional Pearson product-moment correlation and the Spearman rank-order correlation, respectively, between relative bid-ask spreads and market capitalizations.

(a) Pearson Correlation = -59.5%; Spearman Correlation = -99.3%.

(b) Pearson Correlation = -99.3%; Spearman Correlation = -59.5%.

(c) Pearson Correlation = +59.5%; Spearman Correlation = +99.3%.

(d) Pearson Correlation = +99.3%; Spearman Correlation = +59.5%.

(e) None of the above could possibly be correct.

267. Estimate the IR of an active portfolio manager who follows 225 stocks, but updates forecasts only four times per year. Assume the correlation between realized and forecast active returns is a meagre 2%.

(a) IR=0.02

(b) IR=0.30

(c) IR=0.60

(d) IR=4.24

(e) IR=18

268. When discussing buy-and-hold strategies in *Foundations*, we said that an extra 1% return per annum over the time until your retirement would add roughly half as much again to the final value of your investment. This was roughly true for credible rates of return, e.g., 8% per annum compared with 7% per annum gives a 49.2% boost to your final value at a horizon of 43 years. This statement assumes, however, only a single lump sum deposit made at $t = 0$ and compounded for 43 years. This is not how people save. People are much more likely to save as a growing annuity. That is, people save proportion p of their income each year where their income grows at rate g per annum.

So, tell me, what is the effect on the final value of your investment if the interest rate moves from 7% per annum to 8% per annum, and over a horizon of 43 years you make a deposit at the end of each year (starting one year from now) but your deposit grows at a rate of 4% per annum?

(a) A 85.3% boost to your final value.

(b) A 49.2% boost to your final value.

(c) A 33.0% boost to your final value.

(d) A 27.3% boost to your final value.

(e) A 14.7% drop in your final value.

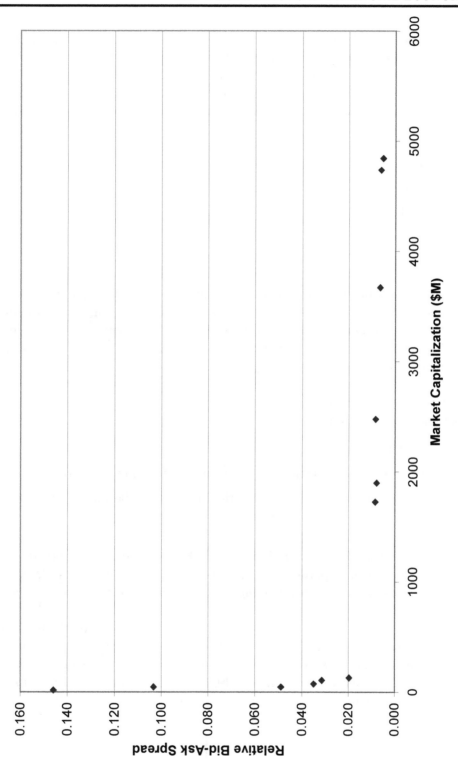

Figure 1.14: Relative Bid-Ask Spread versus Market Capitalization

Relative spread versus market capitalization for a dozen N.Z. stocks sampled
during 2009–2010.

269. Look at the centralized limit order book (CLOB) for MHI in Table 1.18. Suppose that these prices and quantities are available to you now. Suppose you submit a market order to sell 5,000 shares of MHI, and that your order is the only order being sent in to be executed against the CLOB as shown in Table 1.18. What will you receive in total for the 5,000 shares? Please ignore any commissions or exchange fees.

(a) $5,384.27

(b) $5,400.00

(c) $5,450.00

(d) Less than any of the above numbers.

(e) More than any of the above numbers.

270. Ignore the previous question. Look again at the CLOB for MHI in Table 1.18. Suppose that these prices and quantities are available to you now. Suppose you submit a limit order to sell 5,000 shares of MHI. What will you receive in total for the 5,000 shares and when will you get it? Please ignore any commissions or exchange fees.

(a) $5,384.27 immediately.

(b) $5,400.00 immediately.

(c) $5,450.00 immediately.

(d) I cannot answer the question until you tell me the limit price for the order.

(e) No, even if you tell me the limit price, I may still be unable to answer the question with any precision.

271. Look again at the CLOB for MHI in Table 1.18. Ignore any other questions about MHI in this section. Suppose that these prices and quantities are available to you now and you are the only one trading today. Assume your broker charges you a commission of 30 bps but with a minimum commission of $30 per trade (e.g., see Table 1.12 on p. 81). Note that a "round trip trade" is one where you open and then close a position. Assume that you submit a market order to buy 1,000 shares. Almost immediately after your order is executed you change your mind and submit a market order to sell your 1,000 shares. How much worse off are you after this round trip trade than you were before it?

(a) $11.51 worse off.

(b) $16.51 worse off.

(c) $60.00 worse off.

(d) $65.00 worse off.

(e) $70.00 worse off.

MHI

Last: **$1.090** ⬆1 0.9%
VWAP: **$1.086**

Michael Hill International Limited Ordinary Shares (MHI-NZX)

Sector: Retailing   **Add to watchlist**

Michael Hill International (MHI-NZ) is a retail jewellery chain with 237 stores between Australia, New Zealand, Canada and the US. MHI employs over 2,000 full and part time staff in retailing, manufacturing and administration and has app...   see more

| Detail | Charts | **Depth** | Profile | Overview | Recommendation | Research PDF |

Depth

as at 14:38:45, Monday 30 April, 2012 (NZT)

| Table | Chart |

Last	Change	Buy	Sell	Open	High	Low	VWAP	Volume	Turnover
$1.090	⬆1 0.9%	$1.080	$1.090	$1.080	$1.090	$1.080	$1.086	4,622	$5,022

Buyers	Buy Quantity	Prices	Prices	Sell Quantity	Sellers
2	3,427	$1.080	$1.090	97,928	2
3	37,310	$1.070	$1.100	34,335	3
3	38,367	$1.060	$1.160	500	1
4	142,400	$1.050			
3	21,058	$1.040			
1	35,000	$1.030			
1	14,000	$1.020			
3	106,500	$1.010			
1	5,000	$1.000			
1	40,000	$0.980			
22	443,062			132,763	6

Table 1.18: Centralized Limit Order Book for MHI NZ

The CLOB for Michael Hill International from April 30, 2012. Source: ASB Securities, used with permission.

272. Look at the centralized limit order book (CLOB) for NZF in Table 1.19. Note that the bid side of the CLOB is empty. Suppose that these prices and quantities are available to you now. Suppose you submit a market order to sell 10,000 shares of NZF, and that your order is the only order being sent in to be executed against the CLOB as shown in Table 1.19. What do you think will happen?

(a) My order will be executed at $0.004 per share.

(b) My order will be held and crossed with another incoming market order to buy if one arrives.

(c) My order will be executed at $0.005 per share because there is plenty of depth available at the ask.

(d) My order will be automatically inserted into the CLOB and show up as a bid for 10,000 shares at $0.004.

(e) My order will be cancelled because there are no bids. The broker might telephone me to ask if I want to change it to a limit order to sell and if so, at what limit price.

273. In the Markowitz problem in Question 3.2.1 we calculated betas relative to the benchmark and plotted historical returns against those betas to see if the security market line (SML) was a straight line. We did not find a straight line because...

(a) Real world investors are not mean-variance optimizers (but theoretical CAPM investors are).

(b) The CAPM is a theory expressed in terms of forward-looking expectations, but we measured only backward-looking returns.

(c) We looked at only a subset of all risky assets, and there is no reason to suppose the CAPM holds on that subset.

(d) Our benchmark portfolio was not mean-variance efficient.

(e) At no time were we testing the CAPM.

274. The Markowitz solution in Question 3.2.1 uses a formula appearing in the "Markowitz Efficient Set Mathematics" section of Chapter 2 of *Foundations*. In the active alpha optimization in Question 3.2.2 the solution to the optimization is the output of a numerical routine in Excel. What is the single most important reason to explain why we had to use numerical techniques for the active alpha optimization rather than using another algebraic formula?

(a) The objective function in the alpha optimization is too complicated.

(b) There are too many constraints in the active alpha optimization.

(c) There are too many choice variables in the active alpha optimization.

(d) There are inequality constraints in the active alpha optimization.

(e) We allowed short selling in the active alpha optimization.

NZF

Last: **$0.006** ↑0 0%

VWAP:

NZF Group Limited Ordinary Shares (NZF-NZX)

Sector: Diversified Financials   **Add to watchlist**

NZF Group Limited (NZF-NZ) is a finance company specializing in residential and commercial property development-based loans, through its subsidiaries in New Zealand.

see more

| Detail | Charts | Depth | Profile | Overview | Recommendation | Research PDF |

Depth

as at 01:35:08, Monday 30 April, 2012 (NZT)

| Table | Chart |

Last	Change	Buy	Sell	Open	High	Low	VWAP	Volume	Turnover
$0.006	↑0 0%	-	$0.005	-	-	-	-	-	-

Buyers	Buy Quantity	Prices	Prices	Sell Quantity	Sellers
			$0.005	25,000	1
			$0.006	409,274	1
			$0.025	250,000	1
			$0.050	250,000	1
				934,274	**4**

Table 1.19: Centralized Limit Order Book for NZF NZ

The CLOB for NZF Group from April 30, 2012. Source: ASB Securities, used with permission.

275. Table 1.20 shows the prices of 10 stocks six months ago, and their prices right now. You currently hold the benchmark which is composed of these 10 stocks (performance also shown). Other things being equal (e.g., transactions costs, betas, market capitalizations), identify the two stocks that are most heavily favored by the price momentum strategy (we want to buy more of these) and the two stocks that are least favored by the price momentum strategy (we want to sell some of our existing holdings of these to finance buying the favored ones).

Ticker	Price 6 Months Ago	Price Now	% change
JKL	68.50	86.82	26.74%
MNO	27.50	26.95	-2.0%
ABC	581.50	565.02	-2.8%
GHI	1316.50	1250.68	-5.0%
YZA	69.50	62.55	-10.0%
DEF	675.50	594.44	-12.0%
STU	97.50	84.83	-13.0%
VWX	132.50	115.28	-13.0%
PQR	67.50	56.03	-17.0%
BCD	163.50	107.91	-34.0%
BENCHMARK	3500.00	3118.50	-10.9%

Table 1.20: Ten Stocks and Benchmark Price Performance over Last Six Months

(a) Most favored: ABC, MNO. Least favored: BCD, PQR.

(b) Most favored: BCD, JKL. Least favored: YZA, DEF.

(c) Most favored: BCD, PQR. Least favored: JKL, MNO.

(d) Most favored: JKL, MNO. Least favored: BCD, PQR.

(e) Most favored: YZA, DEF. Least favored: BCD, JKL.

276. In our Markowitz optimization problem in Question 3.2.1, the Benchmark portfolio plotted just inside the minimum variance frontier of risky assets and had noticeably less risk than any individual stock. The Benchmark portfolio had much less risk than any individual stock because...

(a) The Markowitz optimization is all about reducing risk, and this was reflected in the Benchmark.

(b) The Benchmark portfolio had greatest weight in the least risky stocks, and this was reflected in the low risk of the Benchmark.

(c) The Benchmark portfolio implicitly includes a partial investment in the riskless asset and this reduces its riskiness.

(d) The Benchmark portfolio has a higher ratio of return per unit risk than any other risky asset that was available.

(e) None of the above make any sense.

277. In *Foundations*, we compared a portfolio manager's investment strategy with a positive ex-ante RAA to a CFO's future investment project with a positive NPV. We said that they are similar because:

    (a) Both are forecast to add value.

    (b) Both are risky.

    (c) Both require skill to manage.

    (d) All of the above.

    (e) (b) and (c) only.

278. ANZBY is an ADR for ANZ Bank. Each share of ANZBY corresponds to how many shares of ANZ on the NZX? Hint: On December 20, 2020, ANZBY traded at USD17.69 (Nasdaq), ANZ traded at NZD 24.70 (NZX), and the exchange rate was 0.7105 USD/NZD (read literally), or NZD/USD 0.7105 (using the standard FX quoting convention). (See footnote 2 on p. 63 regarding FX quotes.)

    (a) 1

    (b) 2

    (c) 3

    (d) 4

    (e) 5

279. Suppose an active bond portfolio manager has an IR of 50%. Suppose that she wants to charge expenses and fees totaling 100 bps. Suppose she wants to generate 50 bps of active return after these fees. Assume $\beta = 1$. What level of active risk does she expect that she will need to take on?

    (a) 83.33bps

    (b) 166.67bps

    (c) 200bps

    (d) 250bps

    (e) None of the above.

280. Roughly what would you expect the arithmetic average **intradaily** relative bid-ask spread to be on the largest 50 stocks listed on the NZX during 2017? Unlike *closing* spreads, this average is calculated over the *whole* trading day for each stock, then averaged over trading days, then averaged over all 50 stocks.

    (a) 5–15 bps

    (b) 15–75 bps

    (c) 75–200 bps

    (d) 250–400 bps

    (e) larger than 500 bps

281. ◇ Figure 1.15 gives six candidates, labeled A–F, for the empirical PDF of the daily returns to stock XRO over the three-year period January 2015–December 2017. The normal PDF with the same mean and variance is overlaid. One of the plots shows valid PDFs. Which one is it? Hint: It is not F.

   (a) A
   (b) B
   (c) C
   (d) D
   (e) E
   (f) F

282. In Chapter 2 of *Foundations*, we discuss how big an information ratio (IR) has to be to be considered good. We gave the example of Warren Buffett's 30-year history of performance having an IR of (___?___), which was superior to every U.S. stock having a 30-year history in the CRSP database. Buffett's IR number was what?

   (a) 0.01
   (b) 0.33
   (c) 0.50
   (d) 0.66
   (e) 1.00

283. ◇ If by chance the benchmark portfolio happens to fall exactly upon the ex-post Markowitz frontier, then which of the following best describes the resulting empirical security market line (SML)? (Please assume that the benchmark portfolio does not fall at the global minimum variance point or at the tangency point where the Tobin frontier touches the Markowitz frontier. You will recall that the SML plots mean returns on the y-axis versus betas on the x-axis.)

   (a) The empirical SML using betas calculated relative to the benchmark portfolio will be perfectly linear.
   (b) The empirical SML using betas calculated relative to the benchmark portfolio will be perfectly linear and horizontal.
   (c) The empirical SML using betas calculated relative to the benchmark portfolio will be perfectly linear and vertical.
   (d) The empirical SML using betas calculated relative to the benchmark portfolio will be the same line as the empirical SML calculated using betas calculated relative to the tangency portfolio.
   (e) None of the above.

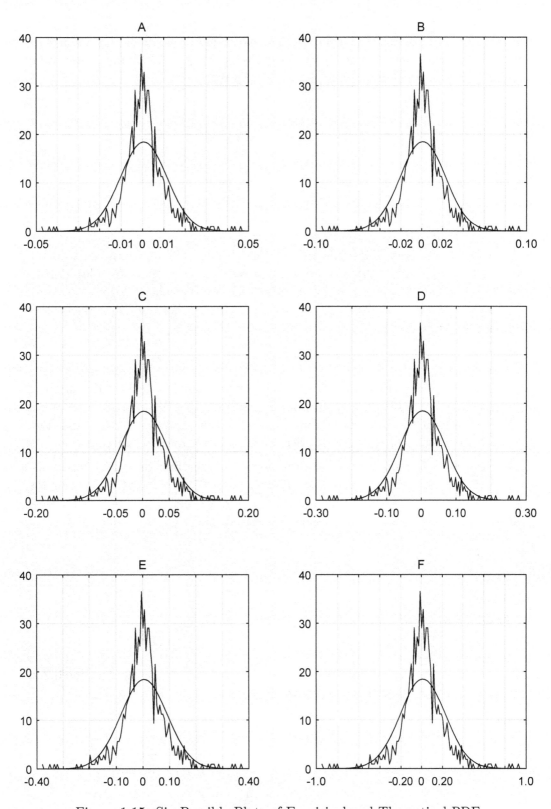

Figure 1.15: Six Possible Plots of Empirical and Theoretical PDFs

284. ◇◇ Figure 1.16 gives six candidates, labeled A–F, for the empirical PDF of the daily returns to the S&P 500 over the 50-year period June 1963–May 2013. The normal PDF with the same mean and variance is overlaid. Which plot shows valid PDFs? Hint: It is not F.

    (a) A

    (b) B

    (c) C

    (d) D

    (e) E

285. The famous mathematician Louis Jean Baptiste Alphonse Bachelier derived and tested an option pricing formula in his PhD thesis in 1900. Bachelier's option pricing formula agrees very closely with prices from the Black-Scholes-Merton formula, but works only for at-the-money options. Bachelier's formula is often used by practitioners to give approximations to Black-Scholes pricing. Bachelier's formula is simply

$$c = p = \frac{S\sigma\sqrt{T-t}}{\sqrt{2\pi}},$$

    where c is call price, p is put price, S is stock price, σ is standard deviation of returns, T is expiration date of the option, t is now, $(T-t)$ is time to expiration, and π is 3.14159265. Bachelier's formula is the same for puts or calls, and does not include interest rates, a strike price, or cumulative normal functions.

    Use Bachelier's formula to estimate the delta (i.e., the first derivative wrt stock price) of an at-the-money call option where $S = 10$, $T - t = 0.50$ (i.e., six months to maturity), and $\sigma = 0.40$. You can use a numerical derivative or an analytical derivative. They should give the same answer. Round to four decimal places.

    (a) 0.7090

    (b) 0.5000

    (c) 0.1128

    (d) 0.0798

    (e) None of the above is correct.

286. Consider the solution portfolio to our active alpha optimization in Question 3.2.2. What must be the sum of the active weights?

    (a) 0.00

    (b) 1.00

    (c) I cannot say without seeing it in front of me, but it must be positive.

    (d) I cannot say without seeing it in front of me, but it must be negative.

    (e) None of the above is correct.

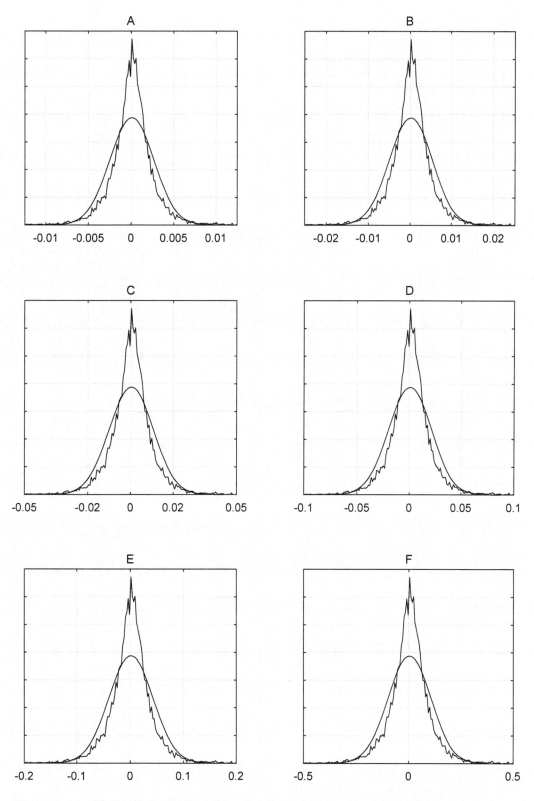

Figure 1.16: S&P 500 Daily Returns: Six Potential Empirical and Theoretical PDFs

287. ◇ Figure 1.17 gives six candidate plots, labeled A, B, C, D, E, and F above the plots. ONE of these shows the empirical PDF for the daily returns to the S&P 500 over the 50-year period June 1963–May 2013. It also has the normal PDF with the same mean and variance overlaid upon it. The other FIVE plots are not valid PDFs. Which plot contains the valid PDFs? Hint: It is not F.

    (a) A

    (b) B

    (c) C

    (d) D

    (e) E

288. ◇ A customer calls you for a quote on an at-the-money 200-day call option on IBM stock. You say the 200-day option is worth $12 per share. The customer calls you back one minute later and asks for a quote on an at-the-money 100-day call option on IBM stock. Assume that U.S. interest rates out to 200-days are virtually nil right now. You say the 100-day option is worth how much

    (a) $6

    (b) $8.49

    (c) $16.97

    (d) You cannot answer without knowing at least one of either the stock price or the volatility.

    (e) None of the above is correct.

289. Table 1.21 gives some relative bid-ask spreads from financial instruments. I used NATO phonetic alphabet code names. Which choice below decodes the names correctly? Note that F=Ford Motor Company, SPY= the SPDR (pronounced "spider") ETF that tracks the S&P 500, GBP/USD is the foreign currency cross rate, FBU=Fletcher Building, and BLT=Blis Technology (small N.Z. stock).

Code Name	Bravo	Charlie	Delta	Echo	Foxtrot
Relative Spread	0.7 bps	2.2 bps	8.1 bps	42 bps	1014 bps

Table 1.21: Relative Spreads on Financial Instruments

    (a) Bravo=F, Charlie=FBU, Delta=BLT, Echo=SPY, Foxtrot=GBP/USD

    (b) Bravo=FBU, Charlie=BLT, Delta=SPY, Echo=GBP/USD, Foxtrot=F

    (c) Bravo=BLT, Charlie=SPY, Delta=GBP/USD, Echo=F, Foxtrot=FBU

    (d) Bravo=SPY, Charlie=GBP/USD, Delta=F, Echo=FBU, Foxtrot=BLT

    (e) Bravo=GBP/USD, Charlie=F, Delta=FBU, Echo=BLT, Foxtrot=SPY

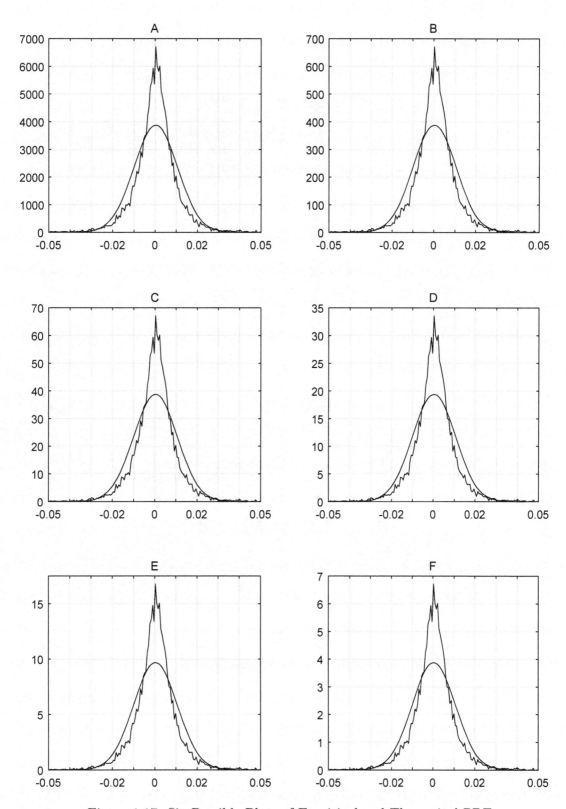

Figure 1.17: Six Possible Plots of Empirical and Theoretical PDFs

290. Figure 1.18 is based on Figure 2.16 from the section of *Foundations* describing the active alpha optimization. Portfolio P^* in Figure 1.18 is our optimum. It appears, however that Portfolio A (with the same level of return as Portfolio P^*), has a lower risk than Portfolio P^*. Portfolio A appears, therefore, to dominate Portfolio P^*. How can this be, if Portfolio P^* is the optimum?

   (a) Portfolio A has a lower standard deviation of returns that Portfolio P^*, but because the standard deviations are less than one, when we square them to get variances, the ranking changes order, and portfolio P^* can then be seen to dominate Portfolio A.

   (b) Portfolio A is irrelevant, and Portfolio P^* is also irrelevant, because Portfolio T is the portfolio we are seeking; Portfolio T has the highest Sharpe ratio of all risky portfolios.

   (c) The budget constraint is missing from Figure 1.18. If we overlay the budget constraint on Figure 1.18, P^* is clearly the optimum.

   (d) Portfolio A is irrelevant, and Portfolio T is also irrelevant, because Figure 1.18 does not show the active space in which the optimization is conducted.

   (e) None of the above is correct.

291. Looking again at Figure 1.18, portfolio T offers a higher Sharpe ratio (i.e., return per unit risk) than portfolio P^*. So, how can P^* be optimal?

   (a) T has a higher Sharpe ratio than P^*, but T treats all components of active risk with an even hand (which is not optimal). T likely also involves short selling and benchmark timing.

   (b) P^* and T offer the same IR in active space, but T is too aggressive.

   (c) P^* has a higher IR than T in the active space of our optimization.

   (d) (a) and (b), but not (c)

   (e) (a) and (c), but not (b)

292. ◇ Looking again at Figure 1.18, Portfolio T is the tangency portfolio. What is it about T that makes it non-optimal in our active-alpha optimization?

   (a) T has too much active risk, and is thus too aggressive in active space (i.e., α-ω space).

   (b) T has a lower Sharpe ratio than P^* in active space (i.e., α-ω space).

   (c) T involves active benchmark timing which we decided to avoid.

   (d) T has a lower Sharpe ratio than P^* in total space (i.e., κ-σ space).

   (e) More than one of (a), (b), (c), (d) are correct.

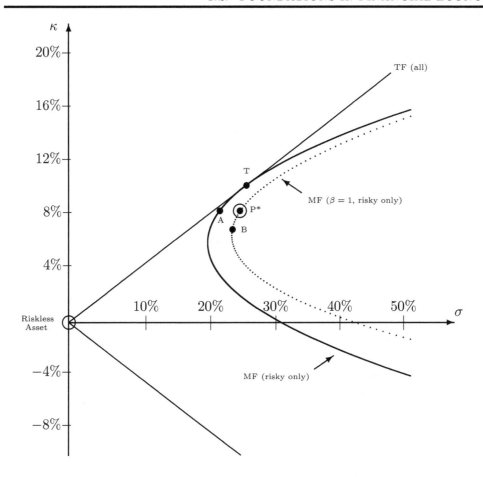

Figure 1.18: Maximizing the Skilled Sharpe Ratio in Total-Return-Risk κ-σ Space

293. Suppose you have $50,000 invested in equal dollar amounts in five stocks: Stock 1, Stock 2, Stock 3, Stock 4, and Stock 5. Suppose I tell you to sell all of Stock 1 and use all the proceeds to double your position in Stock 2. Ignore all T-costs (bid-ask spreads, commissions, price impact, price slippage, exchange fees, etc.). The two-sided turnover, expressed as a relative percentage of initial investment (like the turnover constraint in Question 3.2.2) is given by which ONE of the following?

(a) 10%.

(b) 20%.

(c) 30%.

(d) 40%.

(e) 50%.

294. Figure 1.19 contains two panels. The upper panel shows the sample mean and sample standard deviation of returns to 100 stocks and the Markowitz and Tobin frontiers. The lower panel shows a sample security market line (i.e., sample mean returns plotted against sample betas) for those same 100 stocks (as in Question 3.2.1). The sample betas were calculated for returns relative to a Markowitz frontier portfolio with sample mean return equal to which ONE of the following?

(a) About 4%.

(b) About 7% or 8%.

(c) About 10.0%.

(d) About 12.5%

(e) About 15.0%

295. A "protective put" position is what you have when you...

(a) Are long the stock and long a put option on the stock.

(b) Are short the stock and go short a put option for protection.

(c) Are long a put option and you go short the underlying stock to hedge the position.

(d) Are long the stock, but go short a put option on that stock in order to hedge the position.

(e) None of the above is correct.

296. If we look at a group of put options on a stock that differ only in strike price, then we would expect to see that the higher-strike options have...

(a) Higher option premium and higher relative bid-ask spread.

(b) Higher option premium and lower relative bid-ask spread.

(c) Lower option premium and higher relative bid-ask spread.

(d) Lower option premium and lower relative bid-ask spread.

(e) The answer is not obviously any of the above.

297. In *Foundations*, we gave two reasons why the designated market maker in a NYSE stock does not get to just sit back and collect the quoted bid-ask spread. Which of the following describes that pair of reasons?

(a) Movement in the level of the bid and ask prices (even if the spread itself is constant); price improvement.

(b) Inventory risk; adverse selection (i.e., trading with someone more informed).

(c) Inventory risk; price improvement.

(d) Bid-ask bounce; adverse selection (i.e., trading with someone more informed).

(e) Bid-ask bounce; Movement in the level of the bid and ask prices (even if the spread itself is constant).

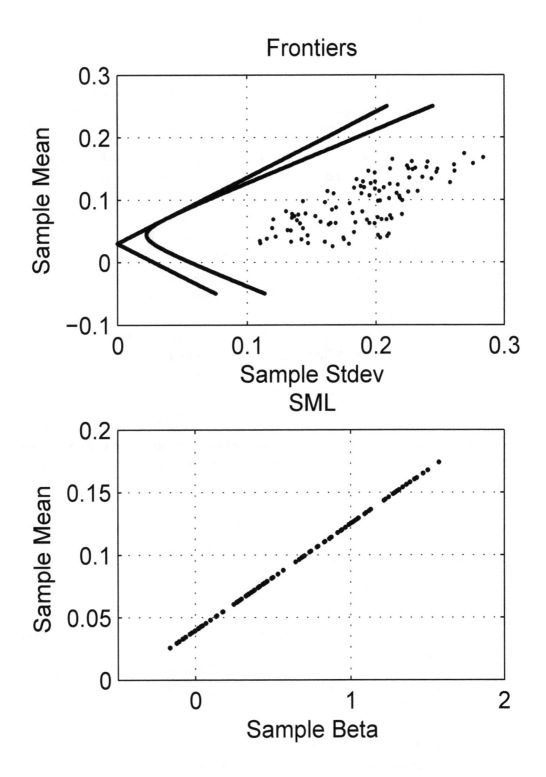

Figure 1.19: Simulated Markowitz and Tobin Frontiers, and SML

298. Telecom Corporation of New Zealand (TEL) paid a final dividend of six cents per share on September 17, 2010. That dividend had an ex-dividend date of September 1, 2010 and a date of record of September 3, 2010 (note the old $T+3$ settlement). That dividend must be incorporated into the returns to TEL when we work out means, standard deviations and higher moments of returns—because the dividend is part of the economic return accruing to the stockholder. Where/how in the time series of prices should we add in that dividend when calculating returns?

   (a) Add it to closing price on September 1 to calculate both the return from August 31 to September 1, and also to calculate the return from September 1 to September 2.

   (b) Add it to closing price on September 1 to calculate the return from August 31 to September 1, but do not add it to the closing price September 1 when calculating the return from September 1 to September 2.

   (c) Add it to closing price on September 17 to calculate both the return from September 16 to September 17, and also to calculate the return from September 17 to September 18.

   (d) Add it to closing price on September 17 to calculate the return from September 16 to September 17, but do not add it to the closing price September 17 when calculating the return from September 17 to September 18.

   (e) None of the above is correct.

299. Suppose an active bond portfolio manager has an IR of 75%. Suppose that she wants to charge expenses and fees totaling 100 bps. Assume $\beta = 1$. Suppose she wants to generate 50 bps of active return after these fees. What level of active risk does she expect that she will need to take on?

   (a) 83.33bps

   (b) 166.67bps

   (c) 200bps

   (d) 250bps

   (e) None of the above.

300. Suppose you have the quantitative active alpha optimization spreadsheet from Question 3.2.2 sitting in front of you. Set T-costs to zero. Suppose you run the optimization using risk aversion $\lambda = 10$. Record the result and then rerun the optimization with $\lambda = 0$. In theory what difference(s) would you expect to see.

   (a) The optimizer will do more turnover with $\lambda = 0$ than with $\lambda = 10$.

   (b) The optimizer will take on more active risk with $\lambda = 0$ than with $\lambda = 10$.

   (c) The optimizer will find a higher alpha portfolio with $\lambda = 0$ than with $\lambda = 10$.

   (d) All of the above are TRUE.

   (e) (a) and (b), but not (c).

301. Let $N(\cdot)$ be the cumulative standard normal function. What is the probability that you will see a 2.5% or bigger move in the broad market stock index of a developed country on a randomly selected day? It might be the U.S., U.K., Japan, Australia or N.Z. Note that it could be an up or down move—we have not specified which. Feel free to assume the average daily return on the index is zero.

    (a) Notably larger than $2[1 - N(2.5)]$.

    (b) Roughly $2[1 - N(2.5)]$.

    (c) Notably smaller than $2[1 - N(2.5)]$.

    (d) Roughly $[1 - N(2.5)]$.

    (e) Between $[1 - N(2.5)]$ and $2[1 - N(2.5)]$.

302. What is the probability that you will see an absolute move of 1% or less in the level of a broad market stock index of a developed country on a randomly selected day? It might be the U.S., U.K., Japan, Australia or New Zealand. Note that it could be an up or down move. We have not specified which. Feel free to assume the average daily return on the index is zero. Note that the area under the standard normal distribution between 0 and 1 is roughly 34%.

    (a) The probability is roughly 68%.

    (b) The probability is roughly 34%.

    (c) The probability is notably larger than 68%.

    (d) The probability is notably smaller than 34%

    (e) We do not have enough information to answer this question.

303. You wish to sell 10,000 shares of Spark (New Zealand) stock. You decide not to submit a market order to sell your stock. Suppose instead that you submit a limit order to sell your stock at the best ask price. Which of the following is the best answer?

    (a) If your limit order is executed, then the economic benefit of the limit order execution over and above the market order execution may be viewed as compensation for providing liquidity to the market.

    (b) If your limit order is executed, then the economic benefit of the limit order execution over and above the market order execution may be viewed as compensation for bearing the risk of non-execution.

    (c) If your limit order is executed, then the economic benefit of the limit order execution over and above the market order execution may be viewed as compensation for bearing the risk of a lack of immediacy in your execution.

    (d) All of the above are correct.

    (e) (a) and (c), but not (b).

304. I ask you to use the Ledoit and Wolf (2004) technique in Question 3.2.4 for the VCV. That exercise asks you to repeat the active alpha optimization from Question 3.2.2 and the backtest from Question 3.2.3 using the Ledoit-Wolf Variance-Covariance (LW-VCV) estimator (much of it is done for you already in the spreadsheets you can download from the Web site for the text). The LW-VCV takes an average of the sample variance-covariance matrix and the constant correlation model VCV (CCM-VCV) matrix. This average is a "shrinkage estimator." Which is the best statement?

    (a) The aim of this shrinkage is to reduce estimation error in the VCV by shrinking the error-prone sample VCV toward the structured CCM-VCV estimator.

    (b) The aim of this shrinkage is to reduce the number of parameters to be estimated in the VCV and thus make it invertible.

    (c) The aim of this shrinkage is to increase error maximization (as discussed by Richard Michaud).

    (d) The aim of this shrinkage is to move eigenvalues toward their mean and produce an invertible VCV.

    (e) All of the above.

305. The S&P 500 index is today at a level of 1361.22 with a dividend yield of 1.72%. Suppose that an investment bank creates an at-the-money (i.e., strike price equals spot price) European-style call option on the index, with one year to expiration. The yield on one-year T-bills (a safe interest rate) is approximately 0.22%. The volatility of returns to the index is approximately 16% per annum. Estimate the delta of the call option. Hint: Use no formula.

    (a) The delta is quite close to 1.00.

    (b) The delta is quite close to 0.75.

    (c) The delta is quite close to 0.50.

    (d) The delta is quite close to 0.25.

    (e) The delta is quite close to 0.00.

306. Your brokerage screen says your sole position is long 100 shares of DIA. Your opinion has reversed. What order(s) do you submit so that your brokerage screen tells you your sole position is short 100 shares of DIA?

    (a) Sell 100 shares and then go short another 100 shares.

    (b) Buy 200 shares.

    (c) Buy 100 shares to cover and then buy another 100 shares.

    (d) Sell 200 shares.

    (e) Short sell 100 shares and then buy another 100 shares.

307. Which of the following statements is/are TRUE?

    (a) It is difficult to reject the null hypothesis that the mean return on a stock is zero.

    (b) Most stocks have daily returns that are not normally distributed.

    (c) Large-capitalization stocks tend to have higher relative bid-ask spreads than small-capitalization stocks.

    (d) All of the above are TRUE.

    (e) One of (a), or (b), or (c) is FALSE.

308. You buy $10,000 worth of N.Z. stock using a 70% "margin lending ratio" (i.e., a 30% margin rate). You buy the stock using $3,000 of your own money and $7,000 borrowed from your broker. Bad news arrives and the stock price immediately plunges 25%. You sell in a panic. What is your rate of return on the transaction? Ignore bid-ask spreads, commissions, exchange fees, and margin interest. Round your answer to two decimal places.

    (a) -83.33%

    (b) -70.00%

    (c) -50.00%

    (d) -42.85%

    (e) -25.00%

309. We described IRs as exceptional, very good, and good. Which of the following best matches our description?

    (a) Exceptional IR=10.00; Very Good IR=5.00; Good IR=1.00.

    (b) Exceptional IR=2.00; Very Good IR=1.00; Good IR=0.50.

    (c) Exceptional IR=1.00; Very Good IR=0.75; Good IR=0.50.

    (d) Exceptional IR=1.00; Very Good IR=0.50; Good IR=0.00.

    (e) Exceptional IR=0.50; Very Good IR=0.00; Good IR=-0.50.

310. In *Foundations*, we said we would do no benchmark timing in our active alpha optimization. What were some of the reasons why we said that?

    (a) Because we have no control over the return on the benchmark. That is, it is not a function of our choice variables.

    (b) Because it is easier to chase one rabbit (i.e., stock selection) than it is to chase two (i.e., stock selection and benchmark timing).

    (c) Because most institutional asset managers do not engage in benchmark timing, and neither will we.

    (d) All of the above.

    (e) (b) and (c) but not (a).

311. ◇◇ You cannot possibly hope to do the calculation for this question in only a few minutes; you need a computer and at least an hour to figure it out. So, your job here is to use every ounce of finance intuition you have to answer this very simple question. I am looking for the sort of answer you can figure out before you touch your calculator or Excel. I recommend that you resist the temptation to touch your calculator for this one.

It is 2010. Three years ago you signed up for a KiwiSaver fund that required only a $20 per week deposit from you but no initial deposit. You got your $1,000 kick-start [old rules] almost immediately. You deposited $20 per week for three years. At the end of each year the government deposited to your account a member tax credit of $52 \times \$20 = \$1,040$ [old rules]. So, you got three of these matches so far. The fund was a conservative cash fund that paid an effective annual rate (EAR) of 5% per annum like a bank account, but with weekly compounding.

Your deposits, however, have earned not just the stable 5% per annum, but also triggered the kick-start and tax credits to parachute into your account. These extra deposits mean that you have earned more than someone putting $20 per week into a bank account yielding the same 5% per annum. So, roughly what was your actual EAR, accounting correctly for the kick-start and the tax credit?

(a) 6% per annum.

(b) 12% per annum.

(c) 18% per annum.

(d) 36% per annum.

(e) 72% per annum.

312. In stock markets (e.g., the NYSE) where there is a designated market maker (DMM), there are at least two reasons why market makers do not always collect the full bid-ask spread. That is, there are at least two reasons why they don't just buy from you at their bid of $1.86, say, and sell to someone else at their ask of $1.87, say, thereby collecting the full one-penny spread in that case. Which of the following is one of those reasons?

(a) The DMM has to move the bid and ask in response to supply and demand. These moves mean that the market maker could easily buy from you at $1.86 but then have to sell to someone else at $1.86, or $1.85, etc.

(b) The DMM gets only *half* the spread, not the *full* spread when they both buy and sell stock because fair value is in the middle of the spread.

(c) The spreads are very tight on liquid stocks, and these tight spreads drive down market maker profits.

(d) The spreads are very wide on illiquid stocks and these wide spreads mean that offsetting trades are few and far between.

(e) Both (a) and (b) above are correct.

313. Suppose you sold short shares of IBM because you think the company is going to collapse. What are some of the day-to-day costs and benefits of holding the short position while you wait for IBM to collapse?

(a) Costs: Earn below-average interest on your margin money, must meet dividend obligation. Benefits: Get to use short sales proceeds to make other investments.

(b) Costs: Earn below-average interest on your margin money. Benefits: Receive dividends.

(c) Costs: Earn below-average interest on your margin money. Benefits: Get to use short sales proceeds to make other investments.

(d) Costs: Must meet dividend obligations. Benefits: Get to use short sales proceeds to make other investments.

(e) None of the above is correct.

314. Suppose I send you to the Bloomberg terminal to obtain dividend payout ratios (DPR) on S&P 100 or S&P/NZX50 stocks. Which of the following is likely to be true?

(a) There will be very little variation in DPRs over the stocks in the index.

(b) The highest DPR you will see for an index stock will be larger than 100%.

(c) It is not possible to have a DPR larger than 100% because then dividends would exceed net income.

(d) All stocks in the index will have a positive DPR.

(e) Some of the Bloomberg DPRs will be negative.

315. I just looked up the price of a put option on a U.S. stock using my Bloomberg terminal. The put option contract covers 100 shares of stock. Bloomberg tells me that the delta of the put option is -0.25 (i.e., -25%). If I am the options market maker who just sold this put option to a trader, what position should I enter in the underlying stock to hedge my exposure to the option I just sold?

(a) I go long 25 shares.

(b) I go short 25 shares.

(c) I go long, but not 25 shares.

(d) I go short, but not 25 shares.

(e) I do not have to hedge it because it was a fair trade (the trader paid me money; I gave the trader an option of equal value).

316. Suppose you buy a stock on the ex-dividend day. Do you expect to get the dividend?

(a) Yes, I am entitled to the dividend.

(b) No, I am NOT entitled to the dividend.

317. Fletcher Building Ltd (FBU) paid an interim dividend of 17 cents per share on April 18, 2012. That dividend had an ex-dividend date of March 28, 2012 and a date of record of March 30, 2012 (note the old $T + 3$ settlement). That dividend should be incorporated into the returns to FBU if we work out means, standard deviations and anything like that—because the dividend is part of the economic return accruing to the stockholder. Where/how in the time series of prices should we add in that dividend when calculating returns?

   (a) We add it to closing price on April 18 to calculate the return from April 17 to April 18, but we did not add it to the closing price April 18 when calculating the return from April 18 to April 19.

   (b) We add it to closing price on April 18 to calculate both the return from April 17 to April 18, and also to calculate the return from April 18 to April 19.

   (c) We add it to closing price on March 28 to calculate the return from March 27 to March 28, but we did not add it to the closing price March 28 when calculating the return from March 28 to March 29.

   (d) We add it to closing price on March 28 to calculate both the return from March 27 to March 28, and also to calculate the return from March 28 to March 29.

   (e) None of the above is correct.

318. Which one of the following was NOT one of the five constraints in the active alpha optimization appearing in Question 3.2.2?

   (a) No short selling in your portfolio ($\vec{h}_P \geq 0$).

   (b) Your portfolio is fully invested in the risky assets ($\vec{h}'_P \vec{\iota} = 1$, where $\vec{\iota}$ is a column of ones).

   (c) There is a constraint on the two-sided turnover in your portfolio ($|\vec{h}_P - \vec{h}_B|'\vec{\iota} \leq U$, for some upper bound U).

   (d) The alphas must be constrained to be benchmark neutral ($\vec{h}'_B \vec{\alpha}_{\text{neut}} = 0$).

   (e) The size of the active positions in your portfolio is constrained ($|\vec{h}_P - \vec{h}_B| \leq L$, for some limit L).

319. In *Foundations* we discussed one scenario where consensus fair value for a security might be outside the bid-ask spread. That scenario was...

   (a) When the market maker has to trade with someone who is more informed (i.e., an adverse selection problem).

   (b) When bid-ask bounce causes prices to jump up and down.

   (c) When heavy demand to buy a stock causes prices to rise.

   (d) When a large market order eats up the depth in the centralized limit order book.

   (e) When inventory risk drives a designated market maker to move the level of the bid-ask spread far from fair value.

320. ◇ In 2011, the NZX conducted a pilot study with five stocks to see whether half-penny tick sizes were preferable to penny tick sizes. We have not really discussed the possible outcomes in *Foundations*, but based on your experience, likely outcomes of the study included...

  (a) Spreads will tend to be tighter with the smaller tick sizes.

  (b) Traders will submit smaller-sized orders because they don't want to send a signal of their intent that is easy to front run via cheaper price priority.

  (c) The smaller tick size won't make the spreads much tighter near the opening of trade each day.

  (d) All of the above.

  (e) Only (a) and (b), but not (c).

321. In the Brandes Partner's 2012 article *Boomers Behaving Badly: A Better Solution to the "Money Death" Problem*, the authors quote Raymond DeVoe Jr as saying "More money has been lost reaching for yield than at the point of a gun." They say that investors determined to generate income may be asking the wrong question. Instead of asking "What investments can generate the $x\%$ yield that will pay me the income I need?," Brandes says they should be asking...

  (a) In practice, how can an individual get a sensible estimate of their real age?

  (b) How can a deferred annuity play a role in helping investors avoid money death?

  (c) How can I take the needed amount out of my portfolio every month without ultimately depleting my assets?

  (d) Where there is both supply and demand, how can the combination of investment and deferred annuity reduce the prospect of money death?

  (e) Is there a way for individuals to insure against their longevity leading to money death, protecting themselves financially from the consequences of a "late death?"

322. Which of the following is the best answer?

  (a) A risk-parity fund is one where the manager has borrowed money and leveraged the bond position so that the bonds and stocks each contribute roughly the same degree of risk to the portfolio.

  (b) The returns to the classic 60/40 stock/bond portfolio are almost perfectly correlated with the returns to an all-stock portfolio. So, a 60/40 stock/bond portfolio does not represent true diversification.

  (c) One reason that leveraged bonds in general, and risk parity in particular, have done very well in the 10 years up to and including 2014 is that we have experienced a secular decline in interest rates.

  (d) All of the above are true.

  (e) Only two of (a), (b), and (c), are true.

323. Environmental, social and governance (ESG) principles for investing refer to finding companies that have embraced a culture of sustainability by adopting a coherent set of corporate policies related to the environment, employees, community, products, and customers. For example, perhaps they promote a work-life balance, avoid suppliers who exploit child labor, aim to reduce emissions or increase water/energy efficiency, engage in more recycling, etc. In general, ESG investing principals...

   (a) are being taken much more seriously in the U.S. than in Europe.

   (b) are being taken much more seriously in Australia than in Europe.

   (c) need better measurement tools to assess how value is being added by ESG factors.

   (d) lead to investments that most studies report as underperforming non-ESG investments.

   (e) constitute a breach of fiduciary duty because they restrict investment opportunities and are therefore likely to produce suboptimal investments, damaging investors' wealth.

324. One of the following is NOT a benefit of trading stocks in the U.S. rather than trading stocks in New Zealand. Which one is it?

   (a) More information is available about the depth of the centralized limit order book in the U.S. than in N.Z.

   (b) U.S. brokerage commissions are lower than N.Z. brokerage commissions.

   (c) U.S. relative bid-ask spreads are smaller than N.Z. relative bid-ask spreads.

   (d) I get faster executions from my U.S. broker than my N.Z. broker.

   (e) I get faster trade confirmations from my U.S. broker than my N.Z. broker.

325. Miss Bebe Nouveaune is 65 years old today. She has $2,000,000 sitting in her KiwiSaver account. She expects to earn 6% per annum in her account after all taxes and fees (that is 50 bps per month). She plans to draw the balance down to zero using monthly withdrawals linked to inflation (i.e., a growing monthly annuity growing at the inflation rate). Inflation is expected to be a steady 2.4% per annum (that is 20 bps per month). Her first withdrawal will be one month from now. She plans to make her last withdrawal, bringing the account down to zero, on her 95th birthday. What will be her first withdrawal? Please choose the best answer.

   (a) $9,103.00

   (b) $60,001.76

   (c) $72,000.29

   (d) $103,289.46

   (e) $111,570.58

326. Equations 1.2, 1.3 and 1.4 give the Black-Scholes-Merton option pricing formula for the value at time-t of a European-style call option expiring at time-T.

$$c(t) = S(t)N(d_1) - e^{-r(T-t)}XN(d_2), \text{ where} \qquad (1.2)$$

$$d_1 = \frac{\ln\left(\frac{S(t)}{X}\right) + (r + \frac{1}{2}\sigma^2)(T-t)}{\sigma\sqrt{T-t}}, \text{ and} \qquad (1.3)$$

$$d_2 = d_1 - \sigma\sqrt{T-t}. \qquad (1.4)$$

Suppose I tell you that $S(t)$, today's stock price, is very high relative to X, the strike price. In that case, the ratio $\frac{S(t)}{X}$ is a big number in Equation 1.3. Keep following that argument and it tells me something about the ratio $\ln\left(\frac{S(t)}{X}\right)$ in Equation 1.3, which tells me something about d_1 in Equation 1.3 and d_2 in Equation 1.4, which then tells me something about $N(d_1)$ and $N(d_2)$ in Equation 1.2, which leads me to conclude that $c(t)$, the call value, is approximately what in Equation 1.2? Note that "$\approx$" means approximately equal to.

(a) $c(t) \approx 0$

(b) $c(t) \approx S(t) - e^{-r(T-t)}X \times \frac{1}{2} = S(t) - \frac{1}{2} \times PV(X)$

(c) $c(t) \approx S(t) \times \frac{1}{2} - e^{-r(T-t)}X = \frac{1}{2} \times S(t) - PV(X)$

(d) $c(t) \approx S(t) \times \frac{1}{2} - e^{-r(T-t)}X \times \frac{1}{2} = \frac{1}{2} \times [S(t) - PV(X)]$

(e) $c(t) \approx S(t) - e^{-r(T-t)}X = S(t) - PV(X)$

327. Why should P/E ratios often be different for different firms?

(a) Firms with higher growth opportunities should have higher P/E ratios, other things being equal.

(b) Firms with more risky possible future earnings should have lower P/E ratios, other things being equal.

(c) Young fast growing firms should have higher P/E ratios than mature slow growing firms, other things being equal.

(d) All of the above are true.

(e) Not all of the above are true.

328. Estimate the IR of an active manager who follows 128 stocks, but updates forecasts only twice per year. Assume the correlation between realized and forecast active returns is 3%.

(a) 0.34

(b) 0.48

(c) 0.68

(d) 0.98

(e) None of the above is correct.

329. Can a portfolio have **no benchmark timing**, and also be **market neutral**?

    (a) Yes, of course, you just need to have $\beta = 1$ and you get both, like the portfolio we formed in Question 3.2.2.

    (b) Yes, of course, you just need to have $\beta = 0$ and you get both, like the long-short portfolio discussed in *Foundations* where we were long \$5,000 in three good stocks and short \$5,000 worth of benchmark-tracking stock.

    (c) No, of course not, no benchmark timing means $\beta = 1$, but market neutral means $\beta = 0$, and you cannot have both these.

    (d) No, of course not, no benchmark timing means $\beta = 0$, but market neutral means $\beta = 1$, and you cannot have both these.

    (e) Yes, it is possible, but it will be difficult to set the portfolio up, and we will have to trade frequently to maintain the required exposures.

330. In Chapter 2 of *Foundations*, I gave you the following equations for finding the Markowitz Frontier of risky assets when there is no riskless asset:

$$\vec{h}_P = \vec{H}\mu_P + \vec{G} \text{ where}$$
$$\vec{H} = \frac{1}{D}\{[C(V^{-1}\vec{\mu}) - A(V^{-1}\vec{\iota})]\},$$
$$\vec{G} = \frac{1}{D}\{[B(V^{-1}\vec{\iota}) - A(V^{-1}\vec{\mu})]\},$$
$$A = \vec{\iota}'V^{-1}\vec{\mu},\ B = \vec{\mu}'V^{-1}\vec{\mu},\ C = \vec{\iota}'V^{-1}\vec{\iota},\ \text{and } D = BC - A^2.$$

You were given $\vec{\mu}$, V, and you had to build $\vec{\iota}$. You then had to solve for the seven unknown quantities appearing to the left of the equals signs: $\vec{h}_P$, $\vec{H}$, $\vec{G}$, A, B, C, D. Tell me the order in which you solved (or could have solved) for these seven unknown quantities.

    (a) $\vec{h}_P, \vec{H}, \vec{G}, A, B, C, D$
    (b) $\vec{h}_P, A, B, C, D, \vec{H}, \vec{G}$
    (c) $A, B, C, D, \vec{H}, \vec{G}, \vec{h}_P$
    (d) $A, B, C, D, \vec{h}_P, \vec{H}, \vec{G}$
    (e) None of the above is reasonable.

331. In the active alpha optimization problem we solved in Question 3.2.2, the objective function was $RTAA = \alpha_P - \lambda_R \cdot \omega_P^2 - TC$. This objective function measures what?

    (a) Risk-adjusted return.
    (b) Choice variables and constraints.
    (c) Expected utility of our active portfolio.
    (d) Return out-performance adjusted for risk and T-costs.
    (e) The CAPM expected return on our portfolio adjusted for costs and risks.

332. If you look at average standard deviation of portfolio return as a function of N, where N is the number of stocks in a portfolio, roughly what reduction in average standard deviation would you expect to see when going from one to four stocks, and when going from one to 10 stocks, respectively? Round to the nearest 5%.

    (a) 10% reduction and 20% reduction, respectively.

    (b) 20% reduction and 30% reduction, respectively.

    (c) 30% reduction and 55% reduction, respectively.

    (d) 50% reduction and 75% reduction, respectively.

    (e) None of the above is close to what we saw.

333. ◇◇ Suppose I find some stock market that trades so nicely that the continuously compounded stock returns are in fact normally distributed, the returns are independent through time, and the distribution is stable. Suppose I estimate the standard deviation of monthly returns σ_m and the standard deviation of daily returns σ_d. What value, roughly speaking, would you expect for the ratio $\frac{\sigma_d}{\sigma_m}$?

    (a) 0.22

    (b) 0.29

    (c) 0.83

    (d) 3.46

    (e) 12.00

334. An "enhanced passive" fund is one where the manager is...?

    (a) Just trying to match the performance of the benchmark.

    (b) Trying to match the performance of the benchmark, but uses "smart trading" to try to capture as little as 10 bps extra alpha per annum.

    (c) Running an active fund, actively trying to beat the market, but has tight controls on active risk and is seeking only to outperform by 100–200 bps per annum.

    (d) Either (b) or (c) could be correct.

    (e) None of the above is correct.

335. If I trade USD100,000 worth of a stock in the U.S., my U.S. broker charges me a USD0.00 commission (as of 2019). If I trade NZD100,000 worth of stock in N.Z., however, my N.Z. broker charges me 30 bps of the value, with a minimum commission of NZD30. How much is the N.Z. commission in that case?

    (a) NZD3

    (b) NZD30

    (c) NZD300

    (d) NZD3000

    (e) NZD30,000

336. In a financial crisis, the correlation between the returns on different assets increases markedly (called "phase locking"). Imagine that you have data for a one-year bull market, and data for a one-year bear market. For each you draw a Markowitz plot showing a snapshot of the year of data including the Markowitz frontier, the Tobin frontier, the tangency portfolio, the individual stocks, and the benchmark index (just like Question 3.2.1). How does the bear market plot compare with the bull market plot?

(a) In the bear market, the benefit of naive diversification will be lower, the individual stocks will plot lower, and the Tobin frontier may be inverted with the tangency point on the bottom half of the Markowitz frontier.

(b) In the bear market, the benefit of naive diversification will be lower, the individual stocks will plot lower, and the Tobin frontier will appear normal way up with the tangency point on the top half of the Markowitz frontier.

(c) In the bear market, the benefit of naive diversification will be greater, the individual stocks will plot lower, and the Tobin frontier may be inverted with the tangency point at the bottom of the Markowitz frontier.

(d) In the bear market, the benefit of naive diversification will be greater, the individual stocks will plot higher, and the Tobin frontier may be inverted with the tangency point at the bottom of the Markowitz frontier.

(e) In the bear market, the benefit of naive diversification will be greater, the individual stocks will plot higher, and the Tobin frontier will appear normal way up with the tangency point on the top half of the Markowitz frontier.

337. When trying to derive an objective function for our active alpha optimization, we arrived at Equation 1.5 as an intermediary step.

$$OBJ2 = \overbrace{[\kappa_B - \lambda_B\sigma_B^2]}^{\text{benchmark}} + \overbrace{[(\beta_P - 1)(\mu_B + \delta_B) - \lambda_{BT}(\beta_P^2 - 1)\sigma_B^2]}^{\text{benchmark timing}} + \overbrace{[\alpha_P - \lambda_R\omega_P^2]}^{\text{stock selection}}$$
(1.5)

We decided to discard the first (benchmark) term because of what?

(a) Long-term investors are resigned to the fact that they must be exposed to benchmark risk over the long term if they are to accumulate wealth, so we do not need this term.

(b) Long-term investors are resigned to the fact that they must be exposed to benchmark risk over the long term if they are to accumulate wealth, so the risk κ_B balances the return σ_B^2 already, and this term is zero.

(c) The benchmark term is not a function of our choice variables, $\vec{h}_P$, so including it or excluding it gives the same solution to our optimization problem.

(d) Direct algebraic expansion and manipulation shows that the first (benchmark) term cancels out with the second (benchmark timing) term. So, we can drop them both.

(e) Both (a) and (c) are correct.

338. In Chapter 2 of *Foundations* we discussed a result from Merton involving accuracy of sample estimators of the mean and variance of returns given a year's worth of data on a stock. Make the same assumptions that Merton makes regarding IID data. If we move from using monthly returns to using daily returns, what will happen to the <u>standard error</u> of the estimator of the annual mean return?

   (a) We cannot say. Not enough information is given.

   (b) It will increase as we move to using daily returns.

   (c) It will decrease as we move to using daily returns.

   (d) It will stay the same as we move to using daily returns.

   (e) In fact, it could go either way and will depend upon the particular sample of data.

339. In the active alpha optimization in Question 3.2.2 we used P/E ratios and dividend yields (DY) to form value-strategy alphas. It is important, however, that the ratios be the correct way up, or we will not be following the correct strategy, and we may end up chasing glamour stocks instead. So, what should we have used for raw alphas?

   (a) $\alpha_{raw,P/E} = \frac{P}{E}$ and $\alpha_{raw,DY} = DY$

   (b) $\alpha_{raw,P/E} = \frac{P}{E}$ and $\alpha_{raw,DY} = \frac{1}{DY}$

   (c) $\alpha_{raw,P/E} = \frac{E}{P}$ and $\alpha_{raw,DY} = DY$

   (d) $\alpha_{raw,P/E} = \frac{E}{P}$ and $\alpha_{raw,DY} = \frac{1}{DY}$

   (e) No, in fact, this question is poorly posed. Any of the above choices would have been fine because all that standardization, Winsorization, neutralization, and re-scaling we did means that whatever we start with, it all leads to the same answer anyway.

340. One of your classmates has suggested the following parameterization of the active alpha objective function from Question 3.2.2, but there is a mistake in it. I want you to tell me where the mistake is. All notation is as used in *Foundations*.

$$RTAA = \alpha_P - \lambda \omega_P^2 - TC$$
$$= \underbrace{\vec{h}_P'\vec{\alpha}}_{A} - \lambda \underbrace{\left[\vec{h}_P'V\vec{h}_P - \vec{h}_B'V\vec{h}_B\right]^2}_{B} - F \cdot \underbrace{\frac{1}{2}}_{C}\underbrace{\left|\vec{h}_P - \vec{h}_B\right|'}_{D}\underbrace{\vec{\gamma}}_{E}$$

   (a) The mistake is in A.

   (b) The mistake is in B.

   (c) The mistake is in C.

   (d) The mistake is in D.

   (e) The mistake is in E.

341. Table 1.22 shows prices that could be used for building momentum alphas in an active alpha optimization like Question 3.2.2. The six-month return based on these prices is also shown. Looking only at raw momentum alphas (i.e., ignoring standardization, Winsorization, neutralization, and re-scaling), which three stocks are the most attractive overweights to a quantitative portfolio manager running a price momentum strategy using these 10 stocks? That is, which three stocks will the manager most wish to overweight?

(a) AIA, RYM, CMO.

(b) SCT, AIA, RYM.

(c) ABA, FBU, BLT.

(d) CEN, FPH, BGR.

(e) None of the above is correct.

Date	FBU	CEN	AIA	FPH	RYM	BGR	ABA	CMO	SCT	BLT
30/06/2010	7.8600	5.6850	1.8750	3.1150	1.9950	1.2750	5.0750	2.1600	1.1850	0.1000
31/12/2010	7.6550	6.2050	2.1750	3.1450	2.2950	1.3750	4.9050	2.4700	1.4250	0.0975
Return	-0.0261	0.0915	0.1600	0.0096	0.1504	0.0784	-0.0335	0.1435	0.2025	-0.0250

Table 1.22: Stock Prices on Two Days, Six Months Apart (10 Stocks)

342. The earnings yield and the P/E ratio appear as a function of the present value of growth opportunities (PVGO) in Equations 1.6 and 1.7. P is today's stock price, E is the earnings next year, r is a discount rate for the earnings, and PVGO is the present value of opportunities for growth in earnings fueled by positive-NPV projects. Now suppose we have a high P/E stock and a low P/E stock. Assume they have the same price, P, and the same discount rate, r. Which stock has the larger proportion of its value (i.e., P) generated by its PVGO?

$$\frac{E}{P} = r\left(1 - \frac{PVGO}{P}\right) \tag{1.6}$$

$$\frac{P}{E} = \frac{1}{r}\left(\frac{1}{1 - \frac{PVGO}{P}}\right) \tag{1.7}$$

(a) The high P/E stock will have a greater proportion of its value generated by its PVGO.

(b) The low P/E stock will have a greater proportion of its value generated by its PVGO.

(c) If they have the same price and the same discount rate r, they will have the same proportion of their value generated by their PVGOs.

(d) We cannot tell. Not enough information is given to answer this question.

(e) The question is not well posed. It does not make sense.

343. Recalling the Markowitz plot from Question 3.2.1, how do we capture the last few percentage points of diversification benefit that take us from the naive diversification of the benchmark index to the optimal diversification of the Markowitz frontier?

    (a) It is very difficult because those plots are backward looking snapshots telling us what we just missed out on. In hindsight it looks easy, but in practice, looking forward, it is darn difficult to extract this.

    (b) This comes down to the 50-year old (or more) question of how to get a better Sharpe ratio than the benchmark. We are attempting this, at least to some extent, with active stock selection, but no sure-fire way to consistently beat the benchmark exists.

    (c) We can do it only by taking on active positions, but then that exposes us to active risk, and we may underperform.

    (d) You must be a very skilled active manager, but most managers are not skilled enough to consistently beat the benchmark after fees and T-costs.

    (e) All of the above are true.

344. A conflict of interest can exist between the agency and proprietary sides of a sell-side brokerage house if...

    (a) The broker is in fact an agency-only business.

    (b) Disintermediation, in the form of electronic trading, is prevalent.

    (c) There is no firewall to stop communication between the agency and proprietary trading desks.

    (d) Tick sizes are sufficiently large to make front running an informed client's trade profitable.

    (e) Fear of price impact means that orders are being cut down into smaller slices and worked during the day.

345. On Monday morning you bought $5,000 worth of a large-capitalization NZX stock on 50% margin from your N.Z. discount broker. Terrible news arrived Monday evening and the stock opened 20% lower on Tuesday morning. You closed out your position immediately. Taking account of spreads, commissions, one day's margin interest, the margin money, and the move in the stock price, give a rough estimate of your loss on the round trip trade.

    (a) I probably lost something like $1,100(i.e., a return something like -22%).

    (b) I probably lost something like $1,100(i.e., a return something like -44%).

    (c) I probably lost something like $2,100(i.e., a return something like -42%).

    (d) I probably lost something like $2,100(i.e., a return something like -84%).

    (e) None of the above is a reasonable answer.

346. There are at least four New Zealand stocks that, if they were U.S. stocks, would be of large enough market capitalization (i.e., size) to be members of the S&P 500 index (mid-2015). They are FBU, TEL, CEN, and AIA. How do the relative bid-ask spreads on these N.Z. stocks compare, on average, with the relative bid-ask spreads on U.S. stocks of similar size that are members of the S&P 500?

    (a) The relative spreads of the N.Z. stocks are smaller than those of the comparably-sized U.S. stocks.

    (b) The relative spreads of the N.Z. and U.S. stocks are about the same, because relative spread is a function of size, and these stocks are the same size.

    (c) The relative spreads of the N.Z. stocks are bigger than those of the comparably-sized U.S. stocks.

    (d) We do not know which way the relationship goes.

    (e) None of the above is true.

347. Suppose that I am short 100 shares of IBM stock, but my opinion has just flipped from being bearish to being bullish. Suppose I submit an order to buy 200 shares of IBM stock. Once my buy order is filled, which ONE of the following best describes my position(s)?

    (a) Short 300 shares. Long 0 shares.

    (b) Short 200 shares. Long 100 shares.

    (c) Short 100 shares. Long 200 shares.

    (d) Short 0 shares. Long 100 shares.

    (e) Short 0 shares. Long 200 shares.

348. ◇ For this question, assume short-term interest rates are zero (that is not far wrong in the U.S. in 2021) and note that Amazon.com (AMZN) does not pay dividends. I describe Louis Bachelier's (1900) option pricing formula in *Basic Black-Scholes* (see the advertisements at the end of this book). It can be used as an approximation to the Black-Scholes formula for pricing at-the-money European-style options. Bachelier's formula is $c = p = \frac{S\sigma\sqrt{T-t}}{\sqrt{2\pi}}$. Suppose you are an options dealer, and you just got off the phone with a client who called you up to get a quote on a two-month at-the-money European-style option on AMZN stock. You quoted her a price of $10 per share. The phone rings again and she now wants a quote on an identical option, except that it is a three-month option. Roughly what price do you quote her? Assume nothing changes except the option maturity.

    (a) $12.25 per share.

    (b) $14.14 per share.

    (c) $15.00 per share.

    (d) $17.32 per share.

    (e) Not enough information is given to answer the question.

349. Which ONE of the following is a sensible statement?

    (a) The S&P 500 index is a tradeable asset.

    (b) The bid-ask spread on the S&P 500 index is very small compared with the bid-ask spread on the largest stock in the S&P/NZX50.

    (c) The stocks that trade on the S&P 500 stock exchange are typically the 500 largest stocks in the U.S.

    (d) The standard deviation of daily returns to the S&P 500 index is close to 1%.

    (e) The stocks in the S&P 500 index trade with wider spreads in N.Z. than in the U.S.

350. Benchmark timing happens when

    (a) My portfolio beta is equal to one.

    (b) My portfolio beta is not equal to one.

    (c) I create a portfolio that passively replicates the behavior of the benchmark index.

    (d) I create a portfolio that actively tries to beat the performance of the benchmark index via stock selection.

    (e) I hold the benchmark stocks and cash, but I impose the constraint that my portfolio beta equals one.

351. At the end of Chapter 2 of *Foundations*, we presented a figure for a proposed asset allocation model for an educated individual investor. Of the eight different allocations mentioned, four are the main "pillars" of the asset allocation model. Which ONE of the following was not one of those four?

    (a) Passive funds (e.g., ETFs or indexed mutual funds).

    (b) Physical real estate.

    (c) Funds in advantaged wrappers (often active).

    (d) Private equity (i.e., ownership of a small business).

    (e) Active funds run by skilled managers (e.g. Warren Buffett, managers in the Shanghai and Shenzhen A-shares market, small-cap fund managers in Australia, etc.).

352. Based on Merton (1980, 1992), we argued something about returns to stocks and trading strategies? Pick the ONE best answer.

    (a) It is difficult to estimate mean returns accurately.

    (b) The variance of returns is typically estimated more accurately than the mean of returns.

    (c) It can be difficult to reject the null hypothesis that the mean return is zero.

    (d) All of the above.

    (e) None of the above.

353. Tables 1.23 and 1.24 show the centralized limit order book (CLOB) for two S&P/NZX50 stocks on April 9, 2014. The stocks are Guinness Peat Group (GPG) and Westpac Banking Corporation (WBC), respectively. On this day, they were the lowest and highest priced members of the NZX50, respectively. Which ONE of the following is the best answer?

(a) GPG had a higher relative bid-ask spread than WBC.

(b) GPG had a lower relative bid-ask spread than WBC.

(c) The relative bid-ask spreads on these two stocks differ by a multiplicative factor of 100 (i.e., one is 100 times the other).

(d) Two of the above answers are true.

(e) None of the above answers is true.

Table 1.23: Centralized Limit Order Book for GPG NZ

The CLOB for Guinness Peat Group PLC from April 9, 2014. Source: ASB Securities, used with permission.

354. Table 1.24 shows the CLOB for S&P/NZX50 stock Westpac Banking Corporation (WBC) on April 9, 2014. Suppose you submit a market order to buy 1,000 shares of WBC, and that your order is the only order being sent in to be executed against the CLOB as shown in Table 1.24. What will you pay in total for the 1,000 shares? Please ignore any commissions or exchange fees.

(a) $36,343.25

(b) $36,500.00

(c) $37,000.00

(d) $37,283.70

(e) None of the above is correct.

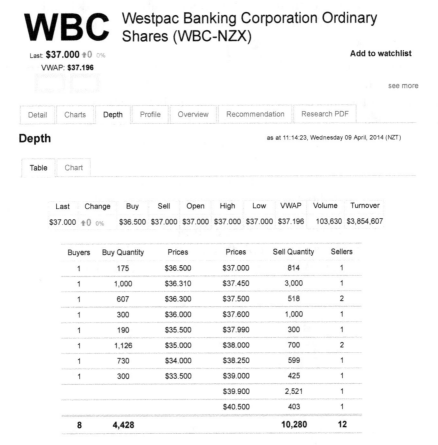

WBC
Westpac Banking Corporation Ordinary Shares (WBC-NZX)

Last: **$37.000** ↑0 0%
VWAP: **$37.196**

Add to watchlist

see more

| Detail | Charts | **Depth** | Profile | Overview | Recommendation | Research PDF |

Depth   as at 11:14:23, Wednesday 09 April, 2014 (NZT)

| Table | Chart |

Last	Change	Buy	Sell	Open	High	Low	VWAP	Volume	Turnover
$37.000 ↑0 0%		$36.500	$37.000	$37.000	$37.000	$37.000	$37.196	103,630	$3,854,607

Buyers	Buy Quantity	Prices	Prices	Sell Quantity	Sellers
1	175	$36.500	$37.000	814	1
1	1,000	$36.310	$37.450	3,000	1
1	607	$36.300	$37.500	518	2
1	300	$36.000	$37.600	1,000	1
1	190	$35.500	$37.990	300	1
1	1,126	$35.000	$38.000	700	2
1	730	$34.000	$38.250	599	1
1	300	$33.500	$39.000	425	1
			$39.900	2,521	1
			$40.500	403	1
8	**4,428**			**10,280**	**12**

Table 1.24: Centralized Limit Order Book for WBC NZ

The CLOB for Westpac Banking Corporation from April 9, 2014. Source: ASB Securities, used with permission.

355. At the end of Chapter 2 in *Foundations*, I gave six good reasons for investing in active funds. Which ONE of the following is NOT one of those six good reasons?

    (a) An active fund manager has very good recent performance, and you choose to invest in that fund because there is a better than a coin-toss probability of persistence in alpha.

    (b) You think that the portfolio manager is genuinely skilled at stock picking (e.g. Warren Buffett, managers in the Shanghai and Shenzhen A-shares market, small-cap fund managers in Australia, etc.).

    (c) Your employer offers you a retirement savings scheme with a menu of funds in a wrapper that is advantaged in some very attractive way (e.g., employer contributions, employer matches, government matches, tax deferral). The menu of funds includes cash and active products, but does not include any passive funds or ETFs.

    (d) You want exposure to benchmark risk in some region, perhaps across borders. No passive fund or ETF exists yet that invests in that region. Active managers, however, run medium-cost funds investing in that region (they are attracted by the fee income). So, you buy into the active fund.

    (e) You want exposure to benchmark risk in some region, typically across borders. You are not legally allowed to trade funds directly in that region, but a local trading platform gives you access to low-cost active funds that invest in that region, so you hold those active funds to get the benchmark exposure.

356. A new firm has an IPO of equity to raise \$10M. They also borrow \$10M from the bank. They buy \$15M in physical plant, and put \$5.0M into cash not immediately needed to run the firm. What is the enterprise value (EV) for this firm?

    (a) \$10.0M.

    (b) \$12.5M.

    (c) \$15.0M.

    (d) \$17.5M.

    (e) \$20.0M.

357. In Question 3.2.1 and Question 3.2.2 you have to calculate the beta of a stock using the formula $\beta_i = \frac{\vec{h}_i' V \vec{h}_B}{\vec{h}_B' V \vec{h}_B}$. What was $\vec{h}_i$ in that context?

    (a) $\vec{h}_i$ was a column vector of ones.

    (b) $\vec{h}_i$ was a row vector of ones.

    (c) $\vec{h}_i$ was a column vector of zeroes.

    (d) $\vec{h}_i$ was a row vector of zeroes.

    (e) None of the above is correct.

358. When discussing Merton's random walk model, we introduced estimators of annual mean and variance of returns based on sub-interval (e.g., daily) returns. The estimator $\hat{\mu}$ of the annual mean return μ had expected value μ (i.e., $\hat{\mu}$ is unbiased) and variance σ^2 (i.e., the uncertainty in our estimator $\hat{\mu}$ does not change as we sample our data more finely). What is the standard error of our estimator $\hat{\mu}$?

    (a) μ

    (b) σ

    (c) $\frac{\sigma}{\sqrt{N}}$

    (d) $\frac{\sigma^2}{N}$

    (e) None of the above is correct, or there is insufficient information given to answer this question.

359. **Benefit of an extra 1% return when depositing a growing annuity.** John and Mary are identical twins. They get jobs at competing financial firms earning identical salaries. John and Mary each deposit an identical growing annuity of annual payments to their respective retirement savings schemes. The growth rate in their dollar deposits is $g = 5\%$ per annum. They make their first deposit at $t = 1$, and their last deposit at $t = 50$ (a total of 50 annual deposits). John earns a steady $R = 7.5\%$ per annum in his scheme. Mary earns a steady $R = 8.5\%$ per annum in her scheme. What is the ratio of Mary's ending balance (at $t = 50$) to John's ending balance (at $t = 50$)? Round the ratio to three decimal places.

    (a) 0.832

    (b) 1.322

    (c) 1.416

    (d) 1.633

    (e) 1.589

360. It is Bebe Nouveaune's 65th birthday today. She has accumulated $2,000,000 retirement savings exactly. She wants to withdraw this money in the form of a growing annuity due, with annual withdrawals starting today. She is planning that her last withdrawal will be on her 95th birthday. She expects to earn $R = 5\%$ per annum in her investment account, and she wants the dollar amount of her annual withdrawals to grow at $g = 3\%$ per annum. How much is her withdrawal today?

    (a) $84,828.83

    (b) $86,898.81

    (c) $89,070.27

    (d) $91,243.75

    (e) None of the above is correct.

361. Why did we neutralize the alphas we fed into the active alpha optimization?

   (a) So that all alphas were on the same scale as each other (i.e., standardized).

   (b) So that any very large alpha values get reduced in size (i.e., $-3 \leq \alpha \leq +3$).

   (c) So that the alphas would neither swamp the other elements of the objective function, nor be swamped by the other elements of the objective function.

   (d) So that the alphas were on the same scale as the returns to the benchmark.

   (e) So that the chasing of alphas would go hand-in-hand with stepping away from the benchmark.

362. A classmate has suggested the following parameterization of the active alpha objective function from Question 3.2.2, but there may be a mistake in it. If there is a mistake, I want you to tell me where the mistake is. All notation is as used in *Foundations*.

$$
\begin{aligned}
RTAA &= \alpha_P - \lambda \omega_P^2 - TC \\
&= \underbrace{\vec{h}_P' \vec{\alpha}}_{A} - \lambda \underbrace{\left[\vec{h}_P' V \vec{h}_P - \vec{h}_B' V \vec{h}_B \right]}_{B} - \underbrace{F \cdot \frac{1}{2}}_{C} \underbrace{\left| \vec{h}_B - \vec{h}_P \right|' \vec{\gamma}}_{D}
\end{aligned}
$$

   (a) The mistake is in A.

   (b) The mistake is in B.

   (c) The mistake is in C.

   (d) The mistake is in D.

   (e) It is Okay. There is no mistake.

363. Today is Bruce's birthday. Bruce is 61 years old. Bruce already has $20 million in the bank (he is a famous former U.S. Olympic athlete). The life expectancy for a 61 year U.S. old male is almost exactly 20 years. Bruce has too much money saved up. So, he has decided to give all his money to charity except for just enough to buy an annuity. Bruce wants to buy an annuity that will make a payment to him today (to live on over the next year). He then wants a payment a year from now, and then a payment on every birthday up to and including his 81st birthday 20 years from now. If Bruce wants to get a $200,000 payment on each birthday starting today, how much money does he need to spend today to buy the annuity if the interest rate is 6% per annum? Round to the nearest dollar.

   (a) $2,493,984

   (b) $2,431,623

   (c) $2,352,815

   (d) $2,293,984

   (e) None of the above answers is correct.

364. Ezra, Collie, and Smith (2009), in their book *The Retirement Plan Solution*, say that for a defined contribution retiree at age 65 who started saving at age 25, we can apply the 10/30/60 rule. Those proportions mean which ONE of the following?

    (a) If you contribute 10% of your savings to a retirement savings scheme, then you can retire and take a comfortable 30-year growing annuity starting at age 60.

    (b) The sum of contributions to your retirement savings scheme are typically made 10% from relatives, 30% from your personal contributions, and 60% from government/employer matches.

    (c) The sum of withdrawals from your retirement savings scheme are typically attributed 10% to relatives, 30% to your personal contributions, and 60% to government/employer matches.

    (d) The sum of withdrawals from your retirement savings are generated 10% by payments into the scheme, 30% by investment earnings before retirement, and 60% by investment earnings after retirement.

    (e) None of the above is correct.

365. Equity holders provide internal equity and hold a direct ownership interest in a firm; Debt holders provide external equity and hold a conditional ownership interest in the firm. Enterprise value is what? Choose the ONE best answer.

    (a) The market capitalization of the company.

    (b) The net cost to you of buying up all the stock of a company at current market prices.

    (c) The net cost to you of buying up all the bonds of a company at current market prices.

    (d) The net cost to you of buying up all the debt of a company at current market prices.

    (e) The net cost to you of buying up all the ownership interests of a company at current market prices.

366. If you were to download a recent year's daily data on the few smallest-capitalization stocks in New Zealand, you would expect their average closing relative bid-ask spread (assuming it exists) to be in the range...

    (a) 5–15 bps.

    (b) 20–65 bps.

    (c) 65–120 bps.

    (d) 120–250 bps.

    (e) Over 250 bps.

367. ◇◇ It is July 2017. Three years ago you signed up for a KiwiSaver fund that required only a $20 per week deposit from you and no initial deposit. You got your $1,000 kick-start [old rules] almost immediately. You deposited $20 per week for three years. At the end of each year the government deposited to your account a half-matching tax credit of $52 \times \$10 = \$520$. So, you got three of these matches so far. The fund was a conservative cash fund that paid an effective annual rate (EAR) of 5% per annum like a bank account, but with weekly compounding.

Your deposits triggered the kick-start and tax credits to parachute into your account. Thus, you have earned more than someone putting $20 per week into a bank account yielding the same 5% per annum. So, roughly what was your actual EAR, accounting correctly for the kick-start and the tax credit? We called this rate a benefit-adjusted EAR (BEAR) in *Foundations*.

(a) 5% per annum.

(b) 10% per annum.

(c) 25% per annum.

(d) 50% per annum.

(e) 75% per annum.

368. An exchange-traded fund (ETF) is ALWAYS what?

(a) A fund tracks a passive index of stocks.

(b) A fund that is very liquid with a very low expense ratio.

(c) A fund that is well diversified.

(d) Each of the above is always true.

(e) None of the above is always true.

369. In Chapter 2 of Foundations we discussed the CAPM, $E(R) = R_F + \beta[E(R_M) - R_F]$, and the market model, $R - R_F = \alpha + \beta(R_M - R_F) + \epsilon$ (where, in practice, we proxy for M). What was the distinction between these two models?

(a) The CAPM is a forward looking theoretical model of expected returns whereas the market model is estimated using historical data.

(b) The structure of the β in the CAPM is not consistent with the structure of the β being estimated by the market model.

(c) The CAPM is a model of the first moment of returns whereas the market model is a model of the second moment of returns.

(d) The CAPM is not a risk model whereas the market model is a simple risk model (i.e., a single index model).

(e) The CAPM is a model of consensus returns, whereas the market model is a model of non-consensus returns used as a basis for our active alpha optimization.

370. In Chapter 2 of *Foundations* we looked at the convergence of the sample mean estimator and the sample standard deviation estimator when sampling from a standard Cauchy distribution ($C = \frac{Z_1}{Z_2}$ for independent standard normal distributions Z_1 and Z_2). These estimators did not converge because...

    (a) The tails of the standard Cauchy distribution are too fat for the population mean and population standard deviation to exist in the first place.

    (b) As we sampled, sometimes a very small observation in the denominator of the $\frac{Z_1}{Z_2}$ ratio would cause the ratio to be very large, which stops the estimators converging.

    (c) The law of large numbers (i.e., either SLLN, or WLLN) does not apply because the assumptions of that law are violated.

    (d) The standard Cauchy distribution is sufficiently il-behaved that if we slice up the pdf into slices of probability mass, and look at the sum of $x_i \cdot p_i$, to try to find the mean for example, this summation does not converge when the number of slices gets big. Similarly for the variance or standard deviation.

    (e) All of the above.

371. You collect a sample of recent dividend payout ratios (DPRs) on the S&P 500 stocks. You find that $N = 382$ of the stocks had positive earnings, and for these stocks the sample average DPR was 0.722 (i.e., just under three quarters of net income was paid out as dividends). The sample standard deviation was 0.978. What is the value to three decimal places of the t-statistic to test the null hypothesis that the average DPR is 100%?

    (a) 14.429

    (b) -5.681

    (c) -5.556

    (d) -5.548

    (e) 0.293

372. When conducting a numerical optimization (e.g., the active alpha optimization problem in Question 3.2.2), you need to launch your optimization from different starting points. Why is this?

    (a) Using a grid search is time consuming in high-dimension problems.

    (b) Analytical solutions may be required when the objective function or the constraints are complex.

    (c) The addition of inequality constraints can make an otherwise simple analytical optimization infeasible.

    (d) Local maxima or minima can confuse the numerical optimizer.

    (e) Once binding constraints are added to an optimization problem, the solution region becomes smaller.

373. Table 1.25 shows the centralized limit order book (CLOB) for SPK on March 5, 2015. Please tell me the relative bid-ask spread, in bps, using absolute spread divided by mid-spread value. Note that the answers below may be rounded.

    (a) 6.1 bps

    (b) 61.3 bps

    (c) 2 bps

    (d) $0.02

    (e) 200 bps

374. Table 1.25 shows the CLOB for SPK on March 5, 2015. Suppose that these prices and quantities are available to you now. Suppose that you submit a market order to sell 5,000 shares of SPK, and that your order is the only order being sent in to be executed against the CLOB as shown in Table 1.25. What will your sales proceeds be? Please ignore any commissions or exchange fees.

    (a) $16,250

    (b) $16,300

    (c) $16,350

    (d) Less than any of the above numbers.

    (e) More than any of the above numbers.

375. Table 1.25 shows the CLOB for SPK on March 5, 2015. Suppose that these prices and quantities are available to you now. Suppose that you submit a limit order to sell 5,000 shares of SPK at $3.26, and that your order is the only order being sent in today to be executed against the CLOB as shown in Table 1.25. What will your sales proceeds be eventually? Please ignore any commissions or exchange fees.

    (a) $16,250

    (b) $16,300

    (c) $16,350

    (d) We cannot say for sure.

    (e) None of the above is correct.

376. The average closing relative bid-ask spreads of the 20 New Zealand stocks in Question 3.2.2 varied from roughly what minimum to roughly what maximum?

    (a) 4 bps to 1040 bps.

    (b) 12 bps to 56 bps.

    (c) 32 bps to 1327 bps.

    (d) 55 bps to 120 bps.

    (e) 75 bps to 345 bps.

SPK Spark New Zealand Limited Ordinary Shares (SPK-NZX)

Last: **$3.250** ⬇4 1.2%

VWAP: **$3.279**

Sector: Telecommunication Services   **Add to watchlist**

Spark New Zealand Limited (SPK-NZ, formerly Telecom Corporation of New Zealand Limited) is a NZ telecommunications service provider, offering a range of services and products to consumers and businesses. The Company operates the followin... see more

Detail   Charts   **Depth**   Profile   Overview   Recommendation   Research PDF

Depth   as at 10:00:31, Thursday 05 March, 2015 (NZDT)

Table   Chart

Last	Change	Buy	Sell	Open	High	Low	VWAP	Volume	Turnover
$3.250	⬇4 1.2%	$3.250	$3.270	$3.250	$3.250	$3.250	$3.279	620,722	$2,035,481

Buyers	Buy Quantity	Prices	Prices	Sell Quantity	Sellers
3	23,136	$3.250	$3.270	57,013	2
1	10,000	$3.205	$3.290	1,000	1
2	64,996	$3.200	$3.300	39,940	4
1	2,936	$3.160	$3.305	5,385	1
1	5,000	$3.125	$3.310	20,000	1
2	27,500	$3.120	$3.320	10,100	2
3	12,500	$3.100	$3.330	20,100	2
1	9,850	$3.095	$3.335	18,857	1
1	3,250	$3.080	$3.340	18,000	3
1	3,252	$3.075	$3.345	9,200	1
16	**162,420**			**199,595**	**18**

The trading and pricing information that appears on this website is provided by the New Zealand Exchange, the Australian Stock Exchange and Chi-X Australia, and is subject to contractual arrangements that expressly prohibit the redistribution of such trading and pricing information. Any redistribution, by any party, constitutes a breach of the Internet Access Terms applying to this website.

Table 1.25: Centralized Limit Order Book for SPK NZ

The CLOB for Spark from March 5, 2015. All prices are in cents per share. Source: ASB Securities, used with permission.

377. In Question 3.2.1 you calculated betas for your stocks relative to the benchmark portfolio B and relative to the tangency portfolio T. Mean returns for the stocks were calculated for you already. You then plotted the betas versus the mean returns. Were you testing the CAPM and what did you find?

    (a) Yes, we were testing the CAPM, and we found that it held for betas relative to T but not for betas relative to B.

    (b) Yes, we were testing the CAPM, and we found that it held for betas relative to B but not for betas relative to T.

    (c) Yes, we were testing the CAPM, and it held for both sets of betas, but perfectly for the betas relative to T and imperfectly for the betas relative to B.

    (d) Yes, we were testing the CAPM, and it held for both sets of betas, but perfectly for the betas relative B and imperfectly for the betas relative to T.

    (e) No, we were not testing the CAPM.

378. The difference between strategic and tactical asset allocation is which ONE of the following?

    (a) Strategic asset allocation is about the high-level decision making (e.g., by the board of trustees of a pension plan), but tactical asset allocation is the day-to-day decision making by the portfolio managers.

    (b) Strategic asset allocation is about choosing beta risk, but tactical asset allocation is about choosing alpha risk.

    (c) Tactical asset allocation is about the high-level decision making (e.g., by the board of trustees of a pension plan), but strategic asset allocation is the day-to-day decision making by the portfolio managers.

    (d) Tactical asset allocation is about choosing beta risk, but strategic asset allocation is about choosing alpha risk.

    (e) (a) and (b) are correct, but neither (c) nor (d) is correct.

379. Suppose that $\vec{h}_P$ and $\vec{h}_I$ are vectors of holdings in an N-stock portfolio P and an N-stock index I, respectively. Suppose the returns to the N stocks are $\vec{R}$ and that $V = V(\vec{R})$ is the variance-covariance matrix of the returns to the stocks. The beta of portfolio P with respect to index I is given by which formula?

    (a) $\vec{h}_P' V \vec{h}_P \big/ \vec{h}_I' V \vec{h}_I$

    (b) $\vec{h}_P' V \vec{h}_I \big/ \vec{h}_I' V \vec{h}_I$

    (c) $\vec{h}_P' V \vec{h}_P \big/ \vec{h}_P' V \vec{h}_P$

    (d) $\vec{h}_P' V \vec{h}_I \big/ \vec{h}_P' V \vec{h}_P$

    (e) $\vec{h}_I' V \vec{h}_I \big/ \vec{h}_P' V \vec{h}_I$

380. Your brokerage screen says that you are long 200 shares of MSFT stock. This is your only position. You want to submit an order or orders to change this so that your brokerage screen says that you short 100 shares of MSFT stock, and that this is your only position. What order or orders should you submit?

    (a) Sell 300 shares of MSFT.
    (b) Short sell 300 shares of MSFT.
    (c) Sell 200 shares of MSFT and then short sell 100 shares of MSFT.
    (d) Buy to cover 200 shares of MSFT and then sell 100 shares of MSFT.
    (e) None of the above is correct.

381. The analytical solution to the Markowitz problem in Question 3.2.1 allowed you to plot a tangency portfolio T. Can T contain any short positions?

    (a) No, because T is on the Markowitz frontier and assets on the Markowitz frontier do not involve short selling.
    (b) No, because T is fully invested.
    (c) No, because assets on the Tobin frontier do not involve short selling.
    (d) Yes, because there is no constraint on short selling in either the Markowitz or Tobin frontiers.
    (e) None of the above is true.

382. Your portfolio of automobile stocks is worth $100,000. You sell $20,000 worth of holdings and use the proceeds to buy $20,000 worth of airline stocks. What is your one-sided turnover? Ignore all transaction costs and taxes.

    (a) 10%
    (b) 20%
    (c) 40%
    (d) 80%
    (e) None of the above is correct.

383. In exploring candidate objective functions for our active alpha optimization, we decided that we needed to break the total risk and total return down into several component parts. Why did we break return and risk into component parts?

    (a) Because our client is likely to have differing degrees of risk aversion toward the different components of risk.
    (b) Because we wanted to distinguish between skilled and unskilled forecasts of risk and return.
    (c) Because we decided that benchmark timing was likely to be futile.
    (d) Because benchmark risk and return are not a function of our choice variables.
    (e) None of the above is true.

384. ◇ In Figure 1.20, the tangency portfolio T is not the optimum (but portfolio P^* is) because T takes on too much active risk for our client. Higher risk aversion pushes the optimum P^* toward the origin, and lower risk aversion pushes the optimum P^* away from the origin. So, would T be the optimum for a risk-neutral client (i.e., one for whom $\lambda = 0$)?

(a) Yes, because the risk-neutral client is not worried about the extra risk in portfolio T.

(b) Yes, because in this case the client has the same risk aversion (i.e., zero) with respect to each source or risk (i.e., benchmark, benchmark timing, and stock selection), and so treating these risks with an even hand (i.e., the same λ) leads to T as the optimum.

(c) Yes, because in this case the iso-utility curves (in fact they are iso-objective function curves) will just touch the budget constraint at T.

(d) All of the above.

(e) None of the above.

385. It is Bebe Nouveaune's 65th birthday today. She has accumulated \$1,500,000 retirement savings exactly. She wants to withdraw this money in the form of a growing annuity due, with annual withdrawals starting today. She is planning that her last withdrawal will be on her 90th birthday. She expects to earn $R = 6\%$ per annum in her investment account, and she wants the dollar amount of her annual withdrawals to grow at $g = 4\%$ per annum. How much is her withdrawal today? There may be some rounding error in my answer.

(a) \$45,007.88

(b) \$72,460.56

(c) \$74,702.01

(d) \$76,808.19

(e) \$79,184.13

386. Suppose I estimate the traditional sample VCV for the S&P 100 (i.e., an index with approximately 100 stocks) using four months of daily returns data on the stocks. In this case, which ONE of the following is the best answer.

(a) The VCV will be estimable (i.e., I can estimate each element of the matrix) and the VCV will be invertible (i.e., its inverse exists and $V \cdot V^{-1} = I$).

(b) The VCV will be estimable but the VCV will not be invertible.

(c) The VCV will be estimable but not enough information is given to conclude whether the VCV will be invertible.

(d) The VCV will be neither estimable nor invertible.

(e) None of the above is correct.

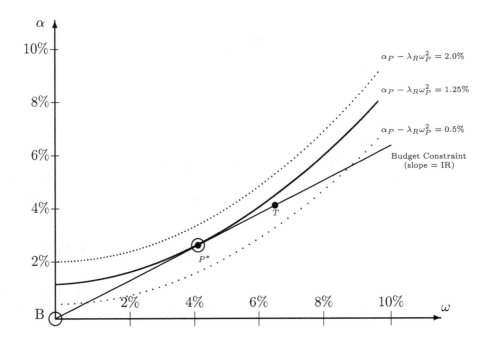

Figure 1.20: Optimization in Active Space

Kahn (1998) says that we may think of the IR of a portfolio manager as a fundamental constant defining the manager. This provides a budget constraint. The budget constraint $IR = \frac{\alpha}{\omega}$ (or $\alpha = IR \cdot \omega$) is plotted here for a manager with an IR of slightly greater than 0.60. "T" is a portfolio that maximizes the skilled Sharpe ratio in total-return-total risk-space. Three parabolas of iso-utility (actually iso-values of the RAA objective function) are shown: $\alpha_P = 0.5\% + \lambda_R \cdot \omega_P^2$, $\alpha_P = 1.25\% + \lambda_R \cdot \omega_P^2$, and $\alpha_P = 2.0\% + \lambda_R \cdot \omega_P^2$. The optimal portfolio P^* is on the straight-line budget constraint, and has the highest possible value of the RAA objective function.

387. Suppose I have one year of price data on the NZD/USD exchange rate, observed every millisecond. Suppose I want to estimate the annual mean return and annual variance of returns to an N.Z. investor buying and holding USD. Then, as we move to higher frequency data (e.g., from monthly to weekly to daily data), the accuracy of the estimator of the annual mean return [does what?] and the accuracy of the estimator of the annual variance of returns [does what?].

    (a) Increases and increases, respectively.

    (b) Increases and decreases, respectively.

    (c) Decreases and increases, respectively.

    (d) Decreases and decreases, respectively.

    (e) None of the above is correct.

388. In Question 3.2.2 (the active alpha optimization) we used both the sample VCV and the Ledoit-Wolf (2004) VCV with a shrinkage target equal to the constant-correlation model. What happens to the diagonal terms of the VCV matrix (i.e., the estimated variances) when we flip from using the sample VCV to using the Ledoit-Wolf (2004) VCV?

    (a) Nothing happens. The variances are the same as those used in the sample VCV matrix.

    (b) The variances are replaced with new, typically different, variances that are constructed assuming all pairs of stocks have the same correlation between their returns.

    (c) We end up with an average of the sample VCV variances and new, typically different, variances constructed assuming all pairs of stocks have the same correlation between their returns.

    (d) We shrink the variances toward a common mean, so that the largest variances are reduced in size and the smallest variances are increased in size.

    (e) None of the above is correct.

389. An "enhanced passive" strategy can be...

    (a) Truly passive indexing, where the manager is just trying to match the benchmark.

    (b) A passive strategy using smart trading that seeks as little as 10 bps alpha per annum.

    (c) An active strategy, but with a tight benchmark and seeking only 50–200 bps alpha per annum.

    (d) An aggressive strategy seeking 500+ bps alpha per annum, for example, at an aggressive hedge fund.

    (e) More than one of the above.

390. The quotes (i.e., the bid and ask prices) for CMO at 2:00PM on Friday April 1, 2016 were \$6.25–\$6.34. How big is the relative spread using our usual definition? Allow for some rounding in the answer.

    (a) \$0.09
    (b) 0.714853%
    (c) 1.419558%
    (d) 1.429706%
    (e) 1.440000%

391. Regarding the empirical security market line (SML), the Roll critique (1977) of tests of the CAPM says that in any test of the CAPM that plots mean returns against betas, an index portfolio (against which betas are calculated) can be chosen so that...

    (a) The empirical SML is linear.
    (b) The empirical SML is not linear.
    (c) The index portfolio is ex-post mean-variance efficient.
    (d) Each of the above is individually true.
    (e) None of the above is correct.

392. The Ledoit-Wolf (2004) VCV estimator takes an average of a very structured VCV estimator (denoted $\mathcal{F}$) and the sample VCV estimator (denoted $\mathcal{S}$). Which of the following is true.

    (a) $\mathcal{F}$ has lots of specification error; $\mathcal{S}$ has lots of specification error.
    (b) $\mathcal{F}$ has lots of specification error; $\mathcal{S}$ has lots of statistical estimation error.
    (c) $\mathcal{F}$ has lots of statistical estimation error; $\mathcal{S}$ has lots of specification error.
    (d) $\mathcal{F}$ has lots of statistical estimation error; $\mathcal{S}$ has lots of statistical estimation error.
    (e) None of the above is correct.

393. In a CLOB-driven market, a "marketable limit order" is one that...

    (a) Already resides deep in the CLOB, away from the current best quotes, waiting to be executed against incoming market orders.
    (b) Already resides in the CLOB at either the best bid or best ask, waiting to be executed against the next incoming market order.
    (c) Is immediately executable against incoming market orders in the CLOB.
    (d) Is immediately executable against existing limit orders in the CLOB.
    (e) Is a new limit order, just submitted, that will now sit at the top of the order book as either the new best ask or the new best bid (that is, it uses price priority to jump ahead of all existing limit orders on one side of the book).

394. P/E ratios are open to manipulation/mis-interpretation because they are sensitive to gearing. So, to overcome this we can instead compare firms using a capital-structure-neutral ratio like what?

    (a) Earnings yield (i.e., E/P).

    (b) P/EBITDA.

    (c) EV/EBITDA.

    (d) EV/revenue.

    (e) Either (c) or (d).

395. Assume that $\vec{h}$ is an $N \times 1$ column vector of holdings in a portfolio and $\vec{\mu}$ is an $N \times 1$ column vector of expected returns. Which of the following is the only one that is both conformal and has a simple sensible economic interpretation?

    (a) $\vec{h}\vec{\mu}$

    (b) $\vec{h}'\vec{\mu}$

    (c) $\vec{h}\vec{\mu}'$

    (d) $\vec{h}'\vec{\mu}'$

    (e) None of the above.

396. Suppose I am looking at a stock and trying to decide whether to invest in it. It pays no dividends. Suppose its P/E ratio is only 8, and the P/E ratio for the market as a whole is 20. Which of the following is the most sensible next step?

    (a) Buy it because that is a great P/E ratio.

    (b) Avoid it because that is a terrible P/E ratio.

    (c) Compare this stock's growth rate in earnings to the P/E ratio of the market.

    (d) Compare this stock's P/E ratio with the P/E ratios of all other stocks in the same industry.

    (e) Compare this stock's P/E ratio with the P/E ratios of other stocks in the same industry, but only if they have a similar level of gearing.

397. The growth in the value of an investment can be expressed using a simple net return (SNR), a simple gross return (SGR), or a continuously-compounded return (CCR). Which ONE of the following statements about these returns is FALSE?

    (a) Adding SNRs can give results that are not economically meaningful.

    (b) If you annualize the arithmetic average of a time series of daily SNRs, the answer is biased downwards relative to realized economic return.

    (c) SGR=1+SNR.

    (d) SGRs compound using multiplication.

    (e) CCRs compound using addition.

398. ◇ A mid-2016 news story reported that the average house price in Auckland N.Z. was \$1,003,144. Assume that a couple have saved a 20% deposit and want to borrow the balance to buy an average Auckland house at this price. Assume the mortgage interest rate is an APR of 6% per annum with monthly compounding (i.e., monthly repayments). Assume a 30-year fixed rate table mortgage (i.e., a level ordinary annuity of repayments). If the first monthly payment must not exceed 28% of the couple's first month's gross income (i.e., before taxes), what minimum annual gross income (taken as 12× the monthly gross income) must the couple be earning? My answers are rounded to the nearest dollar.

(a) \$202,705

(b) \$206,206

(c) \$208,221

(d) \$257,758

(e) None of the above.

399. Suppose you purchase \$10,000 worth of an NZ stock using a 60% margin lending ratio. That is, you use \$4,000 of your own money and \$6,000 borrowed from your broker. Suppose terrible news arrives and the stock immediately falls 50%, and you sell in a panic. What is your rate of return on the transaction? Ignore bid-ask spreads, commissions, exchange fees, and margin interest.

(a) -50%

(b) -60%

(c) -100%

(d) -125%

(e) None of the above is correct.

400. When trying to derive an objective function for our active alpha optimization, we arrived at Equation 1.8 as an intermediary step.

$$OBJ2 = \overbrace{[\kappa_B - \lambda_B\sigma_B^2]}^{\text{benchmark}} + \overbrace{[(\beta_P - 1)(\mu_B + \delta_B) - \lambda_{BT}(\beta_P^2 - 1)\sigma_B^2]}^{\text{benchmark timing}} + \overbrace{[\alpha_P - \lambda_R\omega_P^2]}^{\text{stock selection}}$$
(1.8)

We argued that we could discard the middle term because we are not doing any benchmark timing, but why did we decide to not do any benchmark timing?

(a) Because we fixed β_P equal to 1.

(b) Because the middle term uses benchmark weights rather than our portfolio weights, and is therefore not a function of our choice variables.

(c) Because the benchmark contains too much breadth.

(d) Because practitioners told us that it is futile to try to time the benchmark.

(e) Because λ_{BT} is near zero.

401. In the objective function of the active alpha optimization, the penalties on active risk and T-costs mean that...

    (a) Even a high-alpha stock might not be over-weighted (e.g., if its T-costs are very high).

    (b) We tend to trade less in smaller-capitalization stocks than we would without the penalties.

    (c) Our turnover is lower than it would be without the penalties.

    (d) All of the above.

    (e) None of the above is correct.

402. In his book *One Up on Wall Street* (Lynch and Rothchild, 2000), the famous former fund manager Peter Lynch classifies stocks as slow growers, stalwarts, or fast growers, depending upon the growth rate in their earnings per share (EPS). These classifications correspond to growth rates in EPS of what, respectively?

    (a) 1–2%, 3–5%, and 6–10%, per annum, respectively.

    (b) 1–5%, 5–10%, and 7–15%, per annum, respectively.

    (c) 2–4%, 10–12%, and 20–25%, per annum, respectively.

    (d) 5–10%, 20–30%, and 50–100%, per annum, respectively.

    (e) 0–20%, 20–50%, and 50–200%, per annum, respectively.

403. In *Foundations*, we said that with $\beta_P = 1$, the ex-ante information ratio (IR) is in fact a "Sharpe ratio in active space." What does this statement mean?

    (a) $IR = \frac{\alpha}{\omega}$ where α and ω are the stock selection components of return and risk.

    (b) $IR = \frac{E_{\text{skilled}}(R_P - R_F)}{\sqrt{V(R_P - R_F)}}$ where R_F is the riskless rate.

    (c) $IR = \frac{E_{\text{skilled}}(R_P - R_B)}{\sqrt{V(R_P - R_B)}}$ where R_B is the benchmark return.

    (d) (a) and (b) are correct.

    (e) (a) and (c) are correct.

404. The "market cap" (i.e., market capitalization) of a corporation is usually defined as what?

    (a) The market value of the assets of the corporation.

    (b) Stock price times average daily volume of shares traded.

    (c) The market value of the equity of the corporation.

    (d) The market value of the whole stock market.

    (e) The weight of the stock in the benchmark index.

405. In an interview with the late Jack Bogle, he says that his colleague "Raymond" told him "everything you need to know if you are going to go into the investment business" in just a few words.[3] What were those few words?

    (a) ABC: Always be closing.

    (b) And then what?

    (c) Margin of safety.

    (d) Nobody knows nothing.

    (e) Diversify, buy-and-hold, rebalance.

    (f) Return, risk, fees, liquidity, horizon.

406. The "Fundamental Law of Active Management" says that if we halve the number of independent forecasts of active return we make during a year (e.g., by halving the number of stocks we cover), our information ratio (IR) will roughly:

    (a) be multiplied by 4.

    (b) be multiplied by 2.

    (c) be multiplied by 0.71.

    (d) be multiplied by 0.50.

    (e) stay the same.

407. Nancy Tengler from Heartland Financial, USA, gave a "market monitor" interview on Nightly Business Report on March 3, 2017.[4] What were the common characteristics of the several stocks she thought were attractively priced?

    (a) They pay a dividend yield just below the yield on the S&P 500, their P/E ratios are greater than the P/E on the broad market, and their growth rate in earnings or in dividends is slower than that of the broad market.

    (b) They pay a dividend yield just above the yield on the S&P 500, their P/E ratios are greater than the P/E on the broad market, and their growth rate in earnings or in dividends is faster than that of the broad market.

    (c) They pay a dividend yield just above the yield on the S&P 500, their P/E ratios are less than the P/E on the broad market, and their growth rate in earnings or in dividends is faster than that of the broad market.

    (d) They pay a dividend yield just below the yield on the S&P 500, their P/E ratios are greater than the P/E on the broad market, and their growth rate in earnings or in dividends is faster than that of the broad market.

    (e) They pay a dividend yield just above the yield on the S&P 500, their P/E ratios are less than the P/E on the broad market, and their growth rate in earnings or in dividends is slower than that of the broad market.

---

[3] Available at: `https://www.youtube.com/watch?v=A0gQizOpCyI`

[4] Available at: `http://nbr.com/2017/03/03/nightly-business-report-march-3-2017/` (Go to the 18:25 mark)

408. In the Markowitz optimization in Question 3.2.1, the benchmark portfolio plots just inside the minimum variance frontier of risky assets and has noticeably less risk than any individual stock. The benchmark portfolio has much less risk than any individual stock because of what?

    (a) The benchmark portfolio has greatest weight in the least risky stocks, and this is reflected in the low risk of the benchmark.

    (b) The benchmark portfolio implicitly includes a partial investment in the riskless asset and this reduces its riskiness.

    (c) The benchmark portfolio has a higher ratio of return per unit risk than any other risky asset that was available.

    (d) The Markowitz optimization is all about reducing risk, and this is reflected in the benchmark.

    (e) The benefits of diversification give the benchmark portfolio its low risk.

409. You submit a market order to buy large-capitalization stock FBU on the NZX. Your order is executed. At the execution you pay a commission and you give up part of the bid-ask spread. Identify who earns the commission you pay, and who earns the portion of the bid-ask spread you give up, respectively. Please ignore the NZX fee. Please also ignore any "marriage" trades where the broker is beneficial owner of the stocks sold (which we did not discuss in *Foundations* but you might have seen elsewhere).

    (a) Your brokerage house and the designated market maker, respectively.

    (b) Your brokerage house and another customer with a market order to sell, respectively.

    (c) A designated market maker and the NZX, respectively.

    (d) Your brokerage house and another customer with a limit order to sell, respectively.

    (e) Your brokerage house gets both.

410. I calculated P/E ratios for NZX All Share stocks at the end of 2016. Of the 117 stocks in the index, how many stocks do you think had valid P/E ratios that are positive numbers and less than 300?

    (a) 10 stocks.

    (b) 25 stocks.

    (c) 40 stocks.

    (d) 70 stocks.

    (e) 110 stocks.

411. One of your classmates has suggested the following parameterization of the active alpha objective function from Question 3.2.2, but there is a mistake in it. I want you to tell me where the mistake is.

$$
\begin{aligned}
RTAA &= \alpha_P - \lambda \omega_P^2 - TC \\
&= \underbrace{\vec{h}_P' \vec{\alpha}}_{A} - \lambda \underbrace{\left[\vec{h}_P' V \vec{h}_P - \vec{h}_B' V \vec{h}_B\right]^2}_{B} - \underbrace{\frac{1}{2}}_{C} \underbrace{\left|\vec{h}_P - \vec{h}_B\right|'}_{D} \underbrace{\vec{\gamma}}_{E}
\end{aligned}
$$

(a) The mistake is in A.

(b) The mistake is in B.

(c) The mistake is in C.

(d) The mistake is in D.

(e) The mistake is in E.

412. Which of the following is a current example of a "call market" on the NZX?

(a) The NZX is called to trade at 10A.M. for 30 minutes, and again at 3P.M. for 30 minutes.

(b) The NZX is open for regular trade from 10A.M. to 5P.M.

(c) The NZX allows off-market trades, using prices from the on-market order book trades. During regular trading hours, these trades take place at or within the quotes from the on-market limit order book. The counterparties are typically institutions or high-net-worth individuals.

(d) The NZX introduced an options market on individual stocks in April 2015. These options include call options and put options on Fletcher Building (FBU), Spark (SPK), and Trade Me (TME).

(e) The NZX usually has a brief call auction at the beginning of each day, and at the end of each day, when order imbalances are settled against each other and a market-clearing price is determined.

413. Which of the following attributes would a quantitative portfolio manager be most likely to associate with a value stock? To avoid any ambiguity, in each case assume (somewhat unrealistically) that the comparison is with similarly-levered stocks at the same point in time, in the same industry, and at the same point in their life cycle.

(a) A relatively high P/E ratio.

(b) A relatively high dividend yield.

(c) A relatively high market-to-book ratio (i.e., market value of equity divided by book value of equity).

(d) A relatively high P/CF ratio (i.e., price to cash flow).

(e) A relatively high price-to-sales ratio.

414. Suppose that in an active alpha optimization we compare use of the sample VCV and the Ledoit-Wolf (2004) VCV (with a shrinkage target equal to the constant-correlation model). What happens to the off-diagonal terms of the VCV matrix (i.e., the estimated covariances, but not the variances) when we flip from using the sample VCV to using the Ledoit-Wolf (2004) VCV?

    (a) Nothing happens. The off-diagonal covariances are the same as those used in the sample VCV matrix.

    (b) The off-diagonal covariances are replaced with new, and typically different from the previous, covariances that are constructed assuming all pairs of off-diagonal stocks have the same correlation between their returns.

    (c) We end up with an average of the sample VCV covariances and alternative covariances, where the alternative covariances are constructed assuming all pairs of off-diagonal stocks have the same correlation between their returns.

    (d) We replace the off-diagonal covariances with new, constant, covariances. That is, every off-diagonal term in the Ledoit-Wolf VCV is identical, and equal to some sort of average of the covariances in the sample VCV.

    (e) None of the above is correct.

415. When Hewlett-Packard Enterprise (HPE) made a takeover offer for Nimble Storage Inc. (NMBL), we saw HPE's stock price fall about 1% and NMBL's price rose about 48%, on Tuesday March 7, 2017. Similarly, we saw that when Intel (INTC) made a takeover offer for Mobileye (MBLY), INTC's stock price fell about 2% and MBLY's price rose about 28%, on Monday March 13, 2017. What are the two main reasons why the target stocks' prices rise by so much?

    (a) The acquirer has to overpay slightly in order to outbid any potential rival (a so-called "winners course"), and the target was significantly underpriced initially, which motivated a bid from the acquirer in the first place.

    (b) The acquirer has to "walk up" the limit order book to buy enough stock to gain control, thereby pushing prices up in the process, and limited shares of stock on offer at the available prices merely compounds the problem.

    (c) The acquirer anticipated and factored into its bid the price impact if they had had to buy the target in the open market, and the acquirer is paying for a control premium.

    (d) The board of directors of the target company is likely to reject any offer that is not well above the most recent stock price, and the target company's shareholders are similarly likely to hold out for a better offer if the initial offer is not high enough.

    (e) Upon receipt of a takeover offer, stock market traders are likely to bid the stock price up even higher than the initial offer because they are hopeful that a "bidding war" will emerge, pushing the price even higher than the initial offer, and hand-in-hand with this, many companies currently have large cash holdings and little monitoring oversight on how they spend it, so they tend to overbid.

416. Suppose that $r = 0.05$ is the continuously compounded return on a stock over one year. The simple gross return is how much? Note that I rounded to four decimal places.

    (a) 1.0500

    (b) 0.0500

    (c) 1.0513

    (d) 0.0513

    (e) None of the above.

417. In *Foundations*, when building the objective function for our quantitative active alpha optimization, our motivation for decomposing the first and second moments of returns into three component parts each was what?

    (a) In the real world, fund managers are too aggressive.

    (b) Investors/clients have different risk aversions to different components of risk.

    (c) We wanted to apply the CAPM to each component pair separately.

    (d) All of the above.

    (e) None of the above.

418. You create a stock/bond portfolio that is initially weighted 60% in stocks and 40% in bonds. On Day 1, the stocks go up 5% and the bonds go down 2.5%. On Day 2, the stocks go up 5% and the bonds are flat with a 0% return. You do not rebalance at any time. What is the simple net return to your portfolio on Day 2, rounded to two places as shown?

    (a) 1.00%

    (b) 2.00%

    (c) 3.00%

    (d) 3.09%

    (e) None of the above.

419. I want to estimate a variance-covariance matrix (VCV) using daily returns on the 100 largest U.S. stocks. Suppose I use the most recent four months of daily returns to estimate the sample VCV (assume no missing observations). May I now use this VCV to estimate a historical Markowitz efficient frontier like the one in Question 3.2.1?

    (a) Yes, it will almost certainly work and produce a frontier.

    (b) No, it will certainly not work.

    (c) Not enough information is given to answer the question.

420. Suppose you are multiplying matrices to work out the Tobin frontier part of a Markowitz-type problem. You come to some matrix algebra that looks like this:

$$
\left[\begin{array}{c} \min_{\vec{h}} \vec{h}'V\vec{h} \\ \text{s.t. } \underbrace{\vec{h}'\vec{\mu}}_{\text{risky}} + \underbrace{(1 - \vec{h}'\vec{\iota})R_F}_{\text{riskless}} = \mu_P \end{array} \right] \Rightarrow \left[\vec{h}_P = \underbrace{\frac{\mu_P - R_F}{(\vec{\mu} - R_F\vec{\iota})'V^{-1}(\vec{\mu} - R_F\vec{\iota})}V^{-1}(\vec{\mu} - R_F\vec{\iota})}_{\text{column vector of weight in risky assets for given } \mu_P} \right]
$$

If you have 20 stocks, what are the dimensions of $\left[(\vec{\mu} - R_F\vec{\iota})'V^{-1}(\vec{\mu} - R_F\vec{\iota}) \right]$ and $\left[\frac{\mu_P - R_F}{(\vec{\mu} - R_F\vec{\iota})'V^{-1}(\vec{\mu} - R_F\vec{\iota})}V^{-1}(\vec{\mu} - R_F\vec{\iota}) \right]$, respectively?

(a) 20x1 and 1x1.

(b) 20x1 and 20x1.

(c) 20x1 and 20x20.

(d) 1x1 and 1x1.

(e) 1x1 and 20x1.

421. Suppose you have $2,500 cash in your margin account, and you want to create a dollar-balanced long-short position where you are long Microsoft (MSFT) but short Intel (INTC) in equal dollar amounts. What is the largest magnitude long-short position you can establish assuming we use the traditional margin rates (i.e., 50% for long positions and 150% for short positions) as described in *Foundations*?

(a) $2,500 long MSFT, and $2,500 short INTC.

(b) $5,000 long MSFT, and $5,000 short INTC.

(c) $10,000 long MSFT, and $10,000 short INTC.

(d) $15,000 long MSFT, and $15,000 short INTC.

(e) $20,000 long MSFT, and $20,000 short INTC.

422. In the Markowitz problem we solved in Question 3.2.1, we calculated historical betas and plotted them relative to historical mean returns. Was this a test of the Capital Asset Pricing Model (CAPM)?

(a) Yes, because we estimated betas and returns and plotted them against each other to see if they were linearly related.

(b) No, that particular experiment has nothing to do with whether the CAPM actually holds or not.

(c) No, because the benchmark portfolio was not on the efficient frontier.

(d) Yes, because ultimately real-world betas are calculated relative to market proxies, and that is exactly what we did.

(e) Both (b) and (c) are correct.

423. You see Tesla trading at $300 a share. Tesla delivered 25,418 vehicles in the first quarter of 2017—a record for them. Tesla's stock price has skyrocketed over the last few years, rising to the point where its market capitalization is similar to or more than that of GM and Ford. By comparison, GM sold more than 10 million vehicles during 2016, and Ford sold more than 6.6 million vehicles during 2016. You decide that Tesla's share price is in a speculative bubble and you sell short 100 shares of Tesla, netting sales proceeds of $30,000. Good news arrives, and Tesla's stock price jumps up $50 to $350 per share. You close out your position. Ignoring all T-costs (margin interest, bid-ask spreads, commissions, etc.), what is your dollar gain or loss?

   (a) $5,000 loss.

   (b) $5,000 gain.

   (c) $25,000 loss.

   (d) $25,000 gain.

   (e) None of the above.

424. ◇◇ Suppose that you enter into a contract for difference (CFD), betting on the direction of the S&P 500 index. Assume that your position margin (i.e., the initial margin money you outlay) is $1,000. Assume that the CFD provider offers a margin rate (i.e., [position margin]/[position value]) of 0.20% as discussed in *Foundations*. Assume that you use all your margin money and obtain the full leverage available. Assume that the index moves up by 1% and you close out your position. Ignoring taxes and T-costs, what is your profit?

   (a) $2,000

   (b) $5,000

   (c) $6,000

   (d) $100,000

   (e) $500,000

425. Suppose that you enter into a contract for difference (CFD), betting on the direction of the GBP. Assume that your position margin (i.e., the initial margin money you outlay) is USD1,000. Assume that the CFD provider offers a margin rate (i.e., [position margin]/[position value]) of 0.20% as discussed in *Foundations*. If you use all your margin money, and the full leverage available, what is USD value of the GBP position you can enter?

   (a) $200,000

   (b) $300,000

   (c) $400,000

   (d) $500,000

   (e) None of the above.

426. Which of the following best represents small, medium, and large P/E ratios, respectively, for the NZX market as a whole? Ignore P/E ratios over 300.

    (a) 1, 2, 4
    (b) 1, 5, 10
    (c) 4, 15, 90
    (d) 20, 40, 60
    (e) 20, 100, 250

427. In *Foundations*, we compared a portfolio manager's investment strategy with a positive ex-ante risk-adjusted alpha (RAA) to a chief financial officer's (CFO's) investment project with a positive ex-ante net present value (NPV). We said that they are similar because of what?

    (a) Both will certainly add value.
    (b) Both are risky.
    (c) Both require skill to manage.
    (d) All of the above.
    (e) (b) and (c) only.

428. The Roll critique (1977) of tests of the CAPM says that in any test of the CAPM that plots mean returns against betas, an index portfolio (against which betas are calculated) can be chosen so that...

    (a) The empirical security market line (SML) is linear.
    (b) The empirical SML is not linear.
    (c) The index portfolio is ex-post mean-variance efficient.
    (d) Each of the above is individually true.
    (e) None of the above is correct.

429. In *Foundations*, we said that P/E ratios are open to manipulation/mis-interpretation because they are sensitive to gearing. So, to overcome this we can instead compare firms using a capital-structure-neutral ratio like what?

    (a) EV/EBITDA.
    (b) EV/revenue.
    (c) P/EBITDA.
    (d) Earnings yield (i.e., E/P).
    (e) Either (a) or (b).

430. Consider the solution portfolio $\vec{h}_P$ to our active alpha optimization in Question 3.2.2. What must be the sum of the portfolio weights?

    (a) 0.00

    (b) 1.00

    (c) I cannot say without seeing it in front of me, but it must be positive.

    (d) I cannot say without seeing it in front of me, but it must be negative.

    (e) None of the above is correct.

431. ◇ In another Markowitz optimization, like that in Question 3.2.1, the benchmark portfolio had much lower annualized standard deviation of returns (only 10.3%) than did any individual stock. (The stocks' standard deviations averaged 30.0%, with min 15.6%, and max 70.2%). At the same level of return as the benchmark (an attractive 10.7%), however, a Markowitz frontier portfolio had even less risk, at only 6.9% per annum. At the start of the time period analyzed, and restricting your attention to the benchmark portfolio or the Markowitz frontier portfolio with the same level of return, which portfolio should/can you recommend to a practical real world investor with money to invest in stocks?

    (a) The frontier portfolio is the clear best choice.

    (b) The benchmark portfolio is the clear best choice.

    (c) In fact, the investor is indifferent between these two portfolios.

    (d) In fact, we should recommend an average of these two portfolios, depending upon the risk aversion of the investor. For example, maybe 50% in the frontier portfolio and 50% in the benchmark portfolio.

    (e) No, in fact, none of the above is correct.

432. ◇◇ You and your friend belong to an aggressive KiwiSaver scheme whose effective annual return (EAR) varies a lot from year to year depending upon stock market moves. You are over 18 years of age, and self-employed. So, you qualify for the member tax credit (MTC), but you do not qualify for an employer match. You contribute only the minimum needed each year (i.e., $20 per week) to get the full MTC. Your friend is also over 18, but is contributing more than the minimum required to receive the full MTC, and is employed and also receiving the 3% employer match. Which one of the following is true regarding benefit-adjusted effective annual returns (BEARs)?

    (a) You earn a higher BEAR than your twin.

    (b) You earn a lower BEAR than your twin.

    (c) You earn the same BEAR as your twin.

    (d) Which one of you earns the higher BEAR is going to depend upon whether the stock market goes up or down over the time period analyzed.

    (e) Which one of you earns the higher BEAR is going to depend upon how big your friend's contributions are.

433. ◇ An investor currently receives dividends of roughly $5,000 per month from her portfolio of stocks. If her stocks pay dividends at a rate that matches the average dividend yield on the S&P 500 over the 50-year period from mid-1963 to mid-2013 (see Chapter 1 of *Foundations*), then roughly how much is her portfolio of stocks worth right now?

    (a) Close to $10 million.

    (b) Close to $8 million.

    (c) Close to $6 million.

    (d) Close to $4 million.

    (e) Close to $2 million.

434. Dividend-paying stocks in New Zealand usually pay their dividends how often?

    (a) Annually (i.e., once per year).

    (b) Semi-Annually (i.e., twice per year).

    (c) Quarterly (i.e., four times per year).

    (d) Monthly (i.e., 12 times per year).

    (e) None of the above.

435. ◇ When we estimate recent N.Z. bid-ask spreads to use as a T-cost avoidance term in an active alpha optimization, we should halve the average closing relative bid-ask spread, and then use half of *that* number as a T-cost applied to changes in holding weights. That is, we should quarter the average relative closing bid-ask spread. Why do we halve the original bid-ask spread twice?

    (a) Because for every purchase we make, there is an opposing simultaneous sale. So, we need only report half the spread in the first place. Given that we will also ultimately be selling anything we buy today, we can halve the T-cost again, thus yielding only one quarter of the original spread.

    (b) Because profits are made by buying low (bid) and selling high (ask), and we have to share the difference between those prices with the opposing trader, thus halving the spread. That shared difference is split again with the market maker on the stock exchange. So, we end up using a T-cost of one quarter the original spread.

    (c) Because closing spreads are roughly twice the size of the more attractive in-tradaily spreads at which we might trade, and because, if fair value is in the middle of the spread, then the bid and the ask prices at which we trade are only a half-spread away from fair value.

    (d) No, it is much simpler than any of the above. We halved the spread first because we buy in the middle of the spread. We halved it again because the difference between the middle and the ask (or bid) must be split with an opposing trader.

    (e) None of the above.

436. A stylized fact concerning "mean blur" in returns to individual stocks is that daily stock market data will typically support which ONE of the following?

   (a) The standard deviation of stock returns is typically much bigger than the mean return, and so we rarely reject the null hypothesis that the population mean return is zero.

   (b) The standard deviation of stock returns is typically only slightly larger than the mean return, and so we often reject the null hypothesis that the population mean return is zero.

   (c) The standard deviation of stock returns is typically smaller than the mean return, and so we almost always reject the null hypothesis that the population mean return is zero.

   (d) There is no clear relationship between the size of the standard deviation of stock returns and the size of the mean return, and so a test of the null hypothesis that the population mean return is zero could easily go either way.

   (e) None of the above.

437. A stylized fact concerning the relationship between the volatility of individual stock returns and the market capitalization of individual stocks is that daily stock market data will typically support which ONE of the following?

   (a) Looking across stocks, as market capitalization increases, standard deviation of stock returns tends to decrease, and the relationship is roughly linear.

   (b) Looking across stocks, as market capitalization increases, standard deviation of stock returns tends to increase, and the relationship is roughly linear.

   (c) Looking across stocks, as market capitalization increases, standard deviation of stock returns tends to decrease, and the relationship is non-linear.

   (d) Looking across stocks, as market capitalization increases, standard deviation of stock returns tends to increase, and the relationship is non-linear.

   (e) None of the above.

438. A stylized fact concerning the relationship between the volatility of individual small-cap stock returns and the volatility of individual large-cap stock returns is that daily stock market data will typically support which ONE of the following?

   (a) Individual small-cap stock returns tend to be notably more volatile than individual large-cap stock returns.

   (b) Individual small-cap stock returns tend to be of a roughly similar level of volatility to individual large-cap stock returns.

   (c) Individual small-cap stock returns tend to be of a notably lower level of volatility than individual large-cap stock returns.

   (d) None of the above.

439. ◇ A stylized fact for the first-order autocorrelation of small-cap daily stock returns is that the data typically support which ONE of the following?

(a) Small-cap stock returns often exhibit a positive first-order autocorrelation, and this autocorrelation is often statistically significant.

(b) Small-cap stock returns often exhibit a positive first-order autocorrelation, but this autocorrelation is typically statistically insignificant.

(c) Small-cap stock returns often exhibit a negative first-order autocorrelation, and this autocorrelation is often statistically significant.

(d) Small-cap stock returns often exhibit a negative first-order autocorrelation, but this autocorrelation is typically statistically insignificant.

(e) None of the above is correct. In fact, the autocorrelation mentioned is of varied and unpredictable sign from one small-cap stock to another.

440. A stylized fact concerning excess kurtosis in the distribution of daily stock returns is that daily stock market data will typically support which ONE of the following?

(a) Stock returns typically display negative excess kurtosis (i.e., less kurtosis than a normal distribution), and this excess kurtosis is marginally statistically significant, and often statistically insignificant.

(b) Stock returns typically display negative excess kurtosis (i.e., less kurtosis than a normal distribution), and this excess kurtosis is highly statistically significant.

(c) Stock returns typically display positive excess kurtosis (i.e., leptokurtosis), and this excess kurtosis is marginally statistically significant, and often statistically insignificant.

(d) Stock returns typically display positive excess kurtosis (i.e., leptokurtosis), and this excess kurtosis is highly statistically significant.

(e) None of the above is correct. The excess kurtosis in the returns distributions of stocks is typically of varied and inconsistent sign and significance from one stock to another.

441. ◇ A stylized fact for the skewness of the distribution of daily small-cap stock returns is that the data typically support which ONE of the following?

(a) Small-cap stock returns often exhibit positive skewness of returns, and this skewness is often statistically significant.

(b) Small-cap stock returns often exhibit positive skewness of returns, but this skewness is often statistically insignificant.

(c) Small-cap stock returns often exhibit negative skewness of returns, and this skewness is often statistically significant.

(d) Small-cap stock returns often exhibit negative skewness of returns, but this skewness is often statistically insignificant.

(e) None of the above is correct. In fact, the skewness mentioned is typically varied and of unpredictable sign from one small-cap stock to another.

442. The Web site `https://fundfinder.sorted.org.nz/funds/growth/fees/` lists 48 growth funds and 63 aggressive funds for KiwiSaver (in April 2018). The lowest-fee fund ("Simplicity Growth Fund") charges $f_L = 52$ bps per annum. The highest-fee fund ("Lifestages Growth Fund") charges $f_H = 320$ bps per annum. The holdings of these two funds are, however, surprisingly similar! So, assume that each fund earns a constant $r = 10\%$ per annum before fees. Let us ignore any taxes. Assume that the after-fee annual return is simply $r - f$, where r is the annual before-fee return, and f is the annual fee. Assume that 17-year old Harry invests an inherited lump sum of \$100,000 in the high-fee fund today, and that his twin sister Lydia invests an identical lump sum in the low-fee fund today (i.e., at $t = 0$). They make no more investments, and they hold their funds for 50 years. What is the ratio of ending wealth (i.e., at $t = 50$) in the low-fee fund over ending wealth in the high-fee fund, to three decimal places? Note that there are no KiwiSaver member tax credits in this question.

    (a) 3.453

    (b) 3.368

    (c) 1.130

    (d) 0.302

    (e) 0.222

443. ◇ Assume that you can invest in the two funds in Question 442, with the same quoted returns and fees, but outside of a KiwiSaver wrapper. Assume that the twins make identical annual investments in the form of a level annuity due, with the first investment today, and a total of 50 annual investments (i.e., an investment at $t = 0$, $t = 1$, and so on, up until $t = 49$, where t counts years along the timeline). Fifty years from now (i.e., at $t = 50$), what will be the ratio of ending wealth in the low-fee fund over ending wealth in the high-fee fund, to three decimal places?

    (a) 3.637

    (b) 2.613

    (c) 2.609

    (d) 2.549

    (e) 2.545

444. ◇ You buy an asset for \$1,000,000 and are charged a fee of one-twenty-fifth of a basis point. How much are you charged in dollars?

    (a) \$0.40

    (b) \$4

    (c) \$40

    (d) \$400

    (e) \$4,000

445. When running a numerical optimization, like an active alpha optimization, we need to do what?

   (a) Start the optimization at different values of the choice variables, to see whether the resulting solution is the same. This is to counter the optimizer's tendency to get stuck at local extrema.

   (b) Re-run the optimization when we reach the apparent optimum, because the optimizer may have switched mid-task from an optimization routine that looks far-and-wide to one that looks only at very near values of the choice variables. This is to counter the optimizer's tendency to get stuck at local extrema.

   (c) Check the proposed solution using analytical calculus, to see whether the numerical and analytical solutions match, as they should.

   (d) Re-run the optimization using different choice variables, to see whether the solution remains the same.

   (e) Both (a) and (b), but neither (c) nor (d).

446. Suppose you build an ex-post Markowitz frontier using the vector $\vec{\mu}$ of mean returns and the VCV matrix V of stock returns, both based on two years of data. Would it have been possible on Day 1 of that data set to reliably pick a vector of portfolio weights so as to form a portfolio that would end up on the ex-post Markowitz frontier you plotted?

   (a) Yes, we could have performed the exercise using the previous two years of data (i.e., 2013–2014), and then carried the optimal weights over from that exercise and used them again.

   (b) Yes, we just needed to estimate each of $\vec{\mu}$ and V in advance, pick a level of μ_P, and use the analytic solution to obtain $\vec{h}_P$.

   (c) Yes, it is standard finance industry practice.

   (d) All of the above.

   (e) No, it is impossible, in advance, to pin down the inputs to the analytical solution that leads to a frontier portfolio.

447. Is a stock market index, like the S&P 500 or the S&P/NZX50 an investible asset (i.e., an asset into which an investment can be made)? Note that this is a question about the index itself, rather than the portfolio of stocks underlying the index. Please ignore ETFs, mutual funds, futures contracts, and CFDs (and similar contracts) when answering this question.

   (a) Yes, the index trades on the stock exchange.

   (b) Yes, I can buy the index via a broker.

   (c) Yes, I can buy the index from a market maker.

   (d) Yes, each of the above is true.

   (e) No, none of the above is true.

448. All risk models for estimating a VCV matrix...

   (a) Assume some sort of common themes across stocks.

   (b) Impose some sort of meta-averaging.

   (c) Place structure on the covariances in order to reduce dimensionality of the problem.

   (d) All of the above.

   (e) None of the above.

449. Statistical analysis of daily individual stock returns tends to reveal which of the following?

   (a) Mean returns are small and they are often not statistically different from zero.

   (b) Autocorrelation of returns to small-cap stocks tends to be significantly negative.

   (c) We always or almost always reject normality of daily returns distributions.

   (d) Returns to small-cap stocks tend to be positively skewed.

   (e) All of the above.

450. Suppose that you want to calculate the Sharpe ratio of the return on a portfolio, r_P, relative to the return on T-bills, r_F. You collect a time series of returns $r_P(t)$ and $r_F(t)$. Let $m(\cdot)$ denote the sample mean, and $s(\cdot)$ denote the sample standard deviation. Which of the following is the Sharpe ratio you seek (according to Sharpe [1994])? You may assume that the returns are continuously compounded, though it should not alter your choice. (See also Q. 486 on p. 189.)

   (a) $m(r_P)/s(r_P)$.

   (b) $m(r_P - r_F)/s(r_P)$.

   (c) $m(r_P)/s(r_P - r_F)$.

   (d) $m(r_P - r_F)/s(r_P - r_F)$.

   (e) $m(r_F - r_P)/s(r_F - r_P)$

451. We looked at several variance minimization exercises where the choice variables are a vector of portfolio holdings, say, $\vec{h}_P$. When drawing a picture of the minimum-risk frontier in mean-variance space, the choice variables are where?

   (a) Explicitly on one axis only.

   (b) Explicitly on both axes.

   (c) Implicitly on both axes, but embedded within summary statistic formulae driving the axis values.

   (d) On neither axis, and nowhere to be seen either implicitly or explicitly on either axis because the dimensionality of the problem was too high for them to appear on these axes.

   (e) None of the above.

452. With stocks following different financial years, dividend payments on New Zealand stocks tend to cluster in which months?

    (a) Jan/July and Apr/Oct

    (b) Feb/Aug and May/Nov

    (c) Mar/Sept and Jun/Dec

    (d) Apr/Oct and Jun/Dec

    (e) None of the above.

453. You bought 100 shares of Snapchat (SNAP) during its first day of trading. It went public at $17 per share, opened at $24.00 a share and closed at $24.48. You bought SNAP at the high of the first day: you paid $26.05 per share. There were 217,109,769 shares traded this day. The bid-ask spread when you bought SNAP was $26.00–$26.05. You also paid a commission of $10.00. What are your T-costs as a proportion of the total stock price you paid? Note that the commission is part of the T-costs, but it is not part of the price. Round your answer to the nearest bp.

    (a) 38 bps

    (b) 48 bps.

    (c) 58 bps

    (d) 480 bps

    (e) 576 bps

454. In a March 2017 survey of workers in the U.S., 79% said that they expect to continue working in retirement, with a surprising number planning to work when aged well into their 70s. Ninety percent of these people planning to work into old age had at least one financial reason for doing so. So, let me assume that you have **50 years until retirement**. Assume that you are saving for retirement via a growing ordinary annuity (you save a proportion p of your income each year and your income grows at rate g per annum). What is the **impact on your final wealth** if you can earn an extra 1% return per annum over this 50-year horizon? Note that this is not a KiwiSaver question, so don't worry about a fixed-dollar government match here.

    Please assume your income grows as a steady rate of $g = 4\%$ per annum, and tell me the impact on your final wealth if you could earn $R = 9\%$ per annum rather than $R = 8\%$ per annum. Assume annual cash flows.

    (a) A 17.3% boost to your final wealth.

    (b) A 35.2% boost to your final wealth.

    (c) A 42.1% boost to your final wealth.

    (d) A 50.2% boost to your final wealth.

    (e) A 58.5% boost to your final wealth.

455. The spreadsheet MIN-VAR-OBJ.XLS uses minimization of an objective function that is simply portfolio variance, σ_P^2, subject to the constraint that we be fully invested and that we do not allow short selling. The spreadsheet MAX-UTIL-OBJ.XLS uses, instead, maximization of an objective function that is utility: $E(R_P) - \lambda \sigma_P^2$, subject to the same two constraints. Which of the following is TRUE regarding the utility maximization?

    (a) Very high levels of risk aversion (e.g., $\lambda = 1,000,000$) lead to optimal portfolios on the Markowitz frontier near the global minimum-variance portfolio.

    (b) Assuming risk neutrality (i.e., $\lambda = 0$) leads us to an optimal portfolio on the Markowitz frontier at the individual asset with the highest return.

    (c) The higher is λ, the more assets tend to be included in the optimal portfolio.

    (d) Varying λ from 0 to 1,000,000 traces out solutions on the upper portion only of the Markowitz frontier.

    (e) All of the above are correct.

456. Michaud (1989) describes mean-variance optimizers as "estimation error maximizers" because they overweight (underweight) stocks with

    (a) relatively high (low) estimated returns, negative (positive) covariance of returns with other stocks' returns, and relatively low (high) variances.

    (b) relatively low (high) estimated returns, positive (negative) covariance of returns with other stocks' returns, and relatively high (low) variances.

    (c) relatively low (high) estimated returns, negative (positive) covariance of returns with other stocks' returns, and relatively low (high) variances.

    (d) relatively high (low) estimated returns, positive (negative) covariance of returns with other stocks' returns, and relatively low (high) variances.

    (e) relatively high (low) estimated returns, negative (positive) covariance of returns with other stocks' returns, and relatively high (low) variances.

457. Which one of the following statements about shrinkage estimators of variance-covariance (VCV) matrices is FALSE?

    (a) Extreme estimates of covariances are likely to contain extreme estimation error.

    (b) Shrinking extreme estimates toward some sort of average value is likely to reduce specification error.

    (c) Shrinking extreme estimates toward some sort of average value is likely to reduce estimation error.

    (d) Large positive estimated covariances are likely to be larger than the true population values and large negative estimated covariances are likely to be larger in magnitude than the true population values.

    (e) The Ledoit-Wolf (2004) VCV estimator takes an average of two VCV estimators, one of which has lots of specification error and little estimation error, and the other of which has lots of estimation error and little specification error.

458. Which one of the following tends to DECREASE the P/E ratio of a stock?

  (a) An increase in the forecast growth rate in earnings per share.

  (b) A drop in the expected riskiness of the future earnings per share.

  (c) An increase in the PVGO (i.e., present value of growth opportunities) of the stock as a proportion of price.

  (d) The passage of time, as a company matures.

  (e) More than one of the above.

459. We have the following parameterization of the active alpha objective function from Chapter 2 of *Foundations*. Which answer is FALSE?

$$RTAA \;=\; \underbrace{\vec{h}_P'\vec{\alpha}}_{A} -\lambda\underbrace{\left[\vec{h}_P'V\vec{h}_P - \vec{h}_B'V\vec{h}_B\right]}_{B} -F\cdot\underbrace{\frac{1}{2}}_{C}\,\underbrace{\left|\vec{h}_B - \vec{h}_P\right|}_{D}{}'\underbrace{\vec{\gamma}}_{E}$$

  (a) A is the alpha of portfolio P.

  (b) B is the active risk of portfolio P relative to B.

  (c) C represents the half-spread distance of fair value from the best bid and ask prices.

  (d) D is a vector of the active return of portfolio P relative to B.

  (e) E is a vector of estimated relative bid-ask spreads.

460. The analytical Markowitz frontier solution from Chapter 2 of *Foundations* is:

$$\vec{h}_P \;=\; \vec{h}_P(\mu_P,\vec{\mu},V) \;=\; \vec{H}\mu_P + \vec{G}, \quad\text{where} \tag{1.9}$$

$$\vec{H} \;=\; \frac{1}{D}\left\{\left[C(V^{-1}\vec{\mu}) - A(V^{-1}\vec{\iota})\right]\right\}, \tag{1.10}$$

$$\vec{G} \;=\; \frac{1}{D}\left\{\left[B(V^{-1}\vec{\iota}) - A(V^{-1}\vec{\mu})\right]\right\}, \tag{1.11}$$

$$A \;=\; \vec{\iota}'V^{-1}\vec{\mu},\; B = \vec{\mu}'V^{-1}\vec{\mu},\; C = \vec{\iota}'V^{-1}\vec{\iota},\;\text{and } D = BC - A^2, \tag{1.12}$$

where $\vec{h}_P$ is the argmin. In this case, $\vec{h}_P$ represents what?

  (a) $\vec{h}_P$ is the vector of holdings in the minimum-variance portfolio of risky assets that has the least risk of all possible fully-invested risky asset portfolios.

  (b) $\vec{h}_P$ is the vector of holdings in the tangency portfolio that sits on both the Markowitz and Tobin frontiers.

  (c) $\vec{h}_P$ is the vector of holdings in the fully-invested risky asset portfolio that has $\beta = 1$ relative to the tangency portfolio.

  (d) $\vec{h}_P$ is the vector of holdings in the portfolio of risky assets that has least risk among all fully-invested risky asset portfolios with return μ_P.

  (e) $\vec{h}_P$ is the vector of holdings in the fully-invested portfolio of risky assets with the highest mean return, assuming no short selling.

461. Suppose $\sigma_B = 0.119$ (benchmark annualized standard deviation), $\sigma_P = 0.122$ (portfolio annualized standard deviation), $\beta_P = 1$ (portfolio beta), $\alpha_P = 0.02141$ (forward looking annualized portfolio alpha), and $\lambda = 10$ (residual risk aversion assuming return and risk are in decimals). What is the forward looking RAA (risk-adjusted alpha) **ignoring T-costs**?

(a) -0.247477

(b) 0.014180

(c) -0.008590

(d) 0.020687

(e) None of the above is correct.

462. Suppose that you are an N.Z. citizen, N.Z. resident, over the age of 18, but under the age of 65. Suppose that during the KiwiSaver year (i.e., July 1st to June 30th) you successfully deposit $1,000 into your KiwiSaver scheme, but no more. How much of a member tax credit will your contribution trigger?

(a) $2,000.00

(b) $1042.86

(c) $1,000.00

(d) $521.43

(e) $500.00

463. In the CLOB on the NZX, a "marketable limit order" to BUY is a limit order that is what?

(a) A limit order with a limit price that is better than the best bid, and therefore jumps to the top of the bid side of the book via price priority, where it waits/rests, but it will be first to be executed if an opposing market order arrives next.

(b) A limit order with a limit price that is better than the best ask, and therefore jumps to the top of the ask side of the book via price priority, where it waits/rests, but it will be first to be executed if an opposing market order arrives next.

(c) A limit order with a limit price that is superior to the best bid, and therefore jumps to the top of the bid side of the book via time priority, where it waits/rests, but it will be first to be executed if an opposing market order arrives next.

(d) A limit order with a limit price that is equivalent to the best bid, and therefore jumps to the top of the bid side of the book via price priority, but is made to wait/rest for execution only because previous limit orders at the same price have time priority.

(e) None of the above is correct.

464. If we assume that the beta of our portfolio is one (i.e., $\beta_P = 1$), then the information ratio of our portfolio is given by $IR_P = \frac{\alpha_P}{\omega_P}$. This ratio is what?

   (a) A Sharpe ratio in active space.

   (b) The ratio of return per unit risk in active space.

   (c) The ratio of active return per unit of active risk.

   (d) All of the above.

   (e) both (a) and (b), but neither (c) nor (d).

465. Today is the birthday of Yamamoto Tsunetomo. Yamamoto is 60 years old. Yamamoto already has $10 million in the bank (he is a famous former Japanese samurai). The life expectancy for a 60-year-old Japanese male is almost exactly 25 years. Yamamoto has decided to give all his money to charity except for just enough to buy an annuity. Yamamoto wants to buy an annuity that will make a payment to him today (to live on over the next year). He then wants a payment a year from now, and then a payment on every birthday up to and including his 85th birthday 25 years from now. If Yamamoto wants to get a $200,000 payment on each birthday starting today, how much money does he need to spend today to buy the annuity if the interest rate is 5% per annum? Round to the nearest dollar. Ignore taxes/fees.

   (a) $3,018,789

   (b) $2,875,037

   (c) $2,959,728

   (d) $2,818,789

   (e) None of the above.

466. ◇◇ Recall the Markowitz-Tobin-Tangency analysis from Chapter 2 of *Foundations*. Assume that there are N risky assets and one riskless asset. Restrict our attention to betas calculated relative to the tangency portfolio. Restrict our attention to fully invested portfolios (i.e., all money is in the N risky assets and none is in the riskless asset). Among these risky fully-invested portfolios, some portfolios will have a zero beta relative to the tangency portfolio. Whereabouts in the Markowitz-Tobin-Tangency picture is the least-risky fully-invested zero-beta portfolio?

   (a) It is at the tangency point between the Markowitz and Tobin frontiers.

   (b) It is at the global minimum variance point on the Markowitz frontier.

   (c) It is at the point on the Markowitz frontier that has the same return as the benchmark portfolio.

   (d) It is at the point on the Markowitz frontier that has the same return as the riskless asset.

   (e) It is strictly within the interior of the Markowitz frontier (i.e., it lies strictly to the right of the Markowitz hyperbola).

467. Suppose that portfolio P contains only a **single stock** selected from 20 stocks in your reference benchmark index. If you write the vector of holdings $\vec{h}_P$ using the usual notation, what form does $\vec{h}_P$ take?

    (a) $\vec{h}_P$ is a 20×1 column vector of ones.

    (b) $\vec{h}_P$ is a 1×20 row vector of ones.

    (c) $\vec{h}_P$ is a 20×1 column vector of zeroes.

    (d) $\vec{h}_P$ is the 20×20 identity matrix.

    (e) None of the above is correct.

468. We argued that Benjamin Graham's defensive/passive value strategy was what?

    (a) An active strategy, because he picks only 10–30 stocks, and he cannot expect to include all industries and be diversified within each industry group.

    (b) A relatively passive strategy, because he argues that it is so very difficult to beat the market that we should instead focus on solid companies with little risk of underperformance.

    (c) The closest thing to a passive strategy in his day (recall that Graham died before diversified index funds were available to retail investors).

    (d) All of the above.

    (e) None of the above.

469. ◇ Assume a Gordon-Shapiro dividend growth model. Assume return on equity exceeds required return on equity, $ROE > R$. Does this mean that the present value of growth opportunities is positive: $PVGO > 0$?

    (a) Yes, if $ROE > R$, then value is being created by positive NPV investments.

    (b) No, not necessarily. The retention ratio might be zero, $b = 0$. In this case, no value is being created.

    (c) No, not necessarily. Even if $b > 0$, this might not translate into growing EPS.

470. What is the time-ordering of events for the dividend timeline in New Zealand? Please assume the most recent timeline that came into force in September 2010. (Note that the changes to the N.Z. dividend timeline in March 2016 did not alter the *order* of the events, only their timing.)

    (a) Declaration, Record (i.e., Book Close), Ex-dividend, Payment.

    (b) Declaration, Ex-dividend, Record (i.e., Book Close), Payment.

    (c) Record (i.e., Book Close), Declaration, Ex-dividend, Payment.

    (d) Ex-dividend, Declaration, Record (i.e., Book Close), Payment.

    (e) None of the above is correct.

471. TVM practice: You and your spouse are 25 years old. You just started new jobs earning a *combined* $200,000 per annum. Assume annual pay. So, your first pay will be a total of $200,000 at year end ($t = 1$). You both save a fixed 10% into a new joint retirement savings account. So, your first retirement saving is a deposit of $20,000 at $t = 1$. Your employer contributes nothing. You plan to stay with these jobs and this retirement savings account until you both turn 65 (i.e., your last annual deposit will be at $t = 40$). Your salaries will grow at a steady rate of $g = 6\%$ per annum, driven by promotions and costs of living adjustments linked to inflation. Your investments are forecast to return $R = 7\%$ per annum after all taxes and T-costs. What is the forecast joint balance in your retirement savings accounts immediately after your last deposit? Round your answer to the nearest dollar, and allow that your calculator might give a number a few dollars from the number given by my calculator.

    (a) $3,712,806
    (b) $3,731,497
    (c) $3,992,702
    (d) $4,272,191
    (e) $4,292,191
    (f) $8,582,626
    (g) $8,764,000
    (h) $9,377,480
    (i) $10,033,903
    (j) $10,239,618

472. The term "margin rate" has two popular meanings in investments finance. Which are they?

    (a) The interest rate on a margin loan, and the amount by which revenue exceeds costs on the income statement.

    (b) The margin for error in a valuation model (e.g., so that we do not overpay in an acquisition), and the difference between the total value of securities held in an investor's account and the loan amount from the broker.

    (c) The excess of the earnings yield (i.e., the reciprocal of the P/E ratio) on a stock over the YTM on bonds, and the amount of equity an investor has in their brokerage account.

    (d) The collateral that the holder of a financial instrument has to deposit with a counterparty, and the performance bond deposited by a futures trader.

    (e) The interest rate on a margin loan, and a leverage ratio calculated as position margin over position value.

    (f) The portion of the interest rate on an adjustable-rate mortgage (i.e., ARM) added to the adjustment-index rate, and the amount of equity an investor has in their brokerage account.

473. TVM practice: You and your spouse are 20 years old. You just started new jobs earning a *combined* $100,000 per annum. Assume annual pay arriving at the end of each year. So, your employers pay you a combined total of $100,000 at year end ($t = 1$). You save a fixed 15% into a new retirement savings account (so your first saving is a deposit of $15,000 at $t = 1$). You plan to stay with these jobs and this retirement savings account until you both turn 65 (i.e., you last annual deposit will be at $t = 45$). You forecast that your salaries will grow at a steady rate of 5% per annum, which accounts for promotions and costs of living adjustments linked to inflation. Your retirement savings account is forecast to return $R = 7.5\%$ per annum after all taxes and T-costs. What do you forecast to be the joint balance in your retirement savings accounts immediately after your last deposit? Round your answer to the nearest dollar, and allow that your calculator might give a number a few dollars from that given by my calculator.

(a) $4,633,458

(b) $4,980,968

(c) $5,354,540

(d) $5,369,540

(e) $9,324,224

(f) $9,443,627

(g) $10,151,899

(h) $10,913,291

(i) $11,048,066

474. You buy 100 shares of an NZX stock that is priced at $10 per share. The total cost $1,000. You use $400 of your money (this is your investment) and $600 borrowed from your broker. My U.S. broker cannot lend me such a high proportion of the purchase price; it is a breach of U.S. federal law. My N.Z. broker, however, refers to this as a "60% lending ratio," and is prepared to lend me even more on some stocks. Suppose that the stock price suddenly jumps from $10 per share to $13.50 per share. You close out your position and pay off the loan. What is the rate of return on your investment? Ignore taxes, transaction costs, commissions, and interest on the margin loan.

(a) 14.0%

(b) 17.5%

(c) 21.0%

(d) 35.0%

(e) 70.0%

(f) 75.0%

(g) 87.5%

475. You decide to follow the Bengen retirement savings withdrawal rule. You decide to use Bengen's original 4% per annum safemax withdrawal rate, even though much evidence suggests that this is too aggressive. Assume you are 65 years old today ($t = 0$), and that will make your first withdrawal, of $75,000 as an annual lump sum one year from now ($t = 1$). Assume that inflation is expected to be 1.5% per annum for the next 10 years. What annual withdrawal from your savings do you plan to make three years from now (at time $t = 3$)? Round your answer to the nearest dollar. I strongly recommend that you draw a timeline.

    (a) I cannot answer without knowing the accumulated savings number.

    (b) A dollar number less than $75,000.

    (c) $75,000.

    (d) $76,125.

    (e) $77,267.

    (f) $78,426.

    (g) $79,603.

    (h) A dollar number higher than any of the above.

476. ◇ In Chapter 2 of *Foundations*, in the section on Retirement Planning Rules of Thumb, there is a "You Need to Know" box that uses two different approaches to find a required wealth accumulation for early retirement: a Bengen safemax withdrawal rate calculation and a standard time value of money (TVM) approach. The TVM approach gives an answer of $838,658 and the Bengen approach gives an answer of $1,500,000 (i.e., twice as much required initial wealth). We attributed the difference in answers to mean blur and what?

    (a) Our Bengen approach used a 2% safemax withdrawal rate. If we had used a 4% safemax withdrawal rate instead, the required wealth from the two approaches would have been the same.

    (b) The TVM approach used mean market returns, giving a required wealth answer analogous to the average wealth required to meet our expenses. The Bengen approach, however, relied upon a simulation of all possible returns, and so its safe-wealth answer is analogous to an upper 5% critical value in the distribution of initial wealth required to meet our expenses.

    (c) The Bengen approach failed to assume that there was any interest being earned on the retirement investment portfolio. That is, it assumed that the accumulated wealth was in cash, earning no rate of return. The TVM approach, however, assumed that the accumulated wealth was invested in stocks and bonds earning a reasonable rate of return.

    (d) The TVM approach assumed that the retirement investment portfolio was invested only in stocks, but the Bengen approach assumed that the retirement investment portfolio was invested only in bonds.

    (e) None of the above is correct.

477. You have just retired, aged 35 (at $t = 0$), as part of the FIRE movement. Your annual lump sum expenses are forecast to be $60,000, payable in arrears one year from now (at $t = 1$), at which time you will withdraw the $60,000 from your retirement savings account. Inflation is on track to be a steady 2% per annum, for the foreseeable future. Your wealth, of $1,500,000 is invested in stocks and bonds that yield 7% per annum. You have ignored criticism, and you are following the traditional Bengen 4% rule. How much are you planning to be able to withdraw from your retirement savings account at $t = 5$, five years from now? Round your answer to the nearest dollar. I strongly recommend that you draw a timeline.

(a) $60,000

(b) $64,946

(c) $66,245

(d) $70,192

(e) $72,930

(f) $72,999

(g) $76,577

(h) $78,648

(i) $84,153

(j) None of the above is correct.

478. ◇ You decide to retire by age 35 as part of the FIRE movement. You wish to use the Bengen retirement withdrawal rule. Bengen's original work suggests a 4% withdrawal rule, but you face a much longer retirement period than Bengen intended. What safemax withdrawal rate should you use? To be safe, please ignore the "advisors alpha" that was mentioned in Chapter 2 of *Foundations* (it is a little questionable because it is being promoted by self-interested advisors).

(a) 5% or more, because I expect that I have longer to live than someone retiring at age 60 or age 65.

(b) The original 4% rate because the rule adjusts automatically for inflation, the time value of money, and my long horizon.

(c) A number closer to 3.5%, because Bengen's original data are from the U.S., and they contain a survivorship bias (that is, Bengen's original work was based on U.S. data, but the U.S. financial markets had been unusually successful at the time of Bengen's original work).

(d) A number closer to 3%, because you need to account for both the survivorship bias and fees, but the horizon is unimportant.

(e) A number closer to 2.5% before fees, because you need to account for survivorship bias, and, very importantly, your very long period of time in retirement, but this translates to perhaps 2% after fees.

(f) None of the above is correct.

479. In Chapter 2 of *Foundations* we used the PVGO concept to help understand P/E ratios and valuation of growth stocks. Which of the following is TRUE? Assume that R, mentioned below, is a required return on equity from the CAPM.

   (a) To have a positive PVGO, a company must have both earnings retention (i.e., not all earnings are paid out as dividends) and positive NPV opportunities (i.e., value creation because return on equity $ROE > R$).

   (b) A mature company with no positive NPV investments (i.e., $ROE = R$) and a 100% dividend payout policy (i.e., no earnings retention) will have no growth in EPS. If, however, the company announces a move to earnings retention, then even without positive NPV investments, its stock price should jump up with a PVGO premium to represent the growth in EPS that will result from the subsequent retention-driven expansion of its capital base.

   (c) If a new tech company has many positive NPV projects, but pays out all net profits as dividends, never retaining a penny, then the company can still have a positive PVGO to reflect the active value creation it is engaged in.

   (d) PVGO is to corporate earnings what NPV is to project cash flows.

   (e) All of the above are true.

   (f) Only (b) and (c) above are true.

   (g) None of the above is true.

480. Suppose you want to BUY some FPH stock on the NZX. You are choosing between submitting a market order and a limit order. Assume that the commissions are the same for each. Assume sufficient depth at the best ask price, and no price slippage. Then, when you submit a market order to buy you get an immediate execution (i.e., a benefit), but your order hits the best ask which is a half-spread above mid-spread fair value (i.e., a cost). If you instead submit a limit BUY order with limit price equal to the BEST BID, your cost-benefit trade-off for the limit order is different in what way from that for the market order?

   (a) The benefit of the limit order is an immediate execution, and the cost is potentially having your order executed at a worse price than your chosen limit price.

   (b) The benefit of the limit order is an execution at a half-spread below fair value, and the cost is delayed or possible non-execution if transaction prices rise away from your limit price.

   (c) The benefit of the limit order is an execution at a half-spread above fair value, and the cost is that the price may fall just after you buy the stock.

   (d) The benefit of the limit order is that part of the quantity specified may be immediately marketable, and the cost is that subsequent completion of the execution may take some time.

   (e) The benefit of the limit order is that you get a guaranteed execution at a guaranteed price, but the cost is that if your order is executed over multiple days, in a series of partial fills, you will have to pay multiple commissions.

481. There are problems with the traditional sample VCV matrix as used in Markowitz, Grinold-Kahn, and Black-Litterman approaches. Which one of the following is a FALSE statement about a problem with the traditional sample VCV matrix?

    (a) The traditional sample VCV matrix requires lots of covariances. So many, in fact, that the count of covariances varies quadratically with the count of stocks.

    (b) The traditional sample VCV matrix contains lots of specification error. We would be better off using an average of the sample VCV matrix and another VCV matrix that contains lots of statistical estimation error.

    (c) If we estimate the traditional sample VCV matrix using very recent (i.e., arguably the most relevant) data, then we get so few observations that the covariances will be poorly estimated.

    (d) If we use only recent data, we may get so few observations that there must be linear relationships between the rows of the VCV matrix.

    (e) If there are linear relationships between the rows of the VCV matrix, the VCV matrix must be non-invertible, and of little use to us.

    (f) If we go far enough back in time that we get a long enough time series that the sample VCV matrix is invertible, we are likely using old stale data.

482. The first part of the Black-Litterman optimization approach was developed by Fischer Black to infer equilibrium expected returns on stocks (and on bonds and currencies, though we have focused only on stocks so far). How does Fischer Black address the mean blur problem in estimating expected returns?

    (a) Black turns portfolio mathematics on its head. Instead of inferring a tangency portfolio based on expected returns (as you do in the Markowitz/Tobin problem in Question 3.2.1, Black infers expected returns based on assuming that the benchmark portfolio *is* the tangency portfolio. This is a CAPM-type argument.

    (b) Black exploits the property of the global minimum variance portfolio that it is the only portfolio on the Markowitz frontier whose portfolio weights are not a function of the vector of means, and is thus the only portfolio on the frontier that is immune to mean blur arguments. He treats that as a fixed point, and rotates the frontier about it until no point on the frontier is a function of the vector of mean returns.

    (c) Black applies a CAPM-type argument and he collects expected returns on stocks from traders using a survey of traders' expectations of betas. He needs to supply a riskless rate and a market risk premium to obtain the expected returns using the CAPM.

    (d) Black performs an optimization routine to infer how the VCV matrix needs to change in order that the benchmark portfolio be mean-variance efficient. This then implies what the covariances are, what the betas must be, and therefore what the expected returns on stocks must be via the CAPM.

    (e) None of the above is correct.

483. Suppose that relative bid-ask spreads on the 50 largest N.Z. stocks are averaged across the stocks, and then averaged across each hour of every trading day each year from 2007 to 2017, producing 11 plots (i.e., one for each year). Assume that relative bid-ask spread is on the vertical axis and time during the trading day is on the horizontal axis. All but one of the following ARE patterns in the relative spreads. Which ONE is NOT a pattern in these data?

   (a) A general tendency for spreads to decline over the years, from a minimum during the day of about 75–100 bps in the first two years to a minimum during the day of about 25–35 bps in the last two years.

   (b) A generally shallow U-shape in relative spreads during the day each year.

   (c) Most years, a small kink in the plot close to lunch time.

   (d) Lower spreads at the close than the middle of the day.

   (e) A trend (given by the line of best fit) for relative spreads to decrease over the course of the day.

484. Only ONE of the following is a pattern typically seen in the behavior of relative bid-ask spreads during the trading day and over time in the largest 50 stocks on the NZX from 2007 to 2017. Which ONE is the ACTUAL pattern?

   (a) A dramatic decrease in relative spreads during the 2008 financial crisis.

   (b) A steady increase in relative spreads from 2008 to 2017.

   (c) A trend (given by the line of best fit) for relative spreads to increase over the course of the day.

   (d) Higher spreads at the open than the middle of the day.

   (e) Lower spreads at the close than the middle of the day.

   (f) Nothing noticeable in relative spreads at lunch time.

485. When comparing quantitative portfolio managers to fundamental portfolio managers, which one of the following best describes the *quantitative* managers?

   (a) They have a team of analysts who physically visit the company or phone the managers to talk about earnings, and they value companies using DCF methods.

   (b) They visit companies and ask managers what they are doing and why, ask about prospects for growth in earnings, and try to figure out expected earnings performance relative to competitors.

   (c) They have very few analysts, use signals driven by quantifiable variables, and sit in front of a PC rather than visiting the company.

   (d) They typically do not value companies in absolute terms, but rather rank them and tilt portfolio weights toward (i.e., overweight) the most attractive companies and away from (i.e., underweight) the least attractive companies.

   (e) (a) and (b), but not (c) or (d).

   (f) (c) and (d), but not (a) or (b).

486. Let R_i be the return on a single long-only portfolio. Let R_B be the return on some benchmark index, like the S&P/NZX50. (Note that these returns could be forward-looking expected returns, or backward-looking historical average returns; the answer applies to both cases.) Let $\sigma(\cdot)$ denote standard deviation of whatever is inside the parentheses. Which of the following are Sharpe ratios (according to Sharpe [1994])? (See also Q. 450 on p. 175.)

(a) $\frac{(R_i-R_B)}{\sigma(R_i-R_B)}$

(b) $\frac{R_i}{\sigma(R_i)}$

(c) $\frac{R_B}{\sigma(R_B)}$

(d) All of the above.

(e) $\frac{\sigma(R_i-R_B)}{(R_i-R_B)}$

487. ◇ It is your 22nd birthday. You are saving into a KiwiSaver retirement savings scheme. You forecast that your investments will grow at a rate of 6.5% per annum after all taxes and fees. You forecast that average inflation will be 2.0% per annum between now and age 65. You forecast that your KiwiSaver account will have a balance on your 65th birthday of $2,500,000. Once you reach age 65, you plan to switch to a safer investment option, returning only 4% per annum after all taxes and fees. You plan to withdraw all of your account, down to a zero balance, by making a series of withdrawals. You plan to withdraw the money as a growing annuity of withdrawals from your 65th birthday to your 85th birthday, inclusive of both dates. So, you will withdraw an amount C from your account on your 65th birthday (to be clear, this means that you will have $2,500,000 - C$ left in your account immediately after the first withdrawal). Then you will withdraw $C \times (1 + g)$ on your 66th birthday, $C \times (1 + g)^2$ on your 67th birthday, and so on, where $g = 2\%$ per annum, making a final withdrawal on your 85th birthday. What is the **deflated value of the first withdrawal** C today? Assume deflation using division by $(1 + \pi)^N$ for inflation rate π and period N. That is, what is the value of C in today's dollars? Note that I rounded the final answer, and that your individual calculator may be out by a few pennies.

(a) $91,043.81

(b) $66,302.83

(c) $63,752.72

(d) $63,720.67

(e) $61,269.87

(f) $21,629.87

(g) $39,631.75

(h) None of these answers is within $1,000 of the correct answer.

488. Suppose that you collect returns on 20 stocks, like the returns used in the Markowitz problem in Question 3.2.1. You use all the Markowitz mathematics to locate the Markowitz minimum-variance frontier and the Tobin minimum-variance frontier and the tangency portfolio T. You also locate the benchmark portfolio B using the market capitalization weights. Portfolio B sits strictly inside the Markowitz minimum-variance frontier, exactly like it did on Question 3.2.1. Now, you use the Markowitz mathematics to locate the portfolio on the Markowitz frontier that has the same return as your benchmark portfolio. Let me call this portfolio C. Portfolio C is the optimal (i.e., least-risk) fully-invested risky portfolio with return equal to the return on the benchmark. Suppose that you now calculate betas on each stock i relative to portfolio C, using $\beta_i = \vec{h}_i'V\vec{h}_C \big/ \vec{h}_C V \vec{h}_C$, using the same notation we used *Foundations*. If you plot historical mean returns on stocks versus these betas, the empirical security market line (SML) will be what, as a result of Roll's critique? Choose the best answer.

(a) A perfectly straight line.

(b) A jumble of points.

(c) A perfectly straight line only if $C = T$ (which, in this case, would require that B and T have the same return).

(d) A perfectly straight line only if $C = B$, that is, only if B is on the Markowitz minimum-variance frontier.

(e) We cannot know in advance whether it will be a perfectly straight line or a jumble of points.

(f) A parabola.

(g) A hyperbola.

489. $\diamond$ Suppose that you use R_F, $\vec{h}_B$, V, and a sensible value for μ_B (say, 10% per annum) to implement a Black-Litterman approach to estimate the vector of mean returns to 20 stocks. Suppose that you then estimate the betas of each of your 20 stocks relative to the benchmark portfolio using $\vec{h}_i$, $\vec{h}_B$, and V, using the same formula for beta we used in Chapter 2 of *Foundations*. Suppose that you then plot an empirical security market line (SML) showing the relationship between the Black-Litterman inferred mean returns (on the y-axis) and the betas relative to the benchmark (on the x-axis). This SML will be what?

(a) A jumble of points.

(b) A straight line.

(c) Very close to a straight line, but not a straight line.

(d) A curved frontier like a Markowitz frontier.

(e) A kinked frontier like a Tobin frontier.

(f) We cannot know in advance what shape the empirical SML will take here.

(g) None of the above.

490. Which famous finance person is associated with which famous finance phrase, respectively?

> 1. "Everybody knows something"
> 2. "Nobody knows nothing"
> 3. "Somebody knows something" (in this case, the famous person)

(a) 1. Jack Bogle; 2. Warren Buffett; 3. Peter Lynch.

(b) 1. Jack Bogle; 2. Peter Lynch; 3. Warren Buffett.

(c) 1. Peter Lynch; 2. Warren Buffett; 3. Jack Bogle.

(d) 1. Peter Lynch; 2. Jack Bogle; 3. Warren Buffett.

(e) 1. Warren Buffett; 2. Jack Bogle; 3. Peter Lynch.

(f) 1. Warren Buffett; 2. Peter Lynch; 3. Jack Bogle.

(g) None of the above is correct.

491. Let R be a simple net return (SNR). Let $(1 + R)$ be a simple gross return (SGR), and let $r = ln(1 + R)$ be a continuously compounded return (CCR). Which of the following is TRUE?

(a) Compounding of SNRs uses multiplication of SGRs.

(b) Compounding of CCRs uses addition.

(c) Arithmetic averages of SNRs do not necessarily represent average economic gains.

(d) Arithmetic averages of CCRs do represent average economic gains.

(e) Geometric averages of SNRs (technically, of SGRs) do represent average economic gains.

(f) All of the above are true.

(g) Only three of the above are true.

(h) Only two of the above are true.

492. Fundamental analysis is usually _____ oriented, and technical analysis is usually _____ oriented, respectively. Fill in the blanks.

(a) Quantitative; Non-quantitative.

(b) value; growth.

(c) momentum; reversal.

(d) long-term; short-term.

(e) short-term; long-term.

(f) large-cap; small-cap.

(g) active; passive.

(h) None of the above is correct.

493. ◇ Baker and Powell (2000) survey CFOs of NYSE firms and identify and rank 20 determinants of dividend policy including these six (given in alphabetical order):

1. Concern about maintaining or increasing stock price.

2. Concern that a dividend change may provide a false signal to investors.

3. Investment considerations such as the availability of profitable investment opportunities.

4. Liquidity constraints such as the availability of cash flow.

5. The level of current and expected future earnings.

6. The pattern or continuity of past dividends.

Which two of these determinants were ranked most highly in the survey?

(a) Items 1 and 2.

(b) Items 2 and 3.

(c) Items 3 and 4.

(d) Items 4 and 5.

(e) Items 5 and 6.

(f) None of the above is correct.

494. Which of the following are three T-costs that we *ignored* in the active alpha optimization in Question 3.2.2?

(a) Bid-ask spreads, price impact, and commissions.

(b) Price impact, commissions, and price slippage.

(c) Commissions, price slippage, and bid-ask spreads.

(d) Price slippage, bid-ask spreads, and price impact.

(e) None of the above is a good answer.

495. Our objective function for the active alpha optimization contained three main parts. They are what? You may assume that the beta of the portfolio equals 1.

(a) Active return on our portfolio, a penalty for active risk in our portfolio, and a penalty for transactions costs to rebalance our portfolio.

(b) Benchmark return, a penalty for benchmark risk, and a penalty for holding an active position.

(c) Benchmark risk and return, benchmark timing risk and return, and stock selection risk and return.

(d) Total return on our portfolio, a penalty for total risk on our portfolio, and a penalty for T-costs.

(e) Passive return on our portfolio, a penalty for benchmark risk, and a penalty for relative bid-ask spreads.

496. Dividend policy is complicated. We do, however, know a number of results that seem to be generally true, at least on average. Which ONE of the following is, however, FALSE? Feel free to assume that the broad market is not moving much around any announcements mentioned.

    (a) A company announcing that it is omitting or decreasing dividends after 10 years of paying dividends is likely to see their stock price fall.

    (b) A company announcing that it is initiating dividends after 10 years of not paying dividends is likely to see their stock price rise.

    (c) Because dividend changes are seen as forecasts of subsequent earnings changes, a company announcing increased dividends can expect to see a rise in their "long-run stock price" regardless of underlying profitability.

    (d) Although the proportion of companies paying dividends in the U.S. did drop over the 20 years 1980–2000, aggregate dividends being handed to investors did not decline; it is just that the dividends were concentrated in the largest most profitable firms, and new listings were growth-oriented companies less likely to pay dividends. Since 2001, the proportion of dividend-paying stocks in the U.S. has almost doubled.

    (e) Some companies will borrow money or even forgo a positive NPV project in order to have money on hand to pay the dividend.

497. In the active alpha optimization in Question 3.2.2 we estimated a vector of alphas, $\vec{\alpha}$, for the 20 stocks we used. When standing at the point in time at which these alpha estimates are generated (i.e., the end of the second year of our data), these alphas are what?

    (a) Forecasts of future returns in active space.

    (b) Estimates of ex-post active returns on stocks.

    (c) Estimates of ex-ante total returns on stocks.

    (d) OLS regression intercepts using historical data.

    (e) None of the above is correct.

498. As of mid-2020, roughly what percentage of stocks on the New Zealand Stock Exchange (NZX) pay dividends? This question is about the broader New Zealand stock market (i.e., the roughly 111 stocks in the NZX All Share index), not just the larger-cap S&P/NZX 50 stocks.

    (a) 5–10%

    (b) 20–30%

    (c) 40–55%

    (d) 60–75%

    (e) Over 95%

499. When thinking about PVGO, we usually argue that stocks with very attractive forecast growth rates in earnings per share (EPS) get bid up in price, leading to relatively high P/E ratios. Related to this, which ONE of the following is FALSE.

(a) If we plot P/E ratios versus 3–5 year analyst forecasts of growth in operating earnings for S&P 100 stocks, we should see that higher P/Es tend, on average, to be associated with higher forecast growth rates in EPS.

(b) We should find that, on average, stocks currently classified as growth stocks typically have higher forecast growth rates in EPS than those not classified as growth stocks.

(c) We should find that high P/E ratios are good forecasters of subsequent realized growth rates in EPS. That is, it is easy to identify stocks that will deliver on promised growth in EPS.

(d) We should find that stocks with very high P/E ratios are often involved in projects that investors forecast to have positive NPVs (e.g., self-driving cars, electric vehicles, etc.).

(e) Stocks with very high P/Es are unlikely to be income stocks.

(f) Stocks with a high $PVGO/P$ ratio will tend to have high P/E ratios, assuming the riskiness of the earnings stream is not too high.

500. Which of the following funds would you expect to be the least volatile? That is, which would you expect to have the lowest standard deviation of daily returns?

(a) A fund that goes long stock but also short sells high-beta stocks in sufficient quantity to obtain an overall beta of -1 for the fund.

(b) A dollar-balanced fund that is long $500,000 worth of stock and short $500,000 worth of other stock, so that overall fund beta is zero.

(c) A fund that actively tries to outperform an S&P/NZX 50 benchmark by chasing alpha, and which imposes the restriction that the fund's beta equals 1.

(d) A fund that passively tries to match an S&P/NZX 50 benchmark, and which imposes the restriction that the fund's beta equals 1.

(e) A fund that invests only in low-volatility stocks, like utility stocks.

501. Roughly what would you expect the average *closing* relative bid-ask spread to be on AIA, SPK, FBU, or FPH (i.e., a few of the largest-capitalization N.Z. stocks listed on the NZX)? Assume we collect relative spreads daily over the three years 2017–2019 to calculate the average.

(a) 5–10 bps

(b) 10–25 bps

(c) 50–100 bps

(d) 150–250 bps

(e) Notably over 250 bps

502. Two mutual funds will earn a constant 7.5% per annum gross return. One charges only 25 bps per annum expense ratio; the other charges a 209 bps per annum expense ratio. (These are actual expense numbers I found in N.Z. for two funds with nearly identical holdings.) For a 40-year lump sum investment of $10,000 into each fund, what is the ratio of ending wealth in the low-fee fund over ending wealth in the high-fee fund? Assume that annual net return is $r_n = r_g - e$, where r_g is the gross return and e is the expense ratio. Ignore taxes and other T-costs.

   (a) 2.173

   (b) 1.998

   (c) 1.071

   (d) 0.985

   (e) None of the above is within 0.005 of being correct.

503. Why did we say that there is a problem with the arithmetic averages of simple net returns (SNR)?

   (a) The arithmetic average SNR underestimates the true economic growth represented by the time series of returns.

   (b) The arithmetic average SNR has problems because this average involves multiplication, but SNRs compound using addition only.

   (c) The arithmetic average SNR overestimates the true economic growth represented by the time series of returns.

   (d) The arithmetic average SNR has problems because this average involves addition, but compounding of SNRs requires the use of multiplication.

   (e) (a) and (b).

   (f) (c) and (d).

504. ◇ In Chapter 2 of *Foundations*, we discussed a discrete-time random walk due to Merton (1980). The random walk had the following form:

$$r_n = \mu\tau + \sigma\sqrt{\tau}z_n,$$

where $z_n \sim N(0, 1)$, and τ is the length of each time step. Which one of the following is NOT correct?

   (a) The $\mu\tau$ term is a drift per time step.

   (b) The $\sigma\sqrt{\tau}z_t$ term is a diffusion term per time step.

   (c) The z_t term represents a news arrival process where the news is randomly good or bad.

   (d) The return r_n is a simple net return per time step.

   (e) If we let $\tau \to 0$, the random walk approaches the geometric Brownian motion assumed by Black, Scholes, and Merton in the Black-Scholes-Merton option pricing model.

505. Portfolio manager Peter Lynch gives an old rule of thumb that a fairly priced stock has a P/E ratio _____ its growth rate in earnings and that if the P/E ratio divided by growth rate in earnings is larger than 2 then the stock is _____. Fill in the blanks.

To simplify, assume that the stock does not pay dividends. Note that we must relax when calculating the ratio of P/E to growth rate in earnings because the numerator and denominator are in different units and have different scaling.

(a) roughly equal to; attractive.

(b) larger than; attractive.

(c) smaller than; attractive.

(d) roughly equal to; unattractive.

(e) larger than; unattractive.

(f) smaller than; unattractive.

(g) None of the above is correct.

506. You are an options market maker who just sold an at-the-money call option on a stock (i.e., the strike price is very close to the stock price). In the U.S. and N.Z., exchange-traded options usually cover 100 shares of stock; Assume that is the case here. This option position is the only position you hold. Which of the following makes most sense for you to hedge your options exposure?

(a) Buy 25 shares of stock to hedge the option position.

(b) Sell short 25 shares of stock to hedge the option position.

(c) Buy 50 shares of stock to hedge the option position.

(d) Sell short 50 shares of stock to hedge the option position.

(e) Buy 75 shares of stock to hedge the option position.

(f) Sell short 75 shares of stock to hedge the option position.

507. You are an options market maker. You just sold a deep-in-the-money call option on a stock to a trader. This option has stock price that is very high relative to the strike price. In the U.S. and N.Z., exchange-traded options usually cover 100 shares of stock. Assume that the option you sold covers 100 shares of stock. This option position is the only position you hold. Now you want to hedge your option exposure. Which of the following makes most sense as a hedge?

(a) Buy 25 shares of stock to hedge the option position.

(b) Sell short 25 shares of stock to hedge the option position.

(c) Buy 75 shares of stock to hedge the option position.

(d) Sell short 75 shares of stock to hedge the option position.

(e) Buy 100 shares of stock to hedge the option position.

(f) Sell short 100 shares of stock to hedge the option position.

1.2. FOUNDATIONS II: FINANCIAL ECONOMICS

508. You are a U.S. options trader. You wish to estimate the value of an at-the-money (i.e., stock price equals strike price) three-month call option on BRK.B. This is Berkshire Hathaway Class B stock, managed by the amazing Warren Buffett for 50+ years. BRK.B does not pay dividends. The Black-Scholes formula can be used here, or any formula that *approximates* Black-Scholes pricing.

The option covers 100 shares of stock, and you wish to estimate the *total* value of the option, not the value on a per share basis. (So, you should probably value it on a per share basis first and then multiply your answer by 100). The stock price is $S = \$200$ per share. The volatility is $\sigma = 0.50$. Assume interest rates are zero—it is not far wrong in 2021, and interest rates are the least important input to the Black-Scholes formula anyway. Which one of the following is closest to your estimated total value of your BRK.B option?

(a) $1,000

(b) $2,000

(c) $2,500

(d) $4,000

(e) $6,928

(f) $12,000

509. Two-fund separation (as described in *Foundations*) refers to what?

(a) Choosing two risky assets on the interior of the Markowitz frontier (i.e., to the right of the Markowitz hyperbola), and looking at the portfolio combination curve traced out for those two assets.

(b) Picking two portfolios on the Markowitz frontier that are separate from one another (e.g., the portfolios with weights $\vec{G}$ and weights $\vec{H} + \vec{G}$, respectively, that have returns 0 and 1, respectively, as used in the Markowitz/Tobin problem in Question 3.2.1), and using these weights to generate the entire Markowitz frontier.

(c) Using true diversification arguments to obtain a minimum-risk Markowitz frontier, introducing a riskless asset, and deducing that all investors choose combinations of two "funds": the riskless asset and a single risky portfolio on the Markowitz frontier.

(d) Looking at stocks paired with other candidate risky assets to find the risky pair that offers the best diversification benefits.

(e) The clear distinction between the long-run returns to risky assets (like large-capitalization stocks and small-capitalization stocks) and safer assets (like corporate bonds, long-term government bonds, and T-bills), as seen in the SBBI (Stocks, Bonds, Bills and Inflation) graphs that we looked at in lectures.

510. In the spreadsheet MIN-VAR-OBJ.XLS, I give step-by-step instructions that walk you through some minimizations and some maximizations in order to plot out a feasible investment region in mean-variance space, subject to various constraints which you can change.

    The objective function is portfolio variance (i.e., $\sigma_P^2 = \vec{h}'V\vec{h}$). If we minimize this portfolio variance function for varying level of return μ_P, then we can plot out the mean-variance efficient minimum-risk frontier. We also tried *maximizing* the portfolio variance in order to find the right-hand side boundaries to the feasible set of investments when you cannot go short. (The feasible set looked like a batwing.)

    There were, however, several problems that we encountered where the optimizer did not move the choice variables, and the optimizer concluded, incorrectly, that we were already at some optimum. The important takeaway message(s) for us, especially in reference to implementing the active alpha optimization in Question 3.2.2, were what?

    (a) Always re-run an optimization using a different set of initial conditions, to try to confirm that you found a global optimum, not just a local optimum.

    (b) Do not start any optimization routine using initial values for the choice variables that are equal to the solution to another optimization, because that may be a local optimum for the problem you are solving.

    (c) Minimizing a variance-based objective function is a more stable approach than maximizing a utility-based objective function.

    (d) Both (a) and (b).

    (e) None of the above was a takeaway message from the problems we experienced with the optimizer.

511. In our active alpha optimization in Question 3.2.2 we rebalanced just once, as if we were moving from the benchmark portfolio to our new portfolio. In this situation, the quantity $|\vec{h}_B - \vec{h}_P|'\vec{\iota}$ represented what? (Note that $\vec{\iota}$ is a column vector of ones, "$|\cdot|$" is the absolute value function, $\vec{h}_P$ is the new portfolio weights, and $\vec{h}_B$ is the benchmark portfolio weights.)

    (a) It is the direct measure of transaction costs that we fed into our objective function in Question 3.2.2.

    (b) It is one-sided turnover (i.e., counting just buys or just sells) as a proportion of portfolio value.

    (c) It is two-sided turnover (i.e., counting both buys and sells) as a proportion of portfolio value.

    (d) It is zero; this quantity must be identically zero because there is a purchase for every sale.

    (e) It is the overall active position in the new portfolio.

512. In Chapter 2 of *Foundations*, we compared and contrasted the SPIVA study of index versus active performance in the U.S. and Australian equity markets. Which ONE of the following was NOT one of the results we saw for equity funds?

    (a) As investment horizon increases, the ability of active U.S. fund managers to outperform their benchmark indices decreases fairly steadily, but the Australian results are much more variable.

    (b) At the 15-year horizon, roughly 80–98% of U.S. active fund managers fail to outperform their benchmarks.

    (c) At the 15-year mark, about half of Australian small- and medium-cap managers outperform their benchmarks.

    (d) At the 15-year mark, U.S. small-cap active managers are much more likely to outperform their benchmarks than U.S. large-cap active managers. This is because small-cap stocks present more market inefficiencies than large-cap stocks.

    (e) At the 15-year mark, U.S. value fund managers may have a slight advantage over U.S. growth fund managers in terms of performance relative to their benchmark indices, but both active groups still have something like 90% of managers underperforming their benchmarks.

513. $\diamond$ In the spreadsheet MIN-VAR-OBJ.XLS, portfolio variance (i.e., $\sigma_P^2 = \vec{h}'V\vec{h}$) is minimized for varying level of return μ_P. We used it to trace out a minimum-risk Markowitz frontier. In Chapter 2 of *Foundations*, I give a formula for the solution weights to the Markowitz frontier, which you implemented in the Markowitz/Tobin problem in Question 3.2.1 (with no numerical optimization). Which ONE of the following is TRUE?

    (a) The Markowitz solution in *Foundations* (as used on Question 3.2.1) allows short selling.

    (b) The Markowitz solution in *Foundations* (as used on Question 3.2.1) applies to the no-short-selling case only.

    (c) The Markowitz numerical optimization routine in MIN-VAR-OBJ.XLS is not capable of handling the case where we allow short selling.

    (d) Neither the Markowitz solution in *Foundations* (as used on Question 3.2.1), nor the Excel numerical optimization in MIN-VAR-OBJ.XLS is capable of handling the case where no short selling is allowed.

    (e) Both the Markowitz solution in *Foundations* (as used on Question 3.2.1) and the numerical optimization in MIN-VAR-OBJ.XLS are capable of handling the case where no short selling is allowed.

1.3 Financial Theories and Empirical Evidence

514. The capital asset pricing model (CAPM) and the efficient market hypothesis (EMH) are related in which ways?

   (a) CAPM implies EMH.

   (b) EMH implies CAPM.

   (c) Both CAPM implies EMH and EMH implies CAPM.

   (d) All of the above.

   (e) None of the above.

515. The capital asset pricing model (CAPM) and Black-Scholes-Merton option pricing (BSM) are related in which ways?

   (a) CAPM implies BSM.

   (b) BSM implies CAPM.

   (c) Both CAPM implies BSM and BSM implies CAPM.

   (d) All of the above.

   (e) It is more complicated. In the special case where the time step is infinitesimally short, the CAPM can be used to derive BSM pricing. So, the CAPM implies BSM in this special case, but not in general (e.g., because option betas vary with the passage of time and changing stock price over longer time steps).

516. The random walk hypothesis (RWH) and the geometric martingale hypothesis (GMH) are related in which ways? Assume here that the RWH is the assumption that prices follow a geometric Brownian motion (GBM) with some drift rate μ. Assume that the GMH is that prices follow an unbiased GBM (i.e., $\mu = 0$).

   (a) RWH implies GMH.

   (b) GMH implies RWH.

   (c) Both RWH implies GMH and GMH implies RWH.

   (d) All of the above.

   (e) None of the above.

517. The efficient market hypothesis (EMH) and the random walk hypothesis (RWH) are related in which ways?

   (a) EMH implies RWH.

   (b) RWH implies EMH.

   (c) Both EMH implies RWH and RWH implies EMH.

   (d) All of the above.

   (e) None of the above.

518. In the Markowitz problem we solved in Question 3.2.1, we calculated historical betas and plotted them relative to historical mean returns. Was this a simple test of the CAPM?

    (a) Yes, because we estimated betas and returns and plotted them against each other to see if they were linearly related.

    (b) No, because even though we did look at the relationship between betas and returns, that has got nothing to do with whether the CAPM holds or not.

    (c) Yes, because ultimately real-world betas are calculated relative to market proxies, and that is exactly what we did.

    (d) (a) and (c)

    (e) None of the above is correct.

519. ◇ The three biggest daily percentage moves in the S&P 500 over the 20 years 1990–2010 were all in October 2008 (during the global financial crisis). On October 13, 2008 the S&P 500 rose 11.6%, on October 15, 2008 the S&P 500 fell 9.04%, and on October 28, 2008 the S&P 500 rose 10.8%. The long-run standard deviation of daily returns to the S&P 500 is 1.0%. Suppose daily stock returns are normally distributed with mean zero and standard deviation 1.0% and are independent of each other from one day to the next. Then the probability that on a randomly selected day the S&P 500 would experience a move greater than or equal to the magnitude of the October 28, 2008 rise of 10.8% is roughly what?

    (a) 3 chances in 20 (i.e., 0.15; So, we would expect three moves this big each month).

    (b) 1 chance in 20 (i.e., 0.05; So, we would expect one move this big each month).

    (c) 1 chance in 250 (i.e., 0.004; So, we would expect one move this big each year).

    (d) 3 chances in 5,000 (i.e., 0.0006; So, we would expect three moves this big every 20 years).

    (e) None of the above is correct; it is much less likely than the above answers.

520. The price momentum strategy is a *relative* strategy. What does this mean?

    (a) We look at the weights each stock has in the benchmark, and then we overweight attractive stocks (or underweight unattractive stocks) *relative to* these benchmark weights.

    (b) For any given stock, we look at its most recent price *relative to* its price six months ago, say, in deciding whether to overweight or underweight that stock.

    (c) We score (i.e., rank) stocks based on their recent price performance *relative to* the performance of the other stocks in the benchmark.

    (d) Price momentum is a strategy where the goal is to achieve performance that looks good *relative to* the performance of a quoted benchmark index.

    (e) We rebalance our portfolio by optimizing an objective function that chases forecast price momentum alphas but only does so *relative to* the active risks and T-costs involved in stepping away from the benchmark.

521. This is a theory question. Assume the expected return on the market portfolio is 10% per annum, and the riskless rate is 3% per annum. A stock with a CAPM beta of 0.90 has standard deviation of returns that

    (a) must be higher than the standard deviation of returns to the Market portfolio.

    (b) must be lower than the standard deviation of returns to the Market portfolio.

    (c) could equal the standard deviation of returns to the Market portfolio.

    (d) cannot equal the standard deviation of returns to the Market portfolio but there is not enough information given to determine whether it is higher or lower.

    (e) none of the above is true.

522. When we drew the Markowitz frontier in Question 3.2.1, we saw that the benchmark portfolio plotted on the *interior* of the space bounded by the Markowitz minimum risk frontier. The benchmark portfolio was therefore not mean-variance efficient. Which ONE of the following is correct?

    (a) The benchmark portfolio plotted on the interior because we had only 20 stocks in it. If we had used *all* the stocks on the NZX, then the benchmark would have plotted on the Markowitz frontier.

    (b) The benchmark plotted on the frontier because we were using *historical* "ex-post" returns. If we could have measured *forward looking* "ex-ante" returns, then the benchmark would have plotted on the Markowitz frontier.

    (c) The benchmark portfolio plotted on the interior, rather than on the minimum risk Markowitz frontier only because of the economic cycle (i.e., coming out of a recession). If we had used a more normal time period, the benchmark would have plotted on the Markowitz frontier.

    (d) In fact, it is only measurement error that explains why the benchmark portfolio did not plot on the Markowitz frontier. If we had better estimators of mean and variance and covariance, the benchmark would have been on the Markowitz frontier.

    (e) None of the above is correct.

523. In Question 3.2.1 (the Markowitz problem), we found that the 20-stock benchmark portfolio plotted *strictly within* the minimum risk frontier for risky assets rather than *on* the frontier as in the CAPM theory. This is because

    (a) We used historical returns, rather than forward-looking returns (which we might have obtained by surveying investors).

    (b) There was a recession in N.Z. during our dataset.

    (c) Diversification does not reduce risk as much when most stocks are going down in price.

    (d) Investors are not mean-variance optimizers within this group of stocks.

    (e) Both (a) and (d) are correct.

524. Assume the theoretical CAPM relationship holds. Suppose that the beta of Asset C satisfies $\beta_C < 0$. The CAPM then implies that $E(R_C) < R_F$, where R_C and R_F are the future returns on Asset C and the riskless asset respectively. How can it be that the expected return on Asset C is less than the riskless rate?

   (a) It must be that the market risk premium $[E(R_M) - R_F]$ is negative. Nothing else makes sense.

   (b) Asset C must in fact be another riskless asset.

   (c) Asset C must itself be a very diversified portfolio; so diversified that its expected return is less than the riskless rate.

   (d) Asset C must offer diversification properties so attractive that investors have bid its price up to the point where its expected return is lower than the riskless rate.

   (e) Asset C must be so risky (i.e., high variance of returns) that people find it so unattractive that they have sold it off in such large quantities that it now offers a negative expected return.

525. In the Markowitz problem (Question 3.2.1), we found that historical betas were linearly related to historical mean returns when the reference portfolio for the betas was the tangency portfolio, but not when the reference portfolio for the betas was the benchmark. From a Roll critique perspective, what do you conclude about our attempts to test the CAPM?

   (a) The CAPM holds in theory, but the CAPM does not hold in practice.

   (b) The return on our tangency portfolio is an estimate of the historical return on the CAPM market portfolio.

   (c) Our test of the CAPM was inconclusive.

   (d) We did not test the CAPM.

   (e) None of the above is correct.

526. The Efficient Markets Hypothesis says that easy-to-obtain information should already be reflected in prices. Suppose I download the time series of daily stock prices on IBM for the last 250 trading days. Suppose I use these to work out the correlation between P_t and P_{t-1}. That is, the correlation between the prices on the first 249 days and the last 249 days of my 250-day sample. This tells me whether I can use today's stock price to forecast tomorrow's stock price. Which of the following is a likely number for this correlation?

   (a) 0.995

   (b) 0.750

   (c) 0.500

   (d) 0.000

   (e) -0.500

527. The CAPM is a straight line relationship between expected returns and betas. If I collect daily data for last year on every stock in the S&P/NZX50 index and plot mean returns versus beta (relative to the index), what pattern will I see?

    (a) I will get a perfect straight line.

    (b) I will get something that is quite close to a straight line, but not a perfect straight line.

    (c) I will get a jumble of points that looks nothing like a straight line.

    (d) I will get a clear pattern showing that higher beta gives higher mean return, but it will be curved upward, rather than a straight line.

    (e) None of the above is a good answer.

528. Two-fund separation is when...

    (a) The benchmark and the tangency portfolio are not the same portfolio.

    (b) Markowitz-type investors decide that they want to invest only in combinations of the riskless asset and the world market portfolio of risky assets.

    (c) We calculate portfolio combination curves for portfolios of any two risky assets.

    (d) We look at the difference in performance between an index and an ETF that mimics the index (e.g., the FONZ and the S&P/NZX50 Portfolio Capital Index).

    (e) Markowitz-type investors use stock selection but not benchmark timing.

529. We discussed a criticism of the classic 60/40 portfolio in *Foundations*. The critique said that the 60/40 portfolio is not true diversification because:

    (a) The returns to this portfolio are 98–99% correlated with an all-equity portfolio.

    (b) The fixed income slice of the 60/40 portfolio is in a low-risk market.

    (c) True diversification involves seeking out risky markets lightly correlated or uncorrelated with equities.

    (d) All of the above.

    (e) (a) and (c) above.

530. With a forward-looking theoretical Markowitz mean-variance optimization, and the associated theoretical CAPM relationship, if risky Stock A has $E(R_A) < E(R_M)$, where R_A and R_M are the future returns on Stock A and the market portfolio, respectively, what can you tell me about Stock A's beta, β_A?

    (a) $\beta_A \geq 1$

    (b) $\beta_A = 1$

    (c) $0 < \beta_A < 1$

    (d) $\beta_A < 1$

    (e) $\beta_A < 0$

531. I want to test the CAPM model. Suppose I collect daily returns data for two years on the 50 stocks that are members of the S&P/NZX50. Suppose I calculate average returns on those 50 stocks, and I also calculate the sample betas of those 50 stocks relative to performance of the S&P/NZX50. Suppose I plot the average returns versus the sample betas. Which ONE of the following is TRUE about this plot?

    (a) Finding a straight line indicates that the theoretical CAPM holds.

    (b) Finding a straight line indicates that the theoretical CAPM does not hold.

    (c) Finding a jumble of points (i.e., not a straight line) indicates that the theoretical CAPM holds.

    (d) Finding a jumble of points (i.e., not a straight line) indicates that the theoretical CAPM does not hold.

    (e) None of the above is true.

532. I re-estimated the Markowitz-Tobin frontiers in Question 3.2.1 using data from the middle of the global financial crisis and found that the tangency portfolio was on the lower region of the Markowitz frontier and the "security market line" (relative to the tangency portfolio) was downward sloping. This is because...

    (a) The return on the benchmark portfolio was below the riskless rate.

    (b) Investors were risk seeking, not risk averse during 2007 and 2008.

    (c) Stock prices dropped in advance of the recession, but the riskless rate we used lagged behind at a high rate.

    (d) The Efficient Markets Hypothesis is false, because the marginal investor chose non-optimal investments.

    (e) Investors chose to invest in low-yielding assets in order to be defensive during the Global Credit Crisis.

533. Which of the following best describes the "price momentum" trading strategy?

    (a) Buying stocks that increased in price and selling stocks that decreased in price.

    (b) Overweighting stocks that increased in price over the last 6 months and underweighting stocks that decreased in price over the last 6 months.

    (c) Overweighting those stocks that have increased in price ("winners") over the last 2–3 years and underweighting those stocks that have decreased in price ("losers") over the last 2–3 years.

    (d) Overweighting those stocks that have under-performed the benchmark ("losers") over the last 2–3 years and underweighting those stocks that have over-performed the benchmark ("winners") over the last 2–3 years.

    (e) Overweighting those stocks that have out-performed the benchmark ("winners") over the last 6–9 months and underweighting those stocks that have under-performed the benchmark ("losers") over the last 6–9 months.

This information is for the following THREE questions (Q534–Q536).
Chapter 3 of *Foundations* discusses the size effect in global stocks. The raw data for the test of mean returns are the excess of the continuously compounded daily returns to the global small-cap portfolio over and above the daily returns to the global large-cap portfolio over the sample period 2000–2017. These excess returns data have a mean of 0.00022405, a standard deviation of 0.00437698 (calculated using Bessel's correction—dividing by $N - 1$ instead of N in order for the sample variance to be unbiased), an autocorrelation of 0.00396789, and a sample size of 4,460. On average, there were 251 trading days per year during this time period.

534. Which one of the following is the paired two-sample t-test statistic for the difference in means to the small-cap stocks over and above the large-cap stocks? This t-statistic is calculated ignoring any possible violations of underlying assumptions. Please round your answer to two decimal places.

    (a) 0.05

    (b) 0.81

    (c) 1.02

    (d) 3.42

    (e) 54.16

535. Which one of the following is the t-statistic for the autocorrelation in the excess returns data? Please round your answer to two decimal places.

    (a) 0.26

    (b) 0.91

    (c) 3.42

    (d) 14.36

    (e) 60.54

536. The standard deviation of daily returns to the global small-cap portfolio was 0.01044034 and the standard deviation of daily returns to the global large-cap portfolio was 0.01029635. Each had sample size of 4460. What is the value of the F-statistic to test whether the small-cap portfolio returns were more volatile than the large-cap portfolio returns? To avoid confusion, please put the small-cap number in the numerator, and the large-cap number in the denominator. Please round your answer to three decimal places.

    (a) 1.062

    (b) 1.028

    (c) 1.014

    (d) 1.007

    (e) None of the above.

537. If we restrict our attention to the estimates we saw of the relative market values of equity (E) and debt (D) appearing in the World Market Portfolio of Risky Assets in Chapter 3 of *Foundations*, we find what?

    (a) $E > 2 \times D$

    (b) $2 \times D \geq E > D$

    (c) $E \approx D$ (where "$\approx$" means approximately equal to)

    (d) $D > E \geq \frac{1}{2} \times D$

    (e) $\frac{1}{2} \times D > E$

    (f) None of the above is correct.

538. Eugene Fama and Kenneth French published many research papers during 1992–2017, as part of their "Fama-French critique of the CAPM." They identify economic factors in addition to "The Market" that help to explain stock returns. In Chapter 3 of *Foundations*, we used the arguments of Ferguson and Shockley (2003) to state what?

    (a) Fama and French's results do not provide any evidence against the single-beta CAPM.

    (b) The extra explanatory factors found by Fama and French compensate for the use of poorly estimated proxies for the CAPM market portfolio.

    (c) Best practice capital budgeting use of the single-beta CAPM requires the use of at least some of these extra Fama-French factors, or of a composite market portfolio containing more than just equity.

    (d) All of the above.

    (e) Only some of the above statements are correct, not all of the above.

539. You combine $250,000 of your money with $1,250,000 borrowed from a bank to buy an average $1,500,000 house in Auckland N.Z. Immediately after signing the contract, a news report reveals economic news that causes all Auckland house prices to fall by 20% immediately. In a panic, you sell your house immediately for 20% less than you bought it. What is your rate of return on the investment? Ignore taxes, transaction costs, fees, commissions, and interest on the loan. You may assume that you will not default on your loan.

    (a) -20%

    (b) -60%

    (c) -90%

    (d) -120%

    (e) -150%

    (f) -180%

    (g) None of the above is correct.

1.4 Active Investment Topics

540. In a recent eight-week period, there were four days where the U.S. stock market indexes moved up more than +3.5%. Given your knowledge of the variability of daily returns to indexes, you can conclude that:

   (a) The standard deviation of daily stock returns must be over 3.5%.

   (b) Daily stock returns are not normally distributed.

   (c) The distribution of daily individual stock returns is positively skewed.

   (d) Good days following good days means there is positive autocorrelation in daily stock returns.

   (e) None of the above.

541. Which one of the following is the best definition of the price momentum strategy?

   (a) Go long stocks that have recently risen and go short stocks that have recently fallen.

   (b) Buy stocks that have recently risen and sell stocks that have recently fallen.

   (c) Overweight stocks that have recently risen and under-weight stocks that have recently fallen.

   (d) Overweight stocks that have recently risen relative to the benchmark and under-weight stocks that have recently fallen relative to the benchmark.

   (e) Overweight stocks that have recently fallen relative to the benchmark and under-weight stocks that have recently risen relative to the benchmark.

542. A price momentum strategy over-weights what kind of stocks relative to their benchmark weights? Which is the best ONE answer, holding true regardless of market direction?

   (a) Stocks that have recently dipped down in price and are therefore likely to be value stocks.

   (b) Stocks that have recently fallen in price by much more than the average stock.

   (c) Stocks that have recently risen in price by much more than the average stock.

   (d) Stocks that have recently outperformed the average stock.

   (e) Stocks that have recently underperformed the average stock.

543. Which one of the following is typical of a traditional value stock?

   (a) A stock with a low P/E ratio.

   (b) A stock with a low dividend yield.

   (c) A stock expected to grow its sales dramatically in the future.

   (d) A stock expected to grow its earnings dramatically in the future.

   (e) Either (a) or (b).

544. If we run an active alpha optimization using a glamour alpha built from dividend yield, is our raw alpha just the dividend yield, or is it the negative of dividend yield?

(a) Alpha = dividend yield.

(b) Alpha = negative dividend yield.

(c) Neither (a) nor (b), because you cannot build a glamour alpha using dividend yield.

(d) Either (a) or (b), because the optimizer does not care about the sign.

(e) None of the above.

545. If we run an active alpha optimization using a value alpha built from dividend yield, is our raw alpha just the dividend yield, or is it the negative of dividend yield?

(a) Alpha = dividend yield.

(b) Alpha = negative dividend yield.

(c) Neither (a) nor (b), because you cannot build a value alpha using dividend yield.

(d) Either (a) or (b), because the optimizer does not care about the sign.

(e) None of the above.

546. Which of the following is/are correct for Shariah-compliant investing (SCI)?

(a) SCI sees money only as a *measure* of value, and of no intrinsic value itself. As such no reward in the form of interest should be charged for borrowing it nor earned for lending it.

(b) SCI has existed for over 1400 years.

(c) SCI in halal stocks performed slightly better than traditional western-style investing in stocks during the recent global credit crisis.

(d) All of the above are correct.

(e) Only (a) and (b) above are correct.

547. A "growth" type of investment can be

(a) A glamour stock whose price has been pushed up relative to fundamentals.

(b) A growth company where there is a good possibility of future earnings growth.

(c) A stock whose value has been beaten down relative to fundamentals, but which has good forecast earnings growth.

(d) All of the above.

(e) Only (a) and (b).

548. Many practitioners distinguish between whether stocks are value or growth stocks. Which ONE of the following is FALSE?

   (a) A value stock typically has a higher P/E ratio than its growth rate in earnings (e.g., P/E=20 but growth rate in earnings is 10 percentage points per annum).

   (b) A growth stock is sometimes also a value stock.

   (c) A stock that is expected to grow its earnings dramatically in the future can be correctly referred to as a growth stock.

   (d) A stock that has a very low P/E ratio relative to its peers might be called a growth investment in a New Zealand KiwiSaver scheme.

   (e) A value stock typically has a stock price that is depressed relative to fundamentals when compared with other stocks.

549. An exchange-traded fund (ETF) is always:

   (a) A fund that passively replicates a stock market index.

   (b) A fund that mimics the behavior of a commodity price.

   (c) A fund that tracks a particular sector of the economy.

   (d) A fund that actively trades stocks to try to beat some benchmark.

   (e) A fund that trades on an exchange like a stock.

550. A retail mutual fund that passively replicates the S&P 500 charges a fee of 7 bps per annum. On an investment of $100,000 this is expected to amount to something close to...

   (a) $0.70 per annum

   (b) $7.00 per annum

   (c) $70 per annum

   (d) $700 per annum

   (e) None of the above

551. On April 26, 2012, Vanguard mutual fund group offered both an ETF and a closed end fund that mimic the S&P 500 and charge an annual expense ratio of only 6 bps. Investors had USD114b invested in it (more than three times the market capitalization of the entire NZX at that time). If I put USD10,000 into this fund, roughly how much money will they charge me as an annual expense ratio?

   (a) $0.60

   (b) $6.00

   (c) $60.00

   (d) $600.00

   (e) None of the above is correct.

552. On April 13, 2015, Vanguard offered both an ETF and an open-ended fund mimicking the S&P 500. They charge an annual expense ratio of only 5 bps. Investors had USD208.8b invested in it. (Note that $1b is $1,000,000,000.) Roughly how much money does Vanguard generate per year in fee income from this one fund? Assume the amount invested is stable over the year.

    (a) $1,044,000 (i.e., just over a million dollars).

    (b) $10,440,000 (i.e., just over 10 million dollars).

    (c) $104,400,000 (i.e., just over a hundred million dollars).

    (d) $1,044,000,000 (i.e., just over a billion dollars).

    (e) None of the above is correct.

553. A value stock is usually a stock whose price is depressed relative to fundamentals. This means it might have, for example,...

    (a) A high P/E ratio relative to its peers and a high dividend yield.

    (b) A high P/E ratio relative to its peers and a low dividend yield.

    (c) A low P/E ratio relative to its peers and a high dividend yield.

    (d) A low P/E ratio relative to its peers and a low dividend yield.

    (e) None of the above makes sense.

554. Which of the following would you be surprised to find in a "growth" New Zealand KiwiSaver investment fund?

    (a) A stock that has had excellent earnings performance recently and for which the management are forecasting continued high growth in earnings.

    (b) A stock in the construction industry (which was recently named the fastest growing sector of the New Zealand economy).

    (c) A holding in a listed property trust (i.e., in a fund that trades on the exchange and itself holds direct investments in real estate).

    (d) A holding in corporate bonds.

    (e) I would not be surprised to find any of the above in a "growth" KiwiSaver fund.

555. A major selling point of NZX Smartshares' exchange traded funds (ETFs), and which is not mentioned on their Web site front page (December 2020), is...

    (a) The high returns to ETFs in general.

    (b) The low volatility of the returns to the ETFs.

    (c) The low management expense ratio (i.e., annual fee).

    (d) The passive management which means we need not fear underperformance.

    (e) The low transaction costs associated with the passively managed funds.

556. Growth stocks are attractive because...

   (a) their price has typically been beaten down so far relative to fundamentals that price is expected to grow dramatically in the future when the market comes to its senses.

   (b) they are typically expected to grow their earnings at a high rate relative to the market and their price is expected to trend upwards—hand-in-hand with the earnings growth.

   (c) their P/E ratios are high relative to their projected growth in earnings.

   (d) they have high ratios of fundamental variables to price, e.g., high E/P, C/P, or dividend yield, and thus offer a good return on investment in the form of earnings, cash flow, or dividends.

   (e) More than one of the above answers are correct.

557. The average "conservative" KiwiSaver fund charged an annual fee of 65 bps as at April 27, 2011. Suppose you had $10,000 sitting in a conservative KiwiSaver fund charging this fee. How much do you expect the manager to skim out of your account this year as a total fee? Ignore all other fees.

   (a) $0.65

   (b) $6.50

   (c) $65.00

   (d) $650.00

   (e) $6,500.00

558. Suppose I told you that I just looked at the performance of a passive fund that is meant to be mimicking the behavior of the S&P 500 and I found out that it had an IR equal to 25 over the most recent year. The IR, you will recall, is the Sharpe ratio in active space, and a value of 0.50 is considered good, while a value of 1.0 is considered excellent. Can the IR=25 be correct?

   (a) It is clearly an error in calculation. It is ridiculous to have an IR this high even in an active fund, so in a passive fund it makes no sense at all.

   (b) It is clearly a mistake because IRs are not even defined for passive funds. IRs are only for active funds trying to beat the market.

   (c) It could be correct because the way in which you calculate IRs certainly allows for a result like this in the case of a passive fund.

   (d) It could be correct, but it would require an outstanding active manager running the passive fund.

   (e) It is impossible to say whether such a number could be correct or not. We would need to see the raw data.

559. You just won a lottery and got a \$100,000 tax-free prize. You decide to invest it today ($t = 0$) and you will not touch it for 40 years (i.e., you withdraw the money at $t = 40$). You are choosing between investing in two passive index funds. The funds both have an expected return of 8.5% per annum before expenses. Fund 1 has an annual expense ratio of 50 bps, and Fund 2 has an annual expense ratio of 6 bps. You may assume that the net annual return on each fund is just the 8.5% less the expense ratio. Please ignore taxes and any other T-costs. How much better off do you expect to be at $t = 40$, in dollar terms, if you invest in the low expense ratio fund rather than the high expense ratio fund? Please round to the nearest dollar.

   (a) \$41,967

   (b) \$383,663

   (c) \$472,134

   (d) \$1,697,501

   (e) \$2,211,601

560. In Question 3.2.1 you built Markowitz frontiers and you found that for our 20 stocks, the naive capitalization-weighted benchmark B had less risk than that of any individual stock, and notably less risk than the average risk of the risky stocks. Portfolios on the Markowitz frontier had even less risk still than the naively diversified benchmark. Difficulty in estimating mean returns implies, however, that historical Markowitz frontiers do not, in general, provide forward looking mean-variance benchmark-beating investment guidance. ONE possible exception discussed in *Foundations* was what?

   (a) Cast aside the full Markowitz framework. Accept that the mean returns on all stocks are terribly poorly estimated. So, simply identify and hold what was the historic minimum variance portfolio. Hold for a long time, rebalancing once per annum.

   (b) Buy and hold a portfolio of the 50 largest New Zealand stocks with naive market capitalization weights. Rebalance at least once per year to account for new IPOs and delistings, etc.

   (c) Hold only the five biggest New Zealand stocks, weighted by their market capitalizations, because we noticed that the biggest stocks tend to have the least risk, and are therefore likely to dominate the benchmark from a mean-variance perspective.

   (d) Buy and hold the SPY (SPDR ETF) that tracks the S&P 500 index and charges only a 5 bps expense ratio.

   (e) Buy and hold the Vanguard funds mentioned in *Foundations* that invest in 7,469 stocks and 4,098 bonds spread over 50 countries. They charge a 15 or fewer bps annual expense ratio, thereby providing a better product and at a lower price than most of their competitors. (Numbers as of October, 2016.)

561. I am looking at a stock and trying to decide whether to invest in it. It pays no dividends. Suppose its P/E ratio is 35, and the P/E ratio for the market as a whole is only 12. What would be a sensible next step?

(a) Buy it because that is a great P/E ratio.

(b) Avoid it because that is a terrible P/E ratio.

(c) Look at the stock's projected growth rate in earnings and see how it compares with the stock's P/E ratio.

(d) Look at the P/E of stocks in other industries and see how those ratios compare with this stock's P/E.

(e) None of the above is a sensible next step.

562. Exchange-traded funds (ETFs) have many characteristics that distinguish them from other funds. Which ONE of the following is FALSE for most ETFs?

(a) ETFs must be bought and sold directly from the fund company at end of day prices.

(b) ETFs trade on a stock exchange like a stock.

(c) ETFs can be bought and sold at intradaily prices.

(d) ETFs attempt to replicate the performance of some known index or asset.

(e) ETFs often have lower expense ratios than active funds that try to beat the underlying index or asset being replicated by the ETF.

563. ◇ The New Zealand Superannuation Fund (NZSF) has (late-2016) investment themes of resource sustainability (e.g., timber and rural land), emerging and frontier markets (e.g., Chinese infrastructure), and evolving demand patterns (e.g., because of an aging population). The NZSF mentioned four reasons investors typically expect higher risk-adjusted returns from investment in emerging and frontier markets. These were (in alphabetical order) capital market inefficiencies, diversification benefits, high growth rates (in GDP I think they mean) in these countries, and international investor constraints. They said, however, that only three of these four were reasons for their emerging/frontier investments. What was the ONE reason they said they do NOT use to motivate their emerging/frontier investments?

(a) Capital market inefficiencies.

(b) Diversification benefits.

(c) High growth rates in these countries.

(d) International investor constraints.

(e) None of the above is correct.

564. Smart-beta strategies in stocks are what?

(a) Often a re-packaging of stocks from some popular index.

(b) Often an implicit value or small-capitalization tilt.

(c) Strategies that will not always outperform an index; sometimes they will be out of favor.

(d) Often strategies that use a re-weighting of stocks from an index, and therefore offer no additional diversification benefits to an investor who holds an index fund of those stocks.

(e) All of the above.

565. ◇ I recently compared the returns on exchange-traded funds (ETFs) with the returns on the indices they were meant to follow. The U.S. ETF with ticker symbol SPY followed the S&P 500 index very closely (i.e., regression beta very close to 1, R^2 very close to 1, correlation close to 1, and standard error of beta small). The New Zealand ETF with ticker symbol FNZ did not, however, appear to follow the New Zealand Stock Exchange 50 Portfolio Capital Index (NZSEPOFF) very well at all on a daily basis (i.e., regression beta very far from 1, R^2 much less than 1, correlation well below 1, and standard error of beta large). FNZ does, however, track the NZSEPOFF very well over the long term. What is the most likely primary cause of the very poor day-to-day tracking of NZSEPOFF by FNZ?

(a) High T-costs in New Zealand mean that the difference between transaction prices and net asset value (NAV) can be large on a day-to-day basis. This means that no big traders step in to arbitrage away the difference between the NAV and the price of FNZ.

(b) Price discreteness (i.e., the tick size) in the FNZ that does not exist in the NZSEOFF index leads to variability in the price of FNZ (i.e., jumps on the pricing grid) that does not exist in the index prices.

(c) Compared with the S&P 500, there are relatively frequent adds and drops of stocks from the membership of the NZSEPOFF index. The manager of FNZ must therefore trade into and out of these stocks, whereas the index involves no such trading. The timing and T-costs of these trades introduce extra volatility in FNZ prices not seen in the index.

(d) Having 50 stocks in the NZSEPOFF index makes the influence of any one stock more significant than it would be in the S&P 500. This means that when a stock is added to or dropped from the membership of the NZSEPOFF index, any mistiming in the corresponding trades by the FNZ manager creates extra volatility in the price of FNZ, relative to the comparable volatility seen by the manager of SPY.

(e) High T-costs in New Zealand, coupled with low depth, make it likely that the FNZ manager has to work orders for adds and drops over several days. This creates volatility in the prices of FNZ.

566. The correlation between the returns to U.S. stocks and high-quality U.S. bonds is what during the 1997–2013 period?

    (a) Steady and always negative.

    (b) Steady and always positive.

    (c) Variable and always negative.

    (d) Variable and always positive.

    (e) None of the above.

567. ARCH/GARCH models are widely used by practitioners who are modeling the behavior of FX and stock market returns time series. ARCH/GARCH models are popular because without any extra modelling, they can capture:

    (a) The time series independence in the first moment of returns.

    (b) The time series dependence in the first moment of returns.

    (c) The time series independence in the second moment of returns.

    (d) The time series dependence in the second moment of returns.

    (e) None of the above is correct.

568. Mid-2013, there were roughly how many hedge funds globally?

    (a) 1,000

    (b) 2,000

    (c) 5,000

    (d) 10,000

    (e) Notably more than any of the above numbers.

569. Cash drag is when what happens?

    (a) Illiquidity in small stocks requires that you break up orders into smaller orders and this means that trades drag on for several days relative to trades in liquid stocks.

    (b) Cash positions in your fund mean that you are nimble (i.e., you have money on hand to buy when opportunities arise) but other managers may be dragged down relative to you because they are not so liquid.

    (c) Cash is slow to arrive from counterparties when you sell stock holdings.

    (d) Cash in your margin account earns a below-market interest rate and drags your performance down relative to having that cash in short-term money market instruments.

    (e) Cash holdings in your portfolio dampen fund performance relative to the market's performance.

570. If we use the U.S. SEC definition of investment companies as open-ended funds (OEF), unit investment trusts (UIT), and closed-end funds (CEF), then...

    (a) ETFs fall mostly within the OEF category.

    (b) Mutual funds all fall within the OEF category.

    (c) ETFs and mutual finds overlap within the OEF category.

    (d) Some ETFs are also UITs.

    (e) All of the above except (c).

571. In mid-2020, there were $47.7t AUM in open-ended mutual funds and $6.1t AUM in ETFs globally (where $ is USD). The passive slice of these funds comprised roughly how much?

    (a) $23.9t and $6t, respectively.

    (b) $6.4t and $6t, respectively.

    (c) $3.5t and $6t, respectively.

    (d) $3t and $2t, respectively.

    (e) $1t and $1t, respectively.

572. In mid-2020, global managed funds' AUM were closest to which figure?

    (a) $100t.

    (b) $65t.

    (c) $25t.

    (d) $10t.

    (e) $5t.

573. In mid-2020, global pension assets' AUM were closest to which figure?

    (a) $100t.

    (b) $50t.

    (c) $20t.

    (d) $10t.

    (e) $5t.

574. Fama and French (1991, 1992, 1996) present evidence that SBM and HML factors help to explain stock returns. The implication is what?

    (a) The original single-beta CAPM is invalid because extra factors explain returns.

    (b) The original single-beta CAPM is not necessarily invalid. These results are what we would expect if the original single-beta CAPM were valid.

575. ARCH/GARCH models are widely used by practitioners who are modeling the behavior of financial time series. ARCH/GARCH models are popular because they can capture

    (a) Non-normality in the unconditional distribution of returns (e.g., using normal distributions for conditional returns).

    (b) Time-varying variance in the conditional distribution of returns.

    (c) Non-normality in the conditional distribution of returns (e.g., using scaled t-distributions for conditional returns as discussed in Chapter 3 of *Foundations*).

    (d) All of the above.

    (e) Only (a) and (b).

576. The disposition effect of Shefrin and Statman (1985) is when investors do what?

    (a) Investors dispose of losing stocks very quickly and ride out the winners.

    (b) Investors dispose of winning stocks too soon and ride out the losers.

    (c) Investors "cut the flowers and water the weeds."

    (d) Investors are indifferent toward winners and losers and treat them the same way when they rebalance portfolios.

    (e) Both (b) and (c).

577. In a competitive market, the bid-ask spread is not reduced to zero because the market makers need to be compensated for...

    (a) Order processing costs and adverse selection costs.

    (b) The risk of default by the trader who submitted the order.

    (c) Inventory holding costs/risks.

    (d) (a) and (b), but not (c).

    (e) (a) and (c), but not (b).

578. A stock moves from $10 per share on Monday to $11 a share on Tuesday. What is the simple net return, simple gross return, and continuously-compounded return represented by this price move? My answers are rounded to two decimal places.

    (a) 9.53%, 110.00%, and 10.00%, respectively.

    (b) 110.00%, 10.00%, and 9.53%, respectively.

    (c) 110.00%, 9.53%, and 10.00%, respectively.

    (d) 9.53%, 10.00%, and 110.00%, respectively.

    (e) 10.00%, 110.00%, and 9.53%, respectively.

579. On Friday April 15, 2016, the NZX reported 1,610,697 shares of FBU traded with a total value (of these traded shares) of $13,164,799.64. The open, high, low, and close stock prices were $8.16, $8.21, $8.15, and $8.16. Is the 1,610,697 shares traded a one-sided turnover count or a two-sided turnover count?

    (a) One-sided turnover.

    (b) Two-sided turnover.

    (c) They mean the same thing in this context.

    (d) I need to know the count of buys or the count of sells to be able to answer.

    (e) No, even if I knew the information in (d), it would still be impossible to answer.

580. Which one of the following is always TRUE regarding exchange-traded funds (ETFs)?

    (a) ETFs trade like a stock on the stock exchange.

    (b) ETFs are well diversified investments.

    (c) ETFs are very liquid, trading in large volume with narrow bid-ask spreads.

    (d) ETFs passively follow passive indexes.

    (e) ETFs have low expense ratios (i.e., the annual fee paid to the fund manager).

581. What are some of the events that happen when you short sell a stock? (Assume your broker charges commissions to buy or sell, or short stock; not all do anymore)

    (a) You pay a commission, you pay a small fee to the stock lender via your broker, and you pay any dividends that come due while you are short.

    (b) You pay a commission, you earn interest on the borrowed stock, and you pay any dividends while you are short.

    (c) You usually earn interest on the short sales proceeds, earn dividends on the stock you borrowed, and pay a small fee to the stock lender via your broker.

    (d) You pay interest on the margin loan, you pay a small fee to the stock lender via your broker, and you pay a commission.

    (e) None of the above is fully correct.

582. ◇ There exist levered 3× ETFs designed to return three times the return on the S&P 500 on any given day (the issuers use futures contracts to achieve this outcome). If the levered ETF achieves this goal every day, what should be the correlation between returns to the S&P 500 and returns to the levered 3× ETF?

    (a) +9

    (b) +3

    (c) +1

    (d) +1/3

    (e) +1/9

583. Which of the following are typical annual fees or ranges of annual fees for active mutual funds targeted at retail customers, passive mutual funds targeted at retail customers, smart-beta or factor funds targeted at retail customers, and hedge funds? In 2021, these ranges likely cover 95% of U.S. funds, but extreme-cost funds likely exist beyond each range, and the quoted hedge fund number is a rough average, with one-third of hedge funds still charging 200 bps + 20%.

  (a) Active/Retail 10–85 bps, Passive/Retail 5–25 bps, Smart-beta/Factor 3–10 bps, Hedge 300 bps + 20% of profits (with a high-water mark).

  (b) Active/Retail 25–125 bps, Passive/Retail 3–35 bps, Smart-beta/Factor 2–20 bps, Hedge 300 bps + 20% of profits (with a high-water mark).

  (c) Active/Retail 50–100 bps, Passive/Retail 20–100 bps, Smart-beta/Factor 10–50 bps, Hedge 100 bps + 10% of profits (with a high-water mark).

  (d) Active/Retail 40–250 bps, Passive/Retail 0–75 bps, Smart-beta/Factor 10–60 bps, Hedge 150 bps + 20% of profits (with a high-water mark).

  (e) Active/Retail 100–300 bps, Passive/Retail 25–125 bps, Smart-beta/Factor 15–70 bps, Hedge 100 bps + 10% of profits (with a high-water mark).

584. We can think of the main benefit of diversification as being, loosely speaking, the *relative reduction in risk* that you get in a diversified portfolio *as compared with* an undiversified portfolio. What happens to this main benefit of diversification in a market collapse, like the bear market in equities experienced globally from October 2007 to March 2009?

  (a) This benefit increases noticeably.

  (b) This benefit either stays the same or increases a little.

  (c) This benefit stays about the same because it is independent of market direction.

  (d) This benefit either stays the same or decreases a little.

  (e) This benefit reduces noticeably.

585. The New Zealand Superannuation Fund is mentioned in Chapter 4 of *Foundations*. The "N.Z. Super Fund," as it is known, held roughly NZD52 billion in assets in December 2020. The N.Z. Super Fund is...

  (a) A KiwiSaver scheme provider, which any N.Z. citizen or permanent resident can join.

  (b) A fund that is designed to help provide comprehensive, no-fault personal injury cover for all New Zealand residents and visitors to New Zealand.

  (c) A manager of individual retirement accounts for New Zealanders.

  (d) A superannuation scheme for state sector (i.e., government) employees

  (e) A sovereign wealth fund designed to contribute to the cost of paying New Zealand superannuation entitlements in the future.

586. In 2017, a cutting edge trend in the U.S. equity markets was that record amounts of money were being withdrawn from (___?___) funds and moved instead into (___?___) funds. This trend had been going on for two–three years, but intensified at the end of 2016 and the beginning of 2017, and net fund flows still favored the latter in 2020. The missing words are what, respectively?

   (a) Actively managed funds, passively managed funds

   (b) ETFs, passively managed funds

   (c) Passively managed funds, actively managed funds

   (d) ETFs, actively managed funds

   (e) Passively managed funds, ETFs

587. We identified secular trends in U.S. interest rates over the last 227 years. The average length of these trends was closest to which of the following?

   (a) 1 year.

   (b) 5 years.

   (c) 10 years.

   (d) 30 years.

   (e) 50 years.

588. Even though bond prices fall when interest rates rise, rising rates mean that coupons and repayments of principal may be reinvested at higher yields, thereby increasing subsequent cash flows to a bond fund. If interest rates rise steadily over the next 20 years, we might expect this latter "reinvestment effect" to be most likely to outweigh the initial price effect in bond funds holding which kind of bonds?

   (a) Bonds with long maturity and low coupons.

   (b) Bonds with long maturity and high coupons.

   (c) Bonds with short maturity and low coupons.

   (d) Bonds with short maturity and high coupons.

   (e) All of the above.

589. The "quotes" for a stock are what?

   (a) The most recent transaction prices in that stock.

   (b) The most recent best bid and best ask price for that stock.

   (c) The most recent volume and VWAP for that stock.

   (d) The most recent price and quantity (i.e., count of shares) at which the stock traded.

   (e) The most recent price and dollar volume at which the stock traded.

590. Benjamin Graham's equity screens come in two flavors. What are they?

   (a) Value screens to pick stocks with prices beaten down relative to fundamentals, and growth screens to identify growth stocks with strong prospects for growth in earnings.

   (b) Growth screens to identify growth stocks with strong prospects for growth in earnings, and additional screens that reduce the risk of mis-judgement (e.g., the stock has to have paid dividends, and not made losses, etc.).

   (c) Growth screens to identify stocks with strong prospects for growth in earnings, and diversification screens to make sure that your portfolio is diversified.

   (d) Value screens to pick stocks with low prices relative to fundamentals, and additional screens to reduce the risk of misjudgment (e.g., the stock has to have paid dividends, and not made losses, and be of a large size, etc.).

   (e) None of the above is close to being correct.

591. When implementing the Benjamin Graham equity screens in Question 3.3.1 (see p. 266), which one of the following was NOT one of the screens you were given to choose from? Assume any price comparisons are with quantities on a per share basis.

   (a) Continued dividends for at least the past 20 years.

   (b) No earnings deficit in the past 10 years.

   (c) Ten-year growth of at least one-third in EPS.

   (d) Price no more than 30 times average earnings over the last three years.

   (e) A price that is less than 120% of net tangible assets.

592. ◇ Which ONE of the following is FALSE regarding blockchain technology.

   (a) A blockchain is a distributed ledger, using public/private key cryptography.

   (b) A blockchain is an append-only list of records, and each record is a block.

   (c) Miners compete to validate candidate blocks to be added to the blockchain, and they are rewarded if they validate a block.

   (d) Each new block is linked to previous blocks using cryptographic data involving a cryptographic hash of information associated with the current and previous block.

   (e) Each block contains a single transaction (which is not necessarily a financial transaction; for example, it could be a record of movement of goods, or a revision to a medical record).

593. The COVID-19-driven market panic of 2020:Q1 pushed the level of the major U.S. stock market indices down dramatically. What do you think happened to the average dividend yield of the S&P500 stocks during this general fall in stock prices?

(a) Stayed about the same, because stock prices were down significantly but dividends were also cut significantly.

(b) Stayed about the same, because dividends are "sticky."

(c) Increased notably because stock prices were down notably.

(d) Increased notably because many companies announced compensating dividend increases.

(e) Decreased notably because stock prices were up notably.

(f) Decreased notably because many companies announced dividend cuts.

594. During the COVID-19-driven market panic of 2020:Q1, the level of the major U.S. stock market indices fell dramatically. What do you think happened to 10-year U.S. Treasury bond yields during this fall in stock prices?

(a) Bond yields stayed the same because bonds yields are unrelated to stock market prices.

(b) It is impossible to say because different forces drive stock prices and bond yields.

(c) Bond yields went down, as investors sold off bonds as well as stocks.

(d) Bond yields went down, as investors bought bonds to reduce exposure to other more risky assets.

(e) Bond yields went up, as investors sold off bonds as well as stocks.

(f) Bond yields went up, as investors bought bonds to reduce exposure to other more risky assets.

595. Is Benjamin Graham's original value investing approach an active strategy or a passive strategy? I am referring to the equity screens he proposed for the defensive/passive investor, not those for the aggressive/active/enterprising investor, and I am assuming that he advises no more than about 30 stocks.

(a) He follows a purely passive approach.

(b) He follows a purely active approach.

(c) He uses some active methods to achieve a relatively passive goal. So, there are elements of both active and passive approaches in his method and his goals, respectively.

(d) His approach is neither active nor passive; these terms did not really exist in his day, in the sense we use them today. So, his investment techniques defy categorization.

(e) None of the above is correct.

596. Which one of the following statements does NOT apply to the Benjamin Graham approach to value investing?

    (a) You should follow value investing because identifying growth stocks is too difficult, and if you can identify them, there is a high risk that they will not deliver on their promised growth in EPS

    (b) You should use fundamental analysis. Technical analysis is a joke.

    (c) You should seek non-dividend-paying growth stocks that reinvest all their earnings back into the company to promote growth in earnings.

    (d) You should seek stocks that satisfy two types of criteria/filters. The first is about identifying value stocks (i.e., ones beaten down in price relative to fundamentals) and the second is about controlling risk (i.e., the stocks must have solid financial performance and be of a large size.)

    (e) Graham recommends 10 to 30 stocks. This is active insofar as he is picking stocks rather than holding the market. On the other hand, Graham is so conservative that he argues he is not trying to beat the market. This is a characteristic of passive approaches.

    (f) Graham argues that a single bet on an apparently attractive stock is too risky, but 30 stocks, each of which is attractive, are unlikely to all be dogs.

597. You are an options trader. You are bullish on a stock. You are picking between buying the stock, buying the stock on 50% margin (e.g., you buy a $100 stock using $50 borrowed from your broker), and buying an out-of-the-money call option on the stock. Please ignore the interest rate on any margin borrowing. Please assume the stock pays no dividends. Which of the following is (or are) TRUE?

    (a) Buying the stock on margin involves leverage, but buying a call option on a stock does not involve any sort of leverage.

    (b) If the stock goes up, say, 20% in price, over the course of several months, then whether you bought the stock using margin or you bought an out-of-the-money call option on the stock, both positions magnify (i.e., increase) the percentage gains on the stock.

    (c) Ignoring T-costs (and assuming no margin calls), buying a stock on margin means that the percentage gains or losses on your position are a fixed multiple of the percentage gains or losses on an unlevered stock purchase.

    (d) When you buy a call option on a stock, the time decay in the value of the option (i.e., its drop in price towards its final payoff value, other things being equal), means that even if stock price rises, you are walking up a falling pricing curve and you may lose money.

    (e) If you buy stock using a 50% margin rate, you make the same return as you do if you buy an at-the-money call option on the stock.

    (f) (a) and (b) only.

    (g) (c) and (d) only.

598. Which ONE of the following is FALSE about exchange-traded funds (ETFs)?

(a) ETFs listed on the NZX have designated market makers who must provide liquidity by placing limit orders in the CLOB.

(b) ETFs are popular, but less than 10% of the money invested in managed funds around the globe is in ETFs.

(c) ETFs often have low fees, but high-fee ETFs do exist.

(d) Most of the money invested in ETFs is invested in funds that actively try to beat some benchmark index.

(e) The great Jack Bogle objected to ETFs because they are so easy to trade that you might be tempted to use them to time the market, to your detriment, instead of using them in a long-term buy-and-hold strategy.

(f) You can buy ETFs that mimic popular market indices, FX, gold, diversified portfolios of small-cap stocks, etc.

599. The New Zealand Superannuation Fund (N.Z. Super Fund) has (mid-2020) investment themes of resource sustainability (e.g., timber and rural land), emerging and frontier markets (e.g., Chinese infrastructure), and evolving demand patterns (e.g., high quality protein providers and health and aged-care businesses because of an aging population). What is it that each of these investment themes has in common, as emphasized at `https://www.nzsuperfund.nz/`?

(a) Perceived capital market inefficiencies.

(b) Diversification benefits.

(c) Higher growth rates in earnings in these businesses than others.

(d) International investor constraints.

(e) Lower T-costs in these businesses than in others.

600. What is a dividend reinvestment plan (DRIP)?

(a) A DRIP is a scheme that allows you to strip out and take ownership of the dividends on a stock without ever owning shares of stock.

(b) A DRIP is a scheme that allows you to reinvest some or all of your dividends back into shares of that same stock.

(c) A DRIP is a scheme that automatically converts your dividend income into cash and deposits it directly to your bank account, by-passing your broker.

(d) A DRIP is a broker-sponsored scheme whereby your dividend income on a portfolio of stocks is automatically reinvested into diversified exchange-traded funds (ETFs) to give you a more diversified portfolio.

(e) A DRIP is a Direct Reinvestment of Investment Proceeds scheme whereby maturing certificates of deposit are automatically reinvested for the same term (i.e., "rolled over").

(f) None of the above is correct.

601. Notable differences between defined benefit (DB) and defined contribution (DC) retirement savings schemes are what?

   (a) In DB schemes, the employer bears the investment risk; In DC schemes, the employee bears the investment risk.

   (b) In DB schemes, the employee bears the investment risk; In DC schemes, the employer bears the investment risk.

   (c) DC schemes are becoming increasingly offered; DB schemes are becoming less offered.

   (d) (a) and (c), but not (b).

   (e) (a) and (b), but not (c).

602. **L**ars and **S**milla are picking mutual funds in which to invest equal lump-sum inheritances of $100,000 each. They will hold the investment for 50 years, reinvest all dividends, and pay no taxes at all. Lars chooses to invest in a passively managed Vanguard fund that mimics the behavior of a portfolio of **L**arge-capitalization U.S. stocks. Smilla chooses to invest in a passively managed Vanguard fund that mimics the behavior of a portfolio of **S**mall-capitalization U.S. stocks. The annual expense ratios of the funds are equal and negligible. Historically, on average, small-cap stocks have returned about 200 bps per annum more than large-cap stocks. Assume that 50 years from now, Smilla's investment will be worth S, and Lars' investment will be worth L. If the future looks like the past, roughly what range do you think the ratio of ending values S/L will fall in to? Hint: You need to assume a sensible number for R_L, the long-run return on large-cap stocks.

   (a) 2.4–2.6

   (b) 1.8–2.4

   (c) 1.4–1.8

   (d) 1.0–1.4

   (e) Less than 1.

603. When comparing ETFs with closed-end funds, which one of the following characteristics is unique to an ETF?

   (a) It is a fund that trades on the stock exchange like a stock.

   (b) The value of the assets underlying the fund is reported as the NAV (net asset value).

   (c) There is a bid and an ask for the units that trade on the stock exchange.

   (d) The fund is often, though not always, actively managed, and attempts to outperform some benchmark.

   (e) Units in the fund can be converted into the underlying assets, and the underlying assets can be converted into units of the fund.

604. The buy side and sell side are usually defined as what in the investment management industry?

(a) The bid and ask sides of the limit order book, respectively.

(b) The ask and bid sides of the limit order book, respectively.

(c) Institutional asset managers (i.e., portfolio managers managing assets for institutions), and retail investors (i.e., individuals managing their own money), respectively.

(d) Individual traders who want to buy and sell, respectively.

(e) Investment managers, and financial firms selling investment services to investment managers, respectively.

(f) Traders who submit limit orders, and traders who submit market orders, respectively.

(g) None of the above is correct.

605. Which ONE of the following is closest to the correct estimates of the assets under management (AUM) of different types of global managed funds given in Chapter 4 of *Foundations* as of mid-2020. Note that, in alphabetical order, ETF stands for exchange-traded funds (excluding unit investment trusts and closed-end funds), HF stands for hedge funds, MF stands for open-ended mutual funds, and SWF stands for sovereign wealth funds. All numbers are in trillions of USD ($t), and are rounded to the nearest trillion dollars.

(a) ETF $48t, HF $3t, MF $6t, SWF $18t

(b) ETF $6t, HF $3t, MF $48t, SWF $8t

(c) ETF $8t, HF $6t, MF $3t, SWF $48t

(d) ETF $3t, HF $48t, MF $6t, SWF $8t

(e) ETF $18t, HF $3t, MF $48t, SWF $6t

606. When you sell a stock short, you expose yourself to all but one of the following costs or risks. Which ONE is NOT a cost or risk of short selling?

(a) The company announces terrible earnings, and its stock price collapses.

(b) You may be asked to deposit additional collateral (i.e., additional margin money) if the stock price rises.

(c) You risk losing all your initial margin money, and more, if the stock price moves suddenly against you.

(d) If the stock pays a dividend while you are short, a substitute dividend will be sucked out of your brokerage account and sent to whomever lent you the stock.

(e) You are unlikely to earn any interest on the margin money that must remain in your brokerage account.

(f) You are swimming against the long-term upwards trend of the stock market.

607. Stock markets and FX markets quote their prices in different ways. Which of the following is TRUE?

(a) Stock markets push firm quotes out to you (i.e., ones at which you can trade) during regular trading hours, but you have to query an FX dealer if you want to trade.

(b) Stock market quotes sit there during regular trading hours and are valid until they are revised, but FX quotes are valid for only a very brief window (e.g., 20 seconds).

(c) Stock market quotes are always in the currency of the country of the market, but FX quotes are always expressed in our home currency.

(d) Stock market quotes always have a fixed bid-ask spread, but the width of the FX bid-ask spread varies during the day.

(e) FX market quotes always have a fixed bid-ask spread, but the width of stock market bid-ask spread varies during the day.

(f) (a) and (b) only.

(g) None of the above is correct.

Job Interview Questions: Here are a half-dozen very common and interrelated financial management interview questions from my job interview book:

Question 1: Explain what a discount rate is, and how you would calculate it for a publicly traded company.

Question 2: What is the WACC?

Question 3: How would you estimate a firm's beta?

Question 4: How would you calculate the required rate of return for equity holders for a company? What would you use for a market risk premium?

Question 5: How would you estimate the cost of debt for a company (assume that there is no publicly traded debt for that company outstanding)?

Question 6: Compare the beta of an airport with the beta of a retailer.

Taken from *Heard on The Street: Quantitative Questions from Wall Street Job Interviews,* ©2020 Timothy Falcon Crack. See advertisements at the end of this book.

Chapter 2

Short-Answer Test Questions

2.1 Foundations I: Quantitative

608. Suppose when analyzing kurtosis and skewness for a time series of 250 returns on a stock you find the Z-statistic, $\left[\sqrt{\frac{(N-1)(N-2)(N-3)}{24N(N+1)}} \cdot kurt_{KS}\right]$, takes the value 3.02, and the Z-statistic, $\left[\sqrt{\frac{(N-1)(N-2)}{6N}} \cdot skew_{KS}\right]$, takes the value 0.23. Do you reject normality for returns to this stock at a five percent level of significance? Explain briefly.

609. Suppose I form a t-statistic to test whether the mean of a time series of daily returns to a stock is different from zero. Write down the functional form of the t-statistic. Suppose you have only a short time series of returns, say 20 observations. What assumptions that underlie the t-test might we be most worried about being breached, and which ones, if any, need we not worry much about? Be sure to explain your answers.

610. Suppose when analyzing a time series of daily returns to a stock you find the first order autocorrelation of the daily stock returns is -10.6%. Suppose the sample standard deviation of the daily returns is 22%. How many observations would be required to reject the null that the autocorrelation is zero at a 5% level of significance (assume a two-tailed test).

611. Draw a scatter plot of x_i versus y_i that exhibits dependence, but for which neither the product-moment correlation nor the rank-order correlation will be able to detect a relationship. Explain why not. If you cannot draw the picture, then explain what characteristics the picture would have if you could draw it.

612. When/why would you choose to use a rank-order correlation coefficient rather than a product-moment correlation coefficient?

613. Please distinguish between the standard error of an OLS regression, the standard deviation of the residuals of an OLS regression, and the standard error of the sample mean estimator.

614. Tell me the assumptions that underlie a one sample t-test of the mean for a sample of stock returns. Which assumption are we likely to be least worried about in a small sample? Which assumption are we likely to be least worried about in a large sample?

615. We can think of the expected value of a random variable as a probability-weighted sum of values of the random variable. Please explain briefly with reference to the simple formula $E(X) = \int x f_X(x) dx$, where X is a random variable and $f_X(\cdot)$ is the PDF of X. It may help if you sketch a graph, but that is up to you.

616. Explain the difference between an expected value and a conditional expected value for a random variable. A simple example will do. It need not be from finance.

617. If the returns to stock ABC and stock DEF are negatively correlated, then it must be that ABC tends to rise in price when DEF falls in price. True or False, and give a simple explanation.

618. Define a Student-t distribution.

619. Non-central t-statistics are important in what situation in hypothesis testing? Why does this become important in finance?

620. In what setting in empirical finance, would you worry about Lindley's paradox? How does the paradox manifest itself?

621. What is wrong with assuming that simple net returns to stocks are distributed normal?

622. Suppose I form a t-statistic to test whether the autocorrelation of a time series of daily returns to a stock is different from zero. Write down the functional form of the t-statistic.

623. Some early finance literature addressed multicollinearity problems by pulling an offending independent variable out of the original regression, regressing it upon all the others independent variables (i.e., running a second regression), and then replacing the offending independent variable in the original regression with the residuals from the second regression. Tell me why this is a futile approach to the treatment of multicollinearity.

624. Given a sample of 100 stocks, for how many do you think you would be able to reject the null hypothesis of normality of returns? What causes the rejections? Do the results differ for large- and small-capitalization stocks?

625. From a sample of 511 daily stock returns, suppose we calculate a sample mean daily return of 0.000245, a sample standard deviation of daily returns of 0.009036, and a sample autocorrelation of daily returns of 0.060948.

   (a) Test the null hypothesis that the true mean daily return equals zero. Use a two-sided test with a 5% significance level, give the value of the t-statistic, and state the critical values.

(b) Test the null hypothesis that the true autocorrelation of daily return equals zero. Use a two-sided test with a 5% significance level, give the value of the *t*-statistic, and state the critical values.

626. From a sample of 496 daily stock returns suppose we calculate a sample mean daily return of 0.00090300, a sample standard deviation of daily returns of 0.01143889, and a sample autocorrelation of daily returns of 0.07888326.

(a) Test the null hypothesis that the true mean daily return equals zero. Use a two-sided test with a 5% significance level, state the value of the *t*-statistic, and state the critical values.

(b) Test the null hypothesis that the true autocorrelation of daily returns equals zero. Use a two-sided test with a 10% significance level, state the value of the *t*-statistic, and state the critical values.

627. In Chapter 1 of *Foundations*, I showed an example of two stocks whose simulated prices move up together. The daily returns on the two stocks were, however, almost perfectly negatively correlated. Please explain very briefly how it can be that the returns are almost perfectly negatively correlated when it looks like the stocks' prices are moving together. Limit your answer to at most three sentences; sketch a diagram if it helps.

628. Table 2.1 contains the Skewness and Kurtosis Z-statistics for 10 stocks:
$$Z_{skew} = \left[\sqrt{\frac{(N-1)(N-2)}{6N}} \cdot skew_{KS} \right], \text{ and } Z_{kurt} = \left[\sqrt{\frac{(N-1)(N-2)(N-3)}{24N(N+1)}} \cdot kurt_{KS} \right].$$
You may assume $N = 500$. For how many of the 10 stocks do you reject normality? Explain. Give the ticker symbols of any stocks for which you cannot reject normality.

TICKER	Z_{skew}	Z_{kurt}
ABC	7.8610	24.6390
DEF	-0.2932	3.5868
GHI	0.6276	4.6319
KLM	-0.8385	23.6210
NOP	4.1295	12.2510
QRS	25.9545	182.2593
TUV	-3.6534	45.4627
WXY	6.2286	25.0298
ZZZ	14.9028	62.1418
IBM	51.2507	368.6651

Table 2.1: Skewness and Kurtosis Z-Statistics for 10 stocks

629. The *t*-test for a mean is "distributionally parametric" in small sample, but "distributionally non-parametric" in large sample. Explain what this means in simple terms; two sentences should be enough.

2.2 Foundations II: Financial Economics

630. Do you expect large-cap stocks to have larger or smaller relative bid-ask spreads than small-cap stocks? Please explain your answer.

631. Define dividend yield. Now give me a rough estimate of the average dividend yield of the 10 largest capitalization NYSE or NZX stocks. Now answer the same question, but for 10 very small-capitalization NYSE or NZX stocks.

632. Suppose you have just downloaded the data in Table 2.2 for stock CUB. Each price is the price at the close of trade on that date and CAF is the cumulative adjustment factor. The BUY and SELL columns are closing bid and ask prices respectively. Tell me the rate of return (to a long-term stock holder who was already holding the stock) from the close of trade Friday 18/10/20XY to the close of trade Monday 21/10/20XY (use bid-ask spread mid-points to estimate true value). Do not use the "Price" or "Adjusted Price" columns for any calculation.

Date	Price	CAF	Adjusted Price	VOLUME	BUY	SELL
17/10/20XY	48	1	48	5000	48	50
18/10/20XY	48	1	48	7517	36	50
21/10/20XY	18	3	54	15000	16	22
22/10/20XY	16.5	3	49.5	10000	16	18
23/10/20XY	15	3	45	12000	10	16
24/10/20XY	20	3	60	25000	18	24

Table 2.2: Stock CUB: October 20XY

633. Assume the quotes you see in Table 1.18 (on p. 109) are available to you with no execution risk or price slippage. Suppose you send your broker a market order to sell 97,928 shares. What will be the total dollar proceeds of the sale (ignoring any commission)? Assume that first trade did not happen. Now suppose you send your broker a market order to buy 10,000 shares. What will be the total dollar cost of the purchase (ignoring any commission)? Show all your working!

634. What determines how wide the bid-ask spread will be for S&P/NZX50 stocks on the NZX? Explain carefully.

635. Write down the P/E ratio as a function of the present value of growth opportunities (PVGO). Now suppose we have a high P/E stock and a low P/E stock. Assume they have the same price and the same discount rate. Which stock has the larger proportion of its value generated by its PVGO? Explain.

636. The Ledoit and Wolf (2004) VCV estimator takes an average of the sample VCV and the constant correlation model VCV. This average is a "shrinkage estimator."

   (a) Please explain what is the statistical purpose of the "shrinkage." (one sentence answer expected)

(b) Explain how this purpose is achieved. That is, what purpose does the constant correlation model serve here? (one or two sentence answer expected)

(c) Now tell me what Michaud's "error maximization" is, and how the Ledoit and Wolf VCV estimator may help reduce it. (one or two sentences expected)

637. Suppose Stock A appears in your benchmark with weight 21%. Suppose Stock A appears in your portfolio with weight 20%. What is your active weight in Stock A?

638. Tell me why we said, in *Foundations*, that we would ignore benchmark timing and focus on stock selection in our active alpha optimization.

639. In the active alpha optimization in Question 3.2.2 you are asked to build alphas for 20 stocks, and then to search for an optimum. Tell me

(a) What is the objective function? (keep it simple; do not parameterize it in terms of the choice variables)

(b) Are you maximizing or minimizing the objective function?

(c) What are the choice variables? (name them and give a symbol)

(d) What are the constraints? (as many as you can remember)

640. Suppose $\sigma_B = 0.114$ (benchmark standard deviation), $\sigma_P = 0.118$ (portfolio standard deviation), $\beta_P = 1$ (portfolio beta), $\alpha_P = 0.02974$ (forward looking portfolio alpha), and $\lambda = 10$ (residual risk aversion assuming return and risk are in decimals). What is the forward looking IR (information ratio) and the forward looking RAA (risk-adjusted alpha)? Show your working.

641. Suppose you pick 10 large-cap stocks and download the last year of stock price data on them. Suppose you want to use these data to estimate a historical Markowitz-style efficient frontier (as in Question 3.2.1). Suppose you define the benchmark to be the market-cap-weighted portfolio of the 10 stocks. Suppose you calculate betas for each of the 10 stocks relative to the benchmark portfolio. These are the only betas you calculate.

(a) The formula for the ith stock's beta is $\beta_i = \frac{\vec{h}_i' V \vec{h}_B}{\vec{h}_B' V \vec{h}_B}$. In the case where $i=3$ (i.e., the third stock) write down explicitly the exact value of $\vec{h}_i$.

(b) Please tell me what the numerator (i.e., the top line) and the denominator (i.e., the bottom line) of the ratio in part a. $\left(\text{i.e., } \frac{\vec{h}_i' V \vec{h}_B}{\vec{h}_B' V \vec{h}_B} \right)$ represent.

(c) Will the plot of the mean returns on the stocks versus their betas (i.e., the empirical Security Market Line) be a straight line, or not? Explain briefly but clearly.

642. Describe the time ordering of events for the ex-dividend timeline. Do not worry about the number of days between events, just tell me the ordering through time of the different events or periods. Draw a time-line if it helps.

643. Define price impact. Make up a simple numerical example that involves a market order to buy a stock.

644. It has been said that aiming for 2% annual outperformance of a benchmark does not add much value. Suppose you deposit $10,000 today and you will let it grow for 40 years until you retire. Suppose there is a benchmark portfolio that grows at an average of 6% per annum. Suppose there is an active portfolio that grows at an average of 8% per annum (i.e., 2% outperformance). Assume these are simple net returns. How much better off are you with the active portfolio than the benchmark portfolio after 40 years of annual compounding? Ignore all taxes.

645. Estimate the IR of an active portfolio manager who follows 225 stocks, but updates forecasts only once per year. Assume the correlation between realized and forecast active returns is 4%.

646. Your broker has the commission schedule shown in Table 1.12 on p. 81. You place an online market order to buy 6,000 N.Z. shares and it is executed at $30 per share. Two days later you sell the same 6,000 shares and, by coincidence, your market order is executed at $30 per share. How much commission money did your broker earn from your round trip trade?

647. Sketch a plot of a negatively skewed distribution.

648. ◇◇ You are a summer intern at an investment bank. Figure 2.1 shows a Bloomberg screen grab produced using the command NZT <EQUITY> OV <GO>. Unfortunately, your senior team member sold 10,000 of these options, spilled raspberry jam on this important document (and on the Bloomberg keyboard—disabling it), and then went jogging without taking his phone! You cannot see the option delta but your trading desk needs to know *right now* how many shares of the underlying they need to trade to hedge exposure to the 10,000 options that your team member just sold. Should they be long or short? You have 60 seconds to give them some sort of answer. Note that each option is a plain vanilla American-style put option covering 100 shares, and your firm just sold 10,000 of these options. Get it wrong, and your internship is over; get it right, and they will hire you when you graduate.

649. Suppose that $\vec{h}_P$ is a vector of portfolio weights in a portfolio P that is fully invested in N risky stocks. Write down an expression for the beta of portfolio P relative to a benchmark B, in terms of $\vec{h}_P$, V (the VCV of the N risky stocks' returns), and $\vec{h}_B$ (the vector of weights in the benchmark portfolio).

650. In the active alpha optimization in Question 3.2.2 what is the sum of the active weights? That is, what was $\vec{h}'_{P_A}\vec{\iota}$?

651. Suppose we have N risky stocks. Suppose we locate the Markowitz historical minimum variance frontier, and the tangency portfolio T on the risky asset frontier. Let $\vec{h}_T$ be the $N \times 1$ vector of portfolio weights in the tangency portfolio.

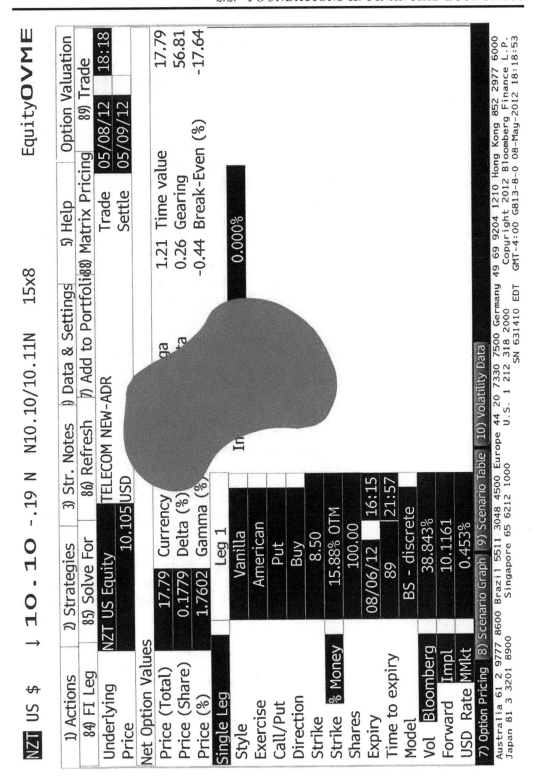

Figure 2.1: Bloomberg Screen: NZT <EQUITY> OV <GO>

An NZT Corporation Bloomberg OV screen from May 8, 2012. Each option covers 100 shares, and your firm just sold 10,000 of these options.

Suppose that, as in Question 3.2.1, the only constraints for any risky asset frontier portfolios P are that $\vec{h}'_P \vec{\imath} = 1$ and that $\vec{h}'_P \vec{\mu} = \mu_p$ for level of return μ_P. Can any of the weights in $\vec{h}_T$ be negative? Can the sum of the weights in $\vec{h}_T$ be different from 1?

652. Suppose I have a vertical column vector of mean returns $\vec{\mu}$ sitting in Excel in CELLS A1:A10, and I have portfolio weights $\vec{h}_P$ sitting in a vertical column vector in CELLS B1:B10, write down the Excel formula for finding the mean return on the portfolio. If you do not use Excel, then write it down in whatever programming language you do use.

653. We wrote down $\beta_P^{(A)}$ and we called it "active beta." Tell me in words what active beta is. What does it measure? When is it zero?

654. What is the difference in the definition of a forward-looking (also called "ex-ante") IR, and an historical (also called "ex-post") IR? Which would you expect to be higher?

655. Tell me in words (i.e., no equations) what I need in a general active alpha optimization objective function if I am a portfolio manager. What appears positively, what appears negatively?

656. Define active portfolio management.

657. What is meant by an "active position" in a portfolio managed for an institutional client.

658. Give a numerical example of the order of magnitude of the risk aversion coefficient λ as seen in Question 3.2.2 for the active alpha optimization. Assume that an alpha of five percent is recorded as 5.

659. The CAPM-type objective function looks like $\mu_P - \lambda_T \sigma_P^2$. Write down the analogous active alpha optimization objective function (assume stock selection but not benchmark timing). Name and define each term. Why did we argue that optimizing the total return total risk objective function was inconsistent with institutional practice.

660. What is benchmark timing?

661. Why might I wish to buy a put option on a stock that I already own?

662. If I am buying a put option for speculative purposes, and if I want my T-costs to be a very small proportion of the price of the put, should I buy a high-strike put or a low-strike put? Explain carefully.

663. Do you expect the relative bid-ask spread on a stock to be larger, smaller, or the same as the relative bid-ask spread on a call option on the stock? Carefully tell me why.

664. Why, when building our active objective function, did we choose to decompose total return and total risk into parts and then pick out some of them and apply different coefficients of risk aversion? In other words, please tell me why we abandoned the candidate objective function $\kappa_P - \lambda_T \sigma^2$ in favor of the active objective function $\alpha_P - \lambda_R \omega_P^2$?

665. Suppose I want to estimate a variance-covariance matrix (VCV) using monthly returns on 100 stocks. Suppose I use monthly returns for five years. Will I have any problem using this VCV to estimate an efficient frontier or solve an active alpha optimization? Please explain.

666. The Sharpe Single Index Model (SIM), the Constant Correlation Model (CCM), and the Structural Risk Model all serve essentially the same purpose. They place additional structure on the VCV. Why do they do this? That is, what is the aim of the models?

667. The MSCI/Barra structural risk model uses two broad categories of factors. Name the categories and name one factor from each category.

668. Why were the alphas constructed to be benchmark neutral in the active alpha optimization?

669. Why would an active portfolio manager care about the results of any event study?

670. Describe dividend imputation. Give a simple numerical example.

671. The research paper by Lintner (1956) says that management does not give unsustainable what? Explain.

672. How can you use a dividend discount model calibration to estimate a discount rate for capital budgeting?

673. The Edwards-Bell-Ohlsen (EBO) model (Edwards and Bell, 1961; Ohlson, 1995; Lee, 1996) attempts to fix some of the problems with the original dividend discount model (DDM). Describe two of the problems that the EBO model tries to fix, and how it tries to fix them. No equations please; just use words.

674. What is a backtest? Name two problems that backtests suffer from, and give a simple example with enough detail to demonstrate that you understand.

675. What is Lindley's paradox?

676. Give an example of analysts "forecasting the past" when it comes to earnings on a stock.

677. Explain what purpose ARCH and GARCH models are designed for? Can you sketch a diagram?

678. Tell me what the RAA is. Explain.

679. The alphas, $\vec{\alpha}$, in the active equity optimization (Question 3.2.2) are constructed to be benchmark neutral. Write down an equation to show me what this means. Do not give me an equation that shows how you construct these alphas, but rather an equation that shows what benchmark neutrality implies for the relationship between the alphas and the weights in the benchmark portfolio. Why do we want the alphas to have this property?

680. Did our active alpha optimization (e.g., Question 3.2.2), require an estimate of the mean returns on the stocks? If so, what for? If not, why not? Explain briefly but clearly.

681. Suppose that your stock picking skill as measured by an IC is 0.03. Suppose you trade 100 stocks and revise your forecasts of active return four times a year. Estimate your IR.

682. Grinold and Kahn (2000, pp. 129–132) give tables of IRs and active risk for both active bond investments and active equity investments. Identify the following statements as TRUE/FALSE with no explanation needed.

   (a) The IRs before fees were similar for the different asset classes.

   (b) Active equity managers charged higher fees than active bond managers.

   (c) The active risk of active bond funds was very low compared with the active risk of active equity funds.

683. What is a skilled forecast of return? Where does it come from? Be brief.

684. We looked at a simple random walk and used it to derive a result due to Merton related to accuracy of sample estimators of means and variances. This result applies quite generally to stock returns data. Tell me the result, but do not show me any of the equations.

685. Give a simple numerical example of the difference between one and two-sided turnover. Is volume of daily trade reported by the NYSE one or two sided?

686. What is a margin trade in a stock? Give a simple numerical example for a buy order.

687. What is the relationship between a firm's PVGO and the NPV of the firm's future investment projects?

688. Suppose I sell a stock two days before the ex-dividend day. Do I get the dividend? Please explain in one sentence; a timeline might help.

689. What is a limit order? A one sentence answer is OK.

690. If I submit a limit order in the U.S. or N.Z., can my trade suffer from price impact? Explain in one or two sentences.

691. Table 2.3 shows market information for New Zealand stock APN on April 04, 2006 and again one week later on April 11, 2006. In both cases the data are observed at around 11AM (i.e., roughly an hour into the trading day). The prices are in cents per share, the volumes and depths are in number of shares, and the turnover is in N.Z. dollars.

	BID	OFFER	LAST	BID DEPTH	OFFER DEPTH	VOLUME	TURN-OVER
APRIL 04, 2006	570	0	565	10000	0	7200	$41,378
APRIL 11, 2006	560	578	584	5000	600	8125	$46,963

Table 2.3: APN Market Quotes on April 04, and April 11, 2006

Each of these questions is independent of each other question. So, please answer each question without assuming the other questions.

(a) On April 11, the last recorded trade in the stock was at a price (i.e., 584) that is outside of the quoted spread (i.e., 560–578). I didn't think you could trade outside the spread in the N.Z. market. Please explain how this is possible? One sentence answer expected.

(b) Using the April 11 quotes, suppose you submit a market order to buy 500 shares of the stock. Will the order be executed? If so, when and at what price will the order be executed? Explain briefly.

(c) Using the April 11 quotes, suppose you submit a limit order to sell 5000 shares of stock at 575. Will the order be executed? If so, when and at what price will the order be executed? Explain briefly.

(d) Using the April 04 quotes, suppose you submit a market order to buy 500 shares of the stock. Will the order be executed? If so, when and at what price will the order be executed? Explain briefly.

(e) Finally, the simplest question you can be asked about a stock price. Did the stock price go up or down from April 04 to April 11? Explain briefly.

692. What is a short sale of a stock? Give a simple example.

693. When you short sell a stock, there are margin requirements. Can you give a simple numerical example of the margin requirements to short sell a stock. Say something also about maintenance margins.

694. What sort of dependent relationships do the two correlation coefficients PPMCC and SROCC identify? [Recall that PPMCC is the traditional Pearson product-moment correlation coefficient (i.e., the traditional standard measure of correlation) and SROCC is Spearman's rank-order correlation coefficient based on ranks].

695. Suppose I want to estimate a variance-covariance matrix (VCV) using daily returns on the 50 largest N.Z. stocks. Suppose I use the most recent 30 trading days of daily returns to estimate the VCV.

(a) Can I now use this VCV to estimate a Markowitz efficient frontier or solve an active space optimization? If yes, please explain why and skip part (b).

(b) If you answered no to (a), tell me why not and give me two suggestions (one sentence each) for how I can fix the problem.

696. A question on numerical derivatives. Table 2.4 gives values of a put option for different possible values of the underlying stock price. The delta is the slope of the plot of put option value (second column of Table 2.4) as a function of stock price (first column of Table 2.4). Delta is also how many shares of stock an options market maker needs to hold to hedge exposure to an option (on one stock) that has been sold to a customer. Assume the stock price is $5 right now, and the market maker just sold a put option covering 100 shares of stock to a customer. Using only the numbers in Table 2.4 and ignoring all T-costs, tell me:

(a) What was the total option premium that the customer paid?

(b) Estimate the number of shares of stock the market maker has to hold to hedge his or her exposure to the options just sold.

Stock Price	Put Option Value
$ 4.0000	$0.9593
$ 4.0100	$0.9497
$ 4.1000	$0.8650
$ 4.2000	$0.7735
$ 4.3000	$0.6853
$ 4.4000	$0.6013
$ 4.5000	$0.5223
$ 4.6000	$0.4489
$ 4.7000	$0.3815
$ 4.8000	$0.3207
$ 4.9000	$0.2665
$ 5.0000	$0.2189
$ 5.0100	$0.2145
$ 5.1000	$0.1777
$ 5.2000	$0.1427
$ 5.3000	$0.1132
$ 5.4000	$0.0889
$ 5.5000	$0.0690
$ 5.6000	$0.0530
$ 5.7000	$0.0402
$ 5.8000	$0.0303
$ 5.9000	$0.0225
$ 6.0000	$0.0166
$ 6.0100	$0.0161

Table 2.4: Stock Price and Put Price (both Dollars Per Share)

697. Suppose that in an active alpha optimization with a bound on the absolute value of active weights of 20%, we optimized to find benchmark standard deviation

$\sigma_B = 0.0921$, portfolio standard deviation $\sigma_P = 0.1012$, and portfolio alpha $\alpha_P = 0.0621$, at the optimum. The historical mean return on the benchmark and portfolio were $\mu_B = 0.2495$, and $\mu_P = 0.2598$, respectively. What is the forward looking IR at this optimum? [Recall that we imposed $\beta_P = 1$.]

698. Estimate the IR of an active portfolio manager who follows 100 stocks, and updates independent forecasts twice per year. Assume the correlation between realized and forecast active returns is only 6%. Is this IR good, very good, or exceptional?

699. In the active alpha optimization in Question 3.2.2 you are asked for an active alpha optimization using T-costs. Name three types of T-costs (that exist in the U.S. or N.Z.) which you ignored and give a one sentence definition of each.

700. A cutting edge new idea in 2006 was called "fundamental indexation." Tell me what it is and what benefits it is supposed to provide. Be sure to mention how these benefits are related to the location of the benchmark in your Markowitz optimization in Question 3.2.1.

701. Table 2.5, below, gives end of day bid (buy) and ask (sell) prices for stock ABC, and the amount of a cash dividend. Tuesday is the ex-dividend date. If you think a stock split took place this week, then you should guess the ratio based on your experiences with actual data. All prices are in cents per share.

Your task: Please work out the daily simple net return on the stock on each day from close of business Monday to close of business Friday. Report the daily returns to at least six decimal places.

Day	Date	Stock BUY Price	Stock SELL Price	Dividend
Mon	January 10	1074	1080	None
Tue	January 11	1020	1024	50
Wed	January 12	1055	1061	None
Thu	January 13	256	260	None
Fri	January 14	268	272	None

Table 2.5: Stock ABC Price and Dividends (Cents Per Share)

702. In *Foundations*, I said that we could think of positive RAA as the capital market portfolio manager's equivalent of a corporate finance CFO's positive NPV investment. I gave six characteristics that the two concepts have in common. Please give me any five of those characteristics. Brief bullet point answers expected.

703. Do you have any evidence from the numerical work you did in Question 3.2.2 that large-cap stocks and small-cap stocks may have different levels of transactions costs when we trade them? If "yes," then please explain why you say that; it should only take one sentence.

704. This example comes from the official N.Z. Tax Authority (IRD) document on Dividend Imputation (IRD274). Suppose a company earns $1,000 profit, and pays corporate tax on the profit at the 33% rate. Suppose the company pays all of the remaining $670 after-tax profit as an after-tax dividend to the shareholder (let us simplify by assuming only one shareholder) and also passes on a $330 imputation credit. Suppose the shareholder has a 33% marginal tax rate.

  (a) What is the shareholder's taxable income from dividends?

  (b) After the payment of all taxes, how much is the after-tax cash dividend? In other words, I am asking whether the shareholder gets to keep exactly the $670 cash dividend, or whether there is some other tax adjustment still to be made. Please explain.

705. Table 2.6 shows the prices of 10 stocks six months ago, and their prices right now. You currently hold the benchmark (performance also shown). Now you want to implement a price momentum strategy by tilting your portfolio weights toward stocks favored by the price momentum strategy and away from those stocks not favored by the strategy. Other things being equal (e.g., T-costs), identify the three stocks which are most heavily favored by the price momentum strategy (we want to buy more of these) and the three stocks which are least favored by the price momentum strategy (we want to sell some of our existing holdings of these to finance buying the favored ones). In each case, tell me their ticker symbols and why you chose them (be brief). You may assume there were no dividends or stock splits over the last six months.

Ticker	Price 6 Months Ago	Price Now	% change
ABC	581.50	476.83	-18.0%
DEF	675.50	594.44	-12.0%
GHI	1316.50	1250.68	-5.0%
JKL	168.50	166.82	-1.0%
MNO	27.50	26.95	-2.0%
PQR	67.50	56.03	-17.0%
STU	97.50	84.83	-13.0%
VWX	132.50	115.28	-13.0%
IBM	69.50	62.55	-10.0%
MSFT	163.50	107.91	-34.0%
BENCHMARK	3300.00	2942.30	-10.8%

Table 2.6: Ten Stocks and Benchmark Price Performance over Last Six Months

706. Active management is composed of one or both of benchmark timing and/or stock selection. Give me a one-sentence definition of benchmark timing, and a one-sentence definition of stock selection.

707. Our original candidate objective function for our active alpha optimization was $\kappa_P - \lambda_T \sigma_P^2$. Tell me what the λ_T is doing in this objective function. That is, what is λ_T, what role does it play, why do we need it? A few sentences are expected; bullet point is fine.

708. Using the same notation as in *Foundations*, write down the equation for the weights in the tangency portfolio of a Markowitz/Tobin optimization. Identify each of the component parts of the equation with arrows and labels. Is it possible for any of the weights to be negative? Must the weights sum to one?

709. We had a two-step procedure when moving from the candidate objective function $\kappa_P - \lambda_T \sigma_P^2$ to the residual "active alpha" objective function $\alpha_P - \lambda_R \omega_P^2$. The first step was to decompose the first and second moment of returns. The second step was to throw away a whole bunch of terms.

    (a) Tell me why we took the first step (two sentences expected).

    (b) Tell me why we took the second step (several bullet points are expected).

710. In *Foundations* I gave you the following equations for finding the Markowitz Frontier of risky assets when there is no riskless asset:

$$\vec{h}_P = \vec{H}\mu_P + \vec{G} \quad \text{where}$$
$$\vec{H} = \frac{1}{D}\left\{[C(V^{-1}\vec{\mu}) - A(V^{-1}\vec{\iota})]\right\},$$
$$\vec{G} = \frac{1}{D}\left\{[B(V^{-1}\vec{\iota}) - A(V^{-1}\vec{\mu})]\right\},$$
$$A = \vec{\iota}'V^{-1}\vec{\mu}, \; B = \vec{\mu}'V^{-1}\vec{\mu}, \; C = \vec{\iota}'V^{-1}\vec{\iota}, \; \text{and } D = BC - A^2.$$

    For Question 3.2.1 you were given $\vec{\mu}$, V, and you had to build $\vec{\iota}$. You then had to solve for the seven unknown quantities appearing to the left of the equals signs: $\vec{h}_P$, $\vec{H}$, $\vec{G}$, A, B, C, D.

    (a) Tell me the order in which you solved for these seven unknown quantities.

    (b) Tell me what is μ_P in the first equation above.

    (c) Tell me what is $\vec{h}_P$ in the first equation above.

2.3   Financial Theories and Empirical Evidence

711. ◇ Tell me three characteristics that differentiate large-capitalization and small-capitalization stocks—apart from their level of capitalization, of course.

712. Is there a relationship between stock price and market capitalization in U.S. or N.Z. stock data? If so, tell me what the relationship is and why it might hold.

713. In a market where there is a designated market maker (like the specialist on the NYSE), what does the width of the bid-ask spread compensate the market maker for? Given your answer to this, and other things being equal, do you expect spreads to be wider for a stock or a broad market index ETF?

714. What is the one application of eigen decomposition that is presented in *Foundations*? Explain in words, with no equations, what the aim of the application was.

715. Is there a relationship between relative bid-ask spread and market capitalization in U.S. or N.Z. Stock data? If so tell me what is the relationship and why.

716. Which of the following are TRUE and which are FALSE? No explanation needed.

   (a) Large-cap stocks tend to have higher return volatility than small-cap stocks.
   (b) Large-cap stocks tend to have less liquidity than small-cap stocks.
   (c) Large-cap stocks tend to have more negatively autocorrelated returns than small stocks.
   (d) Large-cap stocks tend to have more positively skewed return distributions than small-cap stocks.
   (e) Large-cap stocks tend to have larger positive kurtosis of returns than small-cap stocks.

717. Explain the Ferguson-Shockley (2003) argument. Given their argument, what evidence do Fama-French (1992, 1993, 1996, etc.) provide against the CAPM?

2.4 Active Investment Topics

718. Popular exchange-traded funds (ETFs) include ones that track the S&P 500, gold, silver, and oil.

   (a) What is an ETF?
   (b) Pick one of the assets mentioned (i.e., S&500, gold, silver, or oil) and tell me what is attractive about the ETF compared to the asset itself.

719. Distinguish between defined benefit (DB) and defined contribution (DC) retirement plans.

720. Explain why the manager in a DB plan can take on more market risk than an individual investor in a DC plan might choose.

721. Give three reasons why ETFs are important and attractive investment tools.

722. Distinguish between value, glamour and growth stocks. Is growth just bad value?

723. What is a hedge fund?

724. Distinguish between a market neutral long-short fund with a beta near zero and a 130/30 short-extension fund.

725. Give an argument for why we might not be expected to have any apriori economic intuition for what should be the correlation between the returns to stocks and investment grade bonds.

726. Describe the service offered by a DRIP.

727. Explain, with a simple example, why cash drag is a problem for most mutual fund managers.

728. Do you think the manager of a value fund or the manager of a price momentum fund has higher T-costs? Explain.

729. Give the accounting definition of accruals. Define earnings quality. Describe the Sloan (1996) accruals anomaly. Compare and contrast earnings quality and the factor-based investing notion of "quality."

730. Define fundamental indexation and give a simple example. Describe some of the empirical results for the relative performance of fundamental versus traditional indices.

731. What is the diversification puzzle? Statman (2004) gives an argument based on a pyramid of investments. Explain that argument.

732. In Chapter 4 of *Foundations*, I give long-term plots of the level of a stock market index and the log of the level of a stock market index. Explain what the log plot shows that is not shown by the original plot.

Chapter 3

Long-Answer Test Questions

Before working through these problems, please consult the errata for corrections and comments at the Web site www.FoundationsForScientificInvesting.com.

For these problems, or for your employer, or for yourself, when you build a spreadsheet, it should be dynamic and easy to audit. By "dynamic," I mean that if you change one cell in your source data, then every calculation in the spreadsheet should immediately and automatically reflect that change. This means that you never hard-code raw data into a formula. You never copy and paste raw data as values anywhere in any part of the spreadsheet, not even headings or labels. To the best of Excel's abilities, you never run a regression and dump the output as values not driven by source data. To the best of Excel's abilities, every calculation performed has to be a direct consequence of the contents of the raw data. You can use ctrl-grave accent to help look for non-dynamic links. By "easy to audit," I mean that you or anyone else looking at the spreadsheet can figure out what it does and can easily search for errors. So, you should not just throw your workings randomly all over the place, but rather you should order them logically and label them. Raw data should be grouped together and clearly labeled. Neither should you (without good reason) break down simple formulae into component parts that clutter your spreadsheet.

3.1 Time Value of Money

Question 3.1.1: PVA and PVGA

In Chapter 1 of *Foundations*, we mentioned that a one-percentage-point increase in the interest rate earned over a 50-year period adds more than half as much again to your final wealth, based on a lump sum initial deposit. We said, however, that most investors save as an annuity of deposits or a growing annuity of deposits and that this dulls the effect (because the later deposits do not have as much time to compound as the earlier deposits).

1. Show that the future value of a $1 deposit increases by more than half as much again if the constant interest rate earned increases from 8.85%

per annum to 9.95% per annum. Hint: Use $FV(r) = PV(1+r)^T$, where $PV = \$1$, $r = 0.0885$ per annum (and $r' = 0.0985$ per annum), and $T = 50$ years to find the ratio $\frac{FV(r')}{FV(r)}$.

2. Instead of a lump sum initial deposit, assume that the investor deposits an annuity of $1 at $t = 1, \ldots, 49, 50$ (i.e., 50 equally spaced deposits). What is the ratio $\frac{FV(r')}{FV(r)}$ using $FV(r) = PVA(r)(1+r)^T$, where $PVA(r) = \frac{C}{r}\left[1 - \frac{1}{(1+r)^N}\right]$ is the present value of an annuity, $C = \$1$, $r = 0.0885$ per annum (and $r' = 0.0985$ per annum), $T = 50$ years is the date at which we will perform the comparison, and $N = 50$ is the count of the number of deposits in the annuity?

3. Now answer the same question for a growing annuity. The present value of a growing annuity is $PVGA(r) = \frac{C}{r}\left[1 - \left(\frac{1+g}{1+r}\right)^N\right]$. Assume that the deposits grow at $g = 0.03$ per annum (roughly the average annual inflation over the 50 years 1963–2013), that the first deposit is $1 at $t = 1$, and that there are $N = 50$ deposits (i.e., the last deposit is at $t = 50$). Use $FV(r) = PVGA(r)(1+r)^T$, with $T = 50$ years to find the ratio $\frac{FV(r')}{FV(r)}$, using interest rates $r = 0.0885$ and $r' = 0.0985$ per annum.

Answers: I get ratios of 1.579725, 1.426960, and 1.382486, respectively, to six decimal places. So, even with a growing annuity of deposits, one extra percentage point still increases final wealth by more than one-third as much again.

Question 3.1.2: Bank Loan

In the PEAR/TVM discussion in Chapter 2 of *Foundations*, we said that one of the key things to remember when working out loan repayments is that the value of the loan is the same as the present value of the time series of repayments. If, however, a bank that lends out money only ever gets back the economic value of what it lent out, then how, and when, does it ever make an economic profit? The answers to those two questions are rarely mentioned in introductory time value of money classes. First, suppose that a bank loans out $10,000 for a three-year term. Assume that the interest rate is 6% per annum with monthly compounding. Assume the repayments are in the form of an ordinary annuity. We can use the present value of an annuity formula to solve for the monthly repayment. The bank makes money because it took that money from depositors to whom it pays only 3% per annum, with monthly compounding, say. So, from the bank's perspective, when it discounts the monthly loan repayments, it does not get $10,000, but a larger number. What is the monthly loan repayment, and how much is the present value of the bank's economic profit? Second, when does the bank make a profit? That is, suppose the person who borrowed the money defaults on the nth payment. What value of n would let the bank still make a profit? Is it like running a marathon, and if you fall just before the final yards you still lose? Answers: I find monthly loan repayment of $C = \$304.219375$ and present value of economic profit of $\$461.028904$, to six decimal places. To figure out when the last payment has to be for the bank to break even, we just need to equate the amount lent out ($\$10,000$) to the present value of an annuity of T repayments of C, discounting at the bank's APR of $r = 0.03$ (with monthly compounding). So, we need to solve Equation 3.1 for T.

$$10000 = \frac{C}{r/12}\left[1 - \frac{1}{(1+r/12)^T}\right] \tag{3.1}$$

Rearranging Equation 3.1 for T yields Equation 3.2.

$$T = \frac{\log\left[\frac{C}{C - 10000 \cdot \frac{r}{12}}\right]}{\log\left(\frac{r}{12}\right)} \tag{3.2}$$

Evaluating Equation 3.2 at $r = 0.03$ and $C = 304.219375$ (carrying all decimal places) yields $T = 34.343380$ to six decimal places. In other words, if the borrower makes the 35th of the 36 loan repayments, the bank makes a profit. If, however, the borrower makes only 34 or fewer payments, the bank makes a loss. This calculation ignores both the fixed costs of running the bank, and taxes.

Question 3.1.3: PVGA and Retirement

There is an example in the TVM section of Chapter 2 of *Foundations* (see the Retirement Lump Sum section) where Mary is contributing a growing annuity of payments to fund a retirement lump sum at age 65. Please use all the same parameter values as that example, except that I want you to treat the contribution rate, previously 10%, as a plug figure that you will solve for in three different scenarios, described shortly.

I want Mary to contribute enough of her salary to have a lump sum available on her 65th birthday sufficient to fund a retirement annuity for 30 years. Upon her 65th birthday, she will flip her investments into a lower-risk fund, forecast to grow at only 40 bps per month, instead of the 50 bps per month growth she got up to age 65. She will make withdrawals from her account at the end of each month (i.e., 360 withdrawals, with the first withdrawal one month after her 65th birthday). She will make withdrawals in the form of a growing annuity, growing at 25 bps per month (i.e., an APR of 3% per annum with monthly compounding).

In the first scenario, I want you to assume that her first withdrawal is equal to 50% of her last monthly after-tax paycheck, but you are to gross that number up for one month at the same inflation rate of 25 bps per month that we are using for the growing annuity. In this case, we are modeling the first withdrawal as an inflation-adjusted proportion of her last pay packet. Note that her deposits were out of after-tax salary, and we shall assume no further tax is due.

In the second scenario, I want you to take the average monthly U.S. Social Security payment to a retiree of $1,269 paid as of the end of June 2013 (SSA, 2014a) and assume that your income is low enough that this amount is tax free. Assume that the Social Security Administration will apply a COLA of 4.00% per annum (please use a COLA of 32.71 bps per month).[1] Now assume that Mary turns 21 at the end of this month, and inflate the $1,269 from the end of June 2013 to the end of the first month after her 65th birthday, and solve for the contribution rate that allows her to withdraw that inflated payment from her retirement account assuming her withdrawals grow at 25 bps per month thereafter. That is, her first withdrawal is supposed to replicate our forecast of what she should get from Social Security, but thereafter her withdrawals grow at a slower rate than Social Security.

The third scenario is the same as the second, except that I want you to solve for the contribution rate that gives Mary 2.5 times the withdrawal from the second scenario. This is because the Social Security Administration estimates that Social Security payments to retirees form just over a third of their income, and I want you to assume that Mary has nothing else to rely on but her self-made pension.[2]

Hints: First of all, draw a careful timeline with all flows, growth rates, etc. Second, in each of the three cases, there is a closed-form formula for the answer. So, you do not need to use Excel Solver or anything similar. Third, I get a contribution rate of 60.221056% in the first case, 11.899505% in the second case (executed as of November 2013), and 29.748762% in the final case. Mary's salary is growing so quickly that replacing only half of the after-tax amount is a heavy burden on her savings, requiring roughly 60% of her after-tax salary to be saved. To match the projected Social Security payment, she need only contribute about 12%. If she wants income comparable with current retirees, and assuming there will be no Social Security when she retires, and no other source of income, then she needs to contribute nearly 30% to her retirement savings account. In my experience with modeling retirement situations, the pre-retiree with average income usually needs to contribute between 10% and 20% per annum to secure a sensible retirement income.

Question 3.1.4:   BEARs

You sign up for an N.Z. KiwiSaver retirement savings plan. It requires no initial deposit. The government pays to you a matching member tax credit (MTC) of $0.50 for every dollar deposit you make up to a maximum MTC of $521.43 per annum (corresponding to a deposit by you of at least $1,042.86, or $20 per week assuming 365 days per annum and seven days per week). Any KiwiSaver investor aged 18 years or over is eligible for this MTC regardless of

---

[1] Over the 39 years from 1975 to 2013 inclusive, the geometric average COLA was 3.996% per annum, based on numbers taken from SSA (2014b).

[2] The Social Security Administration estimated that Social Security payments to the elderly make up about 39% of their income (SSA, 2014a).

employment status.

Assume there are exactly 52 weeks in a year (so you get at most a $520 MTC). You will need to use weekly interest rates and EARs. There is no good reason to use any APRs. You will need most of the TVM math you ever saw and Excel's solver too. Do not use any pre-programmed Excel TVM commands.

Assume that you deposit $20 into your plan at the end of each week for 52 weeks per annum. At the end of each year the government pays into your plan the MTC equal to half your notional deposits (i.e., MTC=$\frac{1}{2} \times 52 \times \$20 = \$520$). Assume your plan earns a stated EAR after all taxes and fees, and you invest in KiwiSaver for N years.

1. Suppose your fund earned an EAR=5.0% per annum after all taxes and fees. In fact, this is not your return! Your return depends upon your contributions. Your return is higher than someone with a bank account earning an EAR of 5.0% because you got the MTC match and they did not. Similarly, your return is higher than another KiwiSaver investor who made no contributions because you got the MTC match and they did not. The key is that your deposits trigger the arrival of the MTC match benefits. These benefits are therefore part of the return on your investment. Assume $N = 3$ (so you get three matches of $520) and tell me the benefit-adjusted EAR (BEAR) you earned. Make your spreadsheet dynamic so we can vary N (and everything else) easily.

2. What is the BEAR if instead your fund earned an EAR=10.2% per annum?

3. Tell me the BEAR in the EAR=5.0% case, for N=1, 2, 3, 4, 5, 10, 25, 50. Give me a table and a plot. The table can be non-dynamic if you need to use output from Excel's solver.

4. With N=3, how low would the stated EAR have to have been for the calculated BEAR to be zero. This is a breakeven BEAR. To answer this question I copied the tab to a new tab, and set up a new Excel SOLVER optimization in that new tab (otherwise the first Solver setup gets overwritten).

5. Given the typical range of EARs in funds you might choose, and given the size of the BEARs, how important is manager selection?

3.2 Portfolio Theory

Question 3.2.1: Markowitz Exercise

Do not use any numerical optimization package (e.g., Excel's Solver) to work out the solutions to this problem. Rather, I want you to implement the formulae appearing in the "Markowitz Efficient Set Mathematics" section of Chapter 2 of *Foundations*. ♣ Download the spreadsheet MARKOWITZ-DATA.XLS from the Web site for this exercise.[3]

---

[3]Web site: `www.FoundationsForScientificInvesting.com`

I want you to use the estimates of mean returns and the estimate of the VCV in the tab labeled "Means & VCV" in the spreadsheet to generate an ex-post efficient frontier of the stocks. This is a historical frontier; it is not the forward-looking ex-ante frontier that we talk about for the theoretical CAPM or for active alpha optimization. I want you to assume a riskless rate of 2.5%.[4][5]

Please produce the following:

1. A Markowitz-type graph of the historical risky portfolio frontier in sample total return–sample total standard deviation space, together with the Tobin frontier and tangency portfolio. Please note, you are plotting three different concepts on the same picture: Markowitz frontier, Tobin frontier, and tangency portfolio. Each is calculated using the Markowitz mathematics in Chapter 2 of *Foundations*. For the Markowitz and Tobin frontiers, I want the graph to extend from $\mu_P = -5.00$ (i.e., -500%) up to $\mu_P = 5.00$ (i.e., +500%) in steps of 0.25% (i.e., 25 bps). That is, for each of the two frontiers, I want 4001 observations in the data series that you plot spaced at 25-bp intervals from -500% up to $+500\%$. Use an X-Y graph with points not joined by lines and choose the smallest possible marker sizes. You must show both halves of the Tobin frontier (i.e., the kinked lines that touch at the riskless rate).

   - Do not build the Tobin frontier by some ad hoc technique that either includes only a few points connected to make a straight line, or calculates a Sharpe ratio and then deduces the frontier in segments. Rather, you should calculate it using the Markowitz mathematics in Chapter 2 of *Foundations*.

   - Do not deduce betas using some ad hoc technique that assumes a linear relationship between returns and betas, because this technique will fail for half the betas in this exercise. You need to calculate the betas using the equation given in item number 6 below.

   - Do not estimate the location of the tangency portfolio by some ad hoc technique. Rather, you should calculate it using the Markowitz mathematics in Chapter 2 of *Foundations*.

   - When calculating the Tobin frontier variance, note that $R_F \cdot \vec{\iota}$ is not matrix multiplication because it is not conformal. Either use regular multiplication (i.e., $*$ in Excel), or swap the order and use matrix multiplication of $\vec{\iota} \cdot R_F$

   - The analytical solution to the vector of weights $\vec{h}_P$ of a 20-stock portfolio on the Markowitz or Tobin frontiers at any level of return is a 20×1 vector.

---

[4]This rate is reported at `http://www.rbnz.govt.nz/monpol/statements/0090630.html` as being the average official cash rate (OCR) in force over the 2012–2013 period. The OCR is the bank rate, or discount rate, charged by the N.Z. central bank to commercial banks for overnight loans.

[5]Although we are using an average riskless rate over the time period, this is not a look-ahead bias in this context because the entire exercise is done in hindsight. When we carry the minimum variance portfolio weights into the active alpha optimization problem in Question 3.2.6, these data are all observable at the date when the portfolios are formed to avoid any look-ahead biases.

This vector should not appear explicitly anywhere in your spreadsheet for any level of return. Rather, the formula for that vector should be embedded within the formulae for the mean and variance of returns to the frontier portfolios that you plot. See the related discussion in Section 2.6.3 of *Foundations* regarding the absence of the choice variables from the axes of this optimization.

2. Now make a copy of your graph (right click, copy, paste) and rescale to show the region for returns between plus and minus 60%, so that you can see more detail. Adjust the x-axis scale so that there is not lots of space to the right of the frontiers. Force Excel to plot B (i.e., the capitalization-weighted benchmark of the 20 stocks) and as many of the 20 stocks as you can fit on the second Markowitz frontier diagram. Label the stocks and B.

3. For this item, ignore the riskless asset, the Tobin frontier, and the tangency portfolio. "Naive diversification" (also called benchmark diversification) yields the risk reduction offered by B compared with the average risk in the individual stocks. "Optimal diversification" yields the risk reduction offered by frontier portfolios compared with the average risk in individual stocks. Estimate the risk reduction benefit (in units of return, not return squared; that is, examine standard deviations, not variances) from naive and from optimal diversification. Also estimate the incremental risk reduction from optimal diversification over and above that available from naive diversification. This question is purposely vague; use your initiative to answer as you see fit.

4. Identify the tangency portfolio: mean, standard deviation, and vector of portfolio weights identified by ticker symbol. Use Excel to mark this point with a small dot labeled "T" on the graph.

5. Your benchmark is the portfolio of the 20 stocks in the spreadsheet, and the weights come from the market caps in the MARKOWITZ sheet (divide each stock's market capitalization by the sum of the 20 stocks' market caps to get weights). Using this value-weighted benchmark is conceptually no different from a client identifying the stocks it wants in its benchmark. Identify the benchmark portfolio: mean, standard deviation, and vector of portfolio weights identified by ticker symbol. Put this in the same table as the tangency portfolio information so you can read across and see differences in weights. Mark the benchmark with a small dot labeled "B" on the graph.

6. Now, for each of the 20 stocks, calculate the beta of the stock relative to the tangency portfolio, and plot an empirical SML showing these sample betas versus the sample mean returns. Finding a straight line does not guarantee that you are correct, but not finding one guarantees that you are wrong. Plot the graph and give a table with the betas. You do not have to run any time series regressions to find betas! Rather, the beta for stock i relative to portfolio "T" is found using $\beta_i = \frac{\vec{h}_i' V \vec{h}_T}{\vec{h}_T' V \vec{h}_T}$. What exactly is h_i? Go back and re-read Section 2.6.1 of *Foundations* if you do not immediately understand.

7. Repeat the last item, but do it all relative to the benchmark portfolio.[6] Should you expect a straight line? Think about the Roll critique (see Chapter 2 of *Foundations*) when answering.

8. Is the benchmark portfolio mean-variance efficient? Tell me why you can answer this question before you even touch the data.

Question 3.2.2:   Active Alpha Optimization

♣ Download the spreadsheet ACTIVE-ALPHA-DATA.XLS from the Web site for this exercise.[7]

It is time to try to beat the market! We will now execute a forward-looking optimization in active space. We will use the T-cost-adjusted objective function: $\alpha_P - \lambda_R \omega_P^2 - TC$ (see Section 2.7.8 of *Foundations*) for a parameterization of the objective function in terms of the choice variables; note that $\vec{h}_P^*$ is just $\vec{h}_B$ in your implementation because you are starting with benchmark weights, and $F = 1$ because you rebalance only one the first day). I assume that $\lambda_R = 10$ (a moderate level of risk aversion).[8] We will use a 20-stock benchmark built by us. Note that the benchmark weights are calculated using weights at the *end* of the first two years of our sample, that is December 31, 2013, not the beginning of the period as in Question 3.2.1.

You will build two fundamental alphas (value) and one technical alpha (price momentum). You will neutralize the alphas so that they are forecasts of return in active space, and you will rescale them so that they do not swamp the objective function. You will combine them into a single alpha forecast. You will then optimize the objective and choose optimal portfolio weights for each of two levels of restriction on the aggressiveness of the active weights. We will revisit this problem in Question 3.2.3 to see how your portfolios actually performed (i.e., did you beat the market, or did the market beat you?).

We are ignoring methods for building alphas that automatically minimize turnover; that takes a lot of experience. We are also ignoring alpha scaling issues that help to re-map distances between outliers automatically. We are also ignoring cross-sectional alpha scaling issues that optimally rescale alphas to give better forecasts of active return (see Section 4.1.15 of *Foundations*). We are also ignoring building alphas that are turnover-robust to missing observations. We are also ignoring methods for optimally combining multiple alphas. We are also ignoring any attempt to neutralize our alphas beyond benchmark neutrality (e.g., using industries or the components of the old Barra N.Z. risk model). We are also ignoring any attempt to build a better risk model using a MSCI/Barra-type model (though Question 3.2.4 asks for a Ledoit-Wolf (2004) estimator in this context).

---

[6]A necessary, but not sufficient condition for checking that your betas are correct is that for betas calculated relative to some index I, $\vec{\beta}'\vec{h}_I = 1$. If this fails, your betas are incorrect. If it holds, your betas may be correct.

[7]Web site: `www.FoundationsForScientificInvesting.com`

[8]Remember to use $\lambda_R = 0.10$ if returns are in number of percentage points rather than decimals.

In practice, we should have a half-dozen or more alphas combined into a single alpha forecast, and they should be chosen based on backtests of strategies accounting for T-costs, and we should do this with much larger breadth than 20 stocks (Tajaddini, Crack, and Roberts, 2015). We would then revise the alphas every day, and rebalance the portfolio two or three times a week, or whenever the traction with the ex-ante alphas declines enough to trigger a rebalance. In our case, we have three alphas, constructed using only the basic data, and ignoring any backtest, and we will revise our portfolio only once, rebalancing from the benchmark to a constrained optimum. The bottom line is that we are building a "quick-and-dirty" alpha model that ignores all the fine-tuning. So, in practice, we can do much better than whatever we find.

Note that the Markowitz analysis in Question 3.2.1 is simple because there are formulae and I give them to you (see Section 2.6.4 of *Foundations*), but it is complex because you need to identify in the real data which items correspond to the formulae, and then implement the formula using matrix algebra in Excel. In contrast, the active alpha optimization is complex because once you overlay enough constraints, there is no explicit formula that gives the solution, but it is simple because all of the difficult optimization is executed behind the scenes in Excel. All you need to do is build the alphas and set up the optimization problem correctly. If you relax and just follow the step-by-step instructions, it should take only a few hours.

1. I want you to build three sets of alphas. Each is a carefully scaled forecast of returns over and above those associated with the benchmark. You will focus on one type of alpha and build it for all stocks, then move to the next type of alpha and build it for all stocks, and then the last type of alpha and build it for all stocks. The final step will be to combine the types of alpha one stock at a time. We will use basic price and price-ratio data: raw P/E ratios and raw dividend yields for each of our stocks.

2. The first alpha is for P/E ratios. Value stocks tend to outperform the market in many countries and in many time periods. So, let us tilt toward stocks with *low* P/E ratios: let us define the raw P/E alpha for stock i as $\alpha_{raw,i} = \frac{1}{P/E_i}$, where P/E_i is the P/E ratio of stock i, to get the ordering right (we want the more positive alphas to be associated with outperformance).[9]

3. Now we must standardize the alphas. Let $\alpha_{zraw,i} = \frac{\alpha_{raw,i} - \text{mean}(\vec{\alpha}_{raw})}{\text{stdev}(\vec{\alpha}_{raw})}$, where $\text{mean}(\vec{\alpha}_{raw})$ and $\text{stdev}(\vec{\alpha}_{raw})$ are the cross-sectional mean and standard deviation (use $N-1$ because it is a small sample) of the elements of the vector of raw alphas.[10]

---

[9]Obviously, these are E/P ratios (i.e., earnings yields). E/P is much better behaved than P/E because it does not explode when earnings cross zero. Note, however, that we will keep calling them P/E alphas.

[10]In finance, we get three kinds of data sets: time series, cross section, and pooled. Time series is like the history of prices on one stock; cross section is like a snapshot of the returns on each of 50 stocks for one day; pooled is like the history of returns on each of 50 stocks. So, cross-sectional

4. If an outlier is a rubbish observation, then it should be zeroed; if the outlier is genuine, it should be Winsorized at three times the scale of the alphas so it does not have undue influence (named after Charles P. Winsor). Let the Winsorized alphas $\alpha_{win,i}$ be given by $\alpha_{win,i} = \begin{cases} \alpha_{zraw,i} & \text{if } |\alpha_{zraw,i}| \leq 3 \\ 3 & \text{if } \alpha_{zraw,i} > 3 \\ -3 & \text{if } \alpha_{zraw,i} < -3. \end{cases}$

   This is to catch outliers; there are often none in small samples. Check that your Winsorization formula works by overwriting some inputs with big and small positive or negative numbers! This is one of the most common errors made by my students.

5. Neutralization can be with respect to the benchmark and also with respect to industries (unless sparse) and risk model factors. You have to watch out that any alphas that have been zeroed do not now take significant values, and you will also have to re-standardize. Now let $\vec{\alpha}_{neut} = \vec{\alpha}_{win} - (\vec{h}'_B \vec{\alpha}_{win}) \cdot \vec{\beta}$, where $\vec{\alpha}_{win}$ is the column vector of Winsorized alphas, $\vec{h}_B$ is the column vector of weights in the benchmark, $\vec{h}'_B \vec{\alpha}_{win}$ is the benchmark average alpha (recall that the sum of the components in $\vec{h}_B$ is unity), and $\vec{\beta}$ is the column vector of betas of the stocks with respect to the benchmark. These are the neutralized alphas. They may have the wrong scale (we will take care of that at the next step), but they should satisfy $\vec{h}'_B \vec{\alpha}_{neut} = 0$, and this is a check you must perform.[11]

6. We now need to rescale the alphas to have similar scale to the returns. We will scale using the ratio of the benchmark standard deviation to the standard deviation of the alphas. Define $\vec{\alpha}_{neut\text{-}scaled} = \vec{\alpha}_{neut} \times \frac{\sigma_B}{\text{stdev}(\vec{\alpha}_{neut})}$, where $\text{stdev}(\vec{\alpha}_{neut})$ is the cross-sectional standard deviation (use $N-1$ because it is a small sample) of the elements of the vector of neutralized alphas. Recall that $\sigma_B = \sqrt{\vec{h}'_B V \vec{h}_B}$.

7. You should now have 20 standardized, Winsorized, neutralized, re-scaled, P/E-based value alphas: $\vec{\alpha}_{P/E}$. Now we move to the (net) dividend yield (DY) alphas. High-DY stocks are value stocks and often outperform the market. Let the raw dividend yield alphas be simply the dividend yields. Now run through all the same calculations used above to obtain 20 standardized, Winsorized, neutralized, re-scaled, dividend yield alphas: $\vec{\alpha}_{DY}$.

8. Now we move to the price-momentum alphas. Chapter 3 of *Foundations* says that recent relative six-month performance tends to be continued. So,

---

standard deviation just means the standard deviation over the sample (which happens to be a cross-sectional sample).

[11]I can think of only two pathological examples regarding neutralization. First, you have no skill and thus no skilled forecasts. In this case, your raw alphas are all zero, and cannot be normalized, or neutralized. Second, if you do not want to do any benchmark timing, and if your alphas are proportional to the betas: $\vec{\alpha} = \kappa \vec{\beta}$, then you have no alphas. Why? The reason is that alphas proportional to betas (perhaps you think individual stocks will outperform naive forecasts as a linear function of their betas) are indistinguishable from benchmark timing. So, your alphas reduce to zero when we benchmark-neutralize them.

we want to tilt toward the relative winners and away from the relative losers. So, let the raw price-momentum alphas be simply the ratio of the last price in the data set to the price six months earlier (I highlighted in yellow and put bold borders around these prices in the spreadsheet to avoid ambiguity). Now run through all the same calculations to obtain 20 standardized, Winsorized, neutralized, re-scaled, price-momentum alphas: $\vec{\alpha}_{MOM}$.

9. Now define $\vec{\alpha}_{\text{final-raw}} = \frac{\vec{\alpha}_{P/E} + \vec{\alpha}_{DY} + \vec{\alpha}_{MOM}}{3}$. Make sure you get each of the standardized, Winsorized, neutralized, re-scaled alphas in this ratio and not the raw alphas. The final raw alpha is two-thirds value and one-third momentum (many clients trust fundamental alphas more than technical alphas, so we can better sell this weighting to a client; it will not make much of a difference to the outcome, as long as all the ingredients are in there). Now run through exactly the same algebra again to standardize, Winsorize, neutralize, and re-scale. Your final alpha is called $\vec{\alpha}_{\text{final-neut-scaled}}$. The $\vec{\alpha}_{\text{final-neut-scaled}}$ are the 20 alphas for our stocks. They are standardized, Winsorized, neutralized, re-scaled, and ready for the optimizer.

10. You also need to know how to handle the T-costs. Let $\vec{\gamma}$ be the vector of relative bid-ask spreads for the 20 stocks (as appearing already in the spreadsheet), and let $\vec{h}_P$ be the total weight of each stock in the portfolio, then $TC = \frac{1}{2}|\vec{h}_P - \vec{h}_B|'\vec{\gamma}$ is the cost of moving from the benchmark to P (and, yes, that is a modulus sign). Note that $TC \geq 0$ by construction (i.e., it costs money to trade and the only way to get $TC = 0$ is to not trade).

Now set up the spreadsheet so that you can use Excel's Solver to maximize the objective function through choice of the portfolio weights. If you cannot find Solver, then add it in (ask Google how to do that if it is not clear). The remainder of the question should take one-to-three hours to implement with the following constraints.

I think it is easiest to do this using total weights $\vec{h}_P$, but it could be done using active weights (i.e., $\vec{h}_P - \vec{h}_B$); the answer is the same. Note that before overlaying extra constraints, this problem can be solved analytically using calculus, but once you overlay short-selling constraints, turnover constraints, etc., it becomes analytically intractable. So, we must solve it numerically instead. Your problem is, using total weights $\vec{h}_P$, maximize the objective function $\alpha_P - \lambda_R \omega_P^2 - TC$ through choice variable total weights $\vec{h}_P$, where those weights are constrained as follows:

(a) First, so that you do not short sell: $h_{P,i} \geq 0$ for each i, where $h_{P,i}$ is the ith element in the column vector $\vec{h}_P$. So, you want $h_{P,i} \geq 0$ to avoid short selling. Note that vector constraints may be added as a single line in the Excel dialog box.

(b) Second, the weights are constrained so that they sum to one $\vec{h}_P'\vec{\iota} = 1$, where $\vec{\iota}$ is a column vector of ones.[12]

---

[12]So, your active positions are in the 20 stocks only. You are putting no active money (i.e., de-

(c) Third, constrain the active weights to be no greater than 10% in magnitude. That is, $|h_{B,i} - h_{P,i}| \leq 0.10$ for each i. I will also ask you to do this for a 5% bound, but once you can do it for 10%, it is just a matter of changing that one number to re-run the optimization. In the real world, we might have over 100 stocks in the portfolio, and quite small bounds on active weights, possibly setting the bound to be a proportion of the benchmark weights.

(d) Fourth, start your problem with total weights ($\vec{h}_P$) equal to the benchmark weights. You are then to trade away from this to find the optimum. The dollar volume of trade you must perform (counting buys and sells) is equal to the dollar investment in the portfolio (which we never specify here; we would if we were modeling price impact in the T-costs) multiplied by the sum of the absolute values of the active weights. This (two-sided) turnover figure needs to be constrained. We will revise our portfolio exactly once, so I want you to constrain it to be less than or equal to an upper bound of 50% of initial investment. Write down the algebra to figure this out; it is not meant to be immediately obvious. In a real world implementation, we would constrain turnover to a much smaller number, but rebalance two or three times a week, instead of once per year.

(e) Fifth, I want no benchmark timing, so you must constrain the portfolio's beta relative to the benchmark to equal 1.

Now run the optimization and record the following information.

1. A table that gives every alpha you calculated at every step for the 20 stocks, one column per stock, one row per alpha. I have 20 rows of alphas in my table. Give six digits after the decimal place for every alpha.

2. A table with the benchmark weights, the portfolio total weights ($\vec{h}_P$), and the portfolio active weights you got for the optimal portfolio using the final-scaled alpha. One ticker per row, one column per type of weights. Give me one table for each level of active holding constraint: 10%, 5%. Give six digits after the decimal place for each portfolio weight.

3. Report $\alpha = \vec{h}_P{}' \vec{\alpha}$, where $\vec{h}_P{}'$ is the optimal set of choice variables (i.e., portfolio weights), and ω is the level of active risk when the portfolio weights equal $\vec{h}_P{}'$, and $IR = \frac{\alpha}{\omega}$, and $RTAA = \alpha - \lambda\omega^2 - TC$, where $TC = \frac{1}{2}|\vec{h}_P - \vec{h}_B|'\vec{\gamma}$. That is, the ex-ante optimal portfolio alpha, active risk, IR, and objective function.

Aside: What you have created is not static. It is dynamic. So, you should check it by taking it out for a spin! It should behave in predictable ways. For

---

viations from the benchmark) into the riskless asset. Your active positions are fully invested. You have "no active cash." What this means is that your portfolio lies on the equivalent of the "MF ($\beta = 1$)" dotted frontier in Figure 2.16 of *Foundations* (except that Figure 2.16 does not have all the constraints you have).

example, if you use $\lambda' = 100 \times \lambda$, that is, a *very* active-risk-averse client, the optimizer should do almost no turnover and the active weights should be tiny. Conversely, if you use $\lambda' = \frac{\lambda}{100}$, the optimizer should trade like crazy, and hit the turnover constraint, and some of the active weight constraints. Similarly, if you use the original λ, but multiply the T-costs by 10, the optimizer should be reluctant to step far away from the benchmark, and might not want to trade at all (unless there is a low-T-cost-but-high-alpha-and-diversifying stock—not too likely because the largest alphas are usually in the smaller stocks with high T-costs). Now try setting $\beta = 1.1$, or 1.2, or 1.3 etc. Eventually you will come to a beta value that cannot be achieved in a long-only portfolio given the other constraints. Try removing the constraint on β completely. What is the natural β for this strategy? Try removing the long-only constraint. Do you now short the stocks you previously had pushed to zero weights? Try removing the turnover constraint. What is the natural level of turnover?

Question 3.2.3: Active Alpha Optimization: Backtest

We now return to the active portfolios we constructed in Question 3.2.2 to see how they performed over the year after formation. Although I present this as a separate analysis implemented in a different spreadsheet, once you have it up and running, I recommend that you transfer it to the same sheet used in Question 3.2.2, with the optimal solution there feeding in as an input here. That way, if you rerun the optimization in Question 3.2.2, using different parameters or constraints, then as long as you have built everything dynamically, you get to see immediately the impact of those changes on the graph of performance, and on the IRs and the RTAA.

In addition to the benchmark, we will run four portfolios: "P5" (5% active weight from Question 3.2.2), "P10" (10% active weight from Question 3.2.2), "MVP" ($\vec{h}_{MVP}$ from the Markowitz problem in Question 3.2.1), and the VINVA portfolio (a scaled version of $V^{-1}\alpha$, hence the name). See detailed discussion of the MVP portfolio in Question 3.2.6. Note that using the MVP or VINVA portfolios does not impose $\beta_P = 1$, and so we are likely to get excessive active risk from both stock selection and from benchmark timing. Our P5 and P10 portfolios should, however, have betas close to 1.

We must calculate fund values first. Then, we calculate an IR using active returns, and then we calculate an IR using residual returns from a regression. If there is no benchmark timing, these two IRs should be identical. I expect, however, that our initial portfolio probably slipped away from having a beta of 1, and that it ended the year with a small accidental active beta, and I expect the MVP and VINVA portfolios to have betas that are crazy-far from 1. Thus, some of our performance will be attributable to the active beta and the movement in the benchmark rather than our stock picking skills.

Note that MVP and VINVA portfolios often involve short selling. We can instead solve the MVP and VINVA problems with the constraint that there be no short selling if we want a long-only implementation.

In Question 3.2.2, you found the optimum active alpha portfolios by maximizing the objective function $\alpha_P - \lambda \omega_P^2 - TC$ (parameterized in terms of the choice variables $\vec{h}_P$) subject to five constraints. You are going to use the solution to look at portfolio performance over the following 12 months. ♣ So, download the spreadsheet BACK-TEST.XLS from the Web site for this exercise.[13]

The "Returns" tab contains returns I have calculated by accounting for dividends and splits during 2014 (I also filled in some missing data in a way that should not matter).

The initial weights in each of the portfolios (mostly from the solution to Question 3.2.2) are given in the "Weights" tab. I want you to form your portfolios using these percentage weights and using the given stock returns. Assume shares are infinitely divisible. Assume an initial investment of $1,000,000 in each portfolio. Please form the portfolios as of close of business December 31, 2013 using the weights from the Weights tab and run them until December 31, 2014. Note the first trading day in 2014 is not until Jan 3, 2014. So, the return in the sheet for "3-JAN-2014" is the return from close of business Dec 31, 2013 to close of business Jan 3, 2014. These returns, shaded yellow in the sheet, are the first returns you need. You apply them to the opening $1M fund value.

In cases where the return on a stock is missing during 2014, just update your portfolio's position in that stock by keeping the previous day's value of that position. So, you will need an "if" statement there, or something similar.

Historically, my students have great difficulty forming buy-and-hold portfolios when given the beginning weights and the time series of returns on the stocks. So, stop and ask yourself "what happens if I put money into a portfolio and I do not rebalance, but the stock price changes?" You must be very careful in your portfolio construction. The optimal weights from Question 3.2.2 hold only at time 0. As soon as stock prices start moving, however, the weights must change automatically. For example, as the value of AAA rises relative to its peers, its weight in your portfolio increases automatically. The construction is easy to implement, but you must think about it carefully before you implement it. Figure it out before you touch the darn keyboard!

Some of the following has been done for you already in the spreadsheet.

Plot on one graph the value of each of the three portfolios as a function of time from December 31, 2013 (when each portfolio is worth $1,000,000 by construction) up until December 31, 2014. The vertical axis is in dollars; the horizontal axis is dates. Be sure to include a legend. Choose a different line style (solid, dotted, dashed, etc.) for each series.

Now plot a second graph that shows the time series of the dollar value of

---

[13]Web site: www.FoundationsForScientificInvesting.com

the two active portfolios over and above the dollar value of the benchmark portfolio (this will be negative if we lose).

Now we will find the active return IR (i.e., combining stock selection and incidental benchmark timing). Use your time series of portfolio values to calculate three time series of daily continuously compounded (CC) returns: $r_{B,t}, r_{P10,t}, r_{P5,t}, r_{MVP,t}, r_{VINVA,t}$ for all available days in 2014. Now calculate four time series of CC daily active returns: $r_{P,t}^{(A)} \equiv r_{P,t} - r_{B,t}$, for our four active funds over the same time period. Now, for each fund, find the mean $\bar{r}_P^{(A)}$ and standard deviation $s_P^{(A)}$ of the daily CC active returns.

Construct a t-statistic to test the null hypothesis that the mean of the CC daily active returns is zero for each of the four active portfolios, and calculate an IR for each portfolio using these CC active returns (see below for the formulae).

Please create a table that has four columns (one for each of P5, P10, MVP, and VINVA), and the following rows:

- annualized mean active CC return: $251 \cdot \bar{r}_{PK}^{(A)}$

- annualized standard deviation of active CC return: $\sqrt{251} \cdot s_{PK}^{(A)}$

- the IR : $\frac{251 \cdot \bar{r}_{PK}^{(A)}}{\sqrt{251} \cdot s_{PK}^{(A)}}$

- the t-stat of the mean daily CC active returns

Give four decimal places for the IRs and t-stats and six decimal places for the mean and standard deviation.

We chose our active portfolios subject to the constraint that $\beta_P = 1$. However, we did not rebalance our portfolio at all during the 12-month period we ran it. In practice, the alphas depend upon price, and the prices change every day. For example, the P/E alphas change when we get new earnings numbers (at least every six months, and quarterly for the biggest stocks; more frequently if we use estimates). This means that as soon as one day passes, the alphas change from what we worked out in Question 3.2.2. If the alphas change, then so do the optimal weights for the optimization you solved in Question 3.2.2. If the optimal weights change, then we should rebalance subject to the five constraints from Question 3.2.2. The fact that we did not rebalance subject to constraints means both that we did not maintain the portfolios' optimal exposure to and traction with our alphas, and that the constraints were not necessarily satisfied after the passage of time. In particular, the portfolio beta may have drifted away from 1.00, and you may have ended up taking unintentional active benchmark timing bets. That will certainly be true for the MVP and VINVA portfolios.

So, I want to know what portion of your performance is attributable to stock selection (our original goal), and what portion is attributable to benchmark timing (an accident). We are going to break up the alpha into two parts to answer this. How do you do this? You have to run the regression of CC daily excess return on CC daily excess benchmark return as in Equation 3.3.

$$(r_{P10,t} - r_{F,t}) = \alpha_{P10} + \beta_{P10}(r_{B,t} - r_{F,t}) + \epsilon_t, \tag{3.3}$$

where $r_{F,t}$ is our estimate of average daily CC riskless rate over this time period (please use $r_{F,t} = [ln(1 + 0.031875)]/251$), $\hat{\alpha}_{P10}$ is our alpha due to stock selection, and $\hat{\beta}_{P10}$ is our beta.[14] Make your regression dynamic. That is, do not use the regression tool. Rather, code it from first principles. There is a template already in the BACK-TEST.XLS spreadsheet for the P5 portfolio, and other examples in the DYNAMIC-REGRESSION.XLS spreadsheet.

Aside: Can you calculate ex-post alpha and residual risk for the different levels of constraint in the active problem and plot a picture roughly like Figure 2.17 of *Foundations*?

Let us do some algebra to see that Equation 3.3 implies a sensible decomposition of returns into component parts. Plug $\beta_{P10} = 1 + \beta_{P10}^{(A)}$ (i.e., beta equals one plus active beta) into Equation 3.3 and multiply it out as follows:

$$
\begin{aligned}
(r_{P10,t} - r_{F,t}) &= \alpha_{P10} + \beta_{P10}(r_{B,t} - r_{F,t}) + \epsilon_t \\
&= \alpha_{P10} + (1 + \beta_{P10}^{(A)})(r_{B,t} - r_{F,t}) + \epsilon_t \\
&= \alpha_{P10} + (r_{B,t} - r_{F,t}) + \beta_{P10}^{(A)}(r_{B,t} - r_{F,t}) + \epsilon_t \\
\Rightarrow r_{P10,t} &= r_{B,t} + \alpha_{P10} + \beta_{P10}^{(A)}(r_{B,t} - r_{F,t}) + \epsilon_t \\
\Rightarrow r_{P10,t} - r_{B,t} &= \alpha_{P10} + \beta_{P10}^{(A)}(r_{B,t} - r_{F,t}) + \epsilon_t \\
\Rightarrow r_{P10,t}^{(A)} &= \alpha_{P10} + \beta_{P10}^{(A)}(r_{B,t} - r_{F,t}) + \epsilon_t
\end{aligned}
$$

It follows that once we have estimated Equation 3.3, we should find that daily average portfolio return exactly satisfies

$$\bar{r}_{P10} = \bar{r}_B + \hat{\alpha}_{P10} + \hat{\beta}_{P10}^{(A)}(\bar{r}_B - \bar{r}_F) \tag{3.4}$$

(portfolio return = benchmark return + alpha + active beta times excess benchmark return), or equivalently

$$\bar{r}_{P10}^{(A)} = \hat{\alpha}_{P10} + \hat{\beta}_{P10}^{(A)}(\bar{r}_B - \bar{r}_F). \tag{3.5}$$

That is, active return equals alpha plus active beta times excess benchmark return.

We may now work out a pure stock selection IR by taking the ratio of $251\hat{\alpha}_{P10}$ to $\sqrt{251}$ times the standard deviation of the daily CC residuals as in Equation 3.6.

$$\hat{\epsilon}_t = (r_{P10,t} - r_{F,t}) - \hat{\alpha}_{P10} - \hat{\beta}_{P10}(r_{B,t} - r_{F,t}) \tag{3.6}$$

---

[14]I got 3.1875% from http://www.rbnz.govt.nz/monpol/statements/0090630.html as being the average OCR in force over 2014.

Please complete (a)–(d) for each of the four active funds (use the template for the P5 portfolio that is already in BACK-TEST.XLS):

(a) Please report $\hat{\alpha}_{P10}$, $\hat{\beta}_{P10}$, $\hat{\beta}_{P10}^{(A)}$, stdev($\hat{\epsilon}_t$), and $IR = \frac{\alpha}{\omega} = \frac{251 \cdot \hat{\alpha}_{P10}}{\sqrt{251} \cdot \text{stdev}(\hat{\epsilon}_t)}$.

(b) If we multiply Equation 3.4 by 251, we get an annualized breakdown of our return performance into

$$\underbrace{251 \cdot \bar{r}_{P10}}_{\text{return}} = \underbrace{251 \cdot \bar{r}_B}_{\text{benchmark}} + \underbrace{251 \cdot \hat{\alpha}_{P10}}_{\text{alpha}} + \underbrace{\hat{\beta}_{P10}^{(A)}(251 \cdot \bar{r}_B - 251 \cdot \bar{r}_F)}_{\text{active beta} \times \text{excess return on benchmark}} . \quad (3.7)$$

Please calculate and report each of the four labeled items in Equation 3.7 and confirm that the sum of the last three gives the first (I just checked mine and they agree to 15 decimal places; yours must too!).

(c) Looking at Equation 3.7, you should see that the last two terms must add up to give the portfolio's outperformance of the benchmark due to stock selection and benchmark timing, respectively. So, please give me a single sentence summary of the total outperformance and the relative and absolute contributions of the component parts. For example, you might say, "We beat the benchmark by 200 bps, and that was composed of 50 bps of stock selection and 150 bps of accidental benchmark timing," or something like that. See the dynamic text in BACK-TEST.XLS.

(d) Finally, did we beat the market? Did we add value or destroy it? You have to explain your answer here. Your explanation should mention the parts of Equation 3.7: the alpha, beta, return on portfolio, return on benchmark, and the excess return on the benchmark. That, however, is not enough for the same reason that comparing raw cash flows with initial investment is not enough when working out an NPV in corporate finance. For an NPV calculation, you have to risk-adjust the cash flows. That is, you have to discount the cash flows using a penalty for risk. Then, only if the discounted cash inflows exceed the discounted cash outflows does it have a positive NPV and does it add value to the firm. In our portfolio management case, we have to add a penalty for risk and T-costs, and that risk- and T-costs-adjusted excess performance is the RTAA formula. Use $\alpha = 251 \cdot \hat{\alpha}_{P10}$, and $\omega = \sqrt{251} \cdot \text{stdev}(\hat{\epsilon}_t)$ in the RTAA. Feel free to just take $\lambda = 10$ as before and 10 bps for the T-costs; that should be about right.

(e) Now compare and contrast (i.e., what is similar and what is different between) the performance of the active alpha optimization, MVP, and VINVA portfolios. Consider everything you calculated: Plot of performance, the alpha, beta, active beta, active risk, active return IR, residual return IR, etc.

Question 3.2.4: Active Alpha Optimization: Ledoit VCV

Repeat the entire exercise for both Question 3.2.2 and Question 3.2.3, but this time use the Ledoit and Wolf (2004) estimator of the VCV. There is already a toggle set up in the spreadsheets for both questions to allow you to create the Ledoit-Wolf alphas and see the solutions. See *Foundations* for details on the Ledoit and Wolf (2004) estimator. What is the value of $\hat{\rho}$ for the constant correlation model? Let us just make the simplifying assumption that the shrinkage estimator uses convexity parameter $\delta = 0.50$.

In practice, there are several reasons not to expect much of a benefit from using the Ledoit-Wolf shrinkage VCV in this particular case. First, we estimated our sample VCV using only 20 stocks and two years of daily data, but the Ledoit-Wolf estimator is aimed at the converse situation where stocks outnumber time series observations. Second, we averaged the bid-ask quotes when we calculated prices that then gave the returns with which we estimated the VCV. This averaging smoothens out some of the microstructure-induced statistical estimation error. Third, we imposed five constraints on the optimization, including a no short-sales constraint. Jagannathan and Ma (2003) point out that the no short-selling constraint already goes some way toward simulating the effects of a shrinkage estimator.

Question 3.2.5: Active Alpha Optimization: Invert Alphas

Assuming that you correctly worked out the alpha tilt weights, go back and invert the value alphas. That is, go back to Question 3.2.2 and recalculate the P/E and DY alphas as glamour-growth alphas instead of value alphas. Keep momentum as it was. Re-run the active alpha optimization at the two levels of active constraint and then feed the optimal weights into the backtest problem to see whether we underperform or outperform the benchmark. What do you conclude? Does one approach outperform and one underperform, or do both techniques outperform by picking different stocks for different reasons? (Hint: I find that both beat the benchmark, but that the value approach performs best.)

Question 3.2.6: Active Alpha Optimization: P10-MVP Weights

We usually think of the Markowitz frontier as being backward looking and yielding intuition about the benefits of diversification but not much else. Is any part of the Markowitz analysis in Question 3.2.1 useful to us in forming an active portfolio?

We have argued repeatedly that we have difficulty estimating expected returns. In our active alpha optimization (Question 3.2.2), for example, we took pains to ensure that we did not estimate mean returns on stocks. Instead, we estimated only the *active* returns on stocks as a deviation from whatever the naive consensus view was.

Our Markowitz minimum-variance frontier was, however, built using mean *total* returns to every stock. Unfortunately, Black and Litterman (1992) argue that mean-variance optimal portfolio weights are extremely sensitive to the return assumptions. In fact, Chopra and Ziemba (1993) argue that for mean-variance optimizations, errors in means are 10 times as important as errors in variances and covariances, and that errors in variances are twice as important as errors in covariances. These ratios vary with the risk aversion of the investor; for an investor with a very high risk aversion, errors in means are still the most important, but their importance relative to variances and covariances decreases somewhat.

If we want to use some part of the Markowitz minimum-variance frontier to help form active portfolios, this presents three problems: first, mean returns are poorly estimated and mean-variance analysis is extremely sensitive to this issue (Black and Litterman, 1992; Chopra and Ziemba, 1993); second, variances and covariances can be poorly estimated, and this can lead to error-maximization issues (Michaud, 1989); and third, the Markowitz minimum-variance frontier calculations are all backward looking by construction.

With regard to the first problem, is there any part of the Markowitz minimum-variance frontier that does not depend upon the vector of means $\vec{\mu}$? The answer is that yes, the vector of weights in the global minimum-variance portfolio (MVP) (i.e., $\vec{h}_{mvp} = \frac{1}{C}V^{-1}\vec{\iota}$) is immune to the values in $\vec{\mu}$. That is, given the VCV, no matter what you use for $\vec{\mu}$, $\vec{h}_{mvp}$ is unchanged.[15] If we also estimate $\vec{h}_{mvp}$ using a shrinkage estimator for the variance, this should go some way toward addressing the error-maximization problem mentioned above. The third problem is an empirical issue resolved only by interrogating the data: does the MVP portfolio offer any active benefits? Note that $\vec{h}_{mvp}$ minimizes total risk, whereas the optimal holdings in an active alpha optimization come from an optimization that penalizes active risk. So, it is not obvious that the former can replace the latter.

Chow, Hsu, Kalesnik, and Little (2011) test the MVP portfolio in backtests using global stocks over the period 1987–2009 and U.S. stocks over the period 1964–2009. They use a shrinkage estimator of the VCV, no short selling, maximum weights of 5% in any stock, and annual rebalancing. Relative to naive benchmarks, their MVP portfolio reduces standard deviation by about 4–5% per annum and increases mean return by about 1–2% per annum. This gives a relatively good Sharpe ratio of about 0.39–0.49, but terrible tracking error gives a low IR of about 0.12–0.24. High turnover means that something like one-quarter to one-half of the active returns appear to be consumed by T-costs. This is, nevertheless, quite promising.

Unfortunately, we know from the backtest in Question 3.2.2 that the MVP weights introduce a great deal of active risk. So, how about the following pragmatic solution? Take $\vec{h}_{mvp}$ from the Markowitz problem (Question 3.2.1) with or without a Ledoit and Wolf (2004) shrinkage estimator of the VCV. Then

---

[15] Note that there may be a slight inconsistency in saying "given the VCV" if the VCV is a direct function of μ.

take new weights equal to half the P10 weights plus half the MVP weights. Historically, this AAO-MVP portfolio has done quite well by combining the benefits of each technique. How does it do in terms of stock selection IR or RTAA?

3.3 Other Investment Topics

Question 3.3.1: For this question, you will need Graham (2006) plus access to the Bloomberg professional service.

Benjamin Graham's book on value investing *The Intelligent Investor: A Book of Practical Counsel* (Graham, 2006) is described by his former student Warren Buffett as "By far the best book on investing ever written" (quote from the cover of my copy of the book). Graham's book was first published in 1949. It was revised and updated repeatedly until Graham's death in 1976, and the 2006 edition includes a modern commentary on each chapter written by Jason Zweig. Looking back over his life in 1976 (see Butler [1976]), Graham recommended *The Intelligent Investor* as being of more value than his famous *Security Analysis* book (Graham and Dodd, 1934).

Investors and fund managers have used screens for picking stocks for at least 100 years. Graham gives several summarized lists of advice/screens in his book. The lists overlap to some extent and contradict each other to some extent (caused, I think, by repeated partial revisions of the text over many years).

Graham (2006, pp. 114–115) gives four rules for direct investment in the common stocks in the portfolio of the defensive investor.[16] Graham (2006, pp. 337–338) gives seven "statistical requirements" for inclusion of common stocks in the portfolio of the defensive investor. Graham (2006, pp. 385–386) gives five "additional criteria, rather similar to those already suggested for the defensive investor, but not so severe" (these are for the "enterprising investor"). Please also consult the my box mentioning Kahn Brothers' basic equity screens at the end of Section 1.2.2 in *Foundations*.

(a) Select any five stock selection criteria from the lists given by Benjamin Graham or Kahn Brothers. State your criteria clearly.[17]

(b) Use Bloomberg equity screens to shortlist no more than 10 stocks that satisfy your criteria; if you get more than 10 stocks, then choose the first 10

---

[16]Graham refers to a "defensive investor" or "passive investor" as someone who emphasizes the avoidance of serious mistakes or losses and, as a secondary consideration, wishes to minimize effort and frequency of decision making (Graham, 2006, pp. 6, 22). He contrasts this with an "enterprising" or "active" or "aggressive" investor. He argues that the enterprising investor may, over many decades, expect a better return than the defensive investor, but that he has his doubts (Graham, 2006, pp. 6).

[17]See also my discussion of diversification and Graham's margin of safety in Section 2.9.2 of *Foundations*.

in the list.[18] If only one or two stocks satisfy your criteria, then change the criteria because that is not enough stocks to choose from; if more than 50 stocks satisfy the criteria then add more criteria to shorten the list; consider country restrictions to shorten the list if needed. Note that if you miss out the P/E ratio screens, your stock picks will tend to me more "enterprising" than "defensive" (using Graham's terms).

(c) Click on "Results" and pick one stock from the list and explain your stock pick (in 200 words or fewer) in a short sharp sales pitch. For this single stock, you should include printouts of Bloomberg `BQ`, Bloomberg `GP` (last 12 months of daily data), and Bloomberg `DES` (say, just the first page) screens. In your sales pitch, you should also pay attention to Peter Lynch's classifications of stocks (Section 2.3.2 of *Foundations*), our discussion of P/E ratios (Section 2.3.8 of *Foundations*) and P/CF ratios (in Section 2.3.8 of *Foundations*), and anything else we discussed when discussing fundamental analysis.

---

[18]Use Bloomberg command `EQS`. Simple criteria may be added using the visible fields. You can create arbitrarily complicated formulae using the "formula" link (top left of screen). After creating a formula, you can save it and then click on it to add it to your screen. When creating a formula, click in the "enter equation" field and then type `?<GO>` to choose variables. Note that you can cut and paste your formula text to create additional lagged values, etc. Then update. Then click "save and use" and enter a name for the formula. Be patient while Bloomberg screens the data; it could take 10 seconds to add the formula to your screen and give the count. If you mess it up and want to start again, just type `EQS` at the prompt again.

Chapter 4

Suggested Solutions

Suggested solutions to the multiple-choice and short answer questions appear below and at the Web site www.FoundationsForScientificInvesting.com. Solutions to the long-answer questions appear only at the Web site.

4.1 Multiple-Choice Test Solutions

	12345	6789X
00+	cccdc	bbdbc
10+	daebe	eecbd
20+	ebadb	dbcdd
30+	dacab	cbbab
40+	dafbb	abebe
50+	ccbde	dceda
60+	dbaea	cdbba
70+	eaddb	ebded
80+	cacca	aacea
90+	babcc	eaeab

	12345	6789X
100+	ccdce	abeeb
110+	beccc	deeea
120+	baead	eceec
130+	dcdad	cafbe
140+	gcbec	fbeeb
150+	eaced	abdfe
160+	dcdba	cccbc
170+	eebce	bddca
180+	eabde	ccbbe
190+	abacc	ceccd

	12345	6789X
200+	ddbeb	dbedb
210+	eebca	ddaea
220+	bbdbb	aabbb
230+	aaaeb	aeece
240+	bddeb	dedbc
250+	cdcbd	eeeae
260+	dcaed	acdae
270+	eeddd	edaeb
280+	bdacc	acbdd
290+	dedda	babcd

	12345	6789X
300+	acdac	aeace
310+	eaebb	bcded
320+	cdcaa	edbcc
330+	dcadc	aedcb
340+	baecb	ccadb
350+	edbea	cebba
360+	eeade	edeae
370+	cdbad	ceebc
380+	dbaeb	beaed
390+	dbdeb	ebbdd

	12345	6789X
400+	dcecd	ccedd
410+	bebcc	cbdbe
420+	ababd	cedeb
430+	beebc	acacd
440+	aacbe	eeded
450+	ccbbe	abddd
460+	beeda	dedbb
470+	hegge	bbeab
480+	baddf	aeabd
490+	fdeba	cadcb

	12345	6789X
500+	cbfdd	cebcd
510+	cdaae	bebec
520+	ceedd	acbdd
530+	eceda	beddb
540+	ddaba	ddaec
550+	bcced	bccba
560+	cacea	eddee
570+	bbbbd	eeeaa
580+	acdee	addbd
590+	decdc	cgdab

(Note that X=10)

Multiple-Choice Test Solutions (Continued)

	12345	6789X
600+	daeeb	af
610+		
620+		
630+		
640+		
650+		
660+		
670+		
680+		
690+		

(Note that X=10)

4.2   Short-Answer Test Solutions

608. Yes, you reject normality because 3.02 > 1.96. This is a two-tailed test by construction. In the past a quarter of my students argued that the large sample allows us to not reject normality and not only that, but this means the data are in fact normally distributed. This is rubbish. The Z-statistic is distributed standard normal under the null, so 3.02 is a clear rejection at any reasonable level of significance. A large sample, when forming a t-test for a mean (not the situation here, remember, because it is a test of normality), means that a central limit theorem (CLT) kicks in and non-normal data is not a concern as far the assumptions of the t-test are concerned. That is, the data are still non-normal, but as long as they are independent and identically distributed, then the t-statistic is still distributed Student-t. Thus, the large sample does not mean the data are normal, just that their deviation from normality has no impact on the distribution of the t-stat for testing a sample mean (which this question was not even about).

609. $\frac{\bar{X}-\mu_{H_0}}{\sqrt{\frac{s_{N-1}^2}{N}}} \sim t_{N-1}$. The assumptions are normality, independence, and identically distributed data. In small sample, we worry about normality, and we worry about independence, but we do not worry about the identically distributed assumption. ...because, respectively, small sample size means that the CLT will not quite kick in, and financial data may be autocorrelated, but it is unlikely that the distribution changed much in 20 days.

610.

$$\left| \sqrt{N-2} \cdot \frac{\hat{\rho} - 0}{\sqrt{1 - \hat{\rho}^2}} \right| > \text{ critical value of } t_{N-2}.$$

I get $N \geq 341$. Note that if you made a mathematical error that yields a small number of observations, e.g., N=17, then the critical value is no longer correct, and you have an endogeneity problem: you cannot solve for N without the critical value, and you cannot solve for the critical value without N. In this case, you can take iterative guesses until you converge, or produce a table.

611. A circular relationship is neither linear (as searched for by the PPMCC) nor monotone increasing or decreasing (as searched for by the SROCC). Similarly, for a sinusoidal plot over multiple phases.

612. Use SROCC when the relationship is expected to be monotone increasing or monotone decreasing, but there is no reason why it should be linear. For example, relative bid-ask spread versus market capitalization in equities.

613. The standard error of an OLS regression is the square root of the mean sum of squared errors using division by $T - 2$: $\sqrt{\frac{\sum \epsilon_t^2}{T-2}}$. It appears in the calculation of the standard error of $\hat{\beta}$, and in the standard error of $\hat{\alpha}$, and in the standard error of the prediction (i.e., fitted value) of an individual value of y at a given value of x, and in the standard error of the prediction (i.e., fitted value) of the mean value of y at a given value of x.

The standard deviation of the residuals is estimated using $\sqrt{\frac{\sum \epsilon_t^2}{T-1}}$, though division by $T - 2$ would make little difference.

The standard error of the estimator of the mean of X from a sample of size N is given by $\frac{s}{\sqrt{N}}$, where s uses division by $N - 1$.

614. The assumptions are normality, independence, and identically distributed data. In small sample, we worry about normality, and we worry about independence. In large sample we worry about independence and identically distributed data.

615. The integral $E(X) = \int x f_X(x) dx$, where X is a random variable and $f_X(\cdot)$ is the PDF of X is the limiting value of a discrete summation of values of x weighed by probabilities. We can think of the product $f_X(x)dx$ as being like height times width of a small slice of probability mass under the pdf.

616. Conditioning restricts the sample space. Suppose adult male height is normally distributed with mean 69 inches and standard deviation two inches. Then the expected value for height is 69 inches (obtained by integrating probability-weighted height values over the entire distribution). If however, we ask what is the expected height of a person conditional upon being an adult male of above average height, then we recalculate conditional probabilities by doubling the height of the pdf on the domain of heights at or above 69 inches. Then we integrate probability-weighted height values only over the distribution at or above 69 inches using these new conditional probabilities. The answer is $\mu + \sqrt{\frac{2}{\pi}} \cdot \sigma \approx 70.60$ inches in this case.

617. False. If returns to ABC and DEF are negatively correlated, then returns to ABC tend to be above their mean value when returns to DEF tend to be below their mean value.

618. A random variable is distributed Student-t with ν degrees of freedom if it is the ratio of a random variable distributed standard normal to the square root of the ratio of an independent chi-squared random variable to its degrees of freedom ν:
$$\frac{Z}{\sqrt{\chi_\nu^2/\nu}}.$$

619. Non-central t-statistics appear when investigating the behavior of t-tests under the alternative hypothesis. These are important when investigating the power of t-tests.

620. We worry about Lindley's paradox when we have large samples. Standard errors can be so small that we reject the null hypothesis for economically insignificant variations of the data from the null hypothesis. It is a worry in high-frequency data or very long time series.

621. Simple net returns and continuously compounded returns are different ways to express the same economic growth. If we assume that simple net returns are distributed independent normal, then compounded returns are not normal because normality is not closed under multiplication. Also, normally distributed simple net returns allow returns below -100% and thus can lead to negative prices—which usually makes no sense. If, however, we assume that continuously compounded returns are distributed independent normal, then compounded returns are normal because normality is closed under addition.

622. The case of the standard restricted null allows only for $\rho = 0$ under the null hypothesis $\dfrac{\hat{\rho}-0}{\sqrt{1-\hat{\rho}^2}\cdot\sqrt{\frac{1}{N-2}}} \sim t_{N-2}$

When ρ is small and N is large, we may approximate the t-statistic in the standard restricted null case as $\dfrac{\hat{\rho}-0}{\sqrt{\frac{1}{N}}} \sim t_{N-2}$.

In the case of an unrestricted null hypothesis, the above two t-statistics are invalid. The standard Fisher Z-Transform is given by $z = \frac{1}{2}\ln\left(\frac{1+\hat{\rho}}{1-\hat{\rho}}\right)$, $\zeta_{H_0} = \frac{1}{2}\ln\left(\frac{1+\rho_{H_0}}{1-\rho_{H_0}}\right)$, $\dfrac{z-\zeta_{H_0}}{\sqrt{\frac{1}{N-1}+\frac{2}{(N-1)^2}}} \sim N(0,1)$, and for large N, say bigger than 50, we have, $\frac{1}{N-1} + \frac{2}{(N-1)^2} \approx \frac{1}{N-3}$.

623. This approach does not in any way address multicollinearity. Suppose we replace X_3 in the original regression with the residuals e_3 from X_3 regressed on $(1, X_1, X_2)$. The coefficient, standard error, and t-statistic of e_3 in the "orthogonalizing regression" are identical to those of X_3 in the original regression. The residuals of the original regression and the orthogonalizing regression are identical. We were worried about the effect of multicollinearity on the coefficient of X_3 and

its standard error (and t-statistic), but these are all invariant to this orthogonalization. So, we have not combatted multicollinearity in any sense. Note also that this orthogonalizing transformation does not in any sense isolate a "separate effect" of the orthogonalized variable. Note also that the residuals from this final regression are identical to the residuals from the original regression. The R-Squared is also identical, as is the adjusted R-squared, the SSE, the standard error of the regression, and the F-statistic for the regression. See the spreadsheet ♣ INVARIANCE-UNDER-ORTHOGONALIZATION.XLS on the Web site.

624. Out of a sample of 100 stocks I would expect we could reject normality in roughly 95 cases. This is caused by strong excess kurtosis in most stocks, and skewness, typically positive, in most stocks. All results are stronger in small-capitalization stocks.

625. (a) $t = \frac{\bar{X}-\mu}{\sqrt{s^2/N}} = \frac{0.000245-0}{\sqrt{0.009036^2/511}} = 0.6129597$ The critical values are $+1.96$ and -1.96. We cannot reject the null because the t-statistic is between the critical values.

(b) $t \approx \rho \times \sqrt{N} = 0.060948 \times \sqrt{511} = 1.37777$. The critical values are $+1.96$ and -1.96. Slightly different answer for full unrestricted null test. We cannot reject the null because the t-statistic is between the critical values.

626. (a) t=1.7581, critical values $+1.96$, -1.96, not do reject. (b) t=1.7557, critical values $+1.645$, -1.645, reject.

627. The mean daily return to each stock is positive. The return on Stock 1, however, tends to be above its mean return when the return on Stock 2 is below its mean return. Looking at the numerator of the PPMCC we see this gives negative correlation while the positive mean returns give prices that move up together. If you fail to discuss returns relative to their means, or incorrectly talk about prices instead of returns, or used the word "mean" without saying mean what, then your answer is insufficient.

628. Reject normality in all stocks because the Z-statistics are so big.

629. The t-statistic for the mean is driven by the distributional assumption that the raw data are distributed Normal. In small sample, this assumption has been chosen and fixed (i.e., the choice of distribution has been parameterized, or it is distributionally parametric). If this normality assumption does not hold in small sample, then the t-statistic for the mean is not distributed Student-t, and the test is not valid. In large sample, however, even if the normality assumption is violated, then the CLT can kick in and save you if all other assumptions hold and the sample size is large enough (say 50 in the case of kurtotic returns and 200 in the case of skewed returns, though that is an open question). The assumption is still false, the data are still non-normal, the CLT does not change that, but what happens is that it no longer matters that the data are not normal. That is, in large sample the t-statistic is *robust* to (or immune to) the violation of this assumption. So, in

large sample you do not need to choose/fix (i.e., parameterize) the distribution. In large sample, the t-statistic for the mean is thus distributionally non-parametric.

630. Relative bid-ask spread is a measure of liquidity. Large-capitalization stocks tend to have more liquidity than small-capitalization stocks. So, their relative bid-ask spreads tend to be lower (see Figure 1.14 on p. 107). Why are large-capitalization stocks more liquid than small-capitalization stocks? On average, they trade a larger dollar volume per day because they form a larger part of the economy, they are held by more investors, and they are often household names. Note that although large-capitalization stocks tend to have higher prices than small-capitalization stocks, and relative spread has price in the denominator, this is not a good explanation.

631. Dividend yield is dividends divided by price. Which dividends and which price? The most common definition uses trailing 12-month (TTM) cash dividends divided by last price. You can also use anticipated dividends. In the Gordon-Shapiro dividend growth model, you can break required return on the stock, r, say, into the dividend growth component g, say, and a dividend yield component per period D_1/P_0 (i.e., the next dividend divided by current price). In late 2014, the dividend yield on the S&P 500 was sitting at 1.9% per annum, but its average over the 50-year period 1963–2013 was 3.1% per annum, with a high of 6.7% during the recessionary trough in August 1982 and a low of 1.1% at the dotcom bubble peak in August 2000.

Large-capitalization stocks tend to have higher dividend yields than small-capitalization stocks. For example, the dividend yield on the 30 Dow Jones Industrial Average stocks was about 2.5% per annum at the end of 2014.

The very smallest capitalization stocks typically do not pay dividends. so, average dividend yield on a sample of the smallest capitalization stocks will be very close to zero. Note, however, that, as mentioned in *Foundations*, the smallest capitalization stocks that do pay dividends tend to pay a larger dividend yield than the largest capitalization stocks that pay dividends. That is, if you restrict attention only to stocks paying dividends, the plot of dividend yield versus market capitalization is reverse-J-shaped.

In New Zealand, the same general properties hold, but with dividend yields being about 1.5–2 times higher than in the U.S.

632. The initial bid-ask spread mid-point is $(50+36)/2$, but moves to $(22+16)/2$, which must be multiplied by 3. From 43 to 57 is a gain of 32.6%.

633. In a basic CLOB system, you buy at the ask and sell at the bid when you send a market order. You have no opportunity for on-market price improvement because there is typically no DMM. If you sell 97,928 shares, you experience price impact as you walk down the bid side of the order book selling 3,427 shares at \$1.08, 37,310 shares at \$1.07, 38,367 at \$1.06, and the balance of 18,824 at \$1.05. The average price at which you sell must be between the two extremes, at something like

$1.065. Total proceeds are $104,057.08 yielding an average price of $1.0625876, only a quarter of a penny away from our guess. There will be only a single commission for this trade, but we were asked to ignore it.

If you buy 10,000 shares, you experience no price impact, getting all your shares at $1.09 with a total cost of $10,900.

634. The width of the bid-ask spread for S&P/NZX50 stocks is determined by how tight the inner limit orders are. There are no DMMs in S&P/NZX50 stocks.

635. $\frac{P}{E} = \frac{1}{R}\left(\frac{1}{1-\frac{PVGO}{P}}\right)$. With the same R, high P/E goes hand-in-hand with high PVGO. I would accept either a tedious algebraic explanation or the economic explanation that traders bid up the prices of stocks that they think have many growth opportunities (+NPV projects in the future). This pushes up price and gives a high P/E. These are "growth" or "glamour" stocks.

636. (a) Shrinkage is intended to reduce estimation error. (b) CCM is the target. It is a structured estimator which contains few parameters, and shrinking toward it is thus akin to shrinking toward a mean or mean-like central value. (c) Error maximization is when the mean-variance optimizer computer code chases extreme values of the VCV that are extreme because they contain larges errors. The Ledoit-Wolf (2004) estimator address this by reducing those errors. Note, that there are no eigenvalues in this estimator.

637. -1%

638. Most institutional asset managers ignore benchmark timing; the FLAM says stock selection has more breadth and is thus likely to be more successful than benchmark timing; the analysis is much easier without benchmark timing; we are more likely to succeed if we focus on only one task (stock selection), than if we focus on two (stock selection plus benchmark timing)—"chasing one rabbit instead of two" Richard Grinold would say.

639. (a) $\alpha_P - \lambda\omega_P^2 - TC$; (b) maximize; (c) portfolio weights $\vec{h}_P$; (d) $\vec{h}_P \geq 0$, $|\vec{h}_P - \vec{h}_B| \leq$ 0.10 (or 0.01), $|\vec{h}_P - \vec{h}_B|'\vec{\iota} \leq 0.50$, $\vec{h}_P'\vec{\iota} = 1$, $\beta_P = 1$.

640.

$$IR = \frac{\alpha}{\omega} = \frac{0.02974}{\sqrt{\sigma_P^2 - \sigma_B^2}} = \frac{0.02974}{\sqrt{0.118^2 - 0.114^2}} = 0.97626$$

$$RAA = \alpha - \lambda\omega_P^2 = 0.02974 - 10 \cdot 0.000928 = 0.02046$$

Note, if your IR is good, and the portfolio risk is not very much greater than the benchmark risk, then the RAA should be positive; a big negative RAA says you have an error.

641. (a) $\vec{h}_3 = \begin{pmatrix} 0 \\ 0 \\ 1 \\ 0 \\ 0 \\ 0 \\ 0 \\ 0 \\ 0 \\ 0 \end{pmatrix}$

(b) Numerator$=cov(R_i, R_B)$; Denominator$=var(R_B)$

(c) No, because the benchmark is almost certainly not on the mean-variance frontier.

642. Both N.Z. and the U.S. operate on the "ex-rec" regime (with N.Z. moving to this only in September 2010). The timeline is announcement, ex-dividend date, record date, payment date. T+2 settlement was adopted March 2016 in N.Z. and September 2017 in the U.S.

643. Price impact is when your buying (or your selling) is in sufficient quantity that the depth at the ask (or the bid) is insufficient and your order is filled only by executing the balance of the order at less favorable prices. Also called market impact. Your order has an impact on the last price recorded and moves it in the least favorable direction for your upfront cost. An example appears in my answer to Question 633.

644. $10,000 at 6% per annum for 40 years yields $102,857.18; $10,000 at 8% per annum for 40 years yields $217,245.21, more than twice the final wealth. The basic rule of thumb is that for a lump sum, one extra percentage point in annual return yields half as much again at retirement over a 40–50 year horizon. So, two extra percentage points should yield something like double final wealth.

645. Use the FLAM: $IR \approx IC \times \sqrt{BR} = 0.04 \times 15 = 0.60$

646. The broker gets 30bps per trade. So, 30bps of $6,000 \times \$30$ twice. That is $1,080 total.

647. A negatively skewed distribution has its tail out to the direction of the negative end of the x axis. It is also called a left-skewed distribution, because the tail is out to the left. We see right-skewed distribution often in finance. The possible payoffs to a European-style put option, however, should be left skewed as a function of terminal stock price, because they are zero above the strike price, and there is a tail of possible payoffs with low probability for low stock price outcomes.

648. We sold put options covering 1 million shares. We are short the options and need to replicate a long position in the options to establish a hedge. Long a put is like shorting a stock, so we will be going short Δ times 1 million. If the option were

at the money, then $\Delta \approx -1/2$. If the option were deep out of the money, then $\Delta \approx 0$. This option is part way between being at the money and being deep out of the money, so a first-order approximation is that $\Delta \approx -1/4$ and we should short 250,000 shares. That is probably enough for you to keep your internship. To get hired into the graduate role, you might add that Δ attenuates more quickly than you might expect as you move out of the money. So, you probably want to shade that Δ a bit and short only 200,000 shares. In fact, if you could scrape away the raspberry jam, you would see that $\Delta = -0.1588$ (by complete coincidence being equal to the moneyness percentage), and you only need to short 158,800 shares for the delta hedge.

649. $\beta_P = \frac{\vec{h}_P' V \vec{h}_B}{\vec{h}_B' V \vec{h}_B}$.

650. The sum of the active weights is zero. This must be true because the sum of the total weights is one.

651. Yes, some elements of the vector $\vec{h}_T$ can be negative. There was no restriction placed on them being non-negative. No, the sum of the weights in $\vec{h}_T$ must be one, because it is fully invested in risky assets.

652. =MMULT(TRANSPOSE(A1:A10),B1:B10)

653. A non-zero active beta is a benchmark timing tilt. If active beta is positive, then you have a beta larger than 1, and this is an aggressive (even if unintentional) bet that the benchmark will rise by more than expected. Active beta is zero if your beta equals 1.

654. Forward-looking ex-ante IR is forward looking alpha divided by forward looking standard deviation of residual return. It is the optimistic forecast of your return per unit risk in active space. Backward looking ex-post IR is realized alpha (from a regression) divided by realized standard deviation of residual returns. We expect on average the ex-ante IR to be something like twice the realized IR, because ex-ante IR is too rosy in its outlook.

655. Positive: Ex-ante portfolio alpha; Negative: Active risk and T-costs.

656. Active portfolio management is when you take positions in your portfolio different from those in some benchmark. You may be picking individual stocks, based on characteristics you think will lead to outperformance, or you may be tilting your entire portfolio toward a beta higher or lower than one in a macro bet on the broad market.

657. An active position is an overweight or an underweight. For example, you might hold IBM at a weight higher than its weight in the S&P 500 because you think it will be a relative outperformer.

658. $\lambda = 0.10$, for example.

659. The active alpha optimization objective function we used was $RTAA = \alpha_P - \lambda\omega^2 - TC$, where α is the ex-ante active return (outperformance of the benchmark), ω^2 is active risk ($\omega^2 = \sigma_P^2 - \sigma_B^2$ when $\beta_P = 1$), and TC is transaction costs. If you optimize the total risk total return objective function it muddles active risk and benchmark risk in together with each other and does not apply a high enough risk aversion coefficient to the active risk term. So, you end up with active portfolios that contain too much active risk.

660. Benchmark timing is when you have a beta that is not equal to 1.

661. You might buy a put option as downside protection for a stock you already own. This is a "protective put" position. Put-call parity tells us that a put plus the stock equals call plus some other cash position. A call option gives you upside potential and no downside risk (beyond the initial premium, of course); the same is true of owning the put plus the stock.

662. High-priced options tend to have lower relative T-costs. A high-priced put is one with a high strike price, other things being equal, because receiving a higher strike if you exercise is more valuable than receiving a lower strike.

663. The relative bid-ask spread for the stock will typically be a small fraction of the relative bid-ask spread for the option. For example, if the stock's bid-ask spread is 1 penny, the option's bid-ask spread might be 5–20 pennies, or more. Although the option market as a whole is liquid, an individual option on an individual stock is typically not liquid. Relative bid-ask spreads reflect liquidity.

664. The client has different risk aversion to the different components of risk. We need to treat each component with different risk aversion coefficients. After decomposing the risk, we got several terms. The benchmark risk term was not a function of our choice variables, so we dropped it. We argued that we should not be benchmark timing, so we dropped that too.

665. With 60 time series observations and 100 stocks, the standard sample VCV is estimable, but not invertible. You cannot use it in the calculation of the Markowitz efficient frontier (which requires that the VCV be inverted in almost every appearance). A non-invertible sample VCV will, mechanically, still be able to be used in an active alpha optimization, but the results will be untrustworthy.

666. These models all add additional structure in an attempt to reduce estimation error. They all look for meta-relationships or common themes. Using them is akin to shrinking toward a mean or mean-like central value.

667. Industry factors that may be based on the global industry classification system (GICS), for example, Chemicals, Energy Equipment and Services, Metals and Mining, Aerospace and Defense, etc. Risk factors are typically based on academic and practitioner research, for example size, volatility, liquidity, momentum, quality, carry, etc.

668. the alphas are benchmark neutral so that chasing alpha and stepping away from the benchmark go hand in hand. That is, if you passively hold the benchmark, then your alpha is zero, and the only way to generate ex-ante alpha is to step away from the benchmark. Note that the converse is not true. That is, by overweighting positive-alpha stocks, overweighting negative-alpha stocks, and underweighting medium-alpha stocks, for example, you can have $\alpha_P = 0$, when $P \neq B$. ...but why would you ever do that?

669. If an event study tells you that, for example, returns on stocks with low liquidity rise abnormally in the three weeks leading up to an earnings announcement (I am making this up), and if there is a good economic story to go with it, then the portfolio manager might tilt exposure towards those stocks during that period if the returns from doing so outweigh the active risk and the T-costs.

670. In Australia and N.Z., the tax authorities have taken the point of view that if the company has paid taxes on your slice of earnings already, and then paid you a dividend out of the after-tax earnings, then you should declare the pre-tax dividend as a gross dividend on your personal income tax return, combine that gross dividend with other gross taxable income, calculate your taxes due in the normal way, and then offset against those taxes any amount already paid by the company to the tax authority on your behalf. ♣ Download the spreadsheet DIVIDEND-IMPUTATION-EXAMPLE.XLS from the Web site for a worked example.

671. Lintner (1956) says that management does not give unsustainable dividend increases. This is because shareholders will hammer down the price of any stock that cuts or omits its dividends, and management wishes to avoid that outcome.

672. You can build an n-growth rate in dividends model (e.g., the original Gordon-Shapiro single-growth rate in dividends model). Then equate the model stock price to the market stock price, estimate the next dividend and the dividend growth rate(s), and back out the discount rate to use as a cost of equity capital.

673. First, the original DDM requires that the firm pays dividends, but in December 2013, 82.4% of S&P 500 firms paid dividends, and looking across the NYSE, NYSE Alternext, and Nasdaq combined, the average proportion of dividend-paying firms is about 35%. Non-dividend paying firms are more likely to be smaller, younger, neglected, growth, firms. These are just the firms that might present attractive active investment opportunities, but you cannot use the DDM if the firm does not pay dividends. The EBO model uses the clean surplus relation to allow you to use balance sheet information instead of dividend information, thereby allowing valuation of non-dividend paying stocks.

Second, DDMs are about wealth distribution, not wealth creation. Information residing in the balance sheet is, in effect, picked up and spread over future cash flow projections (the exact opposite of capitalization), which are then discounted back to the present. EBO models put that balance sheet wealth creation directly into the valuation model.

674. A backtest is a computer simulation of a trading strategy using historical market databases. It attempts to show you how a trading strategy would have performed if run in the past. One problem with backtests is that they are prone to data snooping. That is, if you over fit your investment strategy by refining and refining your stock selection technique using historical databases until your strategy invests only in stocks that ex-post did very well, then your backtest will look magnificent, but your strategy will fail out of sample. Another problem with backtests is that they love to invest in small illiquid stocks, and you have to account for T-costs and illiquidity (e.g., in the form of price impact) in order to not be lead astray.

675. Lindley's paradox is when very large samples mean that standard errors can be so small that we can reject the null hypothesis for economically insignificant variations of the data from the null hypothesis. It is a worry in high-frequency data or very long time series.

676. Earnings announcements from companies come out after the end of the period they pertain to. There is a small window when analysts are predicting what the announced earnings will be, and are therefore predicting past earnings, rather than future earnings.

677. ARCH and GARCH models are designed to capture time-varying volatility and volatility clustering in financial market returns. A sketch would show periods of high volatility followed by periods of high volatility and periods of low volatility followed by periods of low volatility, with transformations from one to the other in between. In fact, if you fit a GARCH model, say, to your data, and you get a good confident fit with low standard errors on the coefficients, you are likely to find that you cannot actually see the GARCH process in any plot of the data. That is, although the econometric model detects it, your eye might not.

678. The RAA is risk-adjusted alpha: $RAA = \alpha - \lambda\omega^2$. It is the objective function in our active alpha optimization before T-costs are subtracted. It is ex-ante alpha less a penalty for active risk.

679. Benchmark neutral alphas means that $\vec{h}'_B \vec{\alpha} = 0$. We want this property so that a passive portfolio has no alpha, and stepping away from the benchmark goes hand in hand with chasing alpha.

680. No, our active alpha optimization did not require an estimate of mean returns to stocks. Everything was expressed in terms of deviations from the benchmark or deviations from naive consensus forecasts.

681. Use the FLAM: $IR \approx IC \times \sqrt{BR} = 0.03 \times \sqrt{100 \times 4} = 0.60$

682. (a) True, though the equity managers had a higher spread of IRs. (b) False, bond managers charged higher fees. (c) True, bond managers took less active risk than stock managers.

683. A skilled forecast is a forecast different from the naive consensus CAPM-type forecast. Skilled forecasts come from research experience. It may be practitioner research or academic research that identifies characteristics of stocks associated with outperformance.

684. The very general result is that mean returns to stocks are estimated with poor accuracy and variances of stock returns are estimated with good accuracy. The specific result we looked at was that in a sample of fixed length, for example one year, sampling more frequently (e.g., going from monthly to weekly to daily returns) improved the accuracy of the estimator of the variance of returns but had no effect on the accuracy of the estimator of the mean returns.

685. Suppose you have 10 stocks, each with $100,000 invested in them. Suppose I direct you to sell all of Stock 1, and put all the proceeds into Stock 2. Ignore T-costs. Then you will do $100,000 in purchases and $100,000 in sales. If we count only one side of the transactions, the purchases say, they total $100,000 out of a $1,000,000 portfolio, so your one-sided turnover was 10% of the portfolio. If we count purchases and sales, then there was a total of $200,000 in transactions. So, the two-sided turnover was 20%.

686. A margin trade in a stock is when you buy the stock using margin money together with a margin loan from your broker. The classic case is where you buy a $100 stock using $50 of your own money, and $50 borrowed from your broker. Margin trades magnify percentage gains and losses based upon your initial investment.

687. Some authors present PVGO as the present value of all future positive NPV projects, including projects not yet even contemplated. I think, however, that among all those positive NPV projects there are likely some that have been trumped up to look good, and actually have negative NPVs even at the proposal stage, and there are surely projects that will damage firm value. So, I view PVGO as the netting out of the present values of all those *opportunities* for growth in earnings.

688. No, you do not get the dividend because the stock is still trading cum dividend which means the buyer gets the dividend.

689. A buy limit order is an order to buy a specified quantity of stock at or below a specified "limit" price (a sell order would be to sell at or above the limit price).

690. Can a limit order suffer price impact? There are two possible answers to this question. The simple answer is "no" limit orders do not experience price impact, because the limit price is fixed. Contrast this with a market order to buy, for example, where your order can consume the depth at the ask and walk up the CLOB pushing prices against you as your order is filled. A limit order to buy, however, is either executed at or below the limit price or not executed at all, but it never walks up the CLOB experiencing price impact.

The complex answer is that in the case of a limit buy order which may sit at the bid, for example, an increase in demand can move the market away from your limit price. That is, the arrival of market orders to buy can consume depth at the ask, and spur other traders to place limit orders to buy at prices that exceed your limit price (on the bid side). In this case, price impact on the other side of the spread reduces the likelihood that your limit order will be executed and you could argue that your order is suffering as a result of price impact. It is just that it is not price impact created by *your* order being filled. In this case, if you want an execution, then you have to cancel your limit buy and place it with a higher limit price. Technically, this is a new order, and not the old order being executed at a higher price, but you could argue that this is some sort of second-hand price impact.

691. Note that for (b), (c), and (d), I asked if the order will be executed, and if so when and at what price; that is three things.

   (a) It is not possible to trade outside the spread. The spread must have moved since the last trade was executed (584 was either the bid or ask earlier in the day)

   (b) Yes, immediately at 578.

   (c) You cannot tell if it will be executed because the limit order to sell will sit waiting in the limit order book until a sufficiently large market order to buy arrives at which time it will be executed at 575. Note that it might not be executed at all if the market moves down.

   (d) No the market order to buy will not be executed because there is no depth at the ask. The broker will cancel your market order to buy (because the broker has no book to keep that trade in), and they will call you up and ask you if you want to resubmit it as a limit order to buy (which they can keep in the CLOB).

   (e) There were many different possible answers for this because, the question is not well posed. I would accept any of the following: The turnover figures are positive on both days, so trades took place at those "last" prices on those days, and we can see that the last price went up; Turnover divided by volume gives average trade price each day ($5.75 and $5.78, respectively), thus price went up; Bid went down, last went up, and bid-ask spread midpoint went from something larger than 570 down to 569, so it's impossible to say; Fair value is bid-ask spread mid-point. On April 4 it is something higher than 570. On April 11 it is 569. Thus, fair value went down.

692. A short sale of a stock is when you borrow shares of a stock that you do not possess and sell them. For example, I borrow 100 shares of IBM and sell it in the market place at $164 per share. I do this because I hope that the price will fall, and I can buy the stock back later at a lower price, to return to the owner I borrowed it from. My broker takes care of the details. I must pay any dividends that were paid while I was short. The short can be called away from me at the option of the original owner.

693. When I short a stock, I am required to deposit the short sale proceeds into my margin account as collateral. I must, however, have 50% (the classic case) already on deposit as additional collateral (bringing the total to 150%). For example, To short sell IBM at $164 per share, I need to have $82 per share in my brokerage account and then deposit the $164 proceeds also, giving a balance of $246 per share collateral (150% of the selling price). If the stock price moves against me (i.e., rises), then when the cash in my account hits 130% of the (now rising) price, my broker will issue a margin call for me to bring my balance back up to 150% of the new (higher) price. If I fail to do so within 24 hours, the short will be covered by the broker—closing out my position.

694. PPMCC identifies linear relationships and SROCC identified monotone increasing or decreasing relationships.

695. (a) No, I cannot estimate a Markowitz frontier. I should not use the VCV for an active alpha optimization, but mechanically the VCV will work; it is just that it is poor. (b) It is not invertible because $T < N$ (there are insufficient degrees of freedom; there are linear relationships between rows or columns). Suggestions: increase the sample size by going back in time more than 50 days; buy a structural risk model estimator like the Barra models; implement a shrinkage estimator like the eigen decomposition that pushes eigenvalues toward the mean or the Ledoit-Wolf (2004) estimator that shrinks the sample VCV toward a more structured estimator.

696. (a) Put Option value of $0.2189 per share when multiplied by 100 gives $21.89. (b) If it were an option on one share, we would just find delta=rise/run=(0.2145-0.2189)/(5.01-5.00)=-0.44 shares. The option is on 100 shares, so the answer is to hold -44 shares. That is, to be short 44 shares. Note that a graph produced from the table slopes *downwards*, so slope=delta must be negative. The put position is similar to being short stock, not long stock (it loses when stock rises all else being equal). If you sell this position to someone else then you gain when stock rises, so, to hedge you must be short stock, not long (but you did not need to know this to find the answer, you just needed to figure the slope). Note that you have to use the two points I use to estimate the slope because any other pair of points gives a less accurate estimate.

697. $IR = \alpha/\omega$, $\alpha = 0.0621$ is given to you and $\omega = \sqrt{\sigma_P^2 - \sigma_B^2} = \sqrt{0.1012^2 - 0.0921^2} = 0.0419$. Thus IR=1.48.

698. The FLAM says $IR = IC\sqrt{BR} = 0.06\sqrt{100 \times 2} = 0.8485$ between very good and exceptional.

699. For example, commission is the fee you pay your broker for the execution of the trade, price impact is when your market order consumes depth and pushes prices away from your favor as it is executed, margin interest is the interest payment on money borrowed from your broker, taxes are paid to the government

on portfolio profits, and there is typically a small variable exchange fee paid to the NZX/NYSE/Nasdaq etc. for each trade.

700. I asked for three things: what is fundamental indexation, what benefits does it provide, and how are those benefits related to the location of the benchmark in the Markowitz optimization in Question 3.2.1. Fundamental indexation is an innovative index where stocks in a portfolio are weighted using price-insensitive fundamental characteristics (like total sales, total dividends, cash flows, number of employees, etc.) instead of the traditional relative market capitalization approach. It is supposed to improve the ex-post mean variance efficiency of the index portfolio. The cap-weighted benchmark in Question 3.2.1 was far from the efficient frontier (a fundamental index is meant to be closer to the ex-post frontier). Fundamental indexation falls under the "smart-beta" umbrella nowadays.

701. The most common mistake in answering this sort of question is to let the dividend impact more than one day. There are five days. So, there are four returns. If you used the ASK only, or the BID only, then I would give you half marks. The split as 4:1. The simple net returns are: -0.0046425, 0.035225, -0.0245747, 0.0465116.

702. Similarities: We need to take on risk to capture it; we apply a penalty for risk when we work out the value added; we hope the value added is positive; it is difficult to find; and it takes skill to manage.

703. Question 3.2.2 showed higher capitalization stocks have lower relative bid-ask spreads than lower capitalization stocks (I find SROCC$=-95\%$ and that the t-statistic was roughly -8.8!).

704. (a) $1000 in taxable dividend income. (b) Keep all $670 because the tax due ($330) on the income is exactly offset by the tax credit ($330). Note that tax rates may have changed since this question was written, but that the principle is the same.

705. We want to overweight the stocks that outperformed the index, and underweight the stocks that underperformed the index. Asked here for the three extreme of each. So, overweight GHI, JKL, MNO, and underweight MSFT,ABC,PQR.

706. Benchmark timing is when you tilt toward high-beta stocks and away from low-beta stocks when you think the benchmark is going *up* by more than the consensus opinion thinks and tilt toward low-beta stocks and away from high-beta stocks when you think the benchmark is going *down* by more than the consensus opinion thinks. Stock selection is tilting your portfolio toward an overweighting in stocks that you favor for their stock-specific characteristics and toward an underweighting in stocks that you are biased against for their stock-specific characteristics, in an attempt to earn positive residual returns ("alpha").

707. Lambda λ_T is the risk aversion coefficient; it pre-multiplies variance because we need a penalty for risk in the objective function; it also serves the purpose of translating risk (in units of return squared) into units of return.

708. Tangency weights $\vec{h}_T = \frac{V^{-1}(\vec{\mu}-R_F\vec{\iota})}{\vec{\iota}\,'V^{-1}(\vec{\mu}-R_F\vec{\iota})}$. V is the VCV, $\vec{\mu}$ is the vector of mean returns, $\vec{\iota}$ is a conformal vector of ones, R_F is the riskless rate.

Yes, you can have negative weights, but the tangency portfolio is fully invested in risky assets, so the weights sum to one.

709. (a) We decomposed the moments because we realized that in the real world, clients and portfolio managers have different degrees of aversion toward different types of risk. In particular, they fear active risk more than benchmark risk. (b) We discarded the benchmark terms because we have no control over them (they are not a function of our choice variables and thus do not add value), we discarded the benchmark timing terms because in practice very few active managers benchmark time, because it is easier to be successful focusing on only one active approach (stock selection rather than stock selection and benchmark timing), because it makes all the analysis/implementation easier, and because stock selection is more likely to succeed than benchmark timing because it has greater breadth.

710. (a) A, B, C in any order. Then D. Then G and H. Then $\vec{h}_P$. (b) μ_P is the chosen mean level of return for the portfolio we seek on the Markowitz frontier of risky assets. (c) $\vec{h}_P$ is the vector of portfolio weights in the portfolio we seek on the Markowitz frontier of risky assets. In neither (b) nor (c) would I accept that it is the "mean return to the portfolio" or the "weights in the portfolio" unless you say which portfolio.

711. Large-capitalization stocks tend to be more liquid (e.g., smaller relative bid-ask spreads, higher dollar volume, greater depth, less price impact), have smaller absolute bid-ask spreads, have higher stock prices, have returns distributions that are less non-normal, and are less likely to have extremely negatively autocorrelated daily stocks returns, than small-capitalization stocks.

712. It is generally true that large-capitalization stocks have higher stock prices than small-capitalization stocks, in both the U.S. and N.Z.

713. The width of the bid-ask spread (for stocks or options) compensates the market maker for the riskiness of holding inventory while trading with you, for the costs associated with processing your order, and for the risk that you may be better informed than is he or she (i.e., an "adverse selection" cost).

A broadly diversified stock index ETF should have a narrower relative bid-ask spread than the average stock because the market risk is typically lower (giving lower inventory risk), and the adverse selection should be lower.

714. Ledoit (1995) uses an eigen decomposition of the sample VCV matrix. He notes that smallest eigenvalues are biased downwards toward zero, and the largest ones are biased upwards. Ledoit then shrinks the eigenvalues towards their mean value. The smallest eigenvalues get bigger and the largest eigenvalues get smaller. This produces a VCV matrix estimator that is well conditioned and non-singular.

715. It is generally true that large-capitalization stocks have lower relative bid-ask spreads than small-capitalization stocks, in both the U.S. and N.Z.

716. All of (a)–(e) are false.

717. Ferguson-Shockley (2003) argue, basically, that almost all tests of the CAPM are conducted badly. To use an equity only proxy for the CAPM's market portfolio introduces an error because it omits any non-equity slice of the market portfolio. Any variable related to the missing variables (e.g., debt, leverage, financial distress) will proxy for the missing variables and help to explain returns. So, Fama-French (1992, 1993, 1996) *should* find that variables other than beta explain returns. They, therefore, do not present any evidence against the CAPM.

718. (a) An ETF is a fund that is backed by an asset (e.g., a portfolio of stocks, or a commodity) but which trades just like a stock. (b) In the case of gold, the ETF makes it easy to short, avoids storage costs, or insurance or assay costs. It's not enough to say it avoids handling the physical gold; tell me what is bad about that.

719. DB plans specify (or define) the benefit due to the future retiree and the employer typically assumes the risk in meeting that benefit. DC plans specify the contribution that the pre-retiree will make to his/her retirement savings plan and the employee faces a risk that his/her future balance will be insufficient to retire comfortably.

720. The manager of a DB plan can use inter-generational subsidies to ride out the ups and downs of the market. That is, the manager of a DB plan can offer a consistently high benefit to retirees, and assume higher market risk (than does an individual DC plan member) to achieve that end. In good times, the DB manager banks surpluses to meet deficits in bad times, so the DB manager is less risk averse than the individual DC plan member.

721. ETFs often have low T-costs (both management fees and relative bid-ask spreads), ETFs are often well diversified, ETFs give easy access to market sectors, ETFs are often quite liquid (though some are notoriously illiquid), ETFs usually track a passively managed index and avoid the risk of significant manager underperformance, etc. Exceptions exist to all of the above.

722. Value stocks typically have low ratios of fundamentals to price, glamour stocks typically have high ratios of fundamentals to price, a growth stock is typically expected to grow its earnings dramatically in the future (which is not necessarily saying anything about the past). Although likely to have high ratios of price to fundamentals, a growth stock might be correctly priced now, or underpriced, or even overpriced. In the longer run, its price is expected to trend upward following its earnings, regardless of current pricing.

No, growth is not bad value. Indeed, growth and value are not necessarily mutually exclusive terms. For example, if you find a stock that has been beaten down in price relative to its fundamentals, but whose earnings are expected to grow dramatically, then it is both a growth and a value stock.

723. The term hedge fund is undefined. See the discussion in *Foundations*.

724. A market neutral long-short fund may have long and short equity positions that roughly balance. Perhaps every \$1 is used as collateral to go \$1 long and \$1 short. So, the beta is roughly zero. In a 130/30 short-extension fund, however, every \$1 is used to go \$0.30 short and \$1.30 long, giving a beta near one.

725. I argued in *Foundations* that holding investment grade bonds is not a diversifying move. That is, it is not part of the first step of two-fund separation. Rather, it is part of the second step. That is, bonds play the part of an (essentially) riskless asset in a stock-bond portfolio, so that there are no market forces pushing the correlation between stocks and bonds toward any sort of long-run equilibrium.

726. A DRIP allows you to convert dividends received on a stock into additional shares of stock.

727. Mutual fund managers need to have cash on hand. It arrives from investors, and it must be on hand ready for redemptions. Suppose a \$100 million fund has \$5 million in cash on hand. Suppose the market shoots up 20%. The fund's capital gain is only \$19 million because 5% of the fund was in cash that dragged down the capital gain by 5% of the amount of the market's gain. This cash drag can be avoided by equitizing the cash using stock index futures or ETFs.

728. The manager of a momentum fund likely has higher T-costs than the manager of a value fund because the natural level of turnover is higher in the momentum fund.

729. Earnings are reported using accrual accounting. Some of the earnings are cash, and some are non-cash (i.e., accruals). Realized future earnings are related to current earnings. The unexpected component of future realized earnings (the "earnings surprise," let us call it) is positively related to the cash flow component of current earnings and negatively related to the accrual component. Investors fixate on earnings alone and fail to recognize that a large accrual component is bad news (Sloan, 1996).

Sloan (1996) defines accruals as in Equation 4.1, scaled by assets for comparability.

$$
\begin{aligned}
\text{Accruals} = &\ (\text{change in current assets} - \text{change in cash}) - \\
&\ (\text{change in current liabilities} - \text{change in debt included in} \\
&\ \text{current liabilities} - \text{change in income taxes payable}) - \text{de-} \\
&\ \text{preciation and amortization expense, all deflated by average} \\
&\ \text{total assets}
\end{aligned}
\tag{4.1}
$$

In simple terms, cash is high-quality earnings (partly because it is difficult to manipulate) and accruals are low-quality earnings (partly because they are easier to manipulate). This notion of earnings quality was not recognized by investors before Sloan (1996). Note that it is not necessarily a question of manipulation per se, because even without any manipulation or creativity, cash is a higher-quality earning than an accrual.

The systematic risk factor "quality" overlaps with, but is distinct from, earnings quality. Quality is usually evidenced in a stock by some or all of the following: historically high ROE and/or ROA, low leverage, stable earnings and dividend growth, a strong balance sheet, good management and good earnings quality (Ung, Luk, and Kang, 2014). Ung, Luk, and Kang (2014) go one step upstream and describe a quality stock as one with good profitability generation, good earnings quality, and financial robustness.

730. Fundamental indexation is an innovative index where stocks in a portfolio are weighted using price-insensitive fundamental characteristics (like total sales, total dividends, cash flows, number of employees, etc.) instead of the traditional relative market capitalization approach. It is a type of active approach (relative to a capitalization-weighted benchmark). There is considerable evidence that these funds outperform passive capitalization-weighted funds.

731. The diversification puzzle is that investors do not fully diversify even when the cost of doing so is quite low. Statman (2004) argues that some investors hold a pyramid of investments, with a bottom layer designed as a risk-averse fallback to protect them from poverty, and a top layer that often involves risk seeking, in an attempt to get rich.

732. The log plot of market index levels in Chapter 4 of *Foundations* puts all price moves on an even footing. That is, a 10% rise in the index when the index is at level 100, or level 1,000, or level 10,000 takes up the same vertical space on a log plot in each case. So, for example, on the raw levels plot, the dramatic decline in the broad stock market from September 3, 1929 to July 8, 1932 looks negligible when compared with the market decline during the recent global financial crisis, but it totally overshadows the recent decline on the log plot.

Appendix A

Equations for Reference

$$m_r = \frac{1}{N} \sum_{i=1}^{N} [x_i - \bar{x}]^r, \, s = \sqrt{\frac{1}{N-1} \sum_{i=1}^{N} [x_i - \bar{x}]^2}$$

$$skew_{KS} = \frac{N^2}{(N-1)(N-2)} \frac{m_3}{s^3}, \quad Z_{skew} = \sqrt{\frac{(N-1)(N-2)}{6N}} \cdot skew_{KS} \stackrel{A}{\sim} N(0,1),$$

$$kurt_{KS} = \left[\frac{N^2}{(N-1)(N-2)(N-3)} \left(\frac{(N+1)m_4 - 3(N-1)m_2^2}{s^4} \right) \right],$$

$$Z_{kurt} = \sqrt{\frac{(N-1)(N-2)(N-3)}{24N(N+1)}} \cdot kurt_{KS} \stackrel{A}{\sim} N(0,1),$$

$$\hat{\rho}_{xy} = \frac{\sum_{i=1}^{N}(x_i - \bar{x})(y_i - \bar{y})}{\sqrt{\sum_{i=1}^{N}(x_i - \bar{x})^2 \cdot \sum_{i=1}^{N}(y_i - \bar{y})^2}}.$$

$$\frac{\bar{X} - \mu}{\sqrt{\frac{s^2}{N}}} \sim t_{N-1}, \quad \frac{\hat{\rho} - 0}{\sqrt{1 - \hat{\rho}^2} \sqrt{\frac{1}{N-2}}} \sim t_{N-2}.$$

$$z = \frac{1}{2} \ln \left(\frac{1+\hat{\rho}}{1-\hat{\rho}} \right), \quad \zeta_{H_0} = \frac{1}{2} \ln \left(\frac{1+\rho_{H_0}}{1-\rho_{H_0}} \right), \quad \frac{z - \zeta_{H_0}}{\sqrt{\frac{1}{N-1} + \frac{2}{(N-1)^2}}} \sim N(0,1)$$

$$t_k = \frac{N(0,1)}{\sqrt{\frac{\chi_k^2}{k}}}, \quad \chi_\nu^2 = Z_1^2 + Z_2^2 + \cdots + Z_\nu^2, \quad F_{\nu,\eta} = \frac{\chi_\nu^2/\nu}{\chi_\eta^2/\eta}$$

$$c(t) = S(t)e^{-\rho(T-t)}N(d_1) - e^{-r(T-t)}XN(d_2),$$

$$p(t) = e^{-r(T-t)}XN(-d_2) - S(t)e^{-\rho(T-t)}N(-d_1),$$

$$d_1 = \frac{\ln\left(\frac{S(t)}{X}\right) + (r - \rho + \frac{1}{2}\sigma^2)(T-t)}{\sigma\sqrt{T-t}}, \text{ and}$$

$$d_2 = d_1 - \sigma\sqrt{T-t}.$$

$$p = c = \frac{S\sigma\sqrt{T-t}}{\sqrt{2\pi}} \approx 0.4S\sigma\sqrt{T-t}$$

$$R_t = \frac{P_t}{P_{t-1}} - 1, \quad r_t \equiv ln(1 + R_t) = \ln\left(\frac{P_t}{P_{t-1}}\right)$$

$$\vec{R} = \begin{pmatrix} R_1 \\ R_2 \\ \vdots \\ R_N \end{pmatrix}, \vec{h} = \begin{pmatrix} h_1 \\ h_2 \\ \vdots \\ h_N \end{pmatrix}, V = \begin{pmatrix} \sigma_{11} & \sigma_{12} & \cdots & \sigma_{1N} \\ \sigma_{21} & \sigma_{22} & \cdots & \sigma_{2N} \\ \vdots & \vdots & \ddots & \vdots \\ \sigma_{N1} & \sigma_{N2} & \cdots & \sigma_{NN} \end{pmatrix},$$

$$R_P = \vec{h}'\vec{R}, \ E(R_P) = \vec{h}'E(\vec{R}), \text{ and } \sigma_P^2 = \vec{h}'V\vec{h}.$$

$$R_i = R_F + \beta_i(R_B - R_F) + \rho_i,$$

$$R_P = R_F + \beta_P(R_B - R_F) + \rho_P.$$

$$\begin{aligned} R_P - R_B &= (R_P - R_F) - (R_B - R_F) \\ &= [\beta_P(R_B - R_F) + \rho_P] - (R_B - R_F) \\ &= (\beta_P - 1)(R_B - R_F) + \rho_P \\ &= \beta_P^{(A)} \cdot (R_B - R_F) + \rho_P \\ \psi_P &= \sqrt{V(R_P - R_B)} \\ &= \sqrt{(1 - \beta_P)^2 \cdot \sigma_B^2 + \omega_P^2}. \\ \rho_P &= (R_P - R_F) - \beta_P \cdot (R_B - R_F) \\ \omega_P &= \sqrt{V(\rho_P)} = \sqrt{\sigma_P^2 - \beta_P^2\sigma_B^2}. \end{aligned}$$

$$\begin{aligned} \kappa_P &= \overbrace{\kappa_B}^{\text{benchmark return}} + \overbrace{(\beta_P - 1)(\mu_B + \delta_B)}^{\text{benchmark timing}} + \overbrace{\alpha_P}^{\text{stock selection}} \\ \sigma_P^2 &= \underbrace{\sigma_B^2}_{\text{benchmark risk}} + \underbrace{(\beta_P^2 - 1)\sigma_B^2}_{\text{benchmark timing}} + \underbrace{\omega_P^2}_{\text{stock selection}} \end{aligned}$$

$$RAA = \alpha_P - \lambda_R\omega_P^2, \ RTAA = \alpha_P - \lambda_R\omega_P^2 - TC$$

$$\vec{h}_a: \vec{\iota}'\vec{h}_a = 1, \ \mu_a = \vec{h}_a'\vec{\mu}, \ \sigma_a^2 = \vec{h}_a'V\vec{h}_a, \ \sigma_{ab} = \vec{h}_a'V\vec{h}_b.$$

$$\vec{h}_P = \frac{1}{D}\left\{[C(V^{-1}\vec{\mu}) - A(V^{-1}\vec{\iota})]\mu_P + [B(V^{-1}\vec{\iota}) - A(V^{-1}\vec{\mu})]\right\}$$

$$A = \vec{\iota}'V^{-1}\vec{\mu}, \ B = \vec{\mu}'V^{-1}\vec{\mu}, \ C = \vec{\iota}'V^{-1}\vec{\iota}, \text{ and } D = BC - A^2 \text{ (all } (1\times1)).$$

$$\vec{h}_P = \underbrace{\frac{\mu_P - R_F}{(\vec{\mu} - R_F\vec{\iota})'V^{-1}(\vec{\mu} - R_F\vec{\iota})}V^{-1}(\vec{\mu} - R_F\vec{\iota})}_{\text{column vector of weight in risky assets for given }\mu_P}, \ \vec{h}_T = \frac{V^{-1}(\vec{\mu} - R_F\vec{\iota})}{\vec{\iota}'V^{-1}(\vec{\mu} - R_F\vec{\iota})}.$$

$$r_i(t) = \underbrace{\vec{B}_i'}_{(1\times K)} \cdot \underbrace{\vec{R}(t)}_{(K\times1)} + u_i, \qquad V = \underbrace{\mathcal{B}}_{(N\times K)} \cdot \underbrace{F}_{(K\times K)} \underbrace{\mathcal{B}'}_{(K\times N)} + \underbrace{\Delta}_{(N\times N)},$$

$$r_i = \mu\tau + \sigma\sqrt{\tau}\, z_i$$

$$\hat{\mu} = \frac{1}{N}\sum_{i=1}^{N} r_i \bigg/ \tau \; = \; \sum_{i=1}^{N} r_i \; , \quad \hat{\sigma}^2 = \frac{1}{N}\sum_{i=1}^{N} r_i^2 \bigg/ \tau \; = \; \sum_{i=1}^{N} r_i^2$$

$$
\begin{aligned}
E(\hat{\mu}) &= \mu \\
V(\hat{\mu}) &= \sigma^2 \\
E(\hat{\sigma}^2) &= \sigma^2 + \frac{\mu^2}{N} \xrightarrow{N} \sigma^2 \\
V(\hat{\sigma}^2) &= \frac{2\sigma^4}{N} + \frac{4\mu^2\sigma^2}{N} \xrightarrow{N} 0
\end{aligned}
$$

$$
\begin{aligned}
[r_{P10,t} - r_{F,t}] &= \alpha + \beta_{P10}[r_{B,t} - r_{F,t}] + \epsilon_t \\
\Rightarrow r_{P10,t}^{(A)} &= \alpha + \beta_{P10}^{(A)}[r_{B,t} - r_{F,t}] + \epsilon_t \\
\Rightarrow \bar{r}_{P10} &= \bar{r}_B + \hat{\alpha} + \hat{\beta}_{P10}^{(A)}[\bar{r}_B - \bar{r}_F]
\end{aligned}
$$

$$PVA = \frac{C}{R}\left[1 - \frac{1}{(1+R)^N}\right]$$

$$PVGA = \frac{C}{R-g}\left[1 - \left(\frac{1+g}{1+R}\right)^N\right]$$

$$IR = IC \times \sqrt{BR}$$

$$P = \frac{E}{R} + \text{PVGO} \quad \text{and} \quad \frac{P}{E} = \frac{1}{R}\left(\frac{1}{1 - \frac{\text{PVGO}}{P}}\right)$$

$$P_t^* = B_t + \sum_{i=1}^{\infty} \frac{\text{EVA}_{t+i}}{(1+r_e)^i},$$

$$B_{t+1} = B_t + NI_{t+1} - D_{t+1}, \; EVA_{t+i} = NI_{t+1} - r_e B_{t+i-1}$$

$$\frac{P_t^*}{B_t} = 1 + \sum_{i=1}^{\infty}\left[\left(\frac{ROE_{t+i} - r_e}{(1+r_e)^i}\right) \cdot \left(\frac{B_{t+i-1}}{B_t}\right)\right]$$

$$PV = \frac{E(\tilde{c}) - cov(\tilde{c}, R_M) \cdot (E(R_M) - R_F)/\sigma_M^2}{1 + R_F} \quad \text{and} \quad PV = \frac{E^*(\tilde{c})}{1 + R_F},$$

$$
\begin{aligned}
r_{it} &= \alpha_i + \beta_i r_{bt} + u_{it} \\
u_{it}|\mathcal{F}_{i\,t-1} &\sim \mathcal{N}(0, h_{it}) \\
h_{it} &= \gamma_{0i} + \gamma_{1i} u_{i\,t-1}^2 + \gamma_{2i} h_{i\,t-1}.
\end{aligned}
$$

$$(ABM) \quad P_t = \mu + P_{t-1} + \epsilon_t, \quad \epsilon_t \text{ IID } \mathcal{N}(0, \sigma^2)$$

$$(GBM) \quad \ln P_t = \mu + \ln P_{t-1} + \epsilon_t, \quad \epsilon_t \text{ IID } \mathcal{N}(0, \sigma^2)$$

$$[E(P_{t+1}|P_t, P_{t-1}, \dots) = P_t] \Rightarrow [E(P_{t+1} - P_t|P_t, P_{t-1}, \dots) = 0]$$

$$\text{Dimson} \quad R_{j,t} = \alpha + \beta_{-1} R_{M,t-1} + \beta_0 R_{M,t} + \beta_{+1} R_{M,t+1} + \epsilon_{j,t}$$

$$\beta_{Dimson} = \hat{\beta}_{-1} + \hat{\beta}_0 + \hat{\beta}_{+1}$$

Scholes-Williams for each of $\Delta t = -1, 0, 1$, $R_{j,t} = \alpha + \beta_{\Delta t} R_{M,t+\Delta t} + \epsilon_{j,t}$, where

$$\beta_{SW} = \frac{\hat{\beta}_{-1} + \hat{\beta}_0 + \hat{\beta}_{+1}}{1 + 2\hat{\rho}(1)}, \text{ and } \hat{\rho}(1) \text{ is autocorr of index}$$

$$R_{SMB,t} = \left(\frac{R_{S/L,t} + R_{S/M,t} + R_{S/H,t}}{3} \right) - \left(\frac{R_{B/L,t} + R_{B/M,t} + R_{B/H,t}}{3} \right).$$

$$R_{HML,t} = \left(\frac{R_{S/H,t} + R_{B/H,t}}{2} \right) - \left(\frac{R_{S/L,t} + R_{B/L,t}}{2} \right),$$

$$E(R_i) - R_f = b_i[E(R_M) - R_F] + s_i E(SMB) + h_i E(HML)$$

$$R_i - R_f = \alpha_i + b_i(R_M - R_F) + s_i SMB + h_i HML$$

$$R_i = E(R_i) + b_{i1}\delta_1 + \cdots + b_{iK}\delta_K + \epsilon_i, \quad \delta_1 = R_M - E(R_M)$$

$$E(R_i) = \lambda_0 + \lambda_1 b_{i1} + \cdots + \lambda_K b_{iK}, \quad \lambda_1 = E(R_M) - R_F$$

References

Bachelier, Louis, 1900, "Théorie de la Spéculation," *Annales de l'Ecole Normale Supéieure*, Series 3, XVII, pp. 21–86, Gauthier-Villars: Paris. Note that an English translation by A. James Boness appears in Cootner (1964).

Black, Fischer and Robert Litterman, 1992, "Global Portfolio Optimization," *The Financial Analysts Journal*, Vol. 48 No. 5, (September/October), pp. 28–43.

Brandes Partners, 2012, *Boomers Behaving Badly: A Better Solution to the "Money Death" Problem*, White Paper from Brandes Investment Partners, San Diego, CA, January 2012. See http://www.brandes.com/institute

Butler, Hartman L. Jr., 1976, "An Hour with Mr. Graham," A transcribed interview of a taped with Benjamin Graham, recorded March 6, 1976 in La Jolla, California.

Chopra, Vijay K., and William T. Ziemba, 1993, "The Effect of Errors in Means, Variances, and Covariances on Optimal Portfolio Choice," *The Journal of Portfolio Management*, Vol. 19 No. 2, (Winter), pp. 6–11.

Chow, Tzee-man, Jason Hsu, Vitali Kalesnik, and Bryce Little, 2011, "A Survey of Alternative Equity Index Strategies," *The Financial Analysts Journal*, Vol. 67 No. 5, (September/October), pp. 37–57.

Cootner, Paul H., (Ed.), 1964, *The Random Character of Stock Market Prices*, MIT Press: Cambridge, MA.

Damodaran, Aswath, 2019, Excel file histretSP.xls, Available at: http://pages.stern.nyu.edu/~adamodar/ (downloaded December 2019).

Edwards, E.O., and P.W. Bell, 1961, *The Theory and Measurement of Business Income*, University of California Press: Berkeley, CA.

Ezra, Don, Bob Collie, and Matthew X. Smith, 2009, *The Retirement Plan Solution*, John Wiley and Sons: Hoboken, NJ.

Fama, Eugene F., and Kenneth R. French, 1992, "The Cross-Section of Expected Stock Returns," *The Journal of Finance*, Vol. 47 No. 2, (June), pp. 427–465.

Fama, Eugene F., and Kenneth R. French, 1993, "Common Risk Factors in the Returns on Stocks and Bonds," *Journal of Financial Economics*, Vol. 33 No. 1, (February), pp. 3–56.

Fama, Eugene F., and Kenneth R. French, 1996, "Multifactor Explanations of Asset Pricing Anomalies," *The Journal of Finance*, Vol. 51 No. 1, (March), pp. 55–84.

Ferguson, Michael F., and Richard L. Shockley, 2003, "Equilibrium Anomalies," *The Journal of Finance*, Vol. 58 No. 6, (December), pp. 2549–2580.

Graham, Benjamin, 2006, *The Intelligent Investor: A Book of Practical Counsel*, Revised Edition, Harper Collins: New York, NY. (Originally published in 1949, this is Graham's 1973 text annotated by Jason Zweig.)

Graham, Benjamin and David Dodd, 1934, *Security Analysis: The Classic 1934 Edition*, McGraw-Hill: New York, NY.

Grinold, Richard C., and Ronald N. Kahn, 2000, *Active Portfolio Management: Quantitative Theory and Applications*, McGraw-Hill: New York, NY.

Jagannathan, Ravi and Tongshu Ma, 2003, "Risk Reduction in Large Portfolios: Why Imposing the Wrong Constraints Helps," *The Journal of Finance*, Vol. 58 No. 4, (August), pp. 1651–1684.

Kahn, Ronald N., 1998, "Bond Managers Need to Take More Risk," *Journal of Portfolio Management*, Vol. 24 No. 3, (Spring), pp. 70–76.

Ledoit, Olivier Richard Henri, 1995, Essays on Risk and Return in the Stock Market, Thesis (Ph.D.)—Massachusetts Institute of Technology, Sloan School of Management. Available at: `http://hdl.handle.net/1721.1/11875`

Ledoit, Olivier and Michael Wolf, 2004, "Honey, I Shrunk the Sample Covariance Matrix," *Journal of Portfolio Management*, Vol. 30 No. 4, (Summer), pp. 110–119.

Lee, Charles M., 1996, "Measuring Wealth: The Widely Admired Edwards-Bell-Ohlson Valuation Model Provides a Simple but Powerful Way to Compute the Fundamental Values of Publicly Traded Stocks," *CA Magazine*, Vol. 129 No. 3, pp. 32–37.

Lintner, John, 1956, "Distribution of Incomes of Corporations among Dividends, Retained Earnings, and Taxes," *American Economic Review*, Vol. 46 No. 2, pp. 97–113.

Lynch, Peter with John Rothchild, 2000, *One Up on Wall Street*, Simon & Schuster: New York, NY. (Originally published 1989.)

Merton, Robert C., 1980, "On Estimating the Expected Return on the Market: An Exploratory Investigation," *Journal of Financial Economics*, Vol. 8 No. 4, (December), pp. 323–361.

Merton, Robert C., 1992, *Continuous-Time Finance*, Blackwell: Cambridge, MA.

Michaud, Richard O., 1989, "The Markowitz Optimization Enigma: Is 'Optimized' Optimal?," *The Financial Analysts Journal*, Vol. 45 No. 1, (January/February), pp. 31–42.

Ohlson, James, 1995, "Earnings, Book Values, and Dividends in Security Valuation," *Contemporary Accounting Research*, Spring, Vol. 11 No. 2, pp. 661–687.

Sharpe, William F., 1994, "The Sharpe Ratio," *The Journal of Portfolio Management*, Vol. 21 No. 1, (Fall), pp. 49–58.

Shefrin, Hersh and Meir Statman, 1985, "The Disposition to Sell Winners Too Early and Ride Losers Too Long: Theory and Evidence," *The Journal of Finance*, Vol. 40 No. 3, (July), pp. 777–790.

Sloan, Richard G., 1996. "Do stock prices fully reflect information in accruals and cash flows about future earnings?" *The Accounting Review* Vol. 71 No. 3, (July), pp. 289–315.

SSA, 2014a, *Social Security Basic Facts*, Available at: `http://www.ssa.gov/pressoffice/basicfact.htm` (downloaded July 2014).

SSA, 2014b, *Cost-of-Living Adjustments*, Available at:
`http://www.ssa.gov/oact/cola/colaseries.html` (downloaded July 2014).

Statman, Meir, 2004, "The Diversification Puzzle," *The Financial Analysts Journal*, Vol. 60 No. 4, (July-August), pp. 44–53.

Ung, Daniel, Priscilla Luk, and Xiaowei Kang, 2014, "Quality: A Distinct Equity Factor?" Working paper dated July 26, 2014. Available at SSRN's Web site: http://ssrn.com/abstract=2472391

Zwillinger, Daniel, and Stephen Kokoska, 2000, *Standard Probability and Statistics Tables and Formulae*, Chapman & Hall/CRC, New York, NY.

Alphabets and Numerical Equivalences

Greek[a]				NATO Phonetic		Roman (Latin)[a]	
α	A	Alpha	1	A	Alpha	A	50; 500
β	B	Beta	2	B	Bravo	B	300
γ	Γ	Gamma	3	C	Charlie	C	100
δ	Δ	Delta	4	D	Delta	D	500
ϵ	E	Epsilon	5	E	Echo	E	250
ζ	Z	Zeta	7	F	Foxtrot	F	40
η	H	Eta	8	G	Golf	G	400
θ	Θ	Theta	0	H	Hotel	H	200
ι	I	Iota	10	I	India	I	1
κ	K	Kappa	20	J	Juliett	J	_[b]
λ	Λ	Lambda	30	K	Kilo	K	250
μ	M	Mu	40	L	Lima	L	50
ν	N	Nu	50	M	Mike	M	1,000
ξ	Ξ	Xi	60	N	November	N	90
o	O	Omicron	70	O	Oscar	O	11
π	Π	Pi	80	P	Papa	P	400
ρ	R	Rho	100	Q	Quebec	Q	90; 500
σ	Σ	Sigma	200	R	Romeo	R	80
τ	T	Tau	300	S	Sierra	S	7;70
υ	Υ	Upsilon	400	T	Tango	T	160
ϕ	Φ[c]	Phi	500	U	Uniform	U	_[d]
χ	X[c]	Chi	700	V	Victor	V	5
ψ	Ψ[c]	Psi	700	W	Whiskey	W	_[e]
ω	Ω	Omega	800	X	X-Ray	X	10
				Y	Yankee	Y	150
				Z	Zulu	Z	2,000

[a]Some information from Lewis et al. (1942, p1161). The book is out of print and the publisher defunct.

[b]Originally the same as I.

[c]The Greek letters Φ, X, and Ψ were not needed in the medieval Latin alphabet. However, the Romans used them as numerical symbols, writing D (or M), X, and L, respectively.

[d]Originally the same as V.

[e]Not used in medieval Latin.

Index

Winsorized, 256
Wolf, Michael, 126, 156, 157, 164, 177, 232,
        254, 264, 265, 275, 283, 294

$\mathcal{Z}$
zero-beta CAPM, 180
Ziemba, William T., 265, 293
Z_{kurt}, 41, 56, 60, 231
    definition, 289
Z_{skew}, 41, 56, 60, 231
    definition, 289
Zwillinger, Daniel, 295

Foundations for Scientific Investing:
Capital Markets Intuition and
Critical Thinking Skills

Timothy Falcon Crack

PhD (MIT), MCom, PGDipCom, BSc (HONS 1ˢᵗ Class), IMC

The latest edition of this book lays a firm foundation for thinking about and conducting investment. It does this by helping to build capital markets intuition and critical thinking skills.

This book is the product of 25+ years of investment research and experience (academic, personal, and professional), and 20+ years of destructive testing in university classrooms. Although the topic is applied investments, my integration of finance, economics, accounting, pure mathematics, statistics, numerical techniques, and spreadsheets (or programming) make this an ideal capstone course at the advanced undergraduate or masters/MBA level. Most of the material should be accessible to a motivated practitioner or talented individual investor with only high school level mathematics.

Contents include literature reviews in advanced areas, 30+ unanswered research questions suitable for a master's thesis or PhD thesis chapter, an active alpha optimization exercise using actual stock market data, advanced TVM exercises, a review of retirement topics, an extensive discussion of dividends, P/E ratios, transaction costs, the CAPM, and value versus growth versus glamour, and a review of more than 100 years of stock market performance and more than 200 years of interest rates. Special attention is paid to difficult topics like the Roll critique, smart beta, factor-based investing, and Grinold-Kahn versus Black-Litterman models. Every investor needs capital markets intuition and critical thinking skills to conduct confident, deliberate, and skeptical investment. The overarching goal of this book is to help investors build these skills.

The latest edition is available at all reputable online booksellers.

http://www.FoundationsForScientificInvesting.com
timcrack@alum.mit.edu

Heard on The Street: Quantitative Questions from Wall Street Job Interviews

Timothy Falcon Crack

PhD (MIT), MCom, PGDipCom, BSc (HONS 1st Class), IMC

A must read! Now revised annually. Over 225 quantitative questions collected from actual job interviews in investment banking, investment management, and options trading. The interviewers use the same questions year-after-year, and here they are—with solutions!

This is the first and the original book of quantitative questions from finance job interviews. Painstakingly revised over 25 years and 21 editions, *Heard on The Street* has been shaped by feedback from many hundreds of readers. With more than 60,000 copies in print, it is unmatched by any competing book.

These questions come from all types of interviews (investment banking, corporate finance, sales and trading, quant research, etc.), but they are especially likely in quantitative capital markets job interviews. The questions come from all levels of interviews (undergraduate, MS, MBA, PhD), but they are especially likely if you have, or almost have, an MS or MBA. The latest edition includes 225+ non-quantitative actual interview questions, and a new section on interview technique—based partly on Dr. Crack's experiences interviewing candidates for the world's largest institutional asset manager.

The latest edition is available at all reputable online booksellers.

http://www.InvestmentBankingJobInterviews.com/
timcrack@alum.mit.edu

Pocket Heard on The Street

Timothy Falcon Crack

PhD (MIT), MCom, PGDipCom, BSc (HONS 1ˢᵗ Class), IMC

Two pocket-sized editions of finance job interview questions. Compared with the full-sized edition of *Heard on The Street*, these pocket editions are cheaper, physically smaller, and have fewer pages. They contain a careful selection of the best questions from the full-sized edition of *Heard on The Street*. The pocket editions are easy to put in your pocket or purse, and easy to read on the subway, bus, train, or plane! *Pocket Heard on The Street: Quantitative Questions from Finance Job Interviews* is a careful selection of the 75 best quantitative questions taken from the full-sized edition of *Heard on The Street*. Presented with detailed solutions. *Pocket Heard on The Street: Brain Teasers, Thinking Questions, and Non-Quantitative Questions from Finance Job Interviews* is a careful selection of 20 brain teasers, 30 thinking questions, and over 100 non-quantitative questions taken from the full-sized edition of *Heard on The Street*. The brain teasers, and more than half the thinking questions are presented with detailed solutions. Whereas the quantitative questions in the first pocket edition usually require math/stats, the brain teasers and "thinking questions" in the second pocket edition usually require little or no math. The thinking questions fall half-way between brain teasers and true quantitative questions.

The latest editions are available at all reputable online booksellers.

http://www.InvestmentBankingJobInterviews.com/
timcrack@alum.mit.edu

Basic Black-Scholes: Option Pricing and Trading

Timothy Falcon Crack

PhD (MIT), MCom, PGDipCom, BSc (HONS 1st Class), IMC

This book gives extremely clear explanations of Black-Scholes option pricing theory, and discusses direct applications of the theory to option trading. The presentation does not go far beyond basic Black-Scholes for three reasons: First, a novice need not go far beyond Black-Scholes to make money in the options markets; Second, all high-level option pricing theory is simply an extension of Black-Scholes; and Third, there already exist many books that look far beyond Black-Scholes without first laying the firm foundation given here. The trading advice does not go far beyond elementary call and put positions because more complex trades are simply combinations of these. The appendix includes Black-Scholes option pricing code for the HP17B, HP19B, and HP12C. The latest edition includes Bloomberg screens and expanded analysis of Black-Scholes interpretations. The latest edition is also accompanied by two downloadable spreadsheets. The first spreadsheet allows the user to forecast profits and transaction costs for option positions using simple models. The second spreadsheet allows the user to explore option sensitivities including the Greeks.

The latest edition is available at all reputable online booksellers.

http://www.BasicBlackScholes.com/
timcrack@alum.mit.edu

How to Ace Your Business Finance Class: Essential Knowledge and Techniques to Master the Material and Ace Your Exams

Timothy Falcon Crack

PhD (MIT), MCom, PGDipCom, BSc (HONS 1st Class), IMC

This pocket-sized book is aimed at students in their first finance class at the undergraduate, MBA, or executive education level. I use 25 years of experience teaching this material to explain carefully the stumbling blocks that have consistently tripped up students year after year. This gives every student every opportunity to master the material. I also present safe strategies I have developed to help you solve numerical problems. Although these strategies take only an extra minute to implement, they frame each numerical problem so as to increase the likelihood that you detect and fix any errors, while reducing the likelihood that you make any errors in the first place. These techniques also increase the likelihood that you earn partial credit. Although this book is aimed primarily at students, the fact that I focus on essential knowledge and techniques also makes this book useful to instructors. The chapters of the book are as follows: Foundations, Financial Statements, TVM I (One Cash Flow), TVM II (Multiple Cash Flows), Inflation and Indices, Bonds and Interest Rates, Equities and Dividend Discount Models, Capital Budgeting I (Decision Rules), Capital Budgeting II (Cash Flows), Capital Budgeting III (Cost of Capital), Capital Budgeting IV (A Paradox), The CAPM and Interest Rates, Risk and Return, Market Efficiency, Capital Structure, and Dividends.

The latest edition is available at all reputable online booksellers.

www.foundationsforscientificinvesting.com/books.htm
timcrack@alum.mit.edu

24 Essential Tips for Selling Print Replica eBooks on Amazon: How to Capture New Readers by Turning Your Physical Book into an eBook

Timothy Falcon Crack

PhD (MIT), MCom, PGDipCom, BSc (HONS 1st Class), IMC

This eBooklet gives more than two-dozen essential tips that I have accumulated after several years of turning my self-published physical print books into "print replica" eBooks that I sell on Amazon.com.

A print replica eBook uses a simple pdf-formatted text block (i.e., the inside pages of a book, as distinct from its cover.) Most software packages can output pdf files. So, there is no messing around with unfamiliar EPUB or MOBI formatting, HTML code, or reflowable eBooks (i.e., where the book reorganizes itself when the reader re-sizes the text). Nevertheless, some of my advice applies to other formats.

This is not a "How to Write an eBook" book. Instead, I assume that you have already written all the content for your book. My only goal is to help guide you through the tricky process of getting set up to sell print replica eBooks on Amazon.com.

You can follow my eBook advice whether you sell physical books or not. For example, there is no physical print edition of this eBook, but I followed the advice given in it to set it up and sell it on Amazon.

The count of new readers attracted to my eBooks more than compensates for any cannibalization of physical book sales by eBooks. So, if you are not selling your books as eBooks, then you are missing out.

The latest edition is available at all reputable online booksellers.

www.foundationsforscientificinvesting.com/books.htm
timcrack@alum.mit.edu

PUBREF:2020.12.23:14:45.785,181.OU

CPSIA information can be obtained
at www.ICGtesting.com
Printed in the USA
LVHW060857070121
675760LV00011B/351

9 780995 117358